CROSSING BAPTIST BOUNDARIES

A *FESTSCHRIFT* IN HONOR OF

WILLIAM HENRY BRACKNEY

CROSSING BAPTIST BOUNDARIES

A *FESTSCHRIFT* IN HONOR OF

BAPTIST SCHOLAR

WILLIAM HENRY BRACKNEY

ON THE OCCASION OF HIS RETIREMENT

Erich Geldbach, Editor

MERCER UNIVERSITY PRESS
Macon, Georgia
1979–2019
40 Years of Publishing Excellence

MUP/ H970

Published by Mercer University Press
1501 Mercer University Drive
Macon, Georgia 31207

9 8 7 6 5 4 3 2 1

Books published by Mercer University Press are printed on acid-free paper that meets the requirements of the American National Standard for Information Sciences—Permanence of Paper for Printed Library Materials.

The frontispiece portrait was commissioned by McMaster Divinity College at McMaster University, Hamilton, Ontario, Canada and it is hanging in the Divinity School. It was painted by Gregory Furmanczyk. It is used here with permission by McMaster Divinity College.

Printed and bound in Canada by Friesens.

This book is set in Adobe Caslon Pro.

ISBN 978-0-88146-694-2
Cataloging-in-Publication Data is available from the Library of Congress

CONTENTS

PREFACE

This collection of essays is dedicated to William Henry Brackney. Bill, as he is usually called, is a well-known church historian and a researcher of Baptist history and Baptist identity. In Walter Shurden's words, "[H]e knows more Baptists, living or dead, than any other person in the world today." For this reason, it seemed appropriate to have Shurden lead into Bill's many attempts to come to terms with the question of who Baptists are, and Shurden, Minister-at-Large at Mercer University, produced a superb in-depth study. It will prove advantageous to any reader to begin with this *praeludium*. Equally fitting is the *postludium*: After learning from the introductory essay that believer's baptism by immersion is the one Baptist idea that most sums up the Baptist movement, readers are invited to wade into the baptismal water as led by Horace Russell's baptismal sermon. Horace was President of the United Theological College of the West Indies in Kingston, Jamaica, before he moved to the Philadelphia area where at Palmer Theological Seminary he became Professor of Historical Theology and Dean of Chapel. Between the *praeludium* and the *postludium* readers will find a wide variety of topics that in one way or another are related to where Bill left his footprints.

All of the contributors hope that Bill will graciously accept what we humbly and gratefully offer him at the time of his retirement. We wish him health and strength for the time when he will be relieved from the burden of faculty and committee meetings and the busy teaching schedule and can devote more time to his wife and family. We are sure, however, that he will continue to research his beloved field of church history with a special reference to the religious community that is so dear to his heart.

As editor of the volume, it gives me great pleasure to thank all who contributed to this *Festschrift*.

When Bill's wife Kathryn ("Kitty") asked me several years ago if I would serve as editor, I felt greatly honored and without hesitation accepted her invitation as a small token of thanks to Bill. My heartfelt thanks also go to Kitty for her trust and her help.

May Bill with a smile or with a frown, with laughter or with tears read this collection and may he feel inspired by what his friends and colleagues dedicated to him.

Ad multos annos,

Erich Geldbach
Marburg, 20 February 2018

FOREWORD

The work and ministry of William Henry Brackney have been far-ranging. As a historical theologian and ethicist, across his career, our father has sought to explore and advance understanding of the Gospel, Christian faith and its myriad traditions through research, and the honest examination of primary documentation and practices. Dad's academic career and numerous publications are expansive, but beyond the classroom and library, he is a leader whose faith, interests and expertise are also demonstrated locally and globally, in countless hours of volunteer work, learned society and association memberships, pastoral ministry with churches and more. His many graduate students serve in positions of ministry and leadership around the world.

Grounded in biblical theology and teachings, Dr. Brackney, a minister ordained in the Baptist, Methodist and Wesleyan denominations, has served numerous churches, guiding congregations in ministry as well as encouraging them to define their beliefs. Our father has documented and celebrated the diversity of Baptist history and traditions at a denominational level, but also as they are authentically lived in local congregations in countries around the world such as China, Russia and Poland. He is recognized as a Fellow in several international centres: the Institute fur Baptiststudien des Theologischen Seminars, Elstal, Germany, a Lifetime Fellow at Acadia Divinity College, Wolfville, Nova Scotia and a Research Associate at the Oxford Centre for Baptist History and Heritage at Regent's Park College, Oxford, United Kingdom. His research has helped to document the Baptist church's rich historical roots in Atlantic Canada and the colonial United States, as well as Bolivia, England and Germany, and related groups such as the Seventh Day Baptists. The former director of the American Baptist Historical Society and the Acadia Centre for Baptist and Anabaptist Studies, he was also a founder of the Canadian Baptist Historical Society.

In addition to his leadership roles in academia, Dr. Brackney is a veteran Christian leader and administrator, having served with the Canadian Bible Society, including six years as Chairperson of its National Board, as an elected delegate of the United Bible Societies and with organizations such as the Canadian Council of Churches, InterVarsity Christian Fellowship of Canada and commissions of the Baptist World Alliance.

Beyond Dad's pursuits in his primary fields of interest, he has led in efforts to create dialogue, mutual understanding, peace and partnerships across the ecumenical spectrum. Dr. Brackney has participated in national and international theological conversations with leaders from the Orthodox, Anglican and Mennonite churches. At the interfaith level he has led theological dialogues among various religious traditions, including Christian-Muslim conversations, was a founding officer of the Interfaith Spirituality Network of Nova Scotia, and has contributed to ecumenical theological education.

This festschrift honors the career and significant contributions to the fields of Baptist Studies, Post-Reformation Theology and Ethics, made by our father. His gifts in administration, teaching, preaching, research and practice are blended and have been applied with vigor to academic and ministry pursuits alike, creating a legacy of Christian leadership and service for the glory of God and as an inspiration to future generations. Dad's work is anchored in his Christian faith and a genuine passion for the great traditions of the Church, which are vital in understanding who we are and shaping who we will become.

Noel C. Brackney, Ph.D.
Erin A. Brackney Kremkus, MSW
Capt. G. Raphe Brackney, BA, USAF
January 16, 2019

LIST OF CONTRIBUTORS

Clinton Bennett, Professor, Philosophy Department, State University of New York at New Paltz

Chris Chun, Associate Professor of Church History and Chair of Historical Studies, Gateway Seminary

Keith Clements, British Baptist Minister and Retired General Secretary of the Conference of European Churches

Charles W. Deweese, Retired Executive Director, Baptist History and Heritage Society

Paul Fiddes, Professor of Systematic Theology, University of Oxford, Director of Research, Regent's Park College, Oxford

Stanley K. Fowler, Professor of Theological Studies, Heritage Theological Seminary, Cambridge, Ontario, Canada

Erich Geldbach, Retired Professor of Ecumenical Studies, Protestant Faculty of Theology, Ruhr-University Bochum, Germany

Larry Kreitzer, Fellow at Regent's Park College, Oxford; also holds a Research Lectureship within the Faculty of Theology and Religion of the University of Oxford

James Stanley Lemons, Professor (em.) of History, Rhode Island College

Thorwald Lorenzen, Professor at Charles Sturt University, Canberra, Australia, Retired Baptist Minister

Roger H. Prentice, University Chaplain (ret.), Acadia University, Wolfville, Nova Scotia, Canada

John D. Roth, Professor of History, Goshen College, Goshen, Indiana, Director of the Institute for the Study of Global Anabaptism and Editor of *The Mennonite Quarterly Review*

Horace O. Russell, Professor (em.) of Historical Theology and Dean of Chapel, Palmer Theological Seminary of Eastern University, St. David's, Pennsylvania; also Former President of the United Theological College of the West Indies, Kingston, Jamaica

John Shouse, Professor of Christian Theology, Gateway Seminary

Walter B. Shurden, Professor and Minister at Large, Mercer University, Macon, Georgia

Andrea Strübind, Professor of Church History, Carl von Ossietzky University, Oldenburg, Germany

WILLIAM H. BRACKNEY

EDUCATION

Bachelor of Arts (honors) University of Maryland, College Park, Maryland – 1970

Master of Arts in Religion. The Eastern Baptist Theological Seminary, Philadelphia, Pennsylvania – 1972

Master of Arts, Temple University, Philadelphia, Pennsylvania – 1974

Doctor of Philosophy (with distinction). Temple University, Philadelphia, Pennsylvania – 1976

Postgraduate Certificate in Archives Administration. Modern Archives Institute, United States National Archives and Records Service, Washington, D. C. – 1979

ACADEMIC EXPERIENCE

Reading Fellow, Temple University – 1973–74

Teaching Fellow, Temple University, Ambler, PA Campus – 1974–75

Research Fellow, Temple University, Main Campus – 1975–76

Houghton College, Assistant Professor, History Dept. – 1976–79

Colgate Rochester Divinity School, Associate Professor, Church History – 1983–86

Eastern Baptist Theological Seminary, Professor, History of Christianity – 1986–89

Theological Seminary, Ruschlikon CH, Visiting Lecturer – 1985

Hungarian Baptist Seminary, Budapest, Visiting Lecturer – 1985

McMaster Divinity College, Professor, Historical Theology – 1989–2000

McMaster University, Faculty of Theology – 1994–2000

Arthur Turner Training School, NWT, (Anglican) Visiting Lecturer – 1995

Toronto School of Theology Member, Historical, Theological Depts. – 1994–2000

Polish Baptist Seminary at Warsawa, Visiting Lecturer – 1995–1998

Seminario Bautista Boliviano en Cochabamba, Visiting Lecturer 1996

Baylor University, Professor of Religion – 2000–2006

George W. Truett Theological Seminary, Adjunct Professor, Church History – 2001–2006

Acadia University, Divinity College, The Millard R. Cherry Distinguished Professor of Christian Theology and Ethics – 2006–

Hong Kong Baptist Seminary, Visiting Lecturer – 2005

Derwood Deere Lecturer, Golden Gate Baptist Theological Seminary – 2006

George Gallup Lecturer, Dallas Baptist University – 2007

Visiting Lecturer, Logsdon School of Theology, Hardin–Simmons University – 2008
Annual Baptist Heritage Series Lecturer, Campbellsville University – 2008
Invited Regular Columnist, Ethicsdaily.com – 2009–
Visiting Professor, Golden Gate Baptist Theological Seminary – 2012
Adjunct Professor, Dept. of History, Classics, and Religious Studies, Acadia University – 2014–
M.R. Cherry Distinguished Professor of Christian Thought and Ethics, Emeritus – 2017–
Research Fellow, in the McClendon Chair, Faculty of Theology, Vrie Universtat of Amsterdam – 2017–
Research Fellow Centre for Baptist Studies, Regent's Park College, Oxford University – 2017–
Pioneer MacDonald Chair in Baptist Theology and Ethics, Carey Theological College, [affil. College, University of British Columbia] – 2018–
Lifetime Fellow, Acadia Divinity College, Acadia University – 2005
Fellow, Institute fur Baptiststudien, Facultat, Elstal, Germany

ADMINISTRATIVE EXPERIENCE
Executive Director, American Baptist Historical Society – 1979–86
Archivist, American Baptist Churches, USA – 1980–86
Chair, BWA Study Commission on Baptist Heritage – 1985–1990
Vice President and Dean, Eastern Baptist Theological Seminary – 1986–89
Acting President, Eastern Baptist Theological Seminary – 1987
Principal and Dean, McMaster Divinity College – 1989–2000
Chair, Division of Study and Research, Baptist World Alliance – 1990–95
Co–Chair, Baptist–Mennonite International Theological Conversations – 1990–95
Dean of Theology, McMaster University 1993–2000
Chair, Department of Religion, Baylor University – 2000–03
Director, Program in Baptist Studies, Baylor University – 2002–06
Founding Editor, American Baptist Quarterly – 1979
Book Review Editor, American Baptist Quarterly 1983
Member, Editorial Advisory Board, Journal of Church and State – 2002–
Director, Acadia Centre for Baptist and Anabaptist Studies – 2009–
Director, Doctor of Ministry Program, Carey Theo. College – 2017–
Director/Secretary, Believers Church Conferences Committee – 2017–
Chair, Steering Committee to Establish a Regional Interfaith Council in Nova Scotia – 2016–
Chair, [president] National Board of Governors, Canadian Bible Society – 2013–

PRAELUDIUM

WILLIAM H. BRACKNEY'S UNDERSTANDING OF THE BAPTIST IDENTITY

Walter B. Shurden

INTRODUCTION

William H. Brackney is, in my judgment, the unrivaled and foremost Baptist historian in North America for at least the last four decades. Few, if any, Baptist historians in North America of any era have written more extensively, more broadly, or more insightfully on the Baptist people in North America than Brackney. My wager is that he knows more Baptists, living or dead, than any other person in the world today. He also knows more about the history of the Baptists and the sources for that history than any person in the world.

His broad background and vast experience among Baptists of North America also exceeds that of any living Baptist historian or theologian I know. Reared in a hybrid American/Southern Baptist context, he served as vice-president and dean of an American Baptist seminary, Eastern Baptist (now Palmer); as executive director of the American Baptist Historical Society; as principal and dean of a Canadian Baptist seminary, McMaster Divinity College; as chair of the department of religion at Baylor University in Texas, where he became intimately acquainted with both Southern Baptists and the Cooperative Baptist Fellowship; and as distinguished professor at Acadia Divinity College in Nova Scotia since 2006. In addition to this extensive exposure to American Baptists, Canadian Baptists, Southern Baptists, and the Cooperative Baptist Fellowship, Brackney has worked extensively in the Baptist World Alliance, where he became acquainted with Baptist leaders from all over the world. He writes, therefore, from a global as well as continental perspective. Brackney knows all Baptists, not simply one clan of this large and diverse family. This makes him a trusted guide to the meaning of the word "Baptist," and I have no hesitation in calling him the world's preeminent Baptist historian.

The author of numerous books and articles on Baptists, he has written on diverse aspects of Baptist life. The identity of Baptists and their essential principles, however, have been of particular historiographical concern to Brackney throughout his career. In this paper I have reviewed eight of his publications to try to arrive at his understanding of what it means to be a Baptist.[1]

---

[1]The eight writings of Brackney are: William H. Brackney, ed., *Baptist Life and Thought: 1600–1980, A Source Book* (Valley Forge PA: Judson Press, 1983); "'Commonly, (Though Falsely) Called…': Reflections on the Search for Baptist Identity," *Perspectives in Religious*

THE PROBLEM OF BAPTIST IDENTITY ACCORDING TO BRACKNEY

William Brackney wisely introduced almost every one of his discussions of the Baptist identity with statements about the *difficulty* in describing that identity. In a 1983 edited volume Brackney's voice is surely the most prominent of the contributors. His first sentences in the "General Introduction" are as follows: "'Who are the Baptists?' or, more appropriately, 'What are the Baptists?' Either of these questions sparks a lively debate among Baptists and non-Baptists alike."[2] In what some may call his major book on the identity of Baptists, he entitled the introductory chapter "The Problem of Baptist Identity." Again, his opening sentence was, "The issue of identity constitutes a major problem for the Baptists."[3] Continuing to reflect on the difficulty of establishing the Baptist profile in his most recent analysis of Baptist principles and the Baptist identity, he stated, "Baptists are a variegated people with a variegated past."[4]

Brackney identifies reasons for the difficulty. One of those is historical. Baptists differ regarding their origins and beginnings, and their understanding of historical origins impacts their characterization of the Baptist identity. The three theories of Baptist beginnings are the Successionist theory, the Anabaptist Kinship theory, and the English Separatist Descent theory, each with commonalties but also with some distinct differences. Dismissing Successionism as a viable historical approach, Brackney acknowledges some Anabaptist influence while stressing that Baptist origins are rooted in the Puritan Separatist movement of seventeenth-century England.[5] But he then says of Baptists' historical origins, "There will never be an answer which satisfies all or even most Baptists since there is no date, no place, and no person to whom all can look with complete confidence as the *locus classicus* of the movement."[6]

A second factor in establishing Baptist identity, according to Brackney, is

---

Studies 13 (Fall 1986): 67–82; *The Baptists* (Westport CT: Greenwood Press, 1988); *Historical Dictionary of the Baptists* (Lanham MD: The Scarecrow Press, Inc., 1999); *A Genetic History of Baptist Thought* (Macon GA: Mercer University Press, 2004); *Baptists in North America: An Historical Perspective* (Malden MA: Blackwell Publishing, 2006); *Congregation and Campus: Baptists in Higher Education* (Macon GA: Mercer University Press, 2008); and *A Capsule History of Baptist Principles* (Atlanta GA: Baptist History and Heritage Society, 2009). All of these sources will be abbreviated in future footnotes and within the body of the paper.

[2] Brackney, *Baptist Life and Thought*, 15.

[3] Brackney, *The Baptists*, xvii; Brackney goes into some depth on this subject in his article, "'Commonly, (Though Falsely) Called…,'" 67–74.

[4] Brackney, *Capsule History*, 13.

[5] Brackney, *Baptists in North America*, 1; *Baptist Life and Thought*, 23–24; *A Genetic History*, 12.

[6] Brackney, *The Baptists*, xvii.

Baptist pluralism itself. Baptists emerged in distinctly different groups, and that diversity multiplied in later years. General, Particular, and Seventh Day Baptists all appeared in the seventeenth century. Subsequently, one finds several kinds of Baptists in North America alone: Separates, Freewills, black Baptists, Reformed, and Primitive, among others. After the missionary movement dispersed Baptists around the world in the nineteenth century, modifications within the Baptist ethos appeared as Baptists interacted with other cultures and religions.[7]

Baptist ideals constitute a third difficulty in formulating the Baptist identity. In his massive history of Baptist theology, Brackney said, "As part of their emphases upon the priesthood of believers and the competency of the individual soul, the Free Churches began to produce a variegated form of theology."[8] He could justifiably have added the independence of local congregations to that list as a factor that created diversity among Baptists. D.S. Russell, in writing the preface to Brackney's *Historical Dictionary*, said, "Baptists have been likened, somewhat unkindly, to 'a herd of untamed mustangs in an unfenced prairie.' The allusion presumably is to their avowed 'independency,' their alleged 'individualism,' and their unwillingness to be 'controlled' by either ecclesiastical or State authority."[9] Russell goes on to say that such a description is only half of the Baptist story. However, it is enough of the story to create problems in defining the Baptist identity.

The formidable problems in arriving at a Baptist identity never ruled out for Brackney the possibility of discovering that identity. Very significantly, he said, "With all the variety, it would be unfair, however, to characterize Baptists as having no set theology or principles."[10] Notwithstanding the fact that Baptist groups or Baptist churches have never precisely mirrored each other, Brackney asserted, "Enough believers over four centuries have exhibited commonalities that can now be called essential principles."[11] Baptist life and thought may appear to some as hopelessly atomistic and fragmented, but Brackney saw a larger tradition. At one point he described that tradition in summary fashion as a "biblically oriented, Christologically centered, eangelical Christian tradition that values religious experience, congregational identity, and freedom of conscience in a racially and ethnically diverse heritage."[12]

On first glance, one confronts a "problem" even in assessing and describing Brackney's portrayal of the Baptist identity. Brackney has written so much on the subject in such various contexts that his language and categories in describing and

---

[7] Brackney, *Capsule History*, 13.

[8] Brackney, *A Genetic History*, 1.

[9] Brackney, *Historical Dictionary*, xi.

[10] Brackney, *Capsule History*, 13.

[11] Ibid.

[12] Brackney, *A Genetic History*, 528.

characterizing the Baptist identity necessarily change. In his 1986 article where he was proposing a process for establishing the Baptist identity, Brackney seemed to simplify the core of the Baptist identity. He said, "For those who stand outside the ideological and practical squabbling of the people called Baptist and wonder what a Baptist is, there is an answer. What all Baptists have in common is their practice of believer's baptism and the theology which accompanies it."[13] Brackney has been fond of quoting Morgan Edwards, America's first Baptist historian, who said, "Practising believer's baptism is our denominating article."[14]

Two years later, in 1988, in what is surely one of his major expositions on the subject of Baptist identity, Brackney treats five subjects as composing the identity of Baptists: (1) the Bible, (2) the church, (3) the sacraments/ordinances, (4) voluntarism, and (5) religious liberty.[15] In 1999 Brackney produced his *Historical Dictionary of the Baptists,* a book so helpful that it should be near the desk of every Baptist minister, historian, and theologian. In his article on Baptist theology and Baptist theologians, he gives yet another summary of the Baptist identity. "The majority of all Baptists," he said, "emphasize Christian experience, the authority, if not plain interpretation, of Scripture, and the primacy of the local congregation in their determination and articulation of Christian doctrine."[16] Brackney wrote an exhaustive 2008 book on Baptists and higher education in North America. In his first chapter, "The Meaning of Baptist Identity in Higher Education," he again summarizes his understanding of Baptists. He said,

> Baptists have held tenaciously to principles like the direct relation of the human soul to God, the right of private judgment in the interpretation of scripture, liberty of conscience, democracy in political relations, and freedom of thought and liberality in culture and religion. Generally, Baptists place a high value on individual religious experience in conversion, discipleship, and the sacraments/ordinances.[17]

In his most recent work of 2009, Brackney enumerates eleven different principles that summarize the Baptist identity. These eleven are: (1) the Lordship of Christ, (2) the Authority of Scripture, (3) the importance of religious experience, (4) a believer's church, (5) believer's baptism and the Lord's Supper, (6) voluntarism and the independence of the local congregation, (7) the associational principle, (8) principles of ministry, (9) the missionary imperative, (10) religious freedom and separation of church and state, and (11) principles of human rights.[18]

---

[13] Brackney, "'Commonly, (Though Falsely) Called…,'" 79.

[14] Ibid., 80.

[15] Brackney, *The Baptists.* He unpacks the Baptist identity throughout the book.

[16] Brackney, *Historical Dictionary,* 422.

[17] Brackney, *Congregation and Campus,* 2.

[18] Brackney, *Capsule History,* 7–8.

After reading Brackney on the Baptist identity, one may want to ask, "Will the real Bill Brackney please stand up?" However, while one may suppose different Brackneys writing at different times and saying different things, a close reading of his several writings will reveal unusual harmony in his thinking on the subject of Baptist identity. Even though he utilizes different categories in different books, his final profile of the Baptist people is very much the same.

THE DESCRIPTION OF BAPTIST IDENTITY ACCORDING TO BRACKNEY

To arrive at his understanding of the Baptist identity, Brackney excavated numerous Baptists' sources. He refused to confine himself to one genre or one group of Baptists, thinking that one errs in following that truncated approach. Rather, he identified the Baptist vision of Christianity by looking to "confessional statements, the writings of theologians and historians, commentaries, biographies, and institutional and church records."[19] He also analyzed the hymnology of Baptists as a source of Baptist thought.[20] Astutely, he based his understanding of Baptists on both what they said and what they did, on both their talk and their walk.

In profiling Baptists, Brackney never searched for a group of Baptist distinctives that were the sole property of the Baptist people.[21] It is almost impossible, however, to speak of the Baptist identity without reference to some grouping of what he calls Baptist "genes." Taking a cue from Brackney himself, I suggest that Brackney's understanding of who Baptists are and have been may be subsumed under the following three "clusters,"[22] each containing several critically important ideas and actions. These three clusters are (1) Baptists and Authority, (2) Baptists and the Church, and (3) Baptists and Discipleship.

AD 1: BAPTISTS AND AUTHORITY

Brackney's interpretation of where Baptists go for their religious authority is brought together in its most coherent and mature form in his 2009 book, *A Capsule History of Baptist Principles.* He listed three sources of Baptist authority: (1) the Lordship of Christ, (2) the authority of Scripture, and (3) the importance of religious experience.

Regarding the Lordship of Christ, Brackney said, "Christ is the supreme authority in Baptist thought, and this belief takes prime place among historic

---

[19] Ibid., 15. See also, Brackney's *A Genetic History*, 2.

[20] Brackney, *A Genetic History*, 64–104.

[21] Ibid., 4.

[22] Brackney, *Capsule History*, 14.

Baptist principles. The principle of the lordship of Christ brings into focus both theological and ethical dimensions of Baptist experience."[23] Brackney is far from alone in this affirmation, for one can find statements like this from many Baptists.[24] However, this is, as I interpret Brackney, an unusually significant statement. Note that he does not begin his *Capsule History* with the Bible as the supreme authority in Baptist life, as he does in other places.[25] As we shall see, he speaks often and eloquently about the authority of the Bible in Baptist life, but here, in one of his most recent articulations of the Baptist identity, he lifts up Christ as the "supreme authority," saying that the Lordship of Christ "takes prime place among historic Baptist principles."

Brackney alluded to the Christological character of Baptist life often in his other writings. For example, in his *Dictionary*, he lists, without elaboration, the Lordship of Christ as a mark of early Baptists, but he does not lift up the idea as a "supreme" authority for Baptists.[26] In the same book he has a brief paragraph under the article "Christ, Doctrine of," but again without reference to Christ's authority.[27] He implied, without specificity, that the Living Christ was an authority for Baptist life in *Baptists in North America*.[28] However, he makes all of this much more explicit in the concluding chapter of his book on Baptist theology[29] and in *Capsule History*.

But what does Brackney mean by referring to the "Lordship of Christ" as "the supreme authority in Baptist thought"? To answer that question adequately, it may be helpful to know that Brackney is a religiously experiential person. He would eagerly identify, I think, with William E. Hull when Hull said, "When Baptists attempt to understand and interpret their distinctive approach to the Christian faith, they typically do so in terms of experience."[30] Brackney's Baptist experientialism comes out in many places in his writings, but clearly so when he claims Christ as Baptists' supreme authority.

While certainly not all, part of what Brackney is saying is that the Living

---

[23] Ibid., 17.

[24] See Walter B. Shurden, *The Baptist Identity: Four Fragile Freedoms* (Macon GA: Smyth and Helwys Publishing, Inc., 1993) 10–11.

[25] Brackney, *The Baptists*, xvii. On p. 24 of this 1988 publication, Brackney maintains that "the Bible is the sole authority for determining matters related to the Christian faith." This marks a difference, I think, from later writings.

[26] Brackney, *Historical Dictionary*, xxvi.

[27] Ibid., 101, 422.

[28] Brackney, *Baptists in North America*, 2.

[29] Brackney, *A Genetic History*, 527–29.

[30] William E. Hull, *The Meaning of the Baptist Experience* (Brentwood TN: Baptist History and Heritage Society, 2007) 5. Likewise, see Brackney, *Baptists in North America*, 3, where he says, "No one can follow Baptist history very far without appreciating the importance of religious experience." Also see, his *Congregation and Campus*, 2, 417.

Word of God, Christ, is as much an authority for Baptists as the Bible, the written Word of God. He is not placing one authority over against another, and he is making no effort to minimize the prominent place of the Bible in Baptist life. He does say, however, that some Christian traditions have become preoccupied with written texts while "most Baptists sought solace in the living Christ as head of the Church and Lord of the Great Commission."[31]

Baptists have no popes, archbishops, or authoritative ecclesiastical leaders. No one person serves as an authority to point the way for Baptists. Local Baptist churches, Brackney claims, live out their lives hopefully and ideally under the direction of the rule and reign of the Risen Christ. This is Christian experience at its best. Through prayer, meditation, and consultation within the community, local churches seek the mind of Christ in both theological and ethical issues. The imitation of the historical Jesus of Nazareth as He is revealed in Scripture is certainly a Baptist authority, but the risen, living Christ still guides the church today. Baptists, according to Brackney, are a Jesus-people, and Jesus, rather than being closeted in history, lives among them today as a Presence that guides and directs.[32]

If Baptists are a Jesus-people, they are also very much a Bible-people. They are a biblically as well as Christologically oriented people. After the authority of the Lordship of Christ, said Brackney, "The next most recognizable genetic trait among Baptists is undeniably the priority of Scripture."[33] This Baptist historian/theologian has affirmed throughout his long and productive career that the Bible is a major authority in Baptist life. "The Holy Scripture of the Old and New Testaments is the theological bedrock of the Baptist character," he affirmed without equivocation.[34]

He reinforced this idea by pointing to early Baptist theologians and their use of Scripture. For them "scripture was the starting point."[35] Brackney made a thought-provoking point about later liberal Baptist theologians that is often overlooked. They, too, contrary to common understanding, preoccupied themselves with Holy Scripture. The issue in liberal-conservative struggles over the Bible was not that one was biblical and the other unbiblical. The difference was in the approach and interpretation of the Bible, Brackney argued. He also pointed to early Baptist Confessions of Faith that proof-texted almost every phrase with the Bible. The *Second London Confession* of 1677, for example, listed only canonical books

[31] Brackney, *A Genetic History*, 529.

[32] See his fascinating comments about how the Christology principle among Baptists contrasts with other Christian groups concerning the Trinity in ibid. and *Capsule History*, 21.

[33] Brackney, *A Genetic History*, 530.

[34] Brackney, *Capsule History*, 23.

[35] Brackney, *A Genetic History*, 530.

as Scripture, enunciated a Baptist doctrine of Scripture, and supported each theological statement with profuse biblical texts.[36]

While he often pointed to the biblically saturated Baptist Confessions of Faith as evidence of the supreme role of Scripture in Baptist life, he also frequently noted that Baptists were, nevertheless, an anti-creedal people. "For Baptists," he observed, "the written canonical literature replaced the writings of the Church Fathers, the creeds and early confessions, and, of course, the Book of Common Prayer."[37] Brackney took pains to distinguish between confessions of faith, such as Baptists drafted, and the theological creeds of other major denominations. Among other features, he believed creeds to be binding, somewhat unchanging, documents, while confessions were voluntary statements of faith always subject to change.[38]

Another cardinal Baptist emphasis for which Brackney has fondness is the freedom of each individual to interpret the Bible for oneself. Noting that Baptists of the seventeenth century bore kinship to more radical groups such as the Quakers, Seekers, Ranters, and others, he said that what all these groups "had in common was the opportunity to interpret Scripture for themselves in matters of faith and life."[39] Diminishing the idea that only certain gifted or educated persons can provide accurate interpretations of Scripture, Brackney said, "Baptists...believe that all regenerated persons are competent to interpret and understand Scripture for themselves."[40] He was always careful to balance this alleged individualism with the importance of scriptural interpretation within local churches.

An interesting but certainly not unbaptistic wrinkle in Brackney's take on Baptists and the Bible is his apparent fondness for the New Testament itself. He affirms the entire Bible as central to the Baptist identity, but he seems to exalt the New Testament. "All doctrines and practices, individual and corporate, are to be tested in light of Scripture, *particularly the New Testament*,"[41] he said. Doubtless he reflected here an early Baptist approach to Scripture, but he also may be echoing a biblical struggle between fundamentalists and liberals in the Northern Baptist Convention. Locked in a fight over the Bible in the early twentieth century, fundamentalists wanted to adopt the New Hampshire Confession of Faith as a creedal foundation for the denomination. Instead, the denomination adopted by an overwhelming vote to affirm the New Testament as the "all-sufficient ground of our faith and practice."[42]

---

[36] Brackney, *Capsule History*, 24–25.
[37] Brackney, *The Baptists*, 24.
[38] Brackney, *A Genetic History*, 7–14.
[39] Brackney, *Baptists in North America*, 1.
[40] Brackney, *Capsule History*, 28.
[41] Brackney, *The Baptists*, 24. See also, *A Genetic History*, 530.
[42] Brackney, *The Baptists*, 31.

A third expression of Baptist authority for Brackney, though maybe a lesser one than the Lordship of Christ or the Bible, is personal religious experience. "Baptists were among the first Christian denominational traditions to emphasize religious experience," he said. He continued, "In doing so, they broke new ground in stressing the importance of Christian experience over the celebration of sacraments, the affirmation of creeds, or obedience to a system of ethics."[43] Experience, he said, was more than emotions or feelings, for these may lead to a dangerous subjectivity. Rather, "by experience is meant those responses that individuals create or receive through their senses: touch, sight, hearing, and taste."[44]

Religious experience was at the heart of the Baptist understanding of conversion. It was a prerequisite to and a symbol of baptism. It was what gave staying power for obedience to the commands of Christ. It was what created a believers' church. It was communal as well as individual. The Christian faith is not merely knowledge *about* God but a personal acquaintance *with* the Holy One. Brackney insists, joining other Baptist historians and theologians, that one understands Baptists in vain if one does not place personal spiritual experience at the center of Baptist life.

AD 2: BAPTISTS AND THE CHURCH

Much of what Brackney thinks constitutes the Baptist identity centers in ecclesiology. Again, with this conviction he resonates with many Baptist historians and theologians throughout history. Baptists did little in their formative years to create a distinct theology about God, Jesus, the Holy Spirit, the Bible, the atonement, and other such matters. But Baptists have been somewhat distinctive in the way they have theologized and practiced church. In this section I will discuss Brackney's understanding of Baptist ecclesiology under four topics: (1) the meaning of baptism, (2) the nature of the church, (3) the governance of the church, and (4) the associational principle.

Brackney has never liked trying to reduce the Baptist identity to one idea, one characteristic, or one distinctive. He is doubtless right about that. However, if someone put a gun to my head and said, "Tell me what is the *one* Baptist idea that Bill Brackney thinks *most* sums up the Baptist movement or I will shoot," I would not say, "Shoot," although I know he has a multifaceted understanding of the Baptist identity. Rather, I would breathe deeply and say reluctantly, softly, but confidently, "It is believer's baptism by immersion."

In his 1986 article he maintained that "some mainstream Baptists in the United States currently have an identity crisis." Arguing that Baptists have not agreed on historical origins, theological essence, or subsequent denominational

---

[43] Brackney, *Capsule History*, 29–30.

[44] Ibid., 30.

history, he proposed an approach at arriving at an acceptable definition of Baptist identity. Near the end of the article, however, he proposed his own view of describing the Baptist identity by saying, "More than any other characteristic of the Baptist tradition, then, believers' baptism by immersion was the functional essence of historic Baptist identity." He continued, "For those [Baptists] who claimed to reconstitute primitive Christianity, the ordinance [believers' baptism by immersion] spoke literally from the New Testament of the salient issues in the gospel, and of a voluntary personal relationship with Jesus Christ." It was then that he quoted Morgan Edwards, America's first Baptist historian, as saying, "Practising believer's baptism is our denominating article."[45]

Note several features of his statement. "Believers' baptism by immersion was the functional essence of historic Baptist identity," he declares. And Brackney, significantly, adds "immersion" to Edwards' omission of it. Brackney's source is the New Testament, not church tradition. His subject for baptism is a "believer," not one incapable of believing, such as an infant. Many non-Baptists think the major feature of Baptist life is the mode of baptism, immersion. In doing so, however, they overlook Baptists' earliest concern about baptism and that was the subject of baptism. The "believer" has voluntarily entered into a personal relationship with Jesus Christ. Those words, "voluntary" and "personal," signify an experience that is important for Brackney in Baptist life.[46] And he says that believers' baptism by immersion speaks to the "salient issues in the gospel." Doubtless he is referring to the adult nature of baptism, but he is also referencing the symbolism of immersion, the dying to self, symbolized by burial, and the rising to new life, symbolized by resurrection.[47] We may guess at some of what the historian means, but we cannot doubt that believers' baptism by immersion takes a central role in his understanding of the Baptist identity.

Why does Brackney prioritize believers' baptism by immersion as the "functional essence" of Baptist life? He does so because it provides a theological foundation for the Baptist concept of the church, a church composed of people who have willingly, freely, and personally chosen to respond to the merciful invitation of God and follow the Jesus way of life. When early Baptists embraced the idea of a church composed of believers only, they were at the same time rejecting the idea of a geographical parish church. One was born into the parish church, baptized as an infant. However, one had to be "born again" into what Baptists called the "gathered churches" and baptized as one who freely chose the Christian faith.[48] Individuals were "gathered" out of the parish to constitute communities of believers.

---

[45] Brackney, "'Commonly, (Though Falsely) Called...,'" 80.

[46] Brackney, *The Baptists*, xvii.

[47] Brackney, *Capsule History*, 47.

[48] Ibid., 40.

Note the use of the plural above in "gathered churches" and "communities of believers." Brackney recognized that Baptists spoke of the church as both local and universal. However, Baptists have most often spoken of the church as local bodies of believers. Brackney is by no means a fan of Landmarkism, that Baptist movement that ended in narrow sectarianism and excessive localism. An honest historian, however, he recognized an element of truth in Landmark ecclesiology that stressed the church as a local body of believers. He said, "Landmarkists may be faulted for their overly exclusivist understanding of the church, but it is the mark of an ancient Baptist gene to identify local congregations empirically as the people of God."[49]

Another cherished part of Baptist ecclesiology that Brackney vigorously advocates in his writings is the independence or autonomy of local Baptist churches.[50] Adhering to congregational church government as opposed to Presbyterian or Episcopal governance, Baptist churches run their own affairs through a democratic process. Every church member has a voice and a vote. Egalitarianism reigns. The pastor, like all other members, has one vote but no power to dictate. Likewise, no outside powers, no civil or denominational authorities can impose their wills on local Baptist congregations. Outside denominational organizations may withdraw fellowship from local churches, effectively excluding those churches from their own memberships, but those organizations cannot impose their will on local churches.

Brackney believes that Baptist congregational independence is rooted in what he calls the voluntary principle. "Voluntarism" is a critically important word in Brackney's depiction of Baptist life. He has an entire chapter in *The Baptists* called "A New Way: Voluntary Religion," and yet another chapter in his *Capsule History* entitled "Voluntarism and the Independence of the Local Congregation." He explains voluntarism and its relationship to local church rule in this manner:

> In their understanding of human beings, Baptists respond to the idea of spiritual independence under God. It begins with the assumption that human beings are created in God's image and that among their greatest attributes is God-given freedom to make choices. Baptists are quintessential religious voluntarists and the voluntary principle permeates every facet of their life. What follows naturally is the assumption that individuals are accountable directly to God without any mediator for their choices. The theological principle continues with congregations that are free of eternal ecclesiastical or political control and are held mutually accountable under God.[51]

[49] Brackney, *A Genetic History*, 535.
[50] Brackney, *Baptist Life and Thought*, 47.
[51] Brackney, *Baptists in North America*, 2–3.

The Voluntary Principle is at the heart of another of Brackney's Baptist ideas, and that is the Associational Principle.[52] Brackney argues that the Baptist stress on local church independence never made ecclesiastical lone rangers out of Baptists. Baptists are interdependent as well as independent in their organizational life or church polity. This interdependence manifested itself in Baptist life with the formation of Baptist associations.

Several years after the founding of local Baptist churches in the seventeenth century, Baptist churches began grouping themselves into "associations," small geographical regions. They did this for both practical and theological reasons. They wanted to work together in common concerns and also to demonstrate their oneness in Christ. Brackney defined a Baptist association as follows: "The Baptist association is not considered a superior body to the local congregation; rather, an advisory body voluntarily covenanting with local churches for specific tasks."[53] The associational pattern in Baptist polity indicates "how Baptists work together to place fundamental emphasis upon the local congregation while also seeking counsel and opportunities for service in the larger Body of Christ."[54]

The activity of local churches associating together eventually extended beyond local regions to statewide, national, and world organizations. The Associational Principle also permitted Baptists to participate in ecumenical endeavors. Thus, the Associational Principle allowed Baptist churches to cooperate with one another and with other denominations without sacrificing local church autonomy. Brackney, an ecumenical churchman, found this principle especially attractive.

Brackney may have written more words and more frequently than most Baptist historians concerning the interdependence of Baptist churches, but he recognized the limitations and boundaries of the Associational Principle. It never ballooned for Baptists into an Episcopal or even Presbyterian polity. Baptists recoiled at such. With some muscle, he writes, "There is no superior authority above or beyond the local congregation and there is no such thing overall as 'The Baptist Church.'"[55] No other aspect of Baptist church polity reaches the level of importance as does the authority of the local church.

AD 3: BAPTISTS AND DISCIPLESHIP

Brackney reads Baptist sources to discern what Baptists say about what is important to them. He also observes their actions to see what they do, how they

[52] Brackney, *Capsule History*, 59–68; *Baptists in North America*, 3; and *Historical Dictionary*, 29.

[53] Brackney, *Historical Dictionary*, 29.

[54] Brackney, *Capsule History*, 60.

[55] Brackney, *Congregation and Campus*, 3.

live out their faith. We are right to refer to their actions as Baptist discipleship. Two areas of Baptist discipleship are especially important to Brackney as he speaks of the Baptist identity. These two are: (1) religious liberty and (2) the missionary imperative.

Next to their mode of baptism, Baptists, the world over, probably are known best for their passionate commitment to religious liberty. When troubled souls from the margins of society have lamented the absence of religious liberty, Baptists have tended to listen and act. They had themselves emerged onto the stage of history among such troubled souls. After studying Brackney's writings for this paper, I can confidently say that out of his several summary statements on the Baptist identity, I do not know of one that did not include religious liberty. Soul freedom is basic to his understanding of Baptists. He pointed out that behind the idea of religious liberty one finds several terms being used in Baptist life. "The principles of soul freedom, liberty of conscience, religious liberty, separation of church and state, and all their cognates and correlatives are integral to Baptist identity over four centuries of denominational heritage."[56]

When Brackney wrote on religious liberty, he preferred to write on the history of that struggle in Baptist life. He was more likely to write about Helwys, Murtom, Clarke, Backus, and Leland than he was to pen an essay detailing the various aspects of the Baptist interpretation of religious liberty. This was true even of his article on "Religious Liberty" in his *Dictionary*. One can easily tease out of his brief histories, however, much of what he himself thought.

Brackney took pride, as do most Baptists, in the fact that our seventeenth-century forebears in England and America were among the first to plead for complete freedom of conscience.[57] And they pled for that freedom in a context of oppression by both government and religion. In the face of this oppression, Baptists lobbied for a society where one could believe without coercion, practice faith without constraint, and disseminate faith without hindrance.

Baptists promoted their understanding of religious liberty, Brackney contended, by hardwiring it to their Christology and their anthropology.[58] Apparently he was referring to Baptists' often repeated argument that "[t]he Lord Jesus Christ [...] is only Lord of Conscience," or as Thomas Helwys put it in a more theological framework, "God alone is Lord of the conscience." Regarding Baptists' understanding of anthropology and its relationship to religious liberty, they believed that persons were created in God's image with God's gift to make choices, freely and voluntarily. Again to use Brackney's description, "Baptists are

[56] Brackney, *Capsule History*, 90.
[57] Brackney, *Life and Thought*, 78.
[58] Brackney, *A Genetic History*, 536.

quintessential religious voluntarists." Brackney frequently repeated the early Baptist mantra that a person was accountable only to God.[59]

Religious toleration was inadequate. Baptists did not want to be *tolerated*; they wanted to be *liberated* in matters of faith! "Toleration was something connived at," said Brackney, "that is, granted by pressure from a reluctant government or established church."[60] Religious freedom is God-given, freely so! And this freedom was for all people, those of all faiths and those of no faith at all.

A major reason Baptists wanted religious freedom was to speak freely and without restraint about their faith. As much as any Baptist historian I know, Brackney has incorporated evangelism and missions into the profile of the Baptist identity. He writes with enthusiasm about the developments among English Baptists in the last decades of the eighteenth century. Andrew Fuller and William Carey stepped in front of Baptists in 1792 and helped launch the modern missionary movement. Two decades later, Baptists in America organized the Triennial Convention for the expressed purpose of sending missionaries to far-flung parts of the earth. It is a gripping story, and Brackney loves to tell it.

In his history of Baptist theology, Brackney seems to broaden his meaning of mission. "From their earliest gatherings," he said, "Baptists have sensed urgency about their role as God's people and their obligations under the gospel."[61] He then speaks of different ways Baptists have expressed this urgency. For some it has been through obedience to the Great Commission. For others their witness is expressed through worship and service. And then for others this urgency for the gospel has been expressed through works of social activism and ecumenical activities. Observing that Baptists have been "an outwardly directed people," Brackney then contrasted them with some other Christian groups. Quakers, for example, are introspective, while Mennonites are communitarians. Baptists move outward toward the world with resolve and determination.

As he reflected on Baptist missions today, Brackney warned that "Baptists must be clearer in their claims for the finality of Jesus Christ in a pluralistic world of religions, and they must develop better strategies of dialogue and interaction with peoples of other faiths."[62] He also sees religious liberty playing a much greater role in the future because of political regimes that threaten the freedom to evangelize.

A Brief Evaluation of Baptist Identity According to Brackney

[59] Brackney, *Capsule History*, 87.

[60] Ibid., 86.

[61] Brackney, *A Genetic History*, 535.

[62] Brackney, *Capsule History*, 100.

One of the first points to make in assessing Brackney's work on the Baptist identity is to agree with him that there is such. While at first glance the Baptist identity appears to be a theological forest rather than actual trees one can describe, I think Brackney is altogether correct in arguing for a specific identity. Lists and descriptions of Baptists abound. But if one compares those lists, whittling them down to the bare minimum, one would probably end up with a Bible, a believers' church—including believers' baptism by immersion—local church independency, and religious liberty. A fuller description, such as Brackney might propose, is even more helpful.

Are there unique features of the Baptist identity according to Brackney, at least as I have described them here? I would point to three, and these are not so much unique as they are more earnestly stressed. Those three are Christian experience, the associational principle, and the concept of missions. The first is absolutely indispensable in saying who the Baptists are, and Brackney says this as well as any Baptist historian I know. The other two are most helpful in rounding out the Baptist identity.

Does Brackney omit anything critical in describing Baptists? Some of us would look for more attention to the idea of the priesthood of all believers. Other portrayals of Baptist life have made much more of this idea inherited from Luther than does Brackney. However, in a passage where he bemoans the tendency toward authoritarian pastors, he says, "Both the principle of the priesthood of believers and that of individual competence of the soul before God have been jeopardized."[63]

Brackney is keenly aware of the dangers facing the Baptist identity in the future. The Bible can be hijacked by being elevated into a piece of idolatry or stiff-armed to one side as simply another piece of ancient literature. Creedalism can replace the Bible. Religious experience can become radical subjectivity. Localism in church life can become isolationism. The associational principle can morph into a denominational bureaucracy. Religious liberty can be twisted and warped in such a way that it means freedom for me and no one else. And, worst of all, Baptists can end up thinking they are the only ones God has to work with in our broken world.

Finally, reading Brackney on any subject pertaining to Baptists can make one tired. Not because he is boring but because his writing reflects so much extensive and careful work. While I think Brackney has much more to give the Baptist people, I certainly hope that a young Bill Brackney is waiting in the wings to take over the long, hard work of painstaking research and thoughtful interpretation of the Baptist people.

---

[63] Ibid., 101.

SECTION 1

HUMAN RIGHTS

FREE, EQUAL, AND NONVIOLENT: CHRISTIAN FAITH IN CONVERSATION WITH HUMAN RIGHTS

Thorwald Lorenzen

Dates, places, and symbols like "August 6 and 8, 1945," "9/11," "the Anthropocene," "Syria," "Mali and Niger," and "Manus Island" have been imprinted in our minds and souls. They mark the oft frightening and threatening global reality in which we live. And yet, as Christians whose faith is symbolized by events of hope and liberation—the Exodus of the people of God from slavery and the Resurrection of Jesus Christ to new life—we cannot afford the luxury of despair or escape into niches of comfort.

In our time human rights are the only universally available and acceptable moral vision that promise a flourishing human life for *all* people. Human rights are also associated with a comprehensive legal and institutional framework that provides hope for millions of people who are caught in the endless spiral of oppression, exploitation, and poverty. If people of faith, therefore, want to accept responsibility in the public arena, they have to take human rights seriously and develop an attitude towards them.

Baptist Christians, about whose history, theology, and ethics we have learned much from the writings of William Brackney, have good reasons to be involved with the understanding and implementation of human rights. Their very genesis in sixteenth-century continental Europe and seventeenth-century England has to do with the struggle for core human rights such as freedom of conscience and freedom of religion, and with fundamental Western values, such as the separation of Church and State. Brackney has also informed us about the trajectory of human rights in the world's major religions. To honor him, I would like to offer a modest attempt to appreciate human rights from the perspective of Christian faith.

THE QUEST FOR ONTOLOGY

Human rights make ontological claims. Such claims cannot immediately be verified by empirical observation or historical investigation. They speak about "the *inherent* dignity and [...] *inalienable* rights of *all* members of the human family." They assert that "*all* human beings *are born* free and equal in dignity and rights" and that they "are *endowed* with reason and conscience."[1] The intention of these formulations is clear. They want to underline the *universality* of human rights; and they want to assert that the dignity and freedom of the human person *transcends* the authority of human and historical institutions, like the State, the Law, the Church, and human contracts. They want to emphasize that historical institutions neither invented nor granted human dignity, and they therefore cannot take it away. Their noble function is to recognize, understand, and protect it.[2]

It is contentious, however, whether human rights need a moral foundation to underpin their lasting legitimacy and relevance. What does the claim mean that a person has certain "inherent" and "inalienable" rights; that people are "born" with certain rights; that human beings have these rights "by nature"? If people "are endowed with reason and conscience," who or what "endows" them with such?

Traditionally, Natural Law theories have been called upon to provide a universal basis for morality. But such theories have lost their power in the wake of having been used to justify slavery, racism, militarism, sexism, ageism, and nationalism. This loss of credibility poses a serious dilemma.

Jacques Maritain recalls a UNESCO conference where people, despite their different ideological persuasions, agreed on a number of human rights. When questioned about that, they said: "We agree on these rights, providing we are not asked why. With the 'why,' the dispute begins."[3]

While most human-rights declarations leave the question of ontology open, the American Declaration of Independence of 1776 makes an exception by referring to a Creator-God: "We hold these truths to be self-evident, that all men are created equal, that they are endowed by their Creator with certain inalienable Rights, that among these are Life, Liberty, and the pursuit of Happiness."

Max Stackhouse speaks for many when he says: "I want to claim that without the impetus of theological insight, human-rights concepts would not have come to their current widespread recognition, and that they are likely to fade over time if they are not anchored in a universal context-transcending metaphysical

---

[1] The Universal Declaration of Human Rights (UDHR), preamble and article 1 (emphases mine).

[2] The German Constitution (the *Basic Law for the Federal Republic of Germany*), for instance, reads in article 1: "Human dignity shall be inviolable. To respect and protect it shall be the duty of all state authority. The German people therefore acknowledge inviolable and inalienable human rights as the basis of every community, of peace and of justice in the world." In light of this constitutional imperative the German Chancellor, Angela Merkel, had no choice, but to open German borders to people who fled war and persecution.

[3] Jacques Maritain, *Man and the State* (Chicago: University of Chicago Press, 1951) 77. The conflict is described by Nicholas Wolterstorff, *Justice: Rights and Wrongs* (Princeton and Oxford: Princeton University Press, 2008) 1–4.

reality."[4] Nicholas Wolterstorff agrees: "It is impossible to develop a secular account of human dignity adequate for grounding human rights."[5] Stackhouse contends further that if we fail to provide an ontological grounding for human rights, they will erode and there will be "no basis on which to defend the oppressed, the prisoner, the weak, the disposed; to justify civil and political liberties; or to fight for social and economic justice."[6]

It may indeed be the case that the widespread lack of respect for human rights is a direct consequence of their "rationale" being controversial. The recent use of torture during the "war against terror" has shown again that "when the pressure is on" even pace-setting democracies like the United States, Britain, and Australia fall back into moral tribalism and utilitarian self-interest rather than respecting and implementing what they have signed and ratified. It seems to be too easily forgotten that the moral authority of human rights is tested, not when things go well, but when challenging situations need to be confronted and dealt with. Morality commences at the point of pain and at such a point resilience is more likely if an ontological grounding is accepted.

Every culture needs to engage in the quest to seek and find a valid and accepted moral foundation for human rights. Otherwise the danger is great that human rights will be used as entitlements or are functionalized to serve national, economic, and other ideological interests. Since religions often make up the soil and the nourishment in which a culture grows, the religions of the world are challenged with some urgency to consider—from their perspective!—the issue of a moral foundation for universal human rights. I will engage in the debate from the Christian perspective.

Christian Faith and Human Rights

For a long time, Christians and their churches have been apprehensive about human rights. They were suspicious of their secularity and they feared that human

---

[4] Max L. Stackhouse, "Sources and Prospects for Human Rights Ideas: A Christian Perspective," in Jindrich Halama, ed., *The Idea of Human Rights: Traditions and Presence, Proceedings of an International Conference Held in Prague Feb 20–23, 2003,* 183–200 (UK ETF, Praha: 2003) 194.

[5] Wolterstorff, *Justice: Rights and Wrongs*, 325; compare pp. 181 and 361. In chapter 15 of *Justice: Rights and Wrongs*, Wolterstorff discusses and dismisses three secular attempts to provide a moral foundation for human rights. See also Michael J. Perry's *The Idea of Human Rights: Four Inquiries* (Oxford University Press: New York/Oxford, 1998) ch. 1; and also his *Toward a Theory of Human Rights: Religion, Law, Courts* (Cambridge University Press: Cambridge/New York: 2007) ch. 3.

[6] "Why Human Rights Needs God: A Christian Perspective," in Elizabeth M. Bucar and Barbra Barnett, eds., *Does Human Rights Need God?*, 25–47 (Eerdmans: Grand Rapids, 2005) 31, also 36.

rights would question the authority of the church. Even theologians warned that we should be more concerned with God's rights than with human rights. Fortunately, times have changed! These days, many Christians and most Christian denominations welcome the history and praxis of human rights. Christians are engaged on all levels in the implementation of human rights—and they do so for the following reasons.

THE HUMANUM AS *IMAGO DEI*

For Christians, human identity and human worth are not grounded in any *capacity* humans may have—like reason or language or a "soul" or an upright walk—but in the creative, sustaining, and redemptive activity of God. In creation and redemption God relates God's self to each human person and thereby instills in that individual a dignity no one can take away. Christians therefore heartily agree when the Universal Declaration of Human Rights (UDHR), published in 1948, speaks about the "inherent dignity" and "inalienable rights" of human persons, and when it declares in article 1 that "*all* human beings are *born* free and equal in dignity and rights. They are *endowed* with reason and conscience and should act towards one another in a spirit of brotherhood." For Christians human life is the generous and precious gift of God.

At the very outset of the biblical narrative, the creation of humanity is interrelated with the moral demand to *protect* what God has created. The confession that "God created humankind in God's image" is interrelated with the assertion that humans should not do violence to each other because "in his own image God made humankind" (Gen. 1:26–27 and 9:6).

Although the interpretation of *imago dei* (image of God) remains controversial to the present day, Christians confess that God has imbued human beings with dignity and responsibility, and above all with the promises that God will remain passionately involved with what God has created. The Psalmists therefore praise God for having created humans, "crowned them with glory and honor," and for continuing to "think" of them and "regard" them (Psalms 8:4–5, 144:3).

JESUS OF NAZARETH AS *VERE HOMO*

The early Christians took up the *imago dei* trajectory and applied it to *Jesus Christ* and to the *new humanity* that he inaugurated. Jesus Christ is confessed as the "image of God," as the divine Word having become flesh, as "the reflection of God's glory and the exact imprint of God's very being." Indeed "in him the whole fullness of deity dwells bodily" (2 Cor. 4:4, Col. 1:15, John 1:1–14, Heb. 1:3, Col. 2:9). As the real and the true human being, Jesus represents all human beings and at the same time reflects and manifests the nature of God—*vere homo, vere deus* (truly human, truly divine).

With respect to human rights it is important to remember that Jesus' main passion in life was to make human life human. He healed people, he spoke hope into the lives of the oppressed, and he prioritized people over laws, institutions, and traditions. The evangelist Luke captures Jesus' life passion well when he presents Jesus as reading in the temple from the prophet Isaiah and then saying, "Today this scripture has been fulfilled in your hearing" (Luke 4:21):

> The Spirit of the Lord is upon me,
> because he has anointed me to bring good news to the poor.
> He has sent me to proclaim release to the captives
> and recovery of sight to the blind,
> to let the oppressed go free,
> to proclaim the year of the Lord's favor. (Luke 4:18–19)

Justification and Justice

The Reformation emphasis that we are justified not by works, but by faith, indeed by faith alone—*sola gratia, sola fide*—is often reduced to an individualistic confession or doctrinal assertion. In fact, however, it is of immense anthropological significance and social relevance. It asserts, against many trends in our Western cultures, that our human worth and identity are not in what we achieve, produce, and consume, but in who we are as an unconditional gift of God. Indeed, the Christian faith, as far as I know, is the only view of reality that provides for a morality where the most wretched of the earth are of equal worth to the decathlon champion and industrial tycoon.

We humans receive our identity. Faith "comes" to us and it "comes from what is heard, and what is heard comes through the word of Christ" (Gal. 3:23–25, Rom. 10:17). Human dignity, therefore, is derived. It is grounded in God's being for us. When Christians speak of faith and of justification by faith apart from the works of the law, they want to elaborate that human dignity is not grounded in human capacities (reason, language, intelligence, gender, race) and/or achievements (power, wealth, status) but in the fact that human life is God's gift.

Through faith in Jesus Christ human beings become aware that they are created in the image of God. Humanity "is being renewed in knowledge according to the image of its creator" (Col. 3:10). By raising Jesus from death, God relativized the estranging forces of disobedience, pride, and selfishness and renewed God's plans for God's creation: "[...] if anyone is in Christ, there is a new creation: everything old has passed away; see, everything has become *new*!" (2 Cor. 5:17).

Entailed in that new humanity is a new morality: "In that renewal there is no longer Greek and Jew, circumcised and uncircumcised, barbarian, Scythian, slave and free; but Christ is all and in all!" (Col. 3:11, see also Gal. 3:23–28). The Christian confession of being justified by faith alone has therefore an intentional edge against all claims of defining human identity in terms of works, achievements, gender, or race.

Christians need to learn and annunciate more clearly that justification is interlocked with justice. We have thought too much "from above." We have been too concerned with an individualistic salvation and a private spirituality. While it is right and important to proclaim the justification of the sinner, with equal emphasis and pathos we have to show solidarity with the victims of sin. The church has provided sacraments of confession and penance for the sinner, but we have often failed to provide solidarity, hope, and restitution for the victims of sin. Both the sinner and the victim of sin are of equal importance to a compassionate and just God.

Nevertheless, while faith and justice hang together, there is a procedural priority for faith. Faith establishes our personal identity, which precedes our morality and praxis. Our personal identity is grounded in God's relationship to us and our grateful response to God. Christians therefore say that they are "saved by faith" and not "by works," and they emphasize that their engagement for justice is anchored in and resourced by their reconciliation with God.

The same dynamic can be seen in the Jesus Story, the wellspring and content of Christian faith. For Jesus his relationship to God, whom he referred to with the intimate "Abba" (daddy, father), is the ground and content for his relationship to others and for his ministry of healing and justice.

Historical Experience

A further reason why Christians in general and Baptist Christians in particular affirm the importance of human rights is their historical experience of having suffered oppression and persecution by church and state, and having been denied freedom of conscience and religion.

In 2017 we are commemorating 500 years of the Reformation and 100 years of the Russian Revolution.

It is right, of course, to celebrate Martin Luther's influence on church, theology, and society. At the same time, it should not be forgotten that there were also victims of the Reformation.[7] The Magisterial Reformers, for instance, failed to grant to fellow Christians what they claimed for themselves, a conscience freed by faith in Christ and bound to the Word, rather than the pope. In fact, Luther,

[7] For Martin Luther's attitude to the Baptizers (*Täufer*), see Thorwald Lorenzen, "Ecumenism Starts at the 'Point of Pain': Luther and the Victims of the Reformation," *St. Mark's Review* 3/241 (October 2017): 30–49.

Zwingli, Calvin, and their fellow reformers sought and found the help of the State to imprison, ban, burn, and execute thousands of Christians who, like them, wanted to follow the voice of their conscience. This historical experience became an important impetus for claiming freedom of conscience and religious liberty and seeking protection from arbitrary detention and torture. All of these concerns have issued into core human rights today.

And when we remember the Russian Revolution, we must also lament the thousands of Christians, among them many Baptist Christians, who were tortured, imprisoned, and killed for their Christian faith.

Historical experiences like these have fueled the call for freedom of conscience and religion, as well as for other human rights such as the protection from arbitrary arrests and the elimination of torture, all of which have become core human rights today.

Conclusion

The fact that today the established churches have a positive attitude towards human rights is, with some notable exceptions, a rather recent phenomenon. For many centuries the established churches have punished, imprisoned, tortured, exiled, excommunicated, persecuted, and even killed persons who failed to agree with what those churches considered to be important dogmatic or ethical convictions. Both churches and their theologians wanted to protect the moral authority of Christianity against what they perceived as secular humanism.

Fortunately, that time has passed. Today most churches and their representatives are involved with the implementation of human rights, and I have listed the theological reasons why that is so. This should not blind us to the fact, however, that in a number of areas some large churches—one only needs to think of the Southern Baptist Convention and the Roman Catholic Church—fail to give equality to women and still support war as a legitimate way to solve human conflict.

Christian Faith in Dialogue with Human Rights

Every culture, religion, and tradition is challenged to engage with human rights in a creative and constructive way and to implement them in their own settings. Such interaction should reflect the spirit and intention of human rights. It should not serve one's respective self-interest, but must genuinely seek the common good. Human rights are not entitlements. The authority and effect of human rights are measured not by the ones that we find convenient, but by the ones that impinge on our national interest and personal lifestyle. Morality starts at the point of pain!

In that spirit I will now briefly comment on some underlying and integrating values of the human-rights tradition and do so from the Christian perspective.

FREEDOM AS A SOCIAL REALITY

Christians joyously tune into the universal ethos that "*all* human beings are *born free* [...]."[8] Human rights protect people from arbitrary interference by political, social, and religious institutions, and they seek to mark out free spaces in which people can plan their lives, exercise their creativity, and contribute to the common good.

The primary symbols of the Judeo-Christian faith—the Exodus in the Jewish and the Resurrection of Jesus Christ in the Christian tradition—are symbols of freedom. Freedom from slavery. Freedom from the encroaching powers of death. Freedom to celebrate life. The hospitality of God includes the invitation to freedom and liberation.

Nevertheless! The Christian faith sharpens our awareness for a dehumanizing distortion of freedom. In Western cultures, we tend to understand freedom in terms of the eighteenth-century French Revolution. The Declaration of the Rights of Man and of the Citizen (1789) defines freedom as "the power of doing whatever does not injure another" (§ 4).

We tend to overlook the ambivalence and limitations of this understanding of freedom. On the one hand, it has inspired the industrial and scientific revolutions, as well as the economic and political structures on which our Western political and economic strengths and successes are built. Yet, on the other hand, it is widely recognized today that the negative by-product of the Western ideal was that it placed the weak, the underprivileged, and the economically powerless at the mercy of the strong. Capitalism and its modern form of Neo-Liberalism are in a moral crisis today. They do not work for the *common* good. They are not sustainable in the long run. Their unsophisticated trust in market forces, their focus on money and profit, their individualism, and their competitive mentality have even the experts convinced that it can't go on as it is. The problem is, of course, that after the collapse of manifest Socialism in the 1980s, we have no agreed-upon model to lead us out of the crisis.

It is clear, however, that the Western individualistic and competitive understanding of freedom is deficient; it does not serve the *common* good. It fails to recognize adequately the *relational* nature of the human person and the *equality* of all human beings in the context of *one* humanity. It instills in us the impulse to see every other person as a potential enemy who may restrict my individual freedom. Such an individualistic understanding of freedom easily leads to separation and enmity in the human family. People become primarily concerned with stak-

---

[8] UDHR, § 1 (emphases mine).

ing out the frontiers of their self-interest and misuse human rights as entitlements. Concern for the neighbor or for nature is ascribed secondary importance.

Here Christian faith offers a correction. We humans are not self-sufficient islands but relational and social beings. The classic biblical portrayal is well known: "God created humankind in God's image, in the image of God he created them; male and female he created them" (Gen. 1:27). The sociality of being human became individualized by an intentional and unbending focus on the self.[9] Nevertheless, when the Christian community celebrates the reconciliation that God has established through Christ, the communitarian nature of human life is affirmed as in Galatians 3:26–28: "[...] in Christ Jesus you are all children of God through faith. As many of you as were baptized into Christ have clothed yourselves with Christ. There is no longer Jew or Greek, there is no longer slave or free, there is no longer male and female; for all of you are one in Christ Jesus."

Christians joyfully affirm freedom rights, but at the same time we add the extra dimension that, at its deepest level, freedom is a *community experience* in which our human brother or sister is not our potential rival whom we need to fear, but the one whom we need to experience and celebrate true freedom.

The German philosopher Jürgen Habermas puts into words what Martin Luther King, Jr., and Nelson Mandela fleshed out with their lives: "No one is free until we *all* are free."[10] Freedom therefore implies equality and solidarity.

Equality—with a Specific Bent

Equality is a celebrated ideal in the global village. "All human beings are born free and equal in dignity and rights," we read in article 1 of the UDHR. Although we are all different—skin color, gender, education, sexual orientation—such differences must not be used to privilege one over the other. Therefore, human rights emphasize that we are all equal before the law and no one must be discriminated against on account of color or race or gender or sexual orientation or religion.

---

[9] The *individualism* often associated with human rights is a *distortion* rather than the essence of their intention. The fact that they are too often claimed as *entitlements* to further certain interests does not negate their *social* intention. Nicholas Wolterstorff comments that an "ethos of possessive individualism employs the language of rights for its own purposes" (*Justice: Rights and Wrongs*, 388). See also, Wolterstorff's *Justice in Love* (Eerdmans: Grand Rapids, Michigan, 2011) 90–92, 134–38. While individualism remains an ever-present danger, the intention of human rights is to protect human dignity within the network of society and nature.

[10] Jürgen Habermas says it well: "Freedom conceived intersubjectively distinguishes itself from the arbitrary freedom of the isolated individual. No one is free until we all are free" ("A Conversation about God and the World," interview with Eduardo Mendieta, in Jürgen Habermas, *Religion and Rationality: Essays on Reason, God, and Modernity*, ed. Eduardo Mendieta, 147–67 [Cambridge MA: The MIT Press, 2002] 161).

Nevertheless, while equality is the human ideal, inequality is all too often the historical reality. Ask women; ask girls in India and China; ask indigenous people; ask those with disabilities; ask old people; ask refugees; ask Christians in Muslim countries and ask Muslims in Christian countries. The affirmation that "*all* human beings are born free and equal in dignity and rights," is neither obvious nor apparent in our world. Indeed, by looking at the world as it is, there are more reasons for affirming inequality than equality as a "natural" fact.

Christians wholeheartedly affirm and support equality rights—although it is really sad, indeed deplorable, that many churches still refuse to give equality to women and continue to discriminate against people on the basis of gender, race, and color. All that is regrettable. But here I want to make the point that empirical evidence—natural law—does not support a universal ethos of equality. Christians therefore base their commitment to equality not on what human reason perceives in the nature of things, but on God's dealings with humanity as it becomes historically manifest in the Story of Jesus. Christians assert the equality of all people because God has created and redeemed all human beings to be *one* humanity—of course, with interesting and colorful differences!

And yet, for Christians there is a specific bias to equality. Of all ethical theories—and there are many!—it is the Christian understanding of reality that clearly and publicly privileges the victim. Jesus was focused in his activity, and his focus was the victim. In word and deed he revealed to them the justice and compassion of God. "Jesus joins the victims; therein, God joins the victims."[11]

It is consistent with this understanding of reality that the earliest Christian churches located the presence of Christ in the world not only in the preaching of the word and the administration of the sacraments, as Christian churches generally emphasize, but also in the vulnerable child and in the hungry, the stranger and the prisoner (Mark 9:36–37; Matt. 25:31–46). Early Christians confessed that their solidarity with and compassion for victims were reflections of their relation to Christ.

Human life will flourish if we give more room to freedom and equality. Are we not part of the *one* global human family? Why do we have a "firewall" mentality towards refugees? Are they not human beings like us? Do they not deserve a safe space to live? Can there be a conversion, a transfiguration, from a fortress mentality to a mentality of solidarity with our fellow human persons?

Waging Compassionate Solidarity

A third emphasis underpinning human rights is to empower people to participate in shaping their own destiny within the context of nature and society.

---

[11] Wolterstorff, *Justice: Rights and Wrongs,* 110; also Jürgen Moltmann, *Ethics of Hope,* trans. Margaret Kohl (Minneapolis: Fortress Press, 2012) 182.

Therefore not only an elite but "*all* human beings [...] are endowed with reason and conscience," as § 1 of the UDHR says. Most articles of the declaration commence with "everyone" or "no one." "Everyone" has the right to life, liberty, security. "Everyone" is equal before the law, can found a family, and participate in determining the nature of their society. "Everyone" can think freely and pray according to the dictates of their conscience. "No one" shall be tortured or enslaved or arbitrarily detained.

This emphasis on empowering people—all people equally—to use their God-given freedom in shaping their life within the context of nature and society is very conducive to the Christian faith. Christians, therefore, affirm the principle of democracy and its outworking in society. Although many churches are still hierarchically structured and disadvantage people on the basis of gender, sexual orientation, and race, this should be unmasked as a fundamental distortion of the Christian faith. Not only the freedom and equality of all people, but the equal participation of all Christians in the formation of Christian community is fundamental to the Christian faith. Biblically speaking, faith and baptism equalize Christians. The Apostle Paul emphasizes that to "*each* is given the manifestation of the Spirit for the *common good*" (1 Cor. 12:7). Since the Reformation it has become quite common to speak of the priesthood of all believers: "[...] you are a chosen race, a royal priesthood, a holy nation, God's own people, in order that you may proclaim the mighty acts of him who called you out of darkness into his marvelous light" (1 Pet. 2:9; see also 1 Pet. 2:5 and Rev. 1:6, 5:10, and 20:6).

One Humanity

The Judeo-Christian tradition provides a clear rationale for the *universality* of human rights. The God whom Jews and Christians worship is the creator and sustainer "of heaven and earth." The Israelites begin their Holy Scriptures with the creation stories in Genesis 1 and 2, thereby confessing that their God *El* or *YHWH* is not merely a tribal deity, but the creator of all things. Christians affirm that God not only loves the world (Greek: "*cosmos*"), but has reconciled this cosmos with God's self (John 3:16, 2 Cor. 5:17–21). For human beings this means that God "desires *everyone* to be saved and to come to the knowledge of the truth" (1 Tim. 2:4).

Emphasizing the oneness of humanity and, with it, the universality of human rights in no way diminishes cultural diversity and differences. Sameness can be very boring. It is wonderful that the carpet of humanity, if woven from many colors, can contain many interesting patterns. Let every flower bloom in its own beauty. But just as every flower needs air, water, soil, and sunlight to develop its splendor, so every human being needs food, shelter, freedom, equality, and education to become who he or she is. Every human person has the right to a safe space in which he or she can develop into a flourishing member of his or her own culture and of the human family. It is that safe space which human rights want to attain for all people.

Rights of Nature

At the same time, we are becoming increasingly aware of the fact that human life and human history are embedded in nature. God's care encompasses not only humans, but also "the birds of the air and the lilies in the field" (Matt. 6:26–28), and God's spirit "renews the face of the ground" (Psalm 104:30). It is therefore encouraging that within the context of the United Nations there is a growing movement formulating and implementing the rights of nature. For too long humans have treated nature as property to be used and exploited for their own advancement. It is to be welcomed that we are beginning to realize that nature has its own rights to exist and evolve. We ignore those rights at our peril. By showing disrespect for nature, we destroy the very garden that sustains us.

Rights Rather than Charity

Although in Christian circles we talk much about compassion, charity, aid, obligation, duty, and responsibility, "rights language" has the advantage of protecting the dignity of people whose human rights have been denied. Rights language looks at reality from the perspective of those whose dignity is threatened, diminished, or distorted.[12] It challenges us to become aware of the vantage point from which we look at reality. Most ethical theories are agent oriented. They "look" from above. Rights language invites and challenges us to "look" from below, from the perspective of the potential victim.[13]

---

[12] A good example from Australia is the "Mahatma Gandhi Inaugural Oration" (30 January 2012 at the University of New South Wales) of Professor Patrick Dodson, Australia's indigenous "Father" of reconciliation and now Labor Senator in the Australian Parliament: "Under the Howard Coalition Government we saw a shift in reconciliation *away from the rights agenda towards practical reconciliation.* Reconciliation it seemed was redefined as the provision of 'practical' measures to address discrepancies in our socio-economic status, rather than the root causes of our exclusion" (http://www.abc.net.au/tv/bigideas/browse/video_popup.htm?vidURL=/tv/bigideas/stories/2012/02/08/3422644-mediarss-full.xml&vidTitle=Professor Patrick Dodson: Inaugural Gandhi Oration&vidLength=Full, emphasis mine). Nicholas Wolterstorff says the same in different words: "*Moral* obligations will be those *toward* a person or human being, *moral* rights will be those *of* a person or human being" (*Justice: Rights and Wrongs*, 372).

[13] Wolterstorff comments: "To eliminate rights-talk would be to make impossible the coming to speech of *the recipient-dimension of the moral order.*" Again: "The reason the language of rights has proved so powerful in social movements is that it brings *the victims and their moral condition into the light of day*" (*Justice: Rights and Wrongs*, 8–9, emphases mine).

British/European Australians, for instance, are generally prepared to be *charitable* and *generous* toward Aborigines and refugees. Given the Genocide, Refugee, and Torture Conventions, we may also feel *obligated* to give aid to Aborigines, to oppose torture and be sympathetic to the struggle of refugees and asylum seekers. But are we prepared to look at life *through their eyes*? Do we grant them a hermeneutical privilege for understanding reality? Do we recognize the equal dignity and worth of these people as human beings and grant that they have a claim upon us? Are we prepared to acknowledge that if we don't meet that claim, our own dignity is diminished? Are we prepared to recognize that the "other" is an essential part of our common humanity, and that the dignity of our own humanity is at stake when the dignity of others is threatened?

There is, of course, always the danger of misunderstanding and distortion. Too often human rights have been instrumentalized by people and groups to get their own way; they are used as entitlements for venturing one's own cause. We must therefore constantly be aware that being human is a social reality and that human rights name and implement what it means to be human in the context of society and nature.

Nonviolence

The "Doomsday Clock" project was created by those scientists that produced the Atom Bombs that destroyed Hiroshima and Nagasaki. It wants to warn the world of nuclear destruction. It is now only minutes away from midnight, which means that we are as close to nuclear annihilation as ever. The aggressive slanging match between the United States and North Korea, the instability in the Middle East with their nuclear capacities, and the fact that in the history of humanity weapons have been created not only to deter, but to be used, can only heighten the possibility of nuclear war.

The Preamble to the United Nations Charter states: "We the peoples of the United Nations (are) determined to *save succeeding generations from the scourge of war,* which twice in our lifetime has brought untold sorrow to mankind, and to reaffirm faith in fundamental human rights, in the dignity and worth of the human person, in the equal rights of men and women and of nations large and small."

And in article 1 the charter commits the member states of the United Nations "to maintain international peace and security." The UDHR, which was composed in direct response to the inhuman brutalities of the Second World War, refers in its preamble to the "barbarous acts which have outraged the conscience of mankind."

In 1983 the Inter Action Council with over twenty former Heads of State—

including Malcolm Fraser, Helmut Schmidt, Jimmy Carter, Mikhail S. Gorbachev, Pierre Elliott Trudeau, Shimon Peres, and Lee Kuan Yew—was founded to further justice and peace in our world. Their greatest achievement was the handing over to the then United Nations Secretary General Kofi Annan "A Universal Declaration of Human Responsibilities" (1997). A main section in this declaration is entitled "Non-Violence and Respect for Life" (§§ 5–7).

For Christians, God is the "God of Peace" (Rom. 15:33, 16:20; 1 Cor. 14:33; 2 Cor. 13:11; Phil. 4:9; 1 Thess. 5:23; Heb. 13:20) and Jesus Christ is the "Lord of Peace" (2 Thess. 3:16). It is very unfortunate, indeed, that many Christians are still committed to solve human conflicts with violence and war. But the peace movements around the world are gaining vitality. Christians—indeed, people of all religious persuasions—are challenged not to privatize, individualize, and spiritualize the grand narratives of their faith, but in private and in public be committed to a culture of nonviolence. That would be a great contribution that the religions of the world could make to a flourishing future for humanity.

Implementation

The biggest challenge with respect to human rights is the move from theory to implementation. The theory is widely agreed upon. Most nations have ratified at least part of the human-rights package. No nation wants to be seen as disregarding human rights. But the implementation is sadly lacking and when things become difficult, as with the "war against terror," many leaders begin to question the universal application of human rights, as it happened recently with the practice of torture.

Human rights call for implementation. They need to be waged. And we are all called not to look away, but to do our part. The United States Holocaust Memorial Museum features a quote of the German Lutheran Pastor Martin Niemöller (1892–1984), who was an outspoken opponent of the Hitler regime, but who regretted not being engaged for justice earlier:

> First they came for the Communists
> And I did not speak out
> Because I was not a Communist
> Then they came for the Socialists
> And I did not speak out
> Because I was not a Socialist
> Then they came for the trade unionists
> And I did not speak out
> Because I was not a trade unionist
> Then they came for the Jews
> And I did not speak out

Because I was not a Jew
Then they came for me
And there was no one left
To speak out for me

If we affirm freedom as a social reality where the "other" is interesting and important for the flourishing of our own life; where we perceive the "other" not as competitor and potential rival, but a fellow member in the *one* human family; if we affirm a common humanity where all human beings have an inherent dignity and where all human beings are equal; then what else can we do but intentionally take our place in the global human family and accept responsibility for shaping a humane society? But we must do it! Compassionate solidarity must be waged! Our words and deeds must cohere lest we be accused of hypocrisy.

Conclusion

Christian faith includes the struggle for justice and peace. In our time this can best be achieved by affirming universal human rights and engaging with their implementation. I have attempted to show that the Christian narrative includes a constructive, supportive, and critical engagement with human rights.

Most churches today recognize the importance of human rights and the struggle for justice and peace, although it must sadly be admitted that some of the major churches are still lagging behind with the implementation of human rights in their own midst; one only has to think of the equality of women and the support for war.

Yet the challenge is begging us to practice our faith in Jesus Christ by joining the many people and institutions that are engaged in the struggle to implement human rights. Thus we are able to underline that the Christian faith can make creative and helpful contributions to the shaping and implementing of human rights.

RELIGIOUS RIGHTS AND FREEDOMS WITHIN THE BAPTIST TRADITION: THEOLOGICAL FOUNDATIONS

Paul S. Fiddes

1. INTRODUCTION: THREE INTERLOCKING PRINCIPLES

Baptists generally compliment themselves on having a passionate concern for religious liberty. The story they tell is that since their very beginning as a modern Christian movement in the early seventeenth century, they have always defended freedom of religion for all. One recent example of this claim is to be found in a Resolution on Religious Liberty made by the General Council of the Baptist World Alliance at Santiago (2–7 June) 2012, on the anniversary of the publication of Thomas Helwys' *A Short Declaration of the Mystery of Iniquity* (1612), usually recognized as the first defence in the English language of universal freedom of religion. Calling on all Baptist church leaders "to renew urgently the teaching on Religious Liberty for all persons and to serve as advocates in their congregations and communities for the protection of all who wish to worship as their consciences dictate,"[1] it begins with a quotation from the Universal Declaration of Human Rights (1948). It then asserts that "Religious Liberty for all persons has been a foundational Baptist principle for 400 years." In effect, it claims: "The United Nations may have got 'round to saying this in 1948, but we were saying it in 1612." My judgment is that to a large extent the claim to be advocates of religious freedom is true, though there have also been some failures to maintain this principle along the way that Baptists ought to confess. This essay will thus have an element of confession as well as celebration in it.

To understand why Baptists have persisted and sometimes *failed* in making a strong defence of religious liberty, we need to understand the theological foundations they have found for the doctrine. In this essay attention is given to three of them: first, the divine rule (which should be understood as the rule of Christ, representing the sovereignty of God); second, the gift of natural, or "human," rights; and third, respect for conscience. These three principles interweave, interpenetrate, and always work together. I propose to show that their triangulation

[1] *Baptist World Alliance 2012 Yearbook*, Minutes of the General Council Meeting, July 6–7, Santiago, Chile (Washington: Baptist World Alliance, 2012) 150.

has resulted in something recognizably, and perhaps even distinctively, Baptist.

I am delighted to be offering this essay in honour of William Brackney, one of the most distinguished Baptist historians of the present age, and a long-time friend. He himself has often written on the themes of religious liberty and human rights,[2] and I can scarcely hope to add to his immense erudition, as well as his skill in correcting what others have assumed to be the case without paying sufficient attention to the evidence. If I can make any contribution in this area, it might be in the argument towards which this essay works: that the intersection between three foundational principles of religious freedom sets up an overlap between Baptist thinking and a secular "rights-culture," and that it makes possible a valuable dialogue with Islam at our present time. So we make a start on this project where it should begin, with the foundation of the rule of God.

1. The Divine Rule

Baptists broke with the tradition dominant since Constantine that any Christian ruler should try to promote "true religion" within his realms, by the sword if necessary. This was the view of the "Godly prince" or "Godly magistrate," with a God-given responsibility to make sure that subjects within the realm lived and worshipped according to God's ordinances. The particular context in which Baptists appeared was in England, in the wake of the English Reformation, where the king (Henry VIII) had denied that the pope in Rome was in any way the "head" of the church in England, even in a shared headship with the king. The king was the only head in his own regions, though Church of England apologists like Richard Hooker hastened to add that the king or queen was still subordinate to the universal headship of Christ.[3] Moreover, state and church were one body, so that every citizen of the state was also a member of the Church of England.[4]

Against this, Baptists argued that a spiritual realm existed alongside the secular kingdom, so that the authority of the civil power had limits. The godly prince was certainly commissioned by God to maintain peace and justice in the land, but not to rule in the church or in the area of people's relation to God. Echoing Calvin's insistence that Christ was "the only head" of the church,[5] the only Lord in the spiritual realm was Christ, representing the sovereignty of God.

---

[2] See especially Brackney's *Christian Voluntarism: Theology and Praxis* (Grand Rapids MI: Eerdmans, 1997); and also, his *Human Rights and the World's Major Religions. 2. The Christian Tradition* (Westport CT: Greenwood Press, 2005).

[3] Richard Hooker, *Of the Laws of Ecclesiastical Polity*, VIII, iv. 7–9, in *Works*, 2 vols. (Oxford: Clarendon Press, 1885) 2:527–29.

[4] Ibid., i.2, in *Works*, 2:485.

[5] Calvin, *Institutes of the Christian Religion*, IV, vi. 8–10.

Religious freedom is thus grounded in divine rule: on the one hand, every Christian person must be free to be obedient to God as manifest in Christ, and on the other no government should make laws to infringe that freedom. It followed that all people, Christians or not, members of the church or not, should be free to be obedient—or even disobedient—to God.

The person who expressed this earliest and most clearly was Thomas Helwys, in his book *A Short Declaration of the Mystery of Iniquity* (1612), to which the Santiago resolution (above) referred. An often-cited passage runs: "For mens religion to God, is betwixt God and themselves; the King shall not answere for it, neither may the King be jugd betwene God and man. Let them be heretikes, Turcks [i.e., Muslims], Jewes, or whatsoever, it apperteynes not to the earthly power to punish them in the least measure. This is made evident to our lord the King by the scriptures."[6]

In his plea for religious liberty, we see that Helwys advises the king to read scripture. The key verse of Christian scripture to which Helwys refers in this chapter is the statement of Christ in the Gospels that "my kingdom is not of this world" (John 18:36–37), and he interprets it to mean that the state should have no jurisdiction in the "spiritual kingdom" of Christ. With this he links the words of Jesus from the Gospels that "the leader must become like one who serves" (Luke 22:26):

> Doth not the King knowe that the God, of Gods, and Lord of Lords, hath under him made our lord the King an earthly King, and given him all earthly power: and that he hath reserved to himself a heavenly kingdome, a kingdome that is not of this world Joh 18. 36. 37. [...] & that with this kingdome our lord the King hath nothinge to do (by his kingly power) but as a subject himself: and that Christ is King alone, onely High Priest and Cheife Bishop: and there is no King, no Primate, Metropolitane, Archbishop, Lord Spirituall, but Christ onely [...] to exercise authority one over another Luk 22.25. 26. Mat 23.11.12.[7]

While magistrates and kings were to be honoured and obeyed as a permissive divine ordinance to inhibit evil and encourage the good, they were not to make spiritual laws about right belief and worship, nor appoint bishops to do so. God has given to the king [he writes] an "earthly kingdome with all earthly power against the which, none may resist," but "Christ alone is K[ing] of Israell, & sitts vpon Davids Throne, & that the K[ing] ought to be a subiect of his Kingdome."[8] The king simply "can have no power to rule in this spiritual Kingdome of Christ."[9]

---

[6] Thomas Helwys, *A Short Declaration of the Mystery of Iniquity* (n.p.: n.n., 1612) 69.
[7] Helwys, *A Short Declaration*, 41.
[8] Ibid., "The principal matters handled in the Booke," recto.
[9] Ibid., 49.

The rule of Christ is not only *distinguished* from the rule of an earthly monarch, but is perceived to be *different* in manner. The one wields a physical sword, "forcing" obedience through threats of punishment, where the other wields only the "sword of the Spirit," seeking obedience through the "folly" of preaching in the spirit of a Christ who was "lowly and meek."[10] The divine rule is the basis of religious freedom because of its character, exhibited in "one who serves." This is a note developed with particular emphasis by Leonard Busher, perhaps a member of the Helwys congregation, who stresses that the "gentle and merciful law of Christ" displayed in preaching will have much more success in driving out error from hearts and consciences than "fire and sword." Faith, he observes, cannot be commanded.[11]

Unlike continental Anabaptists, English Baptist church members believed they could nevertheless fulfill their Christian calling as civil magistrates and could swear oaths of allegiance to king and country, so it might be claimed that these General Baptists under Helwys showed the beginnings of what the sociologist Ernst Troeltsch came to call a mixture of sect and church in the form of a "Free Church."[12] As far as they were allowed, Baptists wanted to participate actively in the life of the state and society, cooperating with others, and not cut themselves off into a religious ghetto. Helwys' objection is that the king, in establishing the Church of England, has given bishops and archbishops the power to make laws that bind people in the "spiritual kingdom,"[13] with sanction of excommunication, imprisonment, or banishment,[14] and to obey them is to put Christian people in the perilous situation of disobedience to God. It may even, thinks Helwys, lead to a disobedience that imperils their eternal destiny before God.[15]

In this work of Helwys we see the beginning of what has been called a "separation between church and state." It is not the kind of absolute "wall of separation" advocated later by Thomas Jefferson,[16] as Baptists have sometimes understood it to be. After all, the secular ruler is still a servant of God. God is still at

---

[10] Ibid., 46–48.

[11] Leonard Busher, "Religions Peace: Or a Plea for Liberty of Conscience" (London: John Sweeting, 1646), repr. Edward Bean Underhill, ed., *Tracts on Liberty of Conscience and Persecution, 1614–1661* (London: Hanserd Knollys Society, 1846) 16–17. The 1646 edition claims to be a reprint of a first edition printed in 1614, which is not extant. Cf. "The Humble Petition and Representation of the Sufferings of [...] Innocent Subjects, Called by the Name of Anabaptists" (London: Thomas Smith, 1660), repr. in Underhill, ed., *Tracts*, 302.

[12] Ernst Troeltsch, *The Social Teaching of the Christian Churches*, trans. Olive Wyon, 2 vols. (London: George Allen & Unwin, 1950) 708–10, 807–808, 819.

[13] Helwys, *A Short Declaration*, 49–51, 58–59.

[14] Ibid., 65–66.

[15] Ibid., 46.

[16] Thomas Jefferson, "Letter to the Danbury Baptist Association," 1 January 1802, available at http://billofrightsinstitute.org/founding-documents/ (accessed 7 October 2015).

work through rulers, kings, and magistrates in the life of society. Church and state are thus intertwined in complicated ways. It is not inconsistent, for example, for the church to receive money from the state as long as others are also eligible to receive it on the same terms (and some Baptist ministers accepted a salary from the state during the Protectorate of Oliver Cromwell in the mid-seventeenth century). But it does mean that the state is not to interfere in the life of the church, such as in appointing its ministers or bishops, or in decreeing what form of prayer-book is to be used. The test is this: is the rule of Christ being infringed, as he stands in the midst of the congregation? While Baptists have generally argued for the disestablishment of the church, especially the Church of England, the real point is respecting the rule of Christ. Correspondingly, this rule means that the state is not to give privileges to the Church that it denies to others.

With obedience to the rule of Christ we are at the very heart of Baptist ecclesiology: the Baptist conviction is that the risen Christ alone rules in his church, among the people whom he calls and gathers together into a covenant community. The rule of Christ gives the congregation an authority and a freedom to worship as it shares in the threefold office of Christ as prophet, priest, and king.[17] The point was not the modern concept of "autonomy." Rather, the local congregation had "freedom" to order its own affairs because it stood under the direct rule of Christ, whose body it made visible and whose mind it discerned in the meeting of its members for deliberation and corporate exegesis of scripture. Baptists affirmed that the gathering of churches *together* in assemblies was also the body of Christ, and was also subject to the rule of Christ, so that the local congregation should take with great seriousness the finding of the mind of Christ in association life. But they made no attempt to make a regulation to define the relation between these authorities, relying upon the "walking of churches together" in the bonds of trust.[18]

2. Natural Rights

From the mid-eighteenth century onwards, Baptists increasingly found another foundation for religious freedom. They asserted freedom of religion to be a "natural right," later a "human right," given to human be-

[17] *The Confession of Faith of Those Churches Which Are Commonly (Though Falsely) Called Anabaptists* (London: Matthew Simmons, 1644) arts. XXXIII–XXXV, in William L. Lumpkin, ed., *Baptist Confessions of Faith* (Philadelphia: Judson Press, 1959) 165–66; cf. *Confession* (1677) XXVI.7, in Lumpkin, ed., *Baptist Confessions*, 286–87.

[18] See *Confession of Faith* (1644), introduction and art. XLVII, in Lumpkin, ed., *Baptist Confessions*, 155, 168–69: individual congregations are "one body, walking by same rule."

ings by God in creation. Here they took up the mood of the Enlightenment, the American Constitution (1787), the associated Bill of Rights (1791), and the French Declaration of the Rights of Man (1789).

Earlier in the mid-seventeenth century the Leveller John Lilburne, who operated on the edges of the Baptist movement,[19] had coined the language of "free-born rights," among which he included freedom of conscience. By "rights" he generally meant legal rights, "ancient" privileges he claimed to be established by the law of England, privileges that free-born English people inherited but that were being withheld from them by the king and—later—by Cromwell and Parliament as well.[20] But at times he made a leap of thought from "legal" to what we might call "natural rights," and even in modern terms, "human rights," referring to "the privilege, that is, the Right, Due, and Propriety of all the Sons of Adam, *as men*."[21]

Thus, Lilburne may well have helped to get the language of "rights" into the consciousness of Dissenters, but it was John Locke who first clearly identified "natural rights" (based on the classic theological idea of "natural law"), held by virtue of being human, which people did not surrender by entering the social contract of civil society. These rights were notably the right to life, liberty, and property.[22] His main argument in the *Letter Concerning Toleration* (1689) is that people cannot be *deprived* of their civil rights because of their religion. But the idea emerges secondarily that there is a "natural right" of liberty of conscience in matters of religion. He writes:

> These Accusations would soon cease, if the Law of Toleration were once so settled, that all Churches were obliged to lay down Toleration as the Foundation of their own Liberty; and teach that Liberty of Conscience is every mans natural Right, equally belonging to Dissenters as to themselves; and that no body ought to be compelled in matters of Religion, either by Law or Force.[23]

---

[19] His collaborator, Richard Overton, was a General Baptist minister. He also seems to have been a friend of the particular Baptist William Kiffen. See Larry Kreitzer, *William Kiffen and His World*, vols. (Oxford: Regent's Park College, 2010) 1:10–12.

[20] John Lilburne, "Plaine truth without feare or flattery [...] written by I.L." (London: 1647) 12.

[21] John Lilburne, "Londons Liberty in Chaines Discovered, Published by Lieutenant Colonel John Lilburn, Prisoner in the Tower of London" (London: 1646) 19.

[22] John Locke, *Two Treatises of Government* (London: Awnsham Churchill, 1690) bk. 2, ch. 2, ch. 11.

[23] John Locke, *A Letter Concerning Toleration Humbly Submitted.* [...] (London: Awnsham Churchill, 1689) 48.

Locke had a considerable influence among Nonconformists: his *Essay Concerning Human Understanding* (1690) was standard reading in Dissenting Academies from the beginning of the seventeenth century[24] and later in Baptist theological seminaries, while it had been forbidden at Oxford in 1703. In 1744, for example, we find the high Calvinist John Collett Ryland as a student in Bristol Baptist College, making the resolve to "read quite perfectly thro' Mr. Locke's Essay on Hum.[an] Understanding."[25] Baptists took up Locke's arguments and re-cast them more simply as the natural right of religious freedom. Isaac Backus, campaigning against the imposing of special taxes for the maintaining of the Congregationalist Church in Massachusetts, began his "Appeal to the Public for Religious Liberty Against the Oppression of the Present Day" with the warning that "our religious *rights* are encroached upon in this land" (1777). The Particular Baptist Daniel Turner, writing about the "power of election" of elders held by all church members, draws quite casually on the language of "natural rights," so showing how deeply the language had sunk into the Baptist mind by 1758: "if the inspired Apostles paid this regard to the natural rights and liberties of the people, one would think there was still the more reason for us to do so."[26]

The former Secretary of the Bristol (Baptist) Education Society, Thomas Mullett, attended a "Revolution Society" dinner on 24 November 1791, at which Tom Paine was present and records that he was glad to join in congratulating Paine on "his able defence of the Rights of Man," expressing his delight at being present at such a "feast of reason and the flow of Soul."[27] Mullett's acquaintance, Robert Hall, minister at St. Andrew's Street Baptist Church in Cambridge, also offers us a key example of rights language, at a sensitive moment of national life. In 1793 he published "An Apology for the Freedom of the Press and for General Liberty," in the wake of the French Declaration of the Rights of Man, and at the time when Nonconformists still hoped that the declaration would have some impact on English society.[28] Citing Locke, he combines a plea for religious freedom with press freedom as the American Bill of Rights had done only two years previously. In a section entitled "On Theories and the Rights of Man," he maintains:

---

[24] So Alan P.F. Sell, *Philosophy, Dissent, and Nonconformity 1689–1920* (Eugene OR: Wipf and Stock, 2009) 25.

[25] "A Student's Programme in 1744: From the Diary of John Collett Ryland," *Baptist Quarterly* 2/6 (April 1925): 249–52.

[26] Daniel Turner, *A Compendium of Social Religion or the Nature and Constitution of Christian Churches* (London: John Ward, 1758) 38.

[27] Horatio Gates Papers, Emmett Collection, New York Public Library, New York. I owe this reference to Timothy Whelan.

[28] Michael R. Watts, *The Dissenters: Volume 2, The Expansion of Evangelical Nonconformity* (Oxford: Clarendon Press, 1995) 347–49.

> That there are natural rights, or, in other words, a certain liberty which men may exercise, independent of permission from society, can scarcely be doubted by those who comprehend the meaning of the terms. Every man must [...] have a right to worship God after the mode he thinks acceptable; or, in other words, he ought not to be compelled to consult any thing but his own conscience.[29]

Daniel Turner in Abingdon, two years later, and addressing the same turbulent situation in the nation, warns that an appeal to "rights" can be exploited by those who want only to disturb the peace, and yet he still clearly defends the idea.[30]

In the twentieth century, Baptist declarations in favour of religious freedom—especially those published by the Baptist World Alliance—have been uniformly supportive of the modern rights-culture, as spelled out in the UDHR. Article 18 of the UDHR specifies religious freedom as a "human right" alongside freedom of thought and conscience,[31] and this was followed by the "European Convention on Human Rights" (ECHR), article 9; and the "International Covenant on Civil and Political Rights" (ICCPR), article 18. Their language of "human rights" has deeply impressed the Baptist mind.

Indeed, preceding the UDHR, in 1939, the annual sessions of the Southern Baptist Convention, the Northern Baptist Convention, and the (African-American) National Baptist Convention USA, Inc., unanimously approved what was called an "American Baptist Bill of Rights," and this led to the founding of the Baptist Joint Committee on Public Affairs. The text of this bill of rights, including the assertion of religious liberty as a "human right," has unmistakable echoes of its year, with the Nazi threat and looming clouds of war.

> Believing religious liberty to be not only an inalienable human right, but indispensable to human welfare, a Baptist must exercise himself [*sic*] to the utmost maintenance of absolute religious liberty for his Jewish neighbor, his Catholic neighbor, his Protestant neighbor, and for everybody else. Profoundly convinced that any deprivation of this right is a wrong to be challenged, Baptists condemn every form of compulsion in religion

---

[29] *The Works of Robert Hall*, ed. Olinthus Gregory, 6 vols. (London: Holdsworth and Ball, 1832) 3:122.

[30] Daniel Turner, "The Monitor, or a Friendly Address to the People of Great Britain on the Most Effective Means of Deliverance from Our National Calamities, by Theophilus Senex" (Abingdon: R. Watts, 1795) 13, 24.

[31] Article 18 runs: "Everyone has the right to freedom of thought, conscience, and religion; this right includes freedom to change his religion or belief, and freedom, either alone or in community with others and in public or private, to manifest his religion or belief in teaching, practice, worship, and observance."

> or restraint of the free consideration of the claims of religion. We stand for a civil state, "with full liberty in religious concernments."[32]

In the eighteenth and nineteenth centuries there had been little theological reflection by Baptists on natural rights, beyond the belief that they were bestowed by God in creation, but in the twentieth century there appeared a firmer theological grounding. In the first place this was based in the biblical concept of creation in "the image of God." Here, for example, is a declaration from the 13th Baptist World Congress at Stockholm in 1975:

> We believe that God has made humankind *in his own image* and that he endows us with certain human rights which Christians are obliged to affirm, defend, and extend: the right to necessities of life includes the rights of all persons to have access to life, liberty, food, clothing, shelter, health, education, the right to work, and the pursuit of happiness including a quality of life that allows adequate development of human potentialities.[33]

This declaration reaffirms the principles set out in the UDHR, following its wording quite closely, but restoring the religious language of "endowment of rights" by God that had been omitted when the UDHR had itself followed the model of the American Declaration of Independence. The earlier declaration had begun with the ringing statement that human beings are "endowed by their Creator with certain inalienable rights," to which the Baptist Stockholm declaration adds the theological insight that this endowment happened through the making of human beings in the image of God.

An associated theological grounding of human rights to be found occasionally in twentieth-century Baptist thinking is that the image of God includes the imaging of divine rights, human worth mirroring divine worth. So a modern Baptist advocate of human rights, James Wood, writes in a publication of the Baptist Joint Committee:

> If we want to look at the Bible to learn about human rights, as one scholar has observed, "We have to do so in relation to divine rights." These divine rights become the standards for human rights and thus they become for us divine obligations [...]. The concept of human rights has a solid theological foundation in the dignity and worth of the human person created in the image of God.[34]

---

[32] From *The Christian Citizen,* vol. 1, 2007. A Publication of National Ministries, American Baptist Churches USA.

[33] *New People for a New World—Through Christ,* Official Report of the Thirteenth Congress, Stockholm, Sweden, 8–13 July 1975 (Nashville: Broadman Press, 1976) 255.

[34] James E. Wood, *Baptists and Human Rights,* a publication of the BWA's Human

The theologian to whom Wood refers is Helmut Frenz,[35] although a more substantial argument for the grounding of human rights in the rights of God has more recently been made by Nicholas Wolterstorff.[36] Writing in defence of a theological basis for human rights, Wolterstorff also observes acutely that the biblical notion of divine forgiveness of humanity depends upon the concept that God has rights that God is willing to forgo, and that the biblical injunction to human beings to forgive depends upon the same notion of violated and retributive rights.[37] This context of the rights of God may well, as Wood claims, be reflected in the declaration of the Fourteenth Baptist World Congress in Toronto (1980): "Human rights are derived from God—from his nature, his creation, and his commands. Concern for human rights is at the heart of the Christian faith. Every major doctrine is related to human rights, beginning with the biblical revelation of God."[38]

Modern Baptists are also likely to use the language of divine rights in referring to "the Crown Rights of the Redeemer," though there is no evidence that this phrase was used by Baptists before the twentieth century, originating as it did among Scottish Covenanters of the seventeenth century and popularized among the Free Churches of Scotland in the nineteenth.[39] It is surely in tune with what Helwys called the "power and honour" of Jesus,[40] and demonstrates how ideas of "rule" and "right" easily merge with regard to God and his Christ.

Some have urged that there is no need for a particular provision about the right of religious freedom in declarations and conventions about human rights. Religious liberty, it is argued, is sufficiently covered by rights of freedom of speech and of conscience in general. The inclusion of reference to religion in the UDHR took the persistent advocacy of Mrs. Eleanor Roosevelt and Sir Muhammad Zafrulla Khan, a Muslim (Pakistan's ambassador to the UN). Here it may be relevant that in his "Four Freedoms" speech before Congress in 1941, her husband President F.D. Roosevelt had espoused the "right of every person to worship God in his own way." William Brackney suggests that the publishing of the "American Baptist Bill of Rights" may have influenced Roosevelt in this action, and that,

---

Rights Commission (1997) 11.

[35] Helmut Frenz, "Human Rights: A Christian Viewpoint," *Christianity and Crisis* 36 (21 June 1976): 149.

[36] Nicholas Wolterstorff, *Justice: Rights and Wrongs* (Princeton: Princeton University Press, 2008) 65–95, 129–31.

[37] Ibid., 105–107.

[38] *Celebrating Christ's Presence through the Spirit*, Official Report of the Fourteenth Congress, Toronto, Canada, 8–13 July 1980 (Nashville: Broadman Press, 1981) 77.

[39] John Brown, *The History of the Indulgence* (Edinburgh?: s.n. 1678) 135, refers to the "Crown Rights of Christ." I am indebted to Malcolm Yarnell for this reference.

[40] Helwys, *A Short Declaration*, 49.

anyway, the speech "brought cheer to the Baptist community."[41] Baptists have consistently argued for the need of a specific provision for religious freedom. It has been argued by other historians that Baptist influence was possibly responsible for the inclusion of the clause disallowing establishment of religion and allowing "free exercise of religion" in the American Bill of Rights in the first place, this then being enshrined in the First Amendment to the American Constitution.[42]

Baptist linking of freedom of religion with "rights" ought not to be taken for granted. After all, there has recently been a theological protest against the attention given to rights, from thinkers of both established and "free" churches. The objection has been that the anthropocentric emphasis on *human* rights, or "inherent natural rights," does not sit easily with the biblical tradition, which is theocentric, stressing the justice of God and the demand of God for "right order" in the covenant community.[43] The concept of "rights" is also seen as a symptom of possessive individualism, associated with private ownership of property, as in Locke's identification of "natural rights." Moreover, confidence in human rights is said to undermine Christian teleology, or the expectation that justice is a gift of God's kingdom, which is both present and to come.[44] In response, I suggest that while "human rights" is not a strictly *theological* concept in itself, the idea is essential in practice to denote a sphere of discourse in which basic aspects of humanity made in God's image are being defended. It helps to establish an ethos that is consistent with Christian scripture, or it is a "boundary discourse,"[45] which marks out an area of respect for all human beings, based on a worth that has been given them by God.[46] While the ethicist Stanley Hauerwas was earlier highly suspicious of the notion of rights on the kinds of grounds mentioned above, he has in his most recent writings conceded that Christians can—with caution—use the language of rights as part of their moral and theological toolkit, as a "reminder"

---

[41] William H. Brackney, *The Baptists* (Westport CT: Greenwood Press, 1994) 105.

[42] William Warren Sweet, *The Story of Religion in America* (New York: Harper and Brothers, 1950) 193.

[43] Joan Lockwood O'Donovan, "The Concept of Rights in Christian Moral Discourse," in Michael Cromartie, ed., *A Preserving Grace: Protestants, Catholics, and Natural Law* (Grand Rapids: Eerdmans, 1997) 145; similarly, Oliver O'Donovan prefers "right order" to rights although he does not absolutely rule out the concept of "human rights": see his *The Ways of Judgment* (Grand Rapids: Eerdmans, 2005) 139–43, 197–99, 221. See also Stanley Hauerwas, *Fullness of Faith: The Public Significance of Theology* (Mahwah: Paulist Press, 1993) 55–73.

[44] John Milbank sets a (Christian) "community of ends" over against a "community of rights": see his *The Word Made Strange* (Oxford: Blackwell, 1997) 154–55.

[45] The term is advocated by Ethna Regan, *Theology and the Boundary Discourse of Human Rights* (Washington: Georgetown University Press, 2010) 13–14, 178–79.

[46] For the affirmation of worth, see Wolterstorff, *Justice: Rights and Wrongs*, 94–95, 352–60.

of "the thick moral relationships our bodies make possible."[47]

It is striking that Baptists have had the concept of "natural rights" in their toolkit since at least the early eighteenth century. I suggest that, just as with people in oppressive situations today, the concept had practical value in protesting against their marginalization and persecution, whatever its exact theological meaning. But then it acquired theological depth through association with the "rule" of God in Christ, since both "rule" and "right" were grounds for religious freedom. The result has been a Baptist instinct that the right to worship God freely is the very foundation of all other "natural" or human rights, so that it is not sufficient to speak only of the right of freedom of speech, or even of freedom of conscience. Conscience, however, is certainly the third element in the Baptist "triangulation" of reasons for religious freedom.

3. Respect for Conscience

The first theological ground (divine rule) stresses the agency of God, and the second (natural right) a human endowment. The third offers a bridge between them. The appeal to freedom of conscience, which expresses a direct relation of the human spirit to God, has been used to support both other grounds, and enables each to strengthen the other. Indeed, the gradual change in meaning of "conscience" through the years facilitates the development of the idea of "rights," which supplements (and does not replace) the idea of "the rule of Christ."

The idea of conscience that emerges from the theology of the Reformation is supportive of the idea of the "rule of Christ," and is in this way linked with religious freedom. Conscience here is not a matter of individual preference so much as an instrument of the Holy Spirit, at work in the human soul, to create awareness of the demands of God as they are known through revelation in scripture and according to the common mind of the church.[48] Conscience, as Calvin expresses it, is about responsibility in the face of the judgment of God and his Christ,[49] and Baptists argued that forcibly compelling assent hindered this exercise of obedience. So, in a tract arguing against religious persecution published in 1615, usually attributed to John Murton, the author asserts that "my conscience must be satisfied [...] by the word of truth."[50]

We find this kind of appeal to conscience in a comprehensive statement of faith made by the English Baptist congregation that had remained in Amsterdam.

---

[47] Stanley Hauerwas, *The Work of Theology* (Grand Rapids: Eerdmans, 2014) 206.

[48] See John P. Bradbury, "Non-Conformist Conscience? Individual Conscience and the Authority of the Church from John Calvin to the Present," *Ecclesiology* 10/1 (2014): 32–52.

[49] Calvin, *Institutes*, 1:15:2.

[50] John Murton(?), "Objections Answered by Way of Dialogue" (n.p.: n.n., 1615), repr. Underhill, ed., *Tracts*, 103.

In 1612, the same year as the publication of Helwys' book, they declared that civil authority was limited by the rule of Christ exercised over human consciences: "That the magistrate is not by virtue of his office to meddle with religion, or matters of conscience, to force or compel men to this or that form of religion, or doctrine: but to leave Christian religion free, to every man's conscience [...] for Christ only is the king, and lawgiver of the church, and conscience" (James 4:12).[51]

Helwys in England was writing similarly, again linking conscience with the rule of Christ. The king did not possess "by that sword of justice power over his subjects consciences," since that power was a "spirituall power" and "spirituall sword" wielded only by "the King of Kings...[who] requires not anie earthly power to build up his Church."[52] Helwys does not think that conscience is infallible. But the word "conscience" indicates both a God-given ability to discern what God's demands in a particular situation should be, *and* a responsibility to stand before God as judge, who will make clear whether that discernment has been used correctly. Asserting that it is a cruel tyranny to "force men's consciences in their religion to God," he exclaims: "Oh let the K[ing] iudg, is it not most equall, that men should chuse their religion themselves seeing they onely must stand themselves before the iudgment seat of God to answere for themselves, when it shalbe no excuse for them to say, wee were commanded or compelled to be of this religion, by the King, or by them that had authority from him."[53]

Some 150 years later, on another continent, Isaac Backus was making the same link between conscience and the rule of Christ. Calling on members of the Warren Association of churches to refuse either to pay taxes or produce certificates verifying they were approved churches, he first appealed to the text that the Kingdom of Christ was not of this world, and then declared that "we claim and expect the liberty of worshipping God according to our consciences."[54]

Gradually, however, the term "conscience" began to take on the modern sense of a subjective judgment, or decision-making in the light of what the individual believed to be morally proper. In this way an appeal to conscience supports the "natural right" of freedom of religion, and so is often referred to as "the right of conscience," as in John Leland's celebration of "the rights of conscience inalienable."[55] As the UDHR makes clear, it is the right conscientiously to "hold, choose, or change a religion."

---

[51] "Propositions and Conclusions," 84, in Lumpkin, ed., *Baptist Confessions*, 140.

[52] Helwys, *A Short Declaration*, 43–44.

[53] Ibid., 46.

[54] In "Memorial to the First Continental Congress" (1774), cit. Alvah Hovey, *A Memoir of the Life and Times of the Rev. Isaac Backus* (Boston: Gould and Lincoln, 1859) 210.

[55] John Leland, *The Rights of Conscience Inalienable, and Therefore Religious Opinions Not Cognizable by Law* (New London: T. Green and Son, 1791).

In his treatise of 1793, Baptist Robert Hall insisted, as we have already seen, that when it came to worship, "every man...ought not to be compelled to consult any thing but his own conscience." He adds: "The religious opinions of Dissenters are so various, that there is perhaps no point in which they are agreed, except in asserting the *rights of conscience* against all human control and authority. From the time of Queen Elizabeth [...] their views of religious liberty have gradually extended."[56]

Baptists in the twentieth century linked conscience and natural rights in a similar way. J.D. Freeman, speaking from the platform at the First World Congress of the Baptist World Alliance in London, 1905, set the tone by declaring, "In our postulate of soul liberty we affirm the *right* of every human being to exemption in matters of faith and *conscience* from all coercion or intimidation by an earthly power whatsoever."[57] Eleven congresses later, in Tokyo, the assembly declared, "We reaffirm [...] the Baptist concepts of freedom of individual *conscience* and of the worth and inherent *rights* of each human being."[58]

4. Losing the Balance

Baptists will, I suggest, make the most effective defence of religious freedom when the three elements of divine rule, human rights, and conscience have been combined. On the other hand, an overstressing of one at the expense of others *can* lead to a distortion of what this freedom might be.

(a) Over-Emphasis on Divine Rule. This might actually lead to a Baptist failure to extend toleration to all. While stress on the rule of Christ forbids the monarch or government to interfere in the life of the *church*, such as in appointing bishops or decreeing that a prayer book should be used, Baptists did think that divine rule in matters of peace and justice, together with the punishment of "evildoers," had been deputed to the godly magistrate.[59] Without the balance of insisting on natural rights and freedom of conscience, this *can* lead on its own to the idea that the civil power should generally encourage and foster true religion, and discourage false religion.

Among Baptists—and now we come to the element of confession I mentioned right at the beginning—this has occasionally led to a moderation of pleas for full religious toleration. In 1645 Particular Baptist minister John Tombes asserted that magistrates should deal with "abominations" against the first table of the Ten

---

[56] *The Works of Robert Hall*, 3:142.

[57] *The Baptist World Congress, London,* July 11–19, 1905 (London: Baptist Union, 1905) 23.

[58] *Reconciliation through Christ,* Official Report of the Twelfth Congress, Baptist World Alliance, Tokyo, Japan, June 12–18, 1970 (Valley Forge PA: Judson Press, 1971) 248–50.

[59] See *Orthodox Creed* Art. 45, in Lumpkin, ed., *Baptist Confessions*, 331.

Commandments as well as against the second: "Polutheisme [polytheism] and Atheisticall doctrine ought to be restrained, exploded by the Christian Magistrate."[60] Later he extended this lack of toleration to Roman Catholics, "revilers of Christ or deniers of the scriptures." In 1659 Thomas Collier went back on his earlier plea for toleration even to atheists, agreeing that magistrates could punish blasphemy.[61] Imbalance can also occur when appeal is made to conscience only in connection with the rule of Christ and without reference to rights. In the Particular Baptist Confession of 1677, for instance, God is celebrated as "Lord of the Conscience," and in the General Baptist Orthodox Creed of 1679 Christ is similarly "Lord of conscience." But both object only to the imposing of religious obligations if they are not to be found in scripture, which is "the only rule he hath left for the consciences of all men to be ruled, and regulated, and guided by" (1679).[62]

Baptist historian David Bebbington observes that between 1660 and 1700 we get the impression that Baptists were more concerned to argue for religious freedom for themselves and other Dissenters than the universal case earlier advanced.[63] It is perhaps significant that it was in a later age when "rights" were being stressed that the well-known Baptist preacher C.H. Spurgeon argued (in 1880) in favour of Charles Bradlaugh taking his seat in Parliament, even though he was an avowed atheist.[64]

A more modern way that appeal to the rule of God in general society might get unbalanced is in approval of compulsory religious worship on public occasions and in public schools. Isaac Backus approved of compulsory public worship, such as state-sponsored days of fasting and thanksgiving (while his co-Baptist John Leland resolutely opposed them). In both the UK and Australia, Baptists approved of the worship in schools included in education reforms of the twentieth century (the so-called "School Assembly").[65] While in 1962–1963 the Baptist Joint Committee in the United States-endorsed Supreme Court rulings that organized classroom prayer and Bible reading must cease in public schools, in 1982 the Southern Baptist Convention endorsed President Reagan's proposal to reinstate school prayer.

---

[60] John Tombes, *The Ancient Bounds: Or Liberty of Conscience Tenderly Stated, Modestly Asserted, and Mildly Vindicated* (London: 1645) preface, 7.

[61] Thomas Collier, *The Decision & Clearing of the Great Point Now in Controversie* (London: printed for G.C., 1659) 15–16.

[62] Lumpkin, ed., *Baptist Confessions*, 280, 331.

[63] David Bebbington, *Baptists Through the Centuries* (Waco TX: Baylor University Press, 2010) 202.

[64] Patricia Stallings Kruppa, *Charles Haddon Spurgeon: A Preacher's Progress* (New York: Garland Publishing, 1982) 350. Baptists were, however, divided about the "Bradlaugh Case."

[65] See Bebbington, *Baptists*, 209.

(b) Over-Emphasis on Rights and Conscience. An appeal to conscience linked to natural rights will moderate an over-stress on divine rule. But an over-concentration in this area also leads to problems. It has led to individualism, a stress on "possessing" rights, and an autonomy that loses sensitivity to the conscience of others. It is quite proper to pursue claims that the state should act to "accommodate" rights of religion and conscience, even when they are "exceptions" to the general rule of law, and to test these claims against "the public good" in the law-courts.[66] In the United States, the First Amendment granting "free exercise of religion" has been appealed to by certain groups who have claimed "exceptional" treatment so that they can exercise this freedom. Southern Baptists in the 1990s developed such a doctrine of "acommodationism," and used it to promote their social policies, including legislation against abortion and in favour of public prayer. However, law-courts are often a poor way of weighing one person's rights against another. Christians need also to bring their claims for "exception" into the sphere of the rule of God as "Lord of conscience," and to seek widely with others, not just individually or in a narrow interest group, to find the mind of Christ in these matters in the world of today.

The link between conscience and rights was made by the American Baptist E.Y. Mullins in his famous statement of "soul competence," an ability granted by God to make free decisions about Christian faith and worship. "Competency of the soul in religion and under God," he wrote, "may be regarded as the platform of human rights in religion."[67] This has come in for a good deal of criticism among other Baptists recently, however, who think that it has been responsible for an undisciplined individualism, an unbridled sense of autonomy, and a loss of a sense of being part of the Christian community both local and universal.[68] Properly understood, the appeal to conscience must be about the work of the Holy Spirit in the community as well as in the individual.

5. Defence of Universal Liberty of Religion

Despite the deviations I have noticed in a confessional mood above, Baptists have frequently advocated religious freedom for those "of every faiths and no faith,"[69] and this claim has its roots in all three principles of divine rule, human

---

[66] The Beckett Fund for Religious Liberty has been active in promoting such claims for exception on behalf of all faiths.

[67] E.Y. Mullins, *The Axioms of Religion* (Philadelphia: Griffith and Rowland Press, 1908) 77.

[68] "Re-Envisioning Baptist Identity: A Manifesto for Baptist Communities in North America," *Perspectives in Religious Studies* 24/3 (Fall 1997): 303–10.

[69] Sixth Baptist World Congress, Atlanta, Georgia, USA, July 22–28, 1939 (Atlanta: Baptist World Alliance, 1939) 13.

rights, and conscience.

In the seventeenth century the major basis was divine rule, and liberty of conscience in this context; toleration was to be based in the conviction that judgment belonged alone to God. God, rather than human beings, would judge people for the reality of their belief or unbelief, and all people must stand finally before Christ as God's appointed judge. So Helwys insisted that the king could not be "the judge between God and man,"[70] and it was on this basis he called for freedom of religion for all kinds of Christians—including Roman Catholics[71]—Jews, Muslims, and the general class he dubs "heretics."

The example of Helwys was followed by both General and Particular Baptists in the first centuries of Baptist life. Edward Barber (General Baptist) in 1641 insisted that "none" ought to be "compelled to the worship of God by the authoritie of the Magistrate" on the grounds that all must await the Day of Judgment.[72] In 1645 Richard Overton (another General Baptist) asserted that it was "Christs Government over the whole world" that "doth strictly charge the Kings and Rulers of the Earth" to allow "Turkes, Jewes, Pagans, and Infidels, as well as Christians to grow or live together in the Feild of the World until the 'Day of harvest,' or 'Judgment.'"[73] As here, the Parable of the Tares and the Wheat was often alluded to in defence of universal liberty, warning not to forestall the action of the Lord of the harvest. The Particular Baptist Samuel Richardson, arguing for "The Necessity of Toleration" even of "heretics," adds the hope that through gentle persuasion some "tares" might cease to be "strangers" and "become God's people."[74]

Hints of the grounding of universal freedom of religion in the rule of Christ persist into the twentieth century. For example, J.D. Freeman in his speech at the first BWA Congress bases religious liberty "not for ourselves alone but for all men" on "the very essence of our belief" that "Christ is Lord of all."[75] However, in the twentieth and twenty-first centuries the defence of universal religious liberty is more likely to be grounded in the principles of universal rights and conscience. In 1905, for example, Texas Baptists urged the freedom of religion of Jews in Russia, still under the Czarist regime: they declared that they should be "left to the quiet exercise of their heaven-born *right* to worship God according to

[70] Helwys, *A Short Declaration*, 69.

[71] Ibid.

[72] Edward Barber, "To the Kings Most Excellent Maiesty, and the Honourable Court of Parliament the Humble Petition [...]" (n.p.: n.n., 1641) 1 sheet.

[73] Richard Overton, *The Araignement of Mr. Persecution* (n.p.: n.n., 1645) 22.

[74] Samuel Richardson, "The Necessity of Toleration in Matters of Religion" (1647), repr. in Underhill, ed., *Tracts*, 256–59. Overton expresses a similar hope in *The Araignement.*

[75] Baptist World Congress 1905, 23.

their own *consciences*."[76]

The mandate of the Baptist Joint Committee on Public Affairs (1939) linked universal freedom with rights: "Believing religious liberty to be not only an inalienable human right, but indispensable to human welfare, a Baptist must exercise himself to the utmost in the maintenance of absolute religious liberty for his Jewish neighbour, his Catholic neighbour, his Protestant neighbour, and for everybody else."[77]

Similarly, the mandate for the BWA "Commission on Religious Freedom" is at present to "support the BWA and its member bodies in their advocacy for the protection of fundamental human rights for people of all faiths," though it adds, "especially for Baptists and other Christians who experience or face the threat of persecution."[78]

If there is to be a proper theological grounding for this assertion of universal religious freedom, I suggest that Baptists should renew the convictions of the seventeenth century about the root of freedom in the rule of God, but in a form that is appropriate for the theology of our own age. There is perhaps a first move towards this in the resolution from Santiago with which I began, which envisages a possible relation of every human being, whether Christian or not, to some transcendent Otherness, declaring, "Religion can be deeply rooted in the identity of a person and one's relation to the transcendental world expressed in acts of worship and the sharing of one's faith."[79] The practical implications of universal relation to "transcendental" reality are spelled out by a study paper of the Commission on Peace and Justice, meeting at the same time in Santiago, in terms of living in a "plural" society: "Christians are not to be partisan in their concern for religious freedom, but to be active campaigners for religious freedom for all [...] Helwys' stance implies an acceptance of a multi-faith plural society in which he encourages active engagement rather than a withdrawal to the margins, or indeed any attempt to re-establish Christendom."[80]

The question is whether Baptists can share this "active engagement" with others from a theological perspective, and not just on a pragmatic basis. Here, I suggest, we need to return to the triangulation of the three principles of divine rule, human rights, and conscience.

---

[76] Proceedings of the Baptist General Convention of Texas (1905), cited in Bebbington, *Baptists*, 210. My italics.

[77] Wood, *Baptists and Human Rights,* 33.

[78] See www.bwanet.org/programs/freedom-and-justice/religious-freedom (accessed 10 December 2015).

[79] Baptist World Alliance 2012 Yearbook, 150.

[80] Paper by Tony Peck, General Secretary of the European Baptist Federation, "Thomas Helwys—Unlikely Prophet of Universal Religious Freedom," available at www.bwa-baptist-heritage.org/Peck-Helwys-BWA-2012.pdf (accessed 1 October 2016).

6. Common Ground with Others for Religious Freedom

With Muslim dialogue-partners, the greatest common "space" for meeting and conversation is likely to be created by convictions about divine rule and the gift of human conscience. The open letter from Muslim scholars to world Christian leaders, called "A Common Word Between Us and You" (2007), makes appeal to both these concepts, citing especially the Qur'anic text *Aal ' lmran 3:64* and then commenting:

> Clearly, the blessed words: we shall ascribe no partner unto Him relate to the Unity of God. Clearly also, worshipping none but God, relates to being totally devoted to God and hence to the First and Greatest Commandment. According to one of the oldest and most authoritative commentaries (tafsir) on the Holy Qur'an [...] that none of us shall take others for lords beside God, means "that none of us should obey in disobedience to what God has commanded, nor glorify them by prostrating to them in the same way as they prostrate to God." In other words, that Muslims, Christians, and Jews should be free to each follow what God commanded them, and not have "to prostrate before kings and the like,"[81] for God says elsewhere in the Holy Qur'an: Let there be no compulsion in religion [...] (Al-Baqarah, 2:256). This clearly relates to the Second Commandment and to love of the neighbour of which justice and freedom of religion are a crucial part.[82]

Here the command to worship only God, together with the phrase, "We shall ascribe no partner unto him [Allah]," are taken to relate to love of God, and the next phrase, "that none of us shall take others for lords besides God," is related to love of neighbour. Building on the commentary tradition, this last phrase is understood as defending the religious freedom of all people since they need not obey the demands of human lords, kings, or rulers in matters of religion as if they were equal to God. Thus the freedom of Muslims, Christians, and Jews to worship in their own way is not grounded here in a concept of human rights, as would be the case in modern legal discussion. It is rooted explicitly in the sovereignty of God as the supreme Lord, and implicitly in a freedom of conscience "to follow what God has commanded them."

The response of the BWA to *A Common Word* warmly welcomes this theological grounding of religious freedom, and acknowledges that the emphasis of the letter on love of God and neighbour as a motivation for religious freedom

---

[81] *A Common Word* cites Abu Ja'far Muhammad bin Jarir Al-Tabari, *Jami'Al-Bayan fi Ta'wil al-Qur'an* (*Dar al-Kutub al'Ilmiyyah,* Beirut, Lebanon, lst ed., 1992/1412) *tafsir of Aal 'Imran,* 3:64; vol. 3, 299–302.

[82] *A Common Word Between Us and You,* 5-Year Anniversary Edition (Amman: MABDA, 2012) 69–70.

makes a contribution to which Baptists should pay attention. The Baptist response goes on to say that it is, however, difficult to discern whether the letter's view of freedom includes the freedom of people to move from a community of one faith to another of a different faith, under obedience to what is felt to be a command of God.[83] Perhaps reference to the concept of "right," missing from the document, would clarify this; but "rights" as defined by the UDHR are usually seen in the Islamic world as being framed under Western influence.

If, on the other hand, we think about a dialogue with the secular rights-culture of the contemporary world, it is the element of human rights, together with appeal to conscience, that offers a common ground about freedom of religion. However, Baptists will always want to triangulate these with the divine rule, and so place them in a theological context. Then we see that the "conscience" exercised in religious freedom is not a liberal laissez-faire matter but a question of human responsibility before God. An appeal to freedom of conscience will evidently have more force in religious contexts, whether this be Judaeo-Christian or Islamic, when it is set within a "theological" approach of the rights and rule of God.

The Baptist tradition of thought offers the possibility of placing Christian and secular approaches to "rights" side by side, allowing one to illumine the other. This might move discussion forward on two outstanding issues in the debate about the nature and limits of religious freedom. In the first place, it might provide an opportunity to re-state religious freedom as a human right in terms that are not as closely bound to the particular language of Western liberal democracy as the UDHR and its successors, and so open up talk about rights more widely in the Islamic world.

In the second place, bringing in a theological dimension on rights may help to move the concept of religious freedom from the essentially individualistic approach reflected in the UDHR to a more corporate and social concept, which in the Baptist perspective is the righteous rule of God. While this is a perspective shared with Islam, it will also be an essential movement in Western culture towards a caring society and a just world.

[83] Ibid., 217–18, 229–31.

WILLIAM BRACKNEY—LINKING BAPTIST GENETICS, HUMAN RIGHTS, AND OPENNESS TO THE SALVATION OF ALL

Clinton Bennett

INTRODUCTION: THE TRAJECTORY OF BRACKNEY'S THOUGHT

William H. Brackney is not the only Baptist scholar and leader who has embraced interfaith relations and human rights, neither typical spheres of Baptist interest, but his contribution is perhaps especially significant because it extends his important work on Baptist genetics. His commitment to promoting human rights and openness to interfaith dialogue is firmly rooted in his ideas about who Baptists are and what Baptists take with them to these agendas. Linking these may not initially appear obvious. However, the trajectory of Brackney's work leads to establishing a basis for this link. Well aware of traditional Baptist defense of religious freedom and of a wall of separation between Church and state from his extensive work on Baptist history and origins, Brackney subsequently built on this legacy. Belief in the inviolability of the human conscience lies at the core of Baptist defense of religious liberty and of the conviction that government has no jurisdiction over this. Logically, then, alongside championing religious liberty and church-state separation, Baptists should also defend freedom of conscience, and freedom from government intervention, across the whole spectrum of rights. Freedom to be an atheist, to be Muslim, to be whatever people choose to be or realize that this and not that is how they are, which must include sexual orientation and gender identity, are choices that conscience dictates or ways of being that people's innate natures reveal to their self-understanding. Brackney has called religious liberty the foundation for all freedoms.

This is none other than the "soul competency" or "unfettered conscience" that Baptists champion. If people are to be truly free to choose their religion, their choice should be respected. This might not necessarily compel us to see value in all religions, but it does mean that we should speak respectfully about other faiths or our defense of religious liberty will sound strange when we denigrate and even demonize the religious Other. It might also invite us to rethink our theological attitudes lest the foundation of our belief in an inviolable conscience rests on unsafe ground. Not everyone will see that step as necessary but this writer will argue in favor of rethinking soteriology. To contemplate collaboration on social reform or economic justice with those whom we openly describe as "lost" or "in error" would be to try to work with people who might have no wish to work with us. Brackney's personal commitment to and involvement in interfaith human rights collaboration shows that, for him, the link between respectful relations with people of other faiths and social activism has a theological mandate.

After describing Brackney's contribution, this chapter attempts to build on its foundation. It argues that it is inconsistent, first, to defend someone's right to practice a faith while at the same time calling it demonic or futile and, second, to claim that conscience is inviolable while rejoicing in people's murder because you dislike their lifestyle, which you would like to see criminalized. Recent events and some Baptist responses to these in the United States provide a contemporary backdrop to this analysis, although historical examples are described, as will evolution in my personal journey and theological stance combining appreciation for Brackney with narrative theology. From an exclusivist position on salvation, I ended up—although often referred to as a pluralist—finding inclusivism the most compelling Christian theology of religion. Similarly, from a socially conservative stance on issues surrounding sexual orientation and gender identity, I shifted to believing that freedom of choice, or simply freedom to be as nature determines we are, must be defended when this is a matter of personal lifestyle that does not harm others or infringe upon anyone else's liberty. I argue that taking soul-competency to its logical conclusion has consequences for our soteriology and missiology and for what being Christian means in today's world. I intend to follow the direction of the Brackney-trajectory in a way that may extend the boundaries of discourse. Brackney was briefly my departmental chair at Baylor University in Texas. Since then, I had the pleasure of acting as external reader for a doctoral thesis Brackney supervised at Acadia and of maintaining communication with him over many years, sometimes consulting him on questions within his areas of expertise. Brackney contributed a paper to an issue of a journal I guest-edited, and a book, *Studying Christianity* (2010), to my series on critical issues in religious studies.

Brackney's Genetic Scheme for Understanding Baptist DNA

"No single author," comments Keith Harper, "has written as widely about Baptists as William Henry Brackney, and he, too, finds Baptist history a difficult matter" (85). This is because Baptists have had and still have different theologies and emphases, and most of what can be identified as characteristically Baptist also exists in other denominations. Baptists have had their internal disputes and schisms, too. I currently belong to a Baptist body that originated when its founders left the Southern Baptist Convention over several issues, including the role of women in ministry. As Bill J. Leonard, founding dean of Wake Forrest University

School of Divinity (which is now affiliated to my body), says, Baptists are "not the world's best consensus builders" (Harper, 86; Leonard, 15). Brackney refers to disagreement among Baptists on their origins, whether there is an unbroken succession of "Baptists" from the Apostolic era or Baptists began in the 1600s, and about what it means to be Baptist (1994, ix). In the American South, people joke that when three Baptists gather, you will hear four opinions. However, Harper refers to Brackney's *A Genetic History of Baptist Thought* (2004) as pointing in a new direction for understanding Baptist identity. Brackney used "human genetics as a metaphor to explain Baptist development."

According to Brackney, the "hereditary characteristics" of Baptists are Christ-centeredness, the centrality of the Bible, Christian experience, a modified Reformed soteriology, a distinct ecclesiology, and freedom (Brackney, 2004, 527–38). The distinctive Baptist ecclesiology refers both to the autonomy of local congregations and to the Baptist tradition of associationalism through local, regional, and national conventions or unions and, for many, the Baptist World Alliance internationally. In his *The A to Z of the Baptists* (2009), marking 400 years of Baptist existence, Brackney further elaborates on what Baptists mean by freedom of conscience: "Baptists oppose any form of coercion of the conscience" and believe that "the key element in freedom of conscience is the voluntary nature of one's choice" (226). Baptists did not always connect their advocacy for religious liberty, first articulated by Thomas Helwys in *A Short Declaration of the Mystery of Iniquity* (1612), and defense of human rights generally, but Brackney roots this in belief in the inviolability of the conscience as gifted by God, and in the *Imago Dei*—that is to say, in scripture. Below, I shall follow the trajectory of respect for the choices people make into what for many Baptists is the unfamiliar territory of sexual orientation and gender identity.

Yet for Brackney advocacy of human rights is not a task in which Christians must or should engage alone. Invited by Greenwood Press to plan and edit a five-volume Praeger Perspectives series, *Human Rights and the World's Major Religions* (2005), Brackney reached out to scholars across the religions to contribute. A one-volume condensed edition followed in 2013. Brackney describes "the articulation of human rights as a cutting-edge topic in contemporary theology and ethics" (2013b). Since this groundbreaking work, he has encouraged dialogue between religious scholars and leaders from different faiths to find ways of collaborating in the area of peacemaking and human rights. Brackney sees a direct link between belief in "soul competency," which says that every individual should be free to account to God first and to no one else for their moral decisions, and spiritual health and respect for the religions that others practice. In *Studying Christianity* (2010), Brackney refers to contemporary Christians who place less emphasis on "Christianity as a belief system to prepare people for life after death" and more on "the quality of life in the here and now." This has "produced a rich array of writings and projects focused on world peace, justice, human rights, and care for the earth," and may be one way of "interpreting Jesus' promise, 'I have come that you may have life, and have it more abundantly'" (123). Religious leaders, he said, speaking on 2 June 2011 at the Spiritual Diversity Conference and Fair in Halifax, Nova Scotia, need to find ways through interfaith dialogue to create consensus rather than conflict on the urgent issues that confront humanity.

At bottom, the linkage between belief in the inviolability of conscience and support for all freedoms that people have a right to enjoy is rooted in the condition of being human, in what it means to be human. This, for Brackney, is to reflect the image of the divine, the *Imago Dei* (2013a, xi). We are individually free and equal; not only should we be free from government compulsion in matters of religious belief and personal expression, but no one has the right to override our conscience. From the Baptist perspective, the local church, too, recognizes the ultimate freedom of each individual member, including the freedom to interpret scripture. Yet often Baptists have limited their activism to championing religious freedom while demonizing followers of other religions, and even campaigning for legal limits on certain choices that people make or on ways of being human. This implies that some people do not reflect God's image because their choice of religion or of whom they love offends us. Those whose choices differ from ours or who express love differently from us also reflect God's image. Spiritual autonomy is at risk if we insist on imposing the very religious conformity from which the first Baptists dissented by rejecting certain choices as immoral. We reflect God's image, too, as sinners, thus we cannot attribute "wrong choices" to others' sin and claim that our choices are "right" because we have none.

While critical of efforts to remove religion from human-rights discourse and aware that some religious people prefer to talk about "responsibilities" over "rights," Brackney views the Universal Declaration of Human Rights (UDHR), published in 1948, as an inspired document (2013b). He points to that fact that, while drawn up as a secular document, committed Christians played important roles "behind-the-scenes" (2010, 67). If the UDHR does reveal to us God's values and vision for human life, Baptists and all Christians should make compliance a priority in mission as part of the Lukan mandate. This writer has elsewhere proposed that God's revelation is progressive, and that sometimes what Scripture says was meant for us at that point of human maturation, not always for eternity. Even if the Bible can be read as censoring or condemning certain ways of loving, for example, this does not mean that a "righteous government" today should ever execute anyone for loving someone of the same sex, which some Baptists support. Even the authors of the UDHR did not anticipate that gender identity and sexual orientation would become human-rights issues.

A Pilgrimage from Exclusivity to Inclusivity: A Personal Theological Narrative

Although born into an Anglican family, I became a Baptist in my teens and have remained one since then. I learned of the Baptist commitment to religious freedom during instruction for baptism and church membership and remember at the time thinking that this was a legacy of which I could be proud. Later, training for ministry at Northern Baptist College in Manchester (1974–1978), I became interested in the religions of the Indian Sub-Continent, which led me to offer for missionary service with the hope of working in India. Accepted by the Baptist Missionary Society (now BMS World Mission), however, I was posted to Bangladesh. Required to spend a year at the Selly Oak Colleges in Birmingham in preparation, I was excused from much of the standard mission course because I had just graduated with a theology degree from the University of Manchester. Instead of attending courses on Bible, I was given permission to enroll on the University of Birmingham accredited professional certificate in Islam and Christian-Muslim Relations. That and the three years in Bangladesh that followed impacted and shaped the course of my subsequent career. Thinking, teaching, and writing about Islam and Christian-Muslim relations became my main occupation. I have combined this with participating in dialogue with Muslims and community activism, helping mosques and neighborhood associations obtain charitable status and funds for education and social programs. I did, though, attend classes on missiology at Selly Oak by Bishop Lesslie Newbigin (1909–1998), whose subsequent writing on theology of religions became a major influence on my thinking. I went on to serve with Newbigin on several committees of the Birmingham Council of Christian Churches, giving the address when he retired as a vice-president. My exposure to the religions of India, then to Islam, challenged my assumption that Christian faith is the only valid form of religion, and that unless Hindus and Muslims accept Jesus as their personal savior, they are eternally doomed.

My evangelical Baptist upbringing in New South Wales, Australia, had instilled in me the belief that only faith in Christ is saving. There was a strong expectation that Christians must witness their faith at every opportunity, lest by failing to do so someone dies without expressing faith in Jesus. We were expected to interject Christian witnessing into every conversation we had with a non-Christian. This was an imperative, a duty under the Great Commission in Matthew's Gospel. In 1979, as I prepared to leave for Bangladesh, I thought that the Great Commission was the mandate for the work I would undertake as a missionary. At this stage, I had very little exposure to Christian theology of religions, which did not feature prominently in my ministerial formation or even in my mission orientation. I read, however, Bishop Kenneth Cragg's *The Call of the*

Minaret (1956) and *Sandals at the Mosque* (1959), in which he wrestled with what he saw as the spiritual value of Muslim life and what this meant for Christian theology. If God speaks through Qur'an and Bible, how can contradictions be understood? I also discovered and read Lewis Bevan Jones' earlier book, *The People of the Mosque* (1932). Jones, on whom I went on to write my Master's thesis at Birmingham (completed 1985), helped pioneer a more conciliatory, less confrontational Christian approach to Muslims as a missionary in India, where he was born to missionary parents. In later life I came to know and admire Cragg, but I always regarded Jones as especially significant because the latter represented a second-generation Baptist missionary who found it impossible to dismiss Islam out of hand as having no spiritual worth or value. Could a Baptist, *as* a Baptist, look with sympathy on non-Christian religion? To some degree, I took this question with me to Bangladesh, where encountering Muslims raised more questions than it provided answers on the raison d'être for Christian mission vis-à-vis non-Christians who find satisfaction and spiritual fulfilment within their existing religions. Close friendship with Muslims resulted in my thinking that any assumption that I and not they stand in a genuine relationship with God is presumptuous, conceited, and arrogant.

Baptists and Empathy towards Other Religions

Other Baptists have, like Jones, moved away from representing other religions as demonic or as humanly constructed, offering no spiritual nourishment, although it is easier to provide examples of those who share the latter view. Importantly, however, Timothy Richard (1849–1919), who spent 1870–1916 with BMS in China, grew to deeply respect Chinese cultures and religions and focused on befriending those whom he recognized to be "worthy," following Jesus' advice to his disciples as he sent them out to preach at Matthew 10:11: "Whatever town or village you enter, find out who is worthy and stay at his house until you move on." Christians should thus build on and not destroy that which is worthy in every culture because this can prepare the way for Christian faith (see Bohr, 78). Richard had a strained relationship with the BMS. "Christianity," he wrote, "has the power of assimilating all that is good in other religions" (BMS Archives, "Richard to the Committee of the BMS," 12 March 1888; cited by Bohr, 77). On the one hand, this is short of an endorsement of any salvific value in other religions. On the other, it expresses more positivity and respect than Baptists typically did for non-Christian religions. The first detailed work on another religion by a Baptist was William Ward's *Account of the Writings, Religion, and Manners of the Hindoos* (1811). It is not an exaggeration to say that it contains nothing positive about Hinduism across four large volumes. Ward saw no value, no beauty in Hinduism—so much so that the logic of this, he says, is that it should be eradicated.

Hinduism "has no one principle to pacify the conscience" and "not a vestige of real morality...but...raises to a horrid flame all the impure and diabolical passions which raise in the human heart" (vol. 3, 296).

Defending a Hindu's conscience and "soul competency" would seem to be at odds with this negative assessment. More recently, Islam has especially attracted censure and animosity from some Baptists who refuse to acknowledge that Muslims and Christians worship the same God. If Muslims pray to a non-existent deity (since there is indeed but One God), their prayers are futile. Ergun and Emir Caner's *Unveiling Islam* (2002), an immediate bestseller in the aftermath of 9/11, dismisses as "ridiculous" any claim that Christians and Muslims worship the same God (108). Their comment on Muhammad's marriage to Aisha at "age nine" as presenting an "echoing problem" led former Southern Baptist Convention president Jeremy Vines to describe Islam's "founder" as "a demon-possessed pedophile," continuing (quoting from his fellow Baptist Caners), "I can tell you, Allah is not Jehovah either" (12 June 2002; cited by Leonard, 14). Earlier, SBC president Bailey Smith, speaking 22 August 1980, remarked that "God Almighty does not hear the prayer of a Jew... It may be politically expedient, but no one can pray unless he prays through the name of Jesus Christ." He was speaking at the Religious Roundtable's National Affairs Briefing in Dallas. Defending his comment, he later stated, "The only prayer I believe God hears from anybody who has been denying Jesus is, 'Lord, be merciful to me a sinner and save me for Christ's sake'" (Kaylor, 2010). On the anniversary of 9/11 in 2008, Westboro Baptist Church in Topeka, Kansas (unaffiliated to any Baptist association), burned a copy of the Qur'an with a United States flag, alleging that God's wrath is pouring out on the United States for disobeying God's word. Baptists who wish to reach out in friendship to Muslims will have to explain such views, however tentatively related to mainstream Baptists some of these Baptists are. My Muslim friends don't know that. To defend people's freedom to be Muslim and Jewish on the one hand while denigrating their religious beliefs and practices as lacking any value or utility on the other fails to respect their spiritual autonomy. Fanning the flame of Islamophobia, for example, makes Muslims in North America and Europe feel unwanted, insecure, and alienated even where they are active in all walks of life, including high elected offices. What does freedom to practice your religion mean if you face discrimination, hostility, and even calls to ban your co-religionists from entering the state?

The Three Paradigms

By 1987, I had returned to Birmingham, completed my Master's, started doctoral research (completed 1989), and joined the staff of the British Council of Churches as executive secretary of the Committee for Relations with People of

Other Faiths (CROPOF) within the Conference for World Mission division. My post was mainly funded by mission agencies and departments. At that time, Baptists were not sponsors although my appointment was recognized for purposes of continued ministerial accreditation. About this time, I became familiar with the writing of CROPOF member Alan Race, who popularized use of the paradigms, exclusivism, inclusivism, and pluralism to describe three theologies of religions in his *Christians and Religious Pluralism: Patterns in the Christian Theology of Religions* (1983). Brackney refers to these paradigms in *Studying Christianity* (136). The first limits salvation to those who explicitly declare faith in Jesus; the second regards Jesus' role in salvation as central but does not restrict this to self-defined Christians; and the third sees all faiths as valid alternative paths to spiritual fulfillment. The first had dominated mission thinking since the Tambaram World Mission Conference of 1938. Mahatma Gandhi, said Hendrik Kraemer (1888–1965), who proposed the exclusivist paradigm, might be a good man but he was a Hindu and therefore unsaved (1939, 109–13). Persuading people to become Christian, to abandon existing faiths if they have one, is not only the goal of missions but a task of great urgency lest The End come and billions of souls perish. Numbers matter. Good works must take a secondary place, as should fully forming new converts because both divert resources from the primary mission. Nothing must hinder adding numbers to the church. The Church Growth movement developed from this logic. The second paradigm, more or less, became official Roman Catholic thinking after Vatican II due to the influence of Karl Rahner (1904–1984). This leaves salvation to God. The third, associated with John Hick (1922–2012), with whom I later served on the board of the Oxford International Interfaith Centre during my time at Westminster College in Oxford (1992–1998), could perhaps be described as a post-Christian—or even post-Christian imperialism—option, similar in some respects to death-of-God theology. I last heard Hick speak in September 2003 when he gave a public lecture during the Pluralism Summit, held the 6th through the 9th, at Birmingham University. He predicted that pluralism would end up attracting the support of most Christians, drawing an analogy between how Christians had opposed the concept of biological evolution but in the end, in modified form (evolution is not random), this has generally prevailed even among Christians. Similarly, religious pluralism will prevail because it is necessary in our postmodern world for peace and coexistence. The Southern Baptist Convention, though, regards evolution as scientifically unproven and calls for the teaching of creation science in public schools (*Resolution on Scientific Creationism*, 1982).

When I worked at the BCC, a flurry of publications on interfaith relations led one colleague to express jealousy that money seemed to be available for this "growth industry" rather than for their field, although CROPOF was not especially well-funded and neither were most interfaith bodies at the time. Tambaram's fiftieth anniversary stimulated more interest and theological contributions. In missionary circles, much discussion centered on whether the dialogical approach compromised or even betrayed mission. Newbigin's *The Gospel in a Pluralist Society* appeared in 1989. There is no direct reference to Tambaram, but it was very much a response to the conversation on Christianity in relation to the world's religions. What attracted this writer was how Newbigin, for many years a Presbyterian missionary in India, offered an alternative rationale for missions to one of "stemming the fearful cataract of souls going into eternal perdition" (124–25) by criticizing the three-paradigm approach, yet at the same time embracing an aspect of each position. He wrote:

> [my] position is exclusivist in the sense that it affirms the unique truth of the revelation in Jesus Christ, but it is not exclusivist in the sense of denying the possibility of the salvation of the non-Christian. It is inclusivist in the sense that it refuses to limit the saving grace of God to the members of the Christian church, but it rejects the inclusivism which regards the non-Christian religions as vehicles of salvation. It is pluralist in the sense of acknowledging the gracious work of God in the lives of all human beings, but it rejects a pluralism which denies the uniqueness and decisiveness of what God has done in Jesus Christ (182–83).

Examining the New Testament, Newbigin simply did not find there the same concern for results or anxiety about numbers that characterizes Church Growth thought. Paul, he pointed out, never agonizes about results. Instead, in one of his most profoundly missiological passages, he speaks of salvation in eschatological terms and suggests that no one is perfect until the end. God "has consigned all people to disobedience in order that he may have mercy on all" (Rom. 11:32–36). It is then, says Newbigin, that "the fathomless depths of God's wisdom and grace will be revealed" (125). Meanwhile, "creation groans in travail" (Rom. 8:22). Thus, Christians should neither be anxious about their failure nor boast about their success, but should faithfully witness "to the one in whom the whole purpose of God for cosmic history has been revealed" (125). Newbigin preferred to speak of the "logic of mission," predicated on the truthfulness of the message as one that cannot but be proclaimed (or, see below, as I prefer "shared"). We do not control the result. This is the Holy Spirit's task. Some people may join the church, while others may respond in ways that are invisible to us.

Newbigin does not say that mere proclamation is enough; proclamation must be persuasive and culturally sensitive. Evangelists should use strategies that have been proven, while resisting the temptation to control the process. Converts, too, Newbigin argued, must be aware of the ethical dimension of the Gospel, thus "discipling" and "perfecting" cannot be so easily separated. Lacking knowledge of the ethical dimension, converts will focus only on replicating their conversion in others. They will ignore the Gospel command to heal the sick, liberate the oppressed, give sight to the blind, to restore the world to its original perfection (Luke 4:18–20), for only such a world will be acceptable to God. Between 1985 and 1992, I was honorary associate minister of an inner-city, multiracial Baptist congregation in Birmingham, supported by the Baptist Union's Home Mission. Each year, we had to justify continued support and the main criterion was how many new members had joined. Jokingly, we called the published list of how many people churches had baptized the "League Table." The local population was disproportionately elderly, which meant that our statistics were unimpressive. Even though we did attract newcomers, they often replaced members who had passed away. The fact that we provided a wide range of social services to the local community, too, did little to help us meet the criterion for funding, yet arguably we were undertaking biblically mandated mission as faithfully as wealthy churches in suburbia were, which did grow numerically. We also developed excellent relations with our neighboring place of worship, Birmingham Central Mosque. Newbin's comment on the need to disciple new Christians was a response to the Church Growth movements prioritizing the task of bringing people to faith over both social engagement and spending time nurturing new Christians, arguing that these detract from the urgent task of proclamation. Church Growth pioneer Donald McGavran (1897–1990) argued social service runs the risk of substituting "the fruit of the gospel for the gospel" and of advocating that "works of righteousness" are saving (1990, 34). Nothing can be as important, he said, as "the multiplying of cells of reborn Christians" (23).

Newbigin, a lifelong missionary, allowed the possibility that Muslims as Muslims and Hindus as Hindus may be saved. This does sound like Rahner's assertion that "if one believes in the universal salvific purposes of God towards all men in Christ, it need not and really cannot be doubted that gratuitous influences of properly Christian supernatural grace are conceivable in the life of all men" (125). Thus, a non-Christian may experience "the grace of God" without knowing that this grace is being mediated through Jesus Christ. Brackney may or may not share my inclusivist theology of religions, but he does take part in and supports interfaith dialogue. Dialogue begins when people meet each other. Baptists who denigrate other faiths often do so from a distance. Smith did not deny the validity of Jewish prayer in a synagogue. Vines did not insult Muhammad in a mosque. Ward wrote what he did in an India under British colonial rule. Dialogue takes place face-to-face. Yet as conceived by the ecumenical movement that has broadly endorsed interfaith dialogue, it does not preclude but enables Christian witness. This anticipates my suggested revised soteriology. Harper, referring to Leonard, says that the main point of contention over the past generation of Baptists was "conversionist particularism" versus "pluralist libertarianism," or the need to defend the exclusivity of Christian (Baptist) faith claims or remain open to interfaith dialogue (86).

PROPOSING A REVISED SOTERIOLOGY CONSISTENT WITH THE BAPTIST EVANGELICAL LEGACY

In 1981, CROPOF redacted four principles of dialogue from the thirteen contained in the World Council of Churches' Guidelines on Dialogue with People of Living Faiths and Ideologies (1979). Many British churches and denominations have endorsed the principles, quite a few during my tenure as secretary. Promoting these was my main responsibility. After "dialogue begins when people meet," the second principle states that "dialogue depends on mutual trust and mutual understanding." I would want to change "trust" to "respect." Our conversations will not proceed smoothly or end up in human-rights collaboration if we insult our dialogue partners. The BCC's third principle is, in fact, that dialogue makes possible service to the community. Currently, I represent the Alliance of Baptists, with which I am affiliated, on the National Council of Churches USA's Convening Table on Interreligious Relations and Collaboration on Topics of Mutual Concern, which very much aligns with the direction that ecumenical interfaith involvement and thinking have taken for several decades. If we want to work with someone, we shouldn't insult them. Respect does not require agreement. It does call for a certain degree of political correctness. This is currently attracting a great deal of criticism in the United States, where some politicians see being PC as somehow scandalous. Insistence on naming the enemy in the war on terror as "radical Islamic terrorists," for example, does nothing to strengthen our relations with Muslims for whom the acts in which these "terrorists" engage disqualifies them from being Muslim in the first place. Why offend someone with whom we might like to work on, say, improving our community's preschool provision or feeding the house-bound, or on countering the radicalization of young people, or even to share our faith with? Isn't willingness to recognize some "worth" in their religion more likely to engage their interest and willingness to collaborate than an insistence on lack of any value? I once heard a Jewish colleague remark that when Christians speak about love, he prepares to flee and recalls that Gandhi said that what put him off Christianity was Christians. Too often, our actions betray our message. We talk about love, but our demonizing and dehumanizing of others actually express and encourage hostility toward them.

Baptists are committed to proclamation of the gospel. I prefer "sharing the gospel." Proclamation is a monologue. It does not require a personal relationship with those who are targeted. They listen; you speak. Sharing does. Dialogue means to argue a point through to a conclusion, but it cannot be a monologue; it must involve multiple voices. There is every reason in dialogue to talk about our motives and convictions, about our belief that we stand in a relationship with God. That, however, applies to all dialogue partners and begs the question, why should we insist on the reality of our relationship with God while denying that non-Christians can possibly enjoy any such relationship? Jones wrote, "Let us, then, invite the Muslim to explore the phenomena of spiritual experience, his and ours. In his heart, as in ours, the Spirit of the Living God is assuredly at work" (1938, 93).

The fourth principle states that dialogue becomes a medium of authentic witness. This means that we can share our deepest faith convictions and spiritual experiences with our partners, whose response might be to embrace Christianity, just as ours might be to embrace their religious faith. Sharing and witness here are mutual, not one-sided. Baptists have, as Brackney describes in numerous works, championed Calvinist and Arminian soteriology. Calvinists believe that only the elect are saved and that salvation is entirely God's work. Those who are not-elected are eternally lost. Arminians insist that salvation is available to all people and that a free, voluntary response is needed to the gospel. Brackney points out that there is no evidence "of direct dependence of Baptists on Arminius," but that their "emphases on free grace, a free response to the gospel, and a view of Christ's atonement as unlimited in its effects upon humanity" are "frequently described as Arminian" (2009, 33). Thus, attendees at evangelical rallies or at church services are invited to walk to the front, to give their lives to Jesus, to confess their sins and ask Jesus to become their personal lord and savior, which Smith said is the only prayer that God will hear spoken by a non-Christian.

Yet most Baptists also regard salvation as God's work through the Holy Spirit. In practice, though, it becomes a human work dependent both on a preacher proclaiming the gospel and on hearers responding, making a personal, with-the-lips decision for Christ. The Holy Spirit may be understood as inspiring the proclamation and the response, but if there is no human choice involved at all, our souls lack freedom. Talk of "soul competency" is meaningless. It would seem problematic to reconcile belief in "soul competency" with the idea that only an elect is saved since those elected have no say in the matter. Hick saw this as a denial of divine love, asking, "Can we accept the conclusion that the God of love who seeks to save all mankind has nevertheless ordained that men must be saved in such a way that only a small minority can in fact receive this salvation?" (1973, 122–23). Equally, to believe that God predestined people's damnation undermines human freedom. Perhaps a combination of Calvinists' insistence on salvation as God's free-gift with the need for a human turning toward God would preserve "soul competency" and the inviolability of the unfettered conscience. In fact, Baptists have mixed soteriological theologies. Famously, Charles Haddon Spurgeon (1834–1892) said on several occasions, when fellow Calvinists criticized his frequent altar calls inviting sinners to repent, that God should call all his elect and then elect some more (see Fisk, 69). If we separate faith, as God's free-gift of grace, from both the work of sharing the gospel and from the individual's free response to this, the possibility that anyone who turns to God will find himself or herself embraced by his limitless love remains open. They may turn to God as a practicing Hindu or Muslim and experience spiritual renewal without becoming Christian. Failure to share may mean that some miss the opportunity to discover the faith tradition that will best nourish them, so while we should not agonize about results, there is a duty involved here. I readily admit here that while, for me, faith is God's unearned gift, a faith that does not express itself through works is dead (James 2:17), a view that Calvin espoused. The Christian can claim that salvation is always mediated by Jesus whether he is acknowledged or not, which is his or her prerogative. Cragg's soul-searching work on how to make theological sense of Islam as a Christian, for me, is the golden standard in my chosen field. Arguably, while engaging in religious dialogue, it would be a failure of sharing for a Christian to remain silent about that which he or she treasures above everything, his or her spiritual experience, that which gives life meaning, purpose, and value. Leaving salvation to the Holy Spirit means that some will respond in ways we recognize as Christian, while other responses will remain a mystery to us (Newbigin, 1989, 203).

This works best when we ground what we share in our personal experience, rather than insist on doctrinal formulations. On Trinity, for example, we can speak about how our experience of the divine finds expression through Trinitarian language, rather than dogmatize on the absolute need to subscribe to the Nicene Creed. This is certainly consistent with Baptists' non-creedal tradition. God may be Three in One, One without any Persons, or perhaps manifested in three hundred and thirty million ways, but ultimately God is irreducible to number. Jones pointed out, too, "that no Christian claims that even the most widely accepted definition of the Trinity is adequate to the ultimate truth about God, but we do claim that it is a contribution to a better understanding of the mystery of His Nature" (1938, 94–95). Perhaps we need to think of our theological ideas as wholly true about God and the divine-human relationship, yet not the whole truth, leaving room to learn from others' theologies. Unless we think that we are God's equal, there should be room for mystery—even paradox and ambiguity—yet this we know: God's spirit moves within us. Some of our differences may confound and perplex us. Yet collaborating with Hindus and Muslims on making the world peaceful, just, equitable, and sustainable might end up pleasing God more than theological disputation. When Jesus began his ministry, he said that he had come to release prisoners, give sight to the blind, and announce the coming of God's kingdom. Kingdom-building, what I call the Lukan mandate, may be our missiological calling, the *missio Dei*. Yet, as we labor alongside people of other faiths and those of none, we still have a mandate and a responsibility to share our experience of spiritual renewal even as we listen to the experiences of others. While I uphold anyone's right to *disbelieve* in God as fervently as I do people's right to believe, I suspect that some atheists and agnostics who place others' genuine needs above their own—who live simply that others might simply live, by eating enough for their need, not greed (a Gandhi aphorism)—may on the other side of death yet have a chance to accept God's love.

The Unfettered Conscience and Freedom to Be Human as We Understand Our Own Humanity: Extending the Discourse

Devout Muslims and Hindus and others are equally human with ourselves and exercise their unfettered conscience when they live out their lives within their religious communities. Belief in the unfettered conscience means that all human rights are inviolable. For many Baptists and people of faith, defending a woman's reproductive rights will be problematic, yet if she chooses, after a great deal of soul-searching, an abortion, she is exercising the very "soul competency" that Baptists champion. Many Baptists will have difficulty accepting as morally good the lifestyles of those who identify as gay, lesbian, or transgender. Yet, in asserting these identities, people have looked into their souls and into their deepest sense of self and realized who they are in terms of sexuality or gender. For them, despite what anyone else says about deviancy or mental illness, this is who God made them. There are certainly Baptists who believe that homosexuality can be "cured." It took me a long time to feel comfortable with gay rights and transgender identity. I have a sibling who asserted that her gender did not correspond with what her birth certificate records. Initially, my response was not at all affirming. I now regret that I was less than affirming, especially since another sibling has ceased all contact with him. I've realized that what matters for myself and for others is that we are able to freely express who we are without passing judgment on others or being judged ourselves. The state does not have the right to restrict our self-expression, provided it does not harm others. While writing this chapter, the worst mass shooting in American history (so far) took place in an Orlando nightclub popular with the LGBT community. Omar Mateen, an American-born man inspired by ISIS, murdered forty-nine people on 11 June 2016. All agree that this was an act of terror but theories about motive abound, ranging from a hate crime to alleged self-hatred (some say Mateen was gay). Some Baptists praised this horrendous shooting. Pastor Steven Anderson of Faithful Word Baptist Church in Tempe, Arizona, called it "good news" because "homosexuals are a bunch of disgusting people and pedophiles." In killing these women and men, Mateen did what a "righteous government" should do according to Leviticus 20:13. Similarly, Pastor Roger Jimenez of Verity Baptist Church in Sacramento, California, said that the government should round up homosexuals, line them in front of a wall, and "blow their brains out." What did upset him was that Mateen had failed to complete the job. These "Baptists" believe neither in church-state separation nor in soul-competency.

Conclusion

This type of language is as dangerous and sinister as demonizing Muslims, falling far short of respect for the *Imago Dei* in the Orlando victims, or for their freedom to be who they are. The gospel of Jesus is about love, not hate. It is because God loves all people that God gave us our conscience, to accuse or to excuse us before God (Rom. 2:25). Brackney's seeing beyond a shallow, limited, even self-serving advocacy of soul-competency to the duty to champion the whole human-rights agenda, and to look with respect on the religious choices people make, is courageous, prophetic, and biblical.

SOURCES

P. Richard Bohr, "The Legacy of Timothy Richard," in *The International Bulletin of Missionary Research* 24/2 (2000): 75–80.

William H. Brackney, *The Baptists* (New York: Greenwood Press, 1988).

William H. Brackney, *A Genetic History of Baptist Thought: With Special Reference to Baptists in Britain and North America* (Macon GA: Mercer University Press, 2004).

William H. Brackney, *The A to Z of the Baptists* (Lanham: The Scarecrow Press, 2009).

William H. Brackney, *Studying Christianity: The Critical Issues* (London: Continuum, 2010).

William H. Brackney, *Human Rights and the World's Major Religions* (Santa Barbara CA: Praeger, 2013).

William H. Brackney, "Bill Brackney Discusses His Work on Human Rights," Acadia Divinity School, 16 December 2013, http://www.acadiadiv.ca/blog/2013/12/16/bill-brackney- discusses-his-work-on-human-rights.

Ergun Mehmet Caner and Emir Fethi Caner, *Unveiling Islam: An Insider's Look at Muslim Life and Beliefs* (Grand Rapids MI: Kregel Publications, 2009).

Kenneth Cragg, *The Call of the Minaret* (NY: Oxford University Press, 1956).

Kenneth Cragg, *Sandals at the Mosque: The Christian Presence Amid Islam* (London: SCM, 1959).

Keith Harper, *American Denominational History: Perspectives on the Past, Prospects for the Future* (Tuscaloosa AL: University of Alabama Press, 2008).

John Hick, *God and the Universe of Faiths* (London: Macmillan, 1973).

Lewis Bevan Jones, *The People of the Mosque: An Introduction to the Study of Islam with Special Reference to India* (London: SCM, 1932).

Lewis Bevan Jones, *Christianity Explained to Muslims: A Manual for Christian Workers* (Calcutta: YMCA Publishing House, 1939).

Brian Kaylor, "Anniversary of Bailey Smith's Harmful Moment in Baptist-Jewish Relations," *Ethics Daily*, 3 August 2010, http://www.ethicsdaily.com/anniversary-of-bailey-smiths-harmful-moment-in- baptist-jewish-relations-cms-16564 (accessed 21 June 2016).

Hendrik Kraemer, "Continuity or Discontinuity," in *The Authority of the Faith* (London: International Missionary Council and Oxford University Press, 1939) 1–23.

Bill J. Leonard, "Changing a Theology: Baptists, Salvation, and Globalism, Then and Now," in *Distinctively Baptist Essays on Baptist History: A Festschrift in Honor of Walter B. Shurden*, ed. Walter B. Shurden, Marc Alan Jolley, and John D. Pierce (Macon GA: Mercer University Press, 2005) 7–16.

Donald McGavran, *Understanding Church Growth*, rev. and ed. C. Peter Wagner, 3rd ed. (Grand Rapids: Eerdmans, 1990).

Lesslie Newbigin, *The Gospel in a Pluralist Society* (London: SPCK, 1989).

Alan Race, *Christians and Religious Pluralism: Patterns in the Christian Theology of Religions* (London: SCM, 1983).

Karl Rahner, "Christianity and the Non-Christian Religions," in *Theological Investigations*, vol. 5 (New York: Seabury Press, 1966) 115–31.

William Ward, *Account of the Writings, Religion, and Manners of the Hindoos: Including Translations from Their Principal Works*, 4 vols. (Serampore: The Mission-Press, 1811).

SECTION 2

DOGMATICS

NEITHER CALVINIST NOR ARMINIAN, BUT BAPTIST? AN ASSESSMENT OF GRACE AND PERSEVERANCE IN BAPTIST THEOLOGY

Stanley K. Fowler

I am happy to write this chapter in a *Festschrift* for Bill Brackney in appreciation for his scholarship, churchmanship, and friendship. Bill and I were drawn together in 1996, when I was writing my doctoral thesis at Wycliffe College, University of Toronto, and Bill was the principal of McMaster Divinity College in nearby Hamilton. My thesis supervisor accepted an appointment at Oxford University, which left me in search of a new supervisor, and thanks to McMaster's associate status with the Toronto School of Theology, Bill was able to step into that role. Our friendship grew out of our shared interest in the history of Baptist thought, and that continues in spite of our geographic separation. So I offer this study with happy memories of our collaboration on a study of Baptist thought for an Anglican theological college embedded in an ecumenical consortium.

Now to the question at hand: The average member of a Baptist church likely believes that all Baptists affirm the doctrine of eternal security or perseverance of the saints, and this is understandable, given the prominence of this doctrine in much of the Baptist world. There are exceptions, of course, like the General Association of General Baptist Churches and the Free Will Baptists, but they are clearly not the dominant stream of Baptist life, at least in North America. The affirmation that all who are presently regenerate will inherit final salvation can be traced historically to the First and Second London Confessions of the seventeenth century, and in America to the Philadelphia Confession of 1742 (a slightly expanded form of the Second London Confession) and the New Hampshire Confession of 1833. The New Hampshire Confession has influenced many later confessions, including the Baptist Faith and Message in all its iterations, the statement of the General Association of Regular Baptist Churches, and the confession of my own denomination, the Fellowship of Evangelical Baptist Churches in Canada. The precise wording of these confessions varies, but all affirm the same doctrine of perseverance. Some prefer the terminology of "eternal security" and some the terminology of "perseverance of the saints," but there is a common affirmation expressed with two distinct emphases.

This doctrine is a coherent part of the broader Calvinistic system of doctrine. This linkage is explicit in the Second London Confession:

> This perseverance of the Saints depends not upon their own free will; but upon the immutability of the decree of Election flowing from the free and unchangeable love of God the Father; upon the efficacy of the merit and intercession of Jesus Christ and Union with him, the oath of God, the abiding of his Spirit & the seed of God within them, and the nature of the Covenant of Grace from all which ariseth also the certainty and infallibility thereof (ch. XVII).[1]

The logic is clear: God has from eternity past unconditionally chosen particular persons out of the fallen human race for salvation; Christ is the incarnate Son who actualizes in history the eternal purpose of the Father; the Holy Spirit works in a way that infallibly achieves the eternal purpose of election—that is, by a work of irresistible or efficacious grace in the elect that draws all of them to repentance and faith; and the same Spirit who draws them to faith is given to indwell them and efficaciously maintain their faith that leads to final salvation. This logical link to unconditional election and irresistible grace is crucial, because although there are biblical texts that seem to affirm the final salvation of all those who are presently saved, there are probably more texts that seem to question the doctrine. When we are confronted by two groups of biblical texts that seem to contradict each other, as in this case, the synthesis will depend on broader biblical themes—in this case, the wider biblical picture of the relation between divine and human action. In this way, the Calvinistic doctrines of grace and election make the doctrine of final perseverance coherent.

It is not difficult to see how the doctrine of final perseverance makes sense as an implication of Calvinism, but there are many Baptists who affirm final perseverance while denying unconditional election and irresistible grace. This has been stated formally in the Statement of the Traditional Southern Baptist Understanding of God's Plan of Salvation,[2] a document published in 2012 by a group of Southern Baptists expressing their dissent from a resurgent and confident Calvinism within their denomination. I can verify from personal experience that the views expressed in this "Traditional Statement" are held by many Baptists outside the SBC, but this statement is useful as an explicit statement of the position, and it will serve as a focus in this study. We have not only the statement itself, but also a commentary on it by proponents in two issues of the online *Journal for Baptist Theology and Ministry.* The fundamental question is this: Is the doctrine of final perseverance biblically and logically coherent apart from the doctrines of

[1] The confession can be found at_http://baptiststudiesonline.com/wp-content/uploads/2008/08/the-second-london-confession.pdf.

[2] The statement can be found in several places, including the *Journal for Baptist Theology and Ministry* 9/2 (Fall 2012): 14–18.

unconditional election and irresistible grace? The doctrines of unconditional election and irresistible grace are, in reality, two sides of one idea, the former describing the eternal purpose of God and the latter describing the actualizing of that purpose in history. Therefore, for the sake of a clear focus, this study will look specifically at the debate about the nature of grace.

Before turning to the contemporary debate, it is worth noting that the non-Calvinistic affirmation of final perseverance has a historical precedent in the Orthodox Creed of 1678. That confession was adopted by a group of General Baptists who were intent on demonstrating their link to other Protestants such as Presbyterians and Congregationalists. In fact, the full published title of the confession is, *An Orthodox Creed: or a Protestant Confession of Faith, Being an Essay to Unite, and Confirm All True Protestants in the Fundamental Articles of the Christian Religion, against the Errors and Heresies of the Church of ROME.*[3] Although the General Baptists were traditionally Arminian in some ways, they incorporated much of the language of the Westminster Confession into the creed to emphasize their commonalities with Calvinistic Protestants, although there are limits to the commonalities.

Article IX refers to "God's Eternal Purpose in Electing of Christ, and of all that do, or shall believe in him," and later asserts that "God's Eternal Decree doth not oppose his revealed Will in the Gospel, it being but one, not two diverse or contrary Wills." This rejection of a distinction between a revealed will and a secret will indicates a rejection of a particularized election of only some to whom the gospel is offered. Article X asserts that God "foresaw Adam's fall, but did not decree it, yet foreseeing it in his eternal Counsel and Wisdom, did Elect and chuse Jesus Christ, and all that do or shall believe in him, out of that fallen Lump of Mankind." Although there is some ambiguity in the language, this sounds very much like the traditional Arminian doctrine of election based on foreseen faith.

Article XXI treats "Vocation and Effectual Calling," but in spite of the Calvinistic terminology, the concepts appear to be essentially Arminian. The article reads thus:

> Vocation, or Calling, General, or Common, is when God by the means of his Word and Spirit, freely of his own Grace and Goodness, doth ministerially acquaint Mankind with his gracious good purpose of Salvation, by Jesus Christ; inviting and wooing them to come to him, and to accept of Christ revealing unto them the Gospel-Covenant; and those that with Cordial Hearts do improve this common Grace, he in time worketh unfained Faith, and sincere Repentance in them; and by his

[3] A critical edition of the confession is available online at http://baptiststudiesonline.com/wp-content/uploads/2007/02/orthodox-creed.pdf. All quotations in this article are from this edition.

> Grace they come to accept of Christ, as their only Lord and Saviour, with their whole Heart; and God becomes their Father in Christ, and they being then effectually called, are by Faith united to Jesus Christ by Grace unto Salvation.

The crucial point here is that the work of the Spirit that is termed effectual occurs only after the individual sinner has responded positively to the gospel offer via common grace, so that the distinguishing factor in those who are saved is ultimately the human response, not a special work of the Spirit. There is a special work of the Spirit, but it concerns the completion of saving faith in those who have already "improved" the experience of common grace.

Article XXXVI defines the doctrine of perseverance thus: "Those that are effectually called, according to God's eternal Purpose, being justified by Faith, do receive such a measure of the holy Unction, from the Holy Spirit, by which they shall certainly persevere unto Eternal Life." When this is read in isolation, it looks like an affirmation of perseverance rooted in Calvinism, but when "effectual calling" is defined as it is in article XXI, this superficial impression is negated. Nevertheless, the doctrine of the final salvation of all the presently justified is affirmed on the basis of the ongoing work of the indwelling Spirit. Now, this assertion of perseverance guaranteed by a work of the Spirit seems to suggest the reality of irresistible grace in Christian experience, and this is a theme to which I will return when dealing with the current debate.

The challenge for non-Calvinistic defenders of final perseverance is to explain the inner logic of perseverance. If it is true that all those who are presently saved will be saved in the end, then one of two things must be true. Either (1) some who are presently saved by faith may give up their faith and become unbelievers again, but will still be saved; or (2) all who are presently saved by faith will certainly continue in faith and therefore in salvation.

The first of these views preserves a strong sense of human freedom in the experience of salvation, leaving believers free to change their mind, but it requires exegetical gymnastics to correlate it with the biblical witness, and the list of those who hold this view is therefore short. Nevertheless, the view has been defended by Zane Hodges and Charles Stanley, to name two proponents, and it has been expressed organizationally in the Grace Evangelical Society.[4] Hodges explains the shallow, rocky soil in the parable of the sower this way:

> Faith had occurred in the heart the Saviour now described, and not mere passive faith, adequate though that would be, but joyous faith. [...] But alas! The faith by which they appropriated the gift of life had not endured. [...] The faith had not endured. God's gift had! [...] Man, to be

[4] The theology of this society can be found in its online journal at https://faithalone.org/ges-journal/.

> sure, was changeable. The God who gifted him was not! And the gift of life, like every other good and perfect gift, had its origin and source in an immutable giver. [...] Their Master's meaning was plain. The living seed remained in the heart. The faith that received it did not.[5]

Following Hodges' lead, Stanley writes:

> God does not require a constant attitude of faith in order to be saved—only an act of faith. [...] [Hodges] argues convincingly that Satan can completely shipwreck a believer's faith but that this in no way affects the believer's security. [...] The Bible teaches that God's love for His people is of such magnitude that even those who walk away from the faith have not the slightest chance of slipping from His hand.[6]

While the desire to magnify the grace of God and to avoid any sense of salvation based on human merit is certainly commendable, the idea of saved unbelievers is so antithetical to the biblical witness that it is hard to take this view seriously. The Epistle to the Hebrews seems crystal clear on this point, which is to say that those who shrink back from faith will perish and not experience the salvation of their souls (Heb. 10:39). That epistle had already made the point that we are part of God's household only if we hold firmly to our confidence in Christ to the end (3:6, 14). Paul was confident of the salvation of the Corinthians, but only if they held firmly to the message that he preached (1 Cor. 15:1–2). And of course, all the apostles could point back to Jesus, who envisioned that many of his professed disciples would be led astray and turn away from him, but salvation would belong to those who endure to the end (Matt. 24:9–13). Arminians and Calvinists explain apostasy in different ways, but historically they have agreed that there is no final salvation apart from perseverance in faith. The biblical witness points clearly in that direction.

That leaves us, then, with the second view—that is, that all the presently saved will certainly continue in faith and thus in the sphere of salvation. This is clearly more than a simple prediction that as a matter of fact all true believers will continue believing, even though it might have been otherwise. It is rooted in language like that of John 6 (Jesus' promise that he will lose none of those whom the Father has given to him) or John 10 (Jesus' assurance that his sheep are as secure as his grip is strong). In other words, it is rooted in a divine work that guarantees the human response, but none of that negates the equally clear biblical description of faith as a responsible human attitude. God does not repent and believe—*we* do that. This combination of divine monergism and human responsibility is, of

---

[5] Zane Clark Hodges, *The Hungry Inherit* (Chicago: Moody Press, 1972) 60–61.

[6] Charles Stanley, *Eternal Security: Can You Be Sure?* (Nashville: Thomas Nelson, 1990) 80, 91.

course, what we call "compatibilism," and it looks as if this is the only way to explain the idea of final perseverance. But not all agree.

The Traditional Statement of 2012 provides a concise explanation of the Baptist idea of security or assured perseverance in an explicitly non-Calvinistic, incompatibilistic framework. The most relevant parts include the following:

> We deny that grace negates the necessity of a free response of faith or that it cannot be resisted. (Article 4) [...] We deny that election means that, from eternity, God predestined certain people for salvation and others for condemnation. (Article 6) [...] We affirm that God, as an expression of His sovereignty, endows each person with actual free will (the ability to choose between two options), which must be exercised in accepting or rejecting God's gracious call to salvation by the Holy Spirit through the Gospel. We deny that the decision of faith is an act of God rather than a response of the person. We deny that there is an "effectual call" for certain people that is different from a "general call" to any person who hears and understands the Gospel. (Article 8) [...] We affirm that when a person responds in faith to the Gospel, God promises to complete the process of salvation in the believer into eternity. [...] We deny that this Holy Spirit-sealed relationship can ever be broken. We deny even the possibility of apostasy. (Article 9)

I will first note that some of the denials contained in the statement are based on caricatures of Calvinism. Calvinists do not say that grace negates the necessity of faith, nor do they say that the grace of God can never be resisted. What they do say, rightly or wrongly, is that there is a unique work of grace that will not be successfully resisted, a work done only in the elect. With regard to double predestination, Calvinists often emphasize that election and reprobation are asymmetrical, the former based in grace and the latter based in justice. It is also inaccurate to claim that Calvinists define faith as an act of God and not an act of the human person. What they teach is that saving faith is a human response efficaciously evoked by God.

The crucial points are these: an affirmation of some sort of libertarian freedom as inherent in humanity; the denial of a special work of the Spirit done only in those who are going to believe and be saved; and the affirmation that all who believe and are saved now will continue to believe and be saved in the end. The crucial question is whether this complex of beliefs is coherent. Does not this guarantee of continuing faith assume a work of ongoing irresistible grace? And does it not imply that human free will is nullified when the power of contrary choice to disbelieve is eliminated?

Statements of this so-called traditional view are usually very sparse in their explanation of guaranteed continuance in faith. The statement above simply refers to it as a "Holy-Spirit sealed relationship." But this implies that there is an ongoing work of the Spirit that assures continuing faith, even though that faith is clearly our faith, as evidenced by the many biblical exhortations to keep on believing the gospel. So what we have is, in fact, irresistible or efficacious grace in relation to continuing faith, and that presses the question, why not affirm that of initial faith also, as various biblical texts seem to suggest?

In his commentary on the Traditional Statement article on security, Steve Horn says this about the relation to human freedom: "On the Traditionalist view, the true convert has willingly surrendered himself to the sealing, transformational power of the gospel. He has said yes to God's commitment to unending fellowship. There is no going back; the freedom to walk away has been surrendered."[7] This is in many ways an astonishing admission, but it is necessary to hold together the complex of traditionalist beliefs. Is it not odd, though, that the soft libertarian free will that is considered to be a divine gift to all humans is removed at conversion, so that the entrance into salvation actually makes us less human? Is ongoing irresistible grace really less coercive than such grace at the point of conversion?

If, then, it seems that the doctrine of final perseverance can be explained adequately only in relation to a doctrine of irresistible grace, why do "traditional Baptists" reject that doctrine of grace? To assess that, I will summarize the objections to the doctrine articulated by Steve Lemke in his chapter, "A Biblical and Theological Critique of Irresistible Grace," found in the book *Whosoever Will*, edited by Lemke and David Allen; and also the objections given by Braxton Hunter in his "Commentary on Article 8: The Free Will of Man," found in the *Journal for Baptist Theology and Ministry*.

The most directly biblical argument is the appeal to various biblical texts that say God's grace is, in fact, resisted.[8] Lemke points to Old Testament texts that describe the resistance of Israel against God's gracious acts, texts like Hosea 11 or Psalm 81. Luke 7 gives us Jesus' description of the Jews' resistance to God's work through both John the Baptist and Jesus himself. Acts 7 describes Stephen's rebuke of his fellow Jews for their longstanding hardness of heart and resistance to God's overtures of grace. Acts 26 narrates Paul's description of his own resistance to God's purposes. The list could be multiplied, but no amount of texts can put this argument on target, because it seriously distorts the doctrine of irresistible grace. That doctrine does not assert that every work of God's grace is irresistible, but rather asserts that there is a special work of grace that infallibly

---

[7] Steve Horn, "Commentary on Article 9: The Security of the Believer," *JBTM* 10/1 (Spring 2013): 33.

[8] Steve W. Lemke, "A Biblical and Theological Critique of Irresistible Grace," in *Whosoever Will: A Biblical-Theological Critique of Five-Point Calvinism*, ed. David L. Allen and Steve W. Lemke (Nashville: B&H Academic, 2010) 117–19.

evokes the response of faith. The fact of human resistance to grace is not in dispute. The dispute concerns the existence of a gracious work of God done only in the elect that is both necessary and sufficient for faith and salvation.

The broadly theological and philosophical arguments against irresistible grace include the following:

> The doctrine can lead to a denial of the necessity for conversion. If God saves monergistically, then nothing from the human side is ultimately decisive, which makes a personal confession of repentance and faith unnecessary, or at least much less significant than the Bible indicates.[9] Lemke has in view here some Reformed paedobaptists who deny the necessity of an identifiable conversion experience in the lives of "covenant children," but it should be noted that this is not equivalent to a denial of the necessity of repentance and faith for salvation. So while this argument may be relevant concerning some Calvinistic paedobaptists, it has little relevance for Calvinistic Baptists.

The doctrine reverses the order of salvation by putting regeneration prior to conversion, even though Scripture puts faith (conversion) before salvation (including regeneration).[10] The merits of this argument depend to some extent on the definition of regeneration. Although it is true that Calvinists generally posit regeneration as logically prior to conversion, some, like Millard Erickson, have argued (convincingly, in my view) that "regeneration" is in Scripture a comprehensive way of speaking about the experience of spiritual rebirth inclusive of the gift of the indwelling Spirit, and it is accordingly an effect of conversion.[11] There is, to be sure, a work of the Spirit that logically precedes conversion, but that is better phrased as "effectual calling" than as "regeneration." If so, then Lemke's description of the relation between conversion and regeneration can be accepted, while still affirming a work of irresistible grace that brings about conversion.

"Irresistible grace could weaken the significance of preaching the Word of God, evangelism, and missions."[12] There is no point in denying the historical reality of Hyper-Calvinism, with its denial of the universal offer of the gospel, and we can be grateful that Particular Baptists like Andrew Fuller rejected the excesses of John Gill. However, we should also note that the Baptists who rejected Hyper-Calvinism and launched an aggressive program of world evangelism via the Baptist Missionary Society were still Calvinists who rejected false inferences from the basic doctrines of Calvinism. Arguing that Calvinism's emphasis on sovereign grace leads to weaker evangelism is a bit like arguing that Arminianism's

---

[9] Ibid., 132–34.

[10] Ibid., 134–40.

[11] Millard J. Erickson, *Christian Theology*, 3rd ed. (Grand Rapids: Baker, 2013) 863–64.

[12] Lemke, "A Biblical and Theological Critique," 140–45.

emphasis on human freedom leads to open theism.

The doctrine creates questions about the character of God, especially in relation to the problem of evil. In Lemke's words, "The God of hard Calvinism is either disingenuous, cynically making a pseudo-offer of salvation to persons whom He has not given the means to accept, or there is a deep inner conflict within the will of God."[13] At the heart of this objection is the idea that responsibility is limited by ability, so that it appears to be unjust for God to punish unbelievers for not doing what they are unable to do. With regard to the problem of evil, if God is able to efficaciously bring sinners to repentance without destroying their moral agency, but he does not do this, then it is very difficult to absolve him of culpability for the evil in the world.

The doctrine does not provide an adequate account of human freedom. Both Lemke and Hunter argue that compatibilist "freedom" is not genuine freedom in any meaningful sense. While it may be voluntary, it is not free. They both argue for what they call "soft libertarian freedom," as the natural way to explain both the biblical account of human responsibility and the human experience of decision-making.[14]

The doctrine does not provide an adequate view of time and eternity. Lemke assumes that the Pauline reference to divine foreknowledge in Romans 8:29 is about God's precognition of human faith (a debatable assumption in view of the wider biblical usage), and then argues that divine timelessness and divine creation of the laws of logic enable us to make sense of foreseen faith, which is at the same time free.[15] It is hard to see how this particular piece of Lemke's argument can be directed at Calvinist logic. The questions to which divine eternality is the answer, as he expresses them, are all essentially this: "How could God foreknow all things before the foundation of the world and yet allow us genuine libertarian free will?" But this is the question of open theists, not Calvinists. It is also probably true that most Calvinists affirm divine timelessness, so the relevance of this section of his chapter is not at all clear.

The doctrine does not in fact maximize God's sovereignty and glory, no matter what Calvinists say. God's glory is displayed more greatly, it is argued, when his creatures trust and worship him by their free choice, rather than doing so by means of divine coercion. Furthermore, to say that God is sovereign does not in itself describe how God sovereignly chooses to act. God sovereignly chose to create creatures with a kind of libertarian freedom that is the basis for moral responsibility.[16]

---

[13] Ibid., 145.

[14] Ibid., 151. Also, see Braxton Hunter, "Commentary on Article 8: The Free Will of Man," *JBTM* 10/1 (Spring 2013): 21.

[15] Lemke, "A Biblical and Theological Critique," 152–53.

[16] Ibid., 153–62.

To respond in depth to each of these objections is far beyond the scope of this study, and in any case, others have made the positive case for irresistible grace and responded to these and other objections.[17] What I want to argue here is that these kinds of objections to the idea of irresistible grace at conversion also raise serious questions about the coherence of the traditional Baptist description of post-conversion experience.

For example, the arguments based on the trajectory from the doctrine in question can easily be turned against the doctrine of eternal security. Clearly the Calvinistic doctrine of grace has been used in the past to negate the universal offer of the gospel, but it is equally true that the doctrine of eternal security has been used by some to support antinomianism, or at least a lax approach to the demands of discipleship and a false kind of assurance. One must always ask whether inferences are legitimate or not, and to reject a doctrine because of demonstrably negative inferences would nullify eternal security as much as irresistible grace.

If offers of the gospel to non-elect persons are disingenuous because they are certain to be rejected, then what is to be said about exhortations to believers to persevere in faith and remain in Christ, including warnings about the negative consequences of failure to persevere, given that they will certainly not fall away?

The most potent objection to irresistible grace appears to be the argument that it is rooted in a compatibilistic view of human freedom, which seems to be both conceptually illogical and false to human experience. Critics of the doctrine freely use the term "coercive" to describe the action attributed to God by the doctrine. Defining human freedom has been an ongoing debate for millennia, and it will not be settled by this study. It is, I think, the ultimate issue in the debate over open theism, and no resolution of the debate appears to lurk on the horizon. My point here is simply to say that the soft libertarian freedom espoused by traditional Baptists appears to disappear after conversion. Continuing faith is rooted for them in a sealing activity of the Holy Spirit, which negates even the possibility of turning away from faith in Christ, but this makes no sense in the context of libertarian freedom. That kind of freedom demands the power of contrary choice, which implies that the believer has the ability to turn away from faith and become an unbeliever once again. Why is irresistible grace in support of ongoing faith any less a denial of human moral agency than irresistible grace in support of initial faith?

Kenneth Keathley is a Southern Baptist theologian who has thought deeply about these issues and has offered a description of grace that might be a via media in this debate. He recognizes the significance of defining grace when he says,

---

[17] In addition to a long list of systematic theologies written by Calvinists, see Matthew Barrett, *Salvation by Grace:The Case for Effectual Calling and Regeneration* (Phillipsburg NJ: Presbyterian & Reformed, 2013).

"Perhaps more than any other point (including election), the crucial component of Calvinism is effectual calling or, as it is sometimes called, irresistible grace."[18] Keathley proposes what he calls "overcoming grace" that is both monergistic and resistible, so that "salvation is all of grace, and damnation all of sin."[19] Here is his use of an analogy to explain the concept:

> So how does the overcoming grace position understand the workings of the Holy Spirit in bringing a lost person to faith in Jesus Christ? This view can also be called "an ambulatory model" because it understands the sinner's coming to faith as a process by which the Spirit of God carries a person to the point of saving trust. In fact, perhaps an illustration using an ambulance will help. Imagine waking up to find you are being transported by an ambulance to the emergency room. It is clearly evident that your condition requires serious medical help. If you do nothing, you will be delivered to the hospital. However, if for whatever reason you demand to be let out, the driver will comply. He may express regret and give warnings, but he will still let you go. You receive no credit for being taken to the hospital, but you incur the blame for refusing the services of the ambulance.

In this illustration you do not do anything to arrive at the hospital. The only thing you have the ability to do is resist. Any "contribution" made by you is hurtful. Now let the ambulance serve as a metaphor for the work of the Spirit in conversion. If you believe, it is because (and only because) the Holy Spirit brought you to faith. If you do not believe, it is only because you resisted. The only thing you are able to "do" is negative. Thus the ambulatory model provides for a monergistic work of grace that leaves room for the sinner to refuse to accept.[20]

The first thing to be said about this proposal is that it uses the term "monergistic" in an abnormal way. The term normally implies that the actor guarantees the accomplishment of the telos of the action, but that is not the case in this analogy. Here the goal is to get the patient to the hospital, but the ambulance driver only offers the service and achieves the goal only if the patient chooses to allow it. In the soteriological point of this analogy, the goal is repentance and faith, and Calvinists argue that Scripture teaches that the universal human response to God's offer is, in fact, resistance. Given that reality, the crucial person in the analogy would not be the ambulance driver as driver, but the driver (or another person) as the one who persuades the patient to remain in the ambulance. In the end, the ultimately determining factor in the arrival at the hospital is the

[18] Kenneth Keathley, *Salvation and Sovereignty: A Molinist Approach* (Nashville: B&H Academic, 2010) 102.

[19] Ibid., 103.

[20] Ibid., 104.

choice of the patient to remain in the ambulance. As applied to the soteriological question, this is simply an Arminian view of grace, not a via media.

Keathley's analogy could be pushed a bit further. "Salvation" in Scripture is not just what happens at conversion, but is inclusive of all that lies ahead in the new heaven and new earth. So let us suppose that the ambulance is transporting the patient to the end of his life and the ultimate healing of eschatological salvation. In order to defend the "traditional Baptist" doctrine of eternal security, one has to posit that every patient chooses to remain in the ambulance, but that demands a major reconstruction of the analogy in a coercive direction. The analogy makes perfectly good sense for classical Arminian theology, but it falters when used as an explanation of eternal security.

Keathley proposes that the traditional "TULIP" acronym for the "Five Points of Calvinism" be transformed into "ROSES," in which "O" stands for "overcoming grace" (as above) and the "E" stands for "eternal life." His chapter on the latter topic[21] is where one would expect a treatment of final perseverance, but instead he focuses there on assurance rather than perseverance. The two are related, to be sure, but they are not equivalent. Puritans who affirmed final perseverance were nevertheless often caught up in a struggle for assurance, because one can be sure that all who are saved now will be saved in the end without strong assurance that one is, in fact, saved now. The chapter engages debates about the relationship between assurance and sanctification, but there is no attempt to apply the idea of overcoming grace to ongoing Christian experience. I suppose that should come as no surprise, because as argued above, the "traditional Baptist" view of security would demand that the nature of grace change dramatically after conversion in order to guarantee final salvation.

In summary, I am arguing that what has been called the "traditional Baptist" view of soteriology is incoherent in its affirmation of eternal security and denial of irresistible grace. Coherence can be achieved in three ways: (1) Continue to affirm libertarian freedom and accept the reality that some genuine believers will give up their faith, but affirm that they are still saved in spite of their unbelief—i.e., accept the novel view of Zane Hodges and Charles Stanley. I do not expect a mass movement in this direction, given the difficulty of correlating this idea with the warning texts of the New Testament. (2) Continue to affirm libertarian freedom and accept the implication that some genuine believers will choose to desert their faith and, therefore, will forfeit their salvation—i.e., accept Arminian soteriology in its fullness. This is, as I see it, the logical implication of the "traditional Baptist" understanding of human freedom and the nature of grace. On this point I side with Roger Olson, an Arminian Baptist theologian, whose review of the book *Whosoever Will* applauds the authors for their critique of Calvinism and

---

[21] Ibid., 164–90.

chides them for refusing to admit that their soteriology is essentially that of Arminius.[22] The key to making this move is to admit that Arminian theology is not a heretical affirmation of salvation by works and is not foreign to the Baptist tradition. The first Baptists, after all, were generally Arminian in their theology, and that General Baptist tradition continues to our day.[23] (3) Admit that eternal security is coherent only when tied to irresistible grace and compatibilism, and accept Calvinistic soteriology in its fullness. This inference has been at the heart of a significant movement among Southern Baptists in recent history, so much so that "traditional" Southern Baptists felt compelled to respond with the statement noted earlier in this study. My personal view is that the Calvinistic perspective is the most plausible reading of Scripture on these debated points, but the Arminian perspective is at least coherent and deserves respect rather than disdain.

Some of the authors of *Whosoever Will: A Biblical-Theological Critique of Five-Point Calvinism*, noted earlier in this study, described themselves in an online "white paper" entitled "Neither Calvinists nor Arminians but Baptists" as "majoritarian Baptists in the Sandy Creek tradition."[24] The title embodies a category mistake, in that an ecclesiological descriptor is not parallel to soteriological descriptors, but the greater problem is that while they may represent the view of a majority of Southern Baptists, the combination of an Arminian view of grace and a Calvinistic view of perseverance is incoherent.

---

[22] http://www.baptisttheology.org/book-reviews/whosoever-will/.

[23] See, for example, J. Matthew Pinson, *Arminian and Baptist: Explorations in a Theological Tradition* (Nashville: Randall House, 2015); and Stephen M. Ashby, "A Reformed Arminian View," in *Four Views on Eternal Security*, ed. Stanley N. Gundry and J. Matthew Pinson (Grand Rapids: Zondervan, 2002).

[24] The paper can be found on a website sponsored by Southwestern Baptist Theological Seminary at http://www.baptisttheology.org/white-papers/neither-calvinists-nor-arminians-but-baptists/.

THE CHRISTOLOGY OF CANADIAN BAPTIST THEOLOGIAN RUSSELL ALDWINCKLE

John Shouse

I. Introduction

Canadian Baptist theologian Russell Aldwinckle left behind a small but impressive body of work—most of it authored towards the end of or following his thirty-year career at McMaster Divinity College. He told friends that he had simply been too busy to publish during his active teaching years. Aldwinckle's writing is erudite, self-consciously evangelical, pastoral, and ranges comfortably over terrain both contemporary and classic. His work presciently anticipated themes and issues with which theology would engage for decades to come. Consequently, his corpus deserves more attention than it has previously received. His first book, *Death in the Secular City*,[1] addressed the subject of personal eschatology in light of modernity's tacit assumption that this world is the only one that matters.[2] His second book, *More than Man*,[3] anticipated the "Myth of God Incarnate" debate that broke out in British theological circles towards the end of the 1970s.[4] *Jesus—a Savior or the Savior?*[5] foreshadowed issues with which the emerging fields of the theology of religions and comparative theology would grapple. Finally, his *The Logic of the Believing Mind*[6] explored theological epistemology and method.

II. A Brief Biographical Sketch

Russell Foster Aldwinckle was born in Leicester, England, in 1911. He received a B.A. in history at the University of London in 1932 and, in 1936, earned a second B.A.—this time in theology—from Oxford University. His Th.D. was awarded from Strasbourg in 1938. Ten years later, in 1948, he received an M.A.

[1] Russell Aldwinckle, *Death in the Secular City: A Study of the Notion of Life after Death in Contemporary Theology and Philosophy* (Grand Rapids: Eerdmans, 1974).

[2] Ibid., 131.

[3] Russell Aldwinckle, *More Than Man* (Grand Rapids: Eerdmans Publishing Company, 1976).

[4] John Hick, ed., *The Myth of God Incarnate* (Philadelphia: Westminster Press, 1977).

[5] Russell F. Aldwinckle, *Jesus—A Savior or the Savior?: Religious Pluralism in Christian Perspective* (Macon GA: Mercer University Press, 1982).

[6] Russell Aldwinckle, *The Logic of the Believing Mind*, Toronto Studies in Theology, vol. 60 (Lewiston: The Edwin Mellon Press, 1995).

in theology from Oxford. Aldwinckle pastored Hearsall Baptist Church in Coventry from 1939 to 1943, moving on to pastor North Finchley Baptist Church in London until 1947.[7] From 1947 until 1977, he taught Systematic Theology at McMaster and was on the faculty there throughout William Brackney's tenure as principal. Aldwinckle also served as visiting professor at Eastern Baptist, American Baptist, and Southern Baptist Seminaries.

Warm, soft-spoken, and engaging, Aldwinckle was the quintessence of dry wit. He shared once that after coming to McMaster he quickly adopted the "North American custom" of taking coffee with his meal rather than following it. He recalled that during one visit back to Great Britain his waiter studiously ignored his repeated requests for his coffee to be served along with his entrée rather than following it. After a final, insistent appeal, Aldwinckle recalled how his waiter pulled himself up to his full height, peered down his nose, and intoned: "If you insist, I'll bring it. But it isn't right!"[8] On his way home from attending a play at the Shaw Theater Festival in summer 1992, Aldwinckle died in the street of a heart attack in the arms of his wife, Muriel.

III. Theological Method

Aldwinckle's theological method was both sophisticated and informed. He insisted that Christian theological convictions emerge from an interplay between God's actions in history, biblical revelation, ecclesial tradition, and spiritual experience. One of the compelling features of Aldwinckle's theological method was his affirmation that Christian theology can properly proceed only from an informed and balanced matrix of history, interpretation, and Christian living. His appreciation, development, and deployment of this methodological matrix are evident throughout his authorship and is, in this author's opinion, one of the lasting contributions of his theological legacy.

The Dialectic of Faith and History

According to Aldwinckle, it is illegitimate to argue that Christian faith can proceed, on the one hand, independent of any historical judgments or, on the other, that no historical judgments may ever be claimed with certainty.[9] The logic of the Christian faith as a historical religion demands that there be a historical component in its theological affirmations. Some continuity, therefore, must exist

[7] James Leo Garrett, *Baptist Theology: A Four-Century Study* (Macon GA: Mercer University Press, 2009) 652.

[8] Shared with the author in personal conversation.

[9] John McIntyre, *The Shape of Christology* (London: SCM Press, 1966) 120–24; and Peter Carnley, "The Poverty of Historical Skepticism," in *Christ, Faith, & History* (Cambridge: Cambridge University Press) 165–90.

between the church's faith and what can be established by historical research. For Aldwinckle, historical assertions are a necessary and inescapable component of theology. While he understands that there is no "history" without interpretation, he also realizes that the logic of the Christian faith demands that "interpretations" be tethered to actual "events" that have transpired. Aldwinckle recognizes that some historical assertions are necessary in order adequately to affirm the divinity as well as the humanity of Jesus. Aldwinckle is concerned with establishing the viability of the results of modern historical research as a basis for such a confession. As the New Testament writings and the early church move to express the divinity of Jesus in ever more explicit terms, Aldwinckle underscores the importance of establishing to what extent these developments can be rooted in the words, actions, and ministry of Jesus. As such, he anticipates many of the results of the renaissance in Jesus research the "Third Quest" would chronicle in the last decades of the twentieth century. Aldwinckle was able to mine in the work of scholars such as Joachim Jeremias and C.H. Dodd ample justification for affirming that Jesus places not just his proclamation but his person at the center of his message.[10] The contours of the history of Jesus are discernible in such a way, concludes Aldwinckle, that the orthodox confession of the church can be seen to be entirely warranted in the light of the most rigorous historical inquiry.

But while theology is inextricably connected to historical affirmations, Aldwinckle also insisted that faith necessarily goes beyond them. Faith is not constituted by a mere series of historical judgments. Faith's encounter with Jesus Christ involves a dimension other than what can be read in the historical evidence alone. A judgment concerning Jesus' relationship to God cannot be separated from the power of the experience of God to which believers have been brought through him.[11] Furthermore, there is no such thing as interpreted history. "Word" and "event" are inseparably connected. For Aldwinckle, "faith" and" history" stand in a dialectical relationship with one another. Faith is not determined by history, but arises from and is a deeper reading of the truth of history. As Howard Marshall put it, "We interpret evidence in the light of our presuppositions, and we also form our presuppositions in light of the evidence."[12]

While recognizing the interpretive, subjective component of Christian knowledge, Aldwinckle insists that this "dialectic" of "faith and history" does not

---

[10] Aldwinckle, *More Than Man,* 57–59. See also Joachim Jeremias, *New Testament Theology*, Part One, trans. John Bowden (New York: Charles Scribner's Sons, 1971) 57; and C.H. Dodd, *The Founder of Christianity*, (New York: Macmillan, 1970).

[11] Aldwinckle, *More Than Man,* 154.

[12] Ibid., 72.

imply that Christian faith is merely some individual "perspective" free of all objective references and checks.[13] Aldwinckle suggests four criteria by which the experience of faith can be objectively evaluated. Christian faith should be: consistent with what can be known of Jesus by virtue of the most rigorous historical investigation; supported by the way others responded to the same facts; entail no logical or historical contradiction; and compellingly illumine the intelligibility of a person's total experience of reality.[14] Aldwinckle appreciates the virtues of those "christologies from below" whose interest is to trace the stages through which the early church followed as she developed a doctrine of Jesus' divinity, but firmly denies that the movement of faith follows as a logical deduction. "Christological doctrine," Ian Ramsey reminds us, only emerges when "a worshipful situation arises around the acknowledged humanity of Jesus."[15] So, while Christology must attend to affirmations concerning the history of Jesus, there is no transition to the perception of the divinity of Christ that does not involve the movement of faith.[16]

Language and Models in Christological Construction

Aldwinckle's theological method was also prescient with respect to the attention he gave to the interrelationship between religious experience and language. His discussion anticipated many of the insights that would be made by figures in the "Yale School" and the later "post-liberal movement."[17] Aldwinckle insisted that language is inextricably related to experience. The question is not a choice between experience and a consequent linguistic expression of it, but a recognition of the way convictional faith—and the language through which it is expressed—is an inextricable constitutive component of the experience of "meeting Christ."

Aldwinckle understood that theological language regularly requires that speech be stretched beyond its regular usage.[18] In speaking the language of divinity, resources such as "image" and "metaphor" are necessarily involved.[19] Following

---

[13] This objection was articulated most memorably by R.M. Hare, who termed these controlling, individual perspectives that are immune from external reference as "bliks." Antony Flew, R.M. Hare, and Basil Mitchell, "Theology and Falsification," in *New Essays in Philosophical Theology* (New York: Macmillan, 1964).

[14] Aldwinckle, *More Than Man*, 105.

[15] Ian Ramsey, *Words About God* (London: SCM Press Ltd., 1971) 221.

[16] Aldwinckle, *More Than Man*, 106.

[17] George Lindbeck, *The Nature of Doctrine* (Philadelphia: Westminster Press, 1984).

[18] John Macquarrie, *God Talk* (New York: Harper and Row, 1967) 27.

[19] Ian Ramsey, *Models and Mystery* (London: Oxford University Press, 1964) 10. The contrast between "scale" and "analogous" models was made by Max Black in his *Models and Metaphors* (Ithaca: Cornell University Press, 1962) 219–43. Ramsey's development of this distinction was first appropriated for Christology by John McIntyre in *The Shape of Christology*

Austin Farrar and Ian Ramsey, Aldwinckle concluded that images and models allow us to be articulate about mystery. Aldwinckle rejects the attempt to claim for the mystical experience reported in various religions a common factor that transcends all conceptual symbols. The Christian is forced to speak of his or her experience in terms of symbols and to make critical judgments with respect to their adequacy. The affirmation of the divinity of Jesus Christ involves the appropriation of a specific set of symbols.[20] A critical task of Christian theology is to determine how most adequately to speak of that which is perceived by Christian faith.[21] What "models" can be found to express best the meaning of the church's experience of God's presence in Jesus of Nazareth?[22] Aldwinckle finds Ian Ramsey's concept of "disclosure models" a valuable tool. The images of faith are not so much "literal representations" of their object as "structural echoes" that provide access and illumination to mystery.[23]

The attempt to base doctrine on uninterpreted experience is, for Aldwinckle, simply a fantasy. It is only through the dialectical interplay of experience and interpretation that people are able to construe the real at all.[24] Christian experience of the divine is in large measure mediated and engendered through the images of faith.[25] This means that experience itself is conceptually loaded. Images help constitute and construe religious experience. Language, then, is not simply an expression of an experience that itself precedes any verbal component. Aldwinckle would concur with Gordon Kaufmann when he observed: "Our 'religious experience' [...] is never a raw, pre-conceptual, pre-linguistic experience, the undialectical foundation on which theology can be built."[26] Aldwinckle's reflections are very much in concert with Ludwig Wittgenstein's insistence that the difference between believers and unbelievers lies in the different pictures they carry of the world.[27] Religious belief, according to both Wittgenstein and Aldwinckle, is best conceived as a set of regulative pictures that inform all of life.[28] At its heart, then,

---

(London: SCM Press, 1966) 55–81.

[20] Aldwinckle, *More Than Man*, 242.

[21] Aldwinckle, "Worship and Prayer: Principles and Problems," *The Canadian Journal of Theology* XV 3/4 (1960): 162.

[22] Aldwinckle, *More Than Man*, 131.

[23] Ramsey, *Models and Mystery*, 10.

[24] Brian Hebblethwaite, "The Appeal to Experience in Christology," *Christ, Faith, and History: Cambridge Studies in Christology*, ed. S.W. Sykes and J.P. Clayton (London, New York: Cambridge University Press, 1978) 265, 273.

[25] Austin Farrer, *The Glass of Vision* (London: Dacre Press, 1958) 44.

[26] Gordon Kaufman, *An Essay on Theological Method* (Missoula: Scholars Press for the American Academy of Religion, 1975) 6.

[27] Ludwig Wittgenstein, *Lectures on Religious Belief*, ed. Cyril Barrett (Berkeley: University of California Press, 1966) 5.

[28] Ludwig Wittgenstein, *Lectures and Conversations on Aesthetics, Psychology, and Religious*

the Christological task, for Aldwinckle, involves the critique and construction of images through which the church can express, reflect upon, honor, and articulate her soteriological and doxological confession that Jesus is more than simply another man.

IV. The Person of Christ

Aldwinckle locates the basis for affirming the divinity of Jesus in the church's encounter with her risen Lord. During his earthly ministry, the church came to understand Jesus as embodying the full presence of God. The resurrection "confirms" rather than "changes" or "establishes" Jesus' essential status as the "Eternal Son of the Father."

Incarnation

In Jesus Christ, the Christian church confesses that God is met not by proxy but in person. Since Ignatius, this embodiment of God's personal presence in and as Jesus Christ has been called the "Incarnation." For Aldwinckle, the presence of God in the man Jesus is so complete that the difference in degree of Jesus' relationship with His heavenly Father compared with other human beings' relationship with their Creator can only properly be understood as a difference in kind. God is the entire center and determining factor of Jesus' self-consciousness. As such, He is unmistakably "more than man." Christian experience does not look through Jesus to meet God beyond him but meets God in and as Jesus, the Christ. For Aldwinckle, this means that Jesus is an inextricable part of both the Christian definition and experience of God. The incarnation is not just the intensification of God's presence operative everywhere. It tells of the absolutely unique and unparalleled entry of God into a first-order participation in His creation in the life of the man Jesus.

Despite his recognition of the fact of the development of doctrine, Aldwinckle is not particularly concerned with constructing new modes through which to speak of the incarnation. His interest lies in affirming the models most appropriate for Christological understanding and delineating their logical force and status.[29] Consequently, he proceeds to clarify and test the validity of several classic images with which the church has expressed her understanding that, in Jesus Christ, we meet "more than man," but the presence and person of God.

Belief, ed. Cyril Barrett (Berkeley: University of California Press, 1966) 54.

[29] Aldwinckle, *More Than Man*, 130.

INCARNATION AND SOTERIOLOGY

Aldwinckle believes that soteriology provides not just the interest in Christology, but also constitutes a substantial part of the basis for its construction. The confession of the divinity of Jesus cannot be made independently of the experience of the power of God in the believer's relationship to Jesus. Jesus' divinity is not a product of human experience, but the "transforming effects which Jesus has brought in human experience" is an inescapable component for gaining access to who he is.[30] Theologians such as Wolfhart Pannenberg warn that such an approach runs the danger of making Jesus a human projection and leaves Christology without a foundation. Other theologians, such as liberation and feminist, use "appeals to experience" to construct quite different conceptions of incarnation than the one we find in Aldwinckle. He guards against these anthropomorphisms by maintaining that Christian experience is empirical and has an objective character that can be both tested and adjudicated. Aldwinckle presents a devastating critique of any functional Christology that refuses to face the ontological commitments they imply. He argues that if someone acts or functions as God, then it must be God who is acting. While faith is not blind, ultimately the logic of faith is to articulate what it has in the light of sound reason experienced to be true.

INCARNATION AND PREEXISTENCE

Perhaps no single concept is more inextricably tied to the confession of divinity than is the concept of preexistence. Certainly, the church never wished to maintain that the historical man Jesus "existed" before his birth in some bodily form. Instead, Aldwinckle takes a position similar to Wolfhart Pannenberg's in understanding "preexistence" as a way of declaring that what was present in Jesus belonged to the eternal and essential character of God.[31] The logic of "preexistence" carries back into the Godhead the Father-Son relationship that, subsequent to the church's encounter with Jesus, the church confessed to be a necessary characteristic of the eternity of God. This means that God can no longer be conceived as a bare unity. Aldwinckle affirms that the concept of preexistence is warranted, despite the fact that no argument can be made from the Synoptics for Jesus' own consciousness of it. The Father-Son relationship which Jesus does manifest, however, is of such a quality that the full implications cannot be exhausted on the level of Jesus' earthly ministry alone. When viewed along with the believer's experience of faith, there is ample reason to maintain that Jesus could have understood that his relationship to the Father was rooted in the eternity of God.

[30] Ibid., 154.
[31] Ibid., 157.

For Aldwinckle, then, the concept of preexistence is expressive of the fact that the relationship of Father to Son manifested in the history of Jesus must be reflective of a relationship that is from Eternity a part of the Reality of God.[32]

Incarnation and Kenosis

The incarnation of God in Christ was, for Aldwinckle, a unique and unparalleled event. At the same time, he insists the incarnation is also congruent with and an extension of God's continuing activity throughout creation. The ongoing act of creation always involves a giving of the "eternal" towards the "temporal"—a "kenosis" or "pouring out," if you will. Any act of the Biblical God's self-communication of Himself to His creation must, necessarily, involve condescension and humiliation. Therefore, both creation and revelation inevitably involve grace.[33] This movement of self-limitation, which may be described on the cosmic level, must also apply in the particular case of the incarnation. According to Aldwinckle, both reason and revelation would seem to require that there be some form of self-limitation of God for this to occur. The Incarnation is not just a more intense instance of the immanence of God present throughout His creation; it is the personal appropriation of an existence under the limits of creation by the Creator.

Aldwinckle argues that God's continual embrace of His creation is a background for, but is not identical to, God's special act of incarnation in the man Jesus. In light of the best reconstruction of the historical ministry of Jesus and the experience that the church has had of Him, however, Aldwinckle concludes that some form of "divine self-limitation" is the inescapable conclusion that faith must make concerning the nature of God's presence in Jesus. Aldwinckle does not present an elaborate discussion of the kenotic motif. Much fuller treatments can be found in the works of P.T. Forsyth, Vincent Taylor, Oliver Quick, H.R. Mackintosh, etc.[34] Instead, he outlines the conditions from which a kenotic motif

---

[32] Ibid., 158.

[33] Ibid., 150. In this, John Macquarrie echoes this thought in locating the value of the Incarnation in its assertion that the initiative of redemption rests with God (*The Truth of God Incarnate*, ed. Michael Green [Grand Rapids: Eerdmans, 1977] 143).

[34] The school of Kenotic Christology arose in the nineteenth century as an attempt to protect the divinity of Christ while at the same time establishing concretely the conditions of his humanity. Developed in Germany, it later reemerged in a modified form in Britain. In its most extreme form, early kenoticism suggested a cosmic absenteeism—a thirty-year interval in which the second person of the Trinity emptied himself of certain unessential attributes. This raised serious problems for the doctrine of God, as it seemed to portray a complete separation of nature between the persons of the Trinity. Further, in implying that some attributes of God may be "relative" to creation rather than "essential" to Him, it challenged the traditional understanding of the unity and simplicity of God. Although kenoticism has often met with severe

can be seen to be viable. He believes it unnecessary and inappropriate to speak of what attributes are "given up." By speaking of God's "becoming man," a new deed is attributed to God. Limiting the use and exercise of His powers in a way appropriate to a historical and earthly existence in no way implies that God "changed" Himself, or that only "part" of Him became incarnate. While the Person of Jesus did confine the Godhead, the Godhead was fully and completely present in Jesus.[35]

Aldwinckle believes that the concept of "self-limitation," connoted by the word "kenosis," is a necessary and unavoidable resource for Christology.[36] He feels it to be the only possible way of affirming both the divinity of Jesus and the completeness of his humanity as it is presented in the New Testament records. There is simply no alternative, according to Aldwinckle, to affirming some form of "self-limitation," whether the word "kenosis" is used or not.

The charges that have been brought to bear against the kenotic theory are basically two-fold: First, critics argue that kenoticism invariably tends toward tritheism. God is divided into the "beings." Consequently, two-thirds of God is "left out" of the incarnation. Kenoticism, according to this view, succeeds in protecting the humanity but eviscerates the divinity of Jesus. Second, if kenosis tries to emphasize the "unity" of God, it runs the risk of asserting that for a time God "ceased to be God." Can a model of kenosis be formulated that avoids these problems? Aldwinckle believes it can, and this is the task to which he has addressed himself.

Clearly, no development of kenosis can be acceptable in which God ceases

---

criticism, it has continued as a resilient motif in Christological thought. Donald Dawe has made a helpful distinction between kenosis as a "motif" of Christian faith and various kenotic "doctrines" that have been developed in the history of the church. The term "motif" was introduced into theology by Anders Nygren and connotes a broad or recurrent theme that integrates and gives meaning to a work. It can find expression, however, in a variety of particular forms. Dawe believes this distinction serves both to illustrate the depth and vitality of the idea of kenosis, while at the same time establishing a historical continuity between the various kenotic theories and a great underlying theme of the New Testament and the fathers. See Donald Dawe, *The Form of a Servant* (Philadelphia: The Westminster Press, 1963) 19–25.

[35] The turn of the century saw a resurgence of kenotic Christology in the writing of a group of British theologians: A.B. Bruce, Charles Gore, J.B. Lightfoot, H.R. Mackintosh, Oliver Quick, and others. Among the most prominent of these writers was the Congregationalist P.T. Forsyth. Aware of the difficulties involved in a kenotic theory, he also knew that any Christology entails a choice of difficulties. In the attempt to conceptualize the entry of infinite consciousness into finitude, Forsyth argued for the usefulness of the model of "retraction" rather than "abandonment." The possession of attributes is not lost; they come to be expressed in a mode appropriate to that of a creature. It is the true exercise of omnipotence, for example, that the son "set aside the style of God and took the form of a servant." P.T. Forsyth, *The Person and Place of Jesus Christ* (Boston: The Pilgrim Press, 1909) 156.

[36] A.W. Wainwright, *The Trinity in the New Testament* (London: S.P.C.K., 1962), cited in Aldwinckle, *More Than Man*, 163–64.

to be God. By definition, God cannot cease to sustain and secure all that exists. Thus, one is left with the dilemma of the Incarnation: "How could God—infinite in power, knowledge, and wisdom—become a man who was limited in power and knowledge and whose wisdom was the result of a real process of growth and development?"[37] One approach has been to recognize that God's relationship towards His creation always involves some element of "kenosis." The very fact of creation means that God has acted in a way that he restrained and limited Himself. God sustains and indwells His world without annihilating it.[38] It would be surprising if the incarnation were completely unreflective of the way God was experienced as acting elsewhere. Both God's outpouring love and His gracious restraint are manifested in His general relationship to creation. While the incarnation is a peculiar and unique action of God in which it can even be said that God "becomes" man, it must also be said that the incarnation is related to more general ways in which God relates Himself to His world.

Aldwinckle is characteristic of the later kenotic Christologians in maintaining that talk about the incarnation must proceed in an *a posteriori* fashion. One should not ask if the incarnation is possible. It is possible because it has happened. This does not mean, however, that the incarnation is either illogical or irrational. Reason may be used, as it was by Kierkegaard, precisely to show the limits of rationality. If it were possible completely to conceptualize exactly how Jesus Christ could be who he was, then he would not be what the doctrine of the incarnation claims him to be.

In contradistinction to the early kenoticists, later defenders of the doctrine do not see the attributes of God as "accidental" qualities that casually can be laid aside. The act of divine self-limitation is, rather, seen as an additional action of the Godhead. Thus, the limitations accepted by the Son during his earthly existence in no way jeopardize the sustaining or cosmic functions of the Triune God. Aldwinckle sees some form of "self-limitation" required for two reasons. First, an accurate reading of Scripture reveals that Jesus either did not exercise or was not in complete possession of all the attributes of deity. Secondly, Christian faith has experienced in Jesus of Nazareth all the fullness of God. It believes God to be completely present in Jesus.[39] These two facts, taken together, make some concept of divine self-limitation inescapable.

As Aldwinckle develops the case for the kenotic motif, it is more with a view to establishing how this man Jesus could be divine rather than how this God could

---

[37] Aldwinckle, *More Than Man*, 189.

[38] H. Wheeler Robinson, *The Christian Experience of the Holy Spirit* (London: Nisbett & Company, 1928) 82, cited by Aldwinckle, *More Than Man*, 190.

[39] Aldwinckle, *More Than Man,* 192.

be man. Any account of the relationship between a transcendent God to a creation that is granted a real measure of independence and freedom with respect to Him must involve self-limitation on the part of God. To do this, God must exercise deliberate restraint—what H. Wheeler Robinson has called "a kenosis of the spirit."[40] Says Aldwinckle, "If the knowledge of God was as coercive and compelling as [...] our apprehension of the world through the physical senses, [...] then faith as a truly personal act with moral and spiritual significance would be impossible."[41]

According to Aldwinckle, Christian theology does not start with a doctrine of kenosis. Rather, kenoticism emerges inductively as the church reflects on the person and work of Jesus of Nazereth. It uses the language of self-limitation not because of speculative pressure but because of experiential necessity. In Jesus the church confesses that she has met the revelation and presence of the Eternal God. To speak this way might be to invite paradox, but it is to be true to the logic of Christian experience. Consequently, while Christian language might be puzzling to the person who stands outside, from within the circle of faith it is both natural and necessary. While "understanding" the incarnation is admittedly difficult, human reason itself shows that it could not be otherwise. We must speak in models that include concepts of divine self-limitation if we are to speak at all.

V. The Work of Christ

Aldwinckle's consideration of the saving work of Christ proceeds from a perspective both deeply personal and presciently contemporary. As a young adult, his only sister entered an Indian ashram. From that day on she was never again seen by Aldwinckle or any member of their biological family. The occasional letters became less frequent over the years and eventually disappeared altogether. By the time Aldwinckle published his major work on soteriology, he did not know whether his sister was even alive. The subject of the saving significance of Jesus in an increasingly pluralistic world had a personal as well as professional importance for him.[42]

Soteriology and Sin

To speak of salvation is to presuppose a problem that needs to be addressed. Every worldview has a traditioned account of the human dilemma. Oxford theologian Don Cupett critiques the Christian description of humankind as sinners

[40] H. Wheeler Robinson, *Redemption and Revelation* (New York: Harper & Row, 1942) 290ff.

[41] Aldwinckle, *More Than Man*, 87.

[42] See Aldwinckle, *Jesus—A Savior or the Savior?*, unnumbered preface page: Aldwinckle identifies his sister's ashram as "Sri Auburo Ashram in Podichery, India."

in need of redemption as unpersuasive and irrelevant.[43] Aldwinckle dismisses Cupitt's critique as being circular. Christianity may have to make her claims persuasive, but she is not in a specially epistemologically compromised position by making them. The real offense for Cupitt, Aldwinckle argues, is that the Christian doctrine of sin maintains "the bondage of the will and the necessity for an external Savior to secure human release."[44] According to Aldwinckle, every worldview has a diagnosis for the problem of the human condition. Hinduism, Buddhism, and Christianity all agree that there is some basic flaw in human existence as we now know it. "(E)xistence is in some sense separated from its true nature and being the difference lies in the way this separation is understood and what is required to overcome it."[45] The differences between the Christian vision of the consummation and fulfillment of the world in the kingdom of God and other notions of human reconciliation and rehabilitation are vast. For modernists, we are machines to be fixed. For Darwinians, we are animals to be understood. For Freudians, we are sexual beings to be released. For existentialists, we are free beings to be self-created. For Marxists, we are economic beings to be liberated. For Buddhists, we are ripples to be stilled. For Hindus, we are beings to be purified. And for Christians, we are sinful rebels to be redeemed, rescued, reunited, transformed, and loved.

PARTICULARISM AND PLURALISM

Aldwinckle unpacks his "particularist" convictions in direct dialogue with our contemporary pluralist setting. Aldwinckle, again, anticipated concerns only beginning to appear in the broader theological conversation. Paul Knitter, writing in the emerging field of the theology of religions, introduced a rhetorical typology of "Pluralism," "Inclusivism," and "Exclusivism"—also referred to as "Restrictivism," or perhaps most helpfully, "Particularism."[46] Aldwinckle puts clearly the

---

[43] Ibid., 71–72.

[44] Ibid., 84.

[45] Ibid., 140. Aldwinckle is citing here and, then, commenting on John E. Smith, *The Analogy of Experience* (New York: Harper, 1973) ch. 4.

[46] "Pluralists" maintain that there are many paths up the spiritual mountain and that multiple religions provide trustworthy, reliable, and independent access to divine reality. "Inclusivists" affirm that the salvation afforded by Jesus Christ is available in all cultures and all places and all times. Finally, "Particularists" assert the distinctiveness and uniqueness of the redemptive act in the person of Jesus Christ. They make a clear distinction between domains such as "general" and "special" revelation. Alan Race, *Christians and Religious Pluralism: Patterns in the Christian Theology of Religions* (Maryknoll NY: Orbis, 1982). See also Gavin D'Costa, *Theology and Religious Pluralism: The Challenge of Other Religions* (Oxford: Blackwell, 1986); and Dennis Ockholm and Timothy Phillips, *Four Views on Salvation in a Pluralistic World* (Grand Rapids: Zondervan, 1995).

question posed by pluralism: "Can the case be made for the finality, uniqueness, and necessity of Jesus Christ in the project that is involved in human salvation?"[47] To address this issue, Aldwinckle finds it necessary to unpack a host of other questions: "What do we mean by 'salvation'?" "Do we need a Savior in order to be saved?"[48] "What is the role of Jesus in human salvation?"[49] Aldwinckle is committed to maintaining the unique and exclusivist soteriological claims of the Gospel while also engaging in a respectful dialogue with other religions.[50] He observes, however, that adherents of the Pluralist position regularly attempt to resolve religious diversity by invoking assumptions at the outset that disallow the transcendent and personal God of the Bible at the beginning. Pluralists see the life of Jesus as being only representative rather than constitutive of salvation.[51] In the face of such claims, Aldwinckle finds himself identifying with Mary Magdalene at the tomb in assessing that these critiques have "taken away our Lord and we do not know where they have put him."[52]

Aldwinckle commits himself to a clear and uncompromised Particularism. For Aldwinckle, salvation is synonymous with "Christ."[53] Because of human frailty and sin, humanity's own attempt to release itself from its fundamental dilemma is never going to be satisfactory or successful.[54] By contrast, Aldwinckle sees the resources offered by the Christian doctrine of the cross as both rich and rewarding. Jesus' own combining of the motifs of "Son of Man" and "Suffering Servant" result in a theological construction of unparalleled originality and force. Aldwinckle does not equivocate on the particularistic character of Christian salvation. Christian salvation for Aldwinckle is "a truly personal relationship to God mediated through the person of Christ who is the indispensable mediator of that relationship."[55] For Aldwinckle, salvation can never be had apart from a conscious relationship with Jesus Christ.[56] The conscious awareness and willful entrance into relationship with Christ are, by definition, essential to any concept of salvation that can credibly be called "Christian." According to Aldwinckle, "(t)he absoluteness of Jesus Christ means that Christ is constituative of salvation (and) apart from an explicit relationship to Him salvation is impossible."[57] Only

---

[47] Aldwinckle, *Jesus—A Savior or the Savior?*, 195, 199.

[48] Ibid., 202, 207.

[49] Ibid., 200.

[50] Ibid., 65.

[51] Ibid., 179.

[52] Ibid., 205.

[53] Ibid., 186–87.

[54] Ibid., 88.

[55] Ibid., 189.

[56] Ibid., 171.

[57] J.C. Robertson, "A Religion as Particular and Universal: Response to Lonergan's 'Prolegomena,'" *Studies in Religion* 9/1 (1980): 17ff, quoted with agreement in Aldwinckle, *Jesus—*

through participation in the work of Christ can the great exchange be made between God's love and holiness on the one hand and human depravity and sin on the other.[58] Salvation for Christians, by definition, means union with God through Christ.

POST-MORTEM SALVATION

The question that Particularism must address, then, is what becomes of those who, through no fault of their own, never hear the gospel of Jesus. Aldwinckle offers no equivocation. Those who have truly heard the saving name of Jesus and persist in rejection of him must, by definition, be excluded from the salvation that He alone can offer.[59]

Salvation is, for Aldwinckle, a present experience but also a future hope.[60] Aldwinckle leaves open the possibility of Christian salvation being consummated "post-mortem."[61] He writes: "God's saving purpose cannot be regarded as consummated in a negative or positive sense only at the moment of physical death."[62] The possibility of post-mortem salvation allows Aldwinckle to affirm Christian particularism in a pluralistic context. Aldwinckle finds substantial support for this position in figures such as Gregory of Nyssa, Donald Bloesch, and George Beasley-Murray.[63] Nineteenth-century New Testament scholar Peter Lange concludes: "Holy Scripture nowhere teaches the eternal damnation of those who died as heathens or non-Christians; it rather intimates in many passages that forgiveness may be possible beyond the grave, and refers the final decision not to death, but to the day of Christ."[64]

Aldwinckle does close the door on any kind of universalism. He clearly denies that there might be an endless period after death when salvation becomes a

---

A Savior or the Savior?, 187.

[58] Aldwinckle, *Jesus—A Savior or the Savior?*, 109–10.

[59] Ibid., 174.

[60] Ibid., 198.

[61] The hope of post-mortem salvation has enjoyed a long history, although only in recent years has it become more widespread. Previously it has lurked on the fringes of dogmatic possibility. Only recently have orthodox or evangelical Christians expressed interest in it. The post-mortem position agrees with the classic, exclusivist particularist view by affirming that faith must be explicit—that is, a person must consciously understand and accept Jesus Christ as his or her Savior. Post-mortem evangelism also shares with many pluralist positions the concern that condemning people to eternal punishment who have had no opportunity to hear of Christ's redemptive work is unjust and unloving.

[62] Aldwinckle, *Jesus—A Savior or the Savior?*, 189.

[63] Donald G. Bloesch, *Essentials of Evangelical Theology*, 2 vols. (San Francisco: Harper & Row, 1978) 225; and George R. Beasley-Murray, *Baptism in the New Testament* (London: Macmillan, 1962) 258–59.

[64] John Peter Lange, *The First Epistle General of Peter* (New York: Scribner, 1868) 75.

virtual inevitability. There will be a "day of the Lord" where all will be accountable before God.[65] This means there is always a certain agnosticism about Christian salvation. We can never know God's saving purposes in precise detail. Writes Aldwinckle, "The Christian can only work and witness in the faith that God will not permit the end in terms of grace and judgment until all have had the opportunity to behold the Christ free from those personal and ecclesiastical distortions which so often hinder in this world the acknowledgment of him as the one Lord and Savior of humankind."[66]

Aldwinckle presses the point with the test case of Socrates—the figure that remains for all time the paradigm of "intellectual and moral integrity" as well as the indefatigable seeker after truth.[67] To the question as to whether Socrates is "saved," Aldwinckle is both decisive and agnostic. He is decisive that on the basis of the sort of knowledge that Socrates possessed during his earthly existence, salvation is impossible.[68] But that need not rule out a future hope. Aldwinckle puts it this way:

> Why should it be deemed impossible that Socrates and the Christ will one day meet face to face and that Socrates may find in the Son of man and the Son of God the answer to his own restless search. The Christian cannot dogmatize in terms of logical necessities, but he can without inconsistency entertain the larger hope. If the divine love has in the end no option but the negative judgment of final separation from all truth, life, goodness, and love, then God and God alone can make that judgment. We human beings cannot in the meantime "play God" except at the risk of our own condemnation.[69]

For Aldwinckle, then, the claim of the unique, particular, exclusive, and decisive role of Jesus Christ as the sole Savior of the world is not inconsistent with a genuine openness in regard to the destiny of those, whether in the past or the present, who have not yet confessed him as Lord. The future is not indefinitely open. There will be a day of judgment and a final consummation. But until then, we lack complete knowledge of the future, and although we know the terms that have been bought for us by the blood of Christ, we cannot anticipate every contour of God's final judgment.

---

[65] Aldwinckle, *Jesus—A Savior or the Savior?*, 190.

[66] Ibid.

[67] Ibid., 213.

[68] Ibid. Aldwinckle puts to Socrates this probing question: "O Socrates, hast thou yet considered the dire weight of sin and its effects? Have you yet seen the measure of a divine love which speaks [...] through a voluntarily assumed human existence in the life, death, and resurrection of Jesus of Nazareth? O Socrates, with all your splendid integrity, you have not yet seen all the things which God has prepared for them that love him."

[69] Ibid., 214.

VI. Assessment

Russell Aldwinckle has contributed an informed, articulate, and cogent contemporary polemic and apologetic for a contemporary high Christology. He has addressed the question with clarity and conviction as to whether the divinity of Jesus Christ can intelligibly be conceived in light of the most rigorous contemporary standards of knowledge. He has set out to affirm with contemporary tools and in light of contemporary questions how it can be said and what it means to say that Jesus of Nazareth is "more than man." In the end he produces a robust affirmation of Christian Christological orthodoxy in a manner that is at once both bold and humble. He makes the case for Christian exclusivism in a way that is compelling, but also rooted in the gospel of Grace. According to Aldwinckle, while affirming Christian particularism, "(t)he Christian is not making claims for superior intelligence, profounder philosophy, or even superior righteousness. He is simply acknowledging in loving adoration the grace of God actualized in the fact that 'while we were yet sinners Christ died for us.'"[70]

Perhaps Aldwinckle's greatest contribution is in his display and deployment of an intellectually rich and balanced evangelical theological method. He voices and exhibits the way that event, interpretation, and experience are all deeply and profoundly interrelated in the development of Christian doctrine, the formation of Christian convictions, and the entertaining of Christian experience. He places a priority on ways in which events recorded in the Bible and found in the life of the church function to facilitate and constitute human encounter with the divine. Secondly, he displays a rich appreciation for the interrelationship of word and event and the indissolubility of "fact" and interpretation. Specifically, he anticipated the coming discussions in post-liberalism concerning the ways in which language and convictions are catalysts for and formative of experience.[71] He understands, appreciates, and accounts for ways that language affects the interpreter and helps him or her construe the world. Convictions form and guide thoughts, emotions, and even perceptions. Experience does not result from the passive reception of identical impressions, but is constituted by the attitudes, presuppositions, and interpretations that are both brought to and extracted from experience. He understands that language is inextricably related to experience. He shows his debt to Austin Farrer, who called language a "glass of vision." For Farrar—and

---

[70] Ibid.

[71] For an up-to-date and state-of-the art development of this insight, see Kevin Vanhoozer's discussion of "concern-based-construals" in his recent *Remythologizing Theology* (Cambridge: Cambridge University Press, 2010) 408–16.

for Aldwinckle—theology is the analysis and criticism of revealed images. Theology delineates and explores these images, but it does not create them.[72] Aldwinckle combines event and interpretation in an illuminating and convincing way. For Aldwinckle, it is the event of the life, death, and resurrection of Jesus Christ, understood within the context of the reception of the Gospel through faith, that both makes possible and is authenticated by the Christian experience of salvation. The person of Jesus Christ then caused the church to speak in new ways because, in Jesus, an altogether original presence had confronted them. In Jesus Christ, the church decisively understood herself to be encountered personally by the living God. Out of this conviction, the language and witness of the church were forged. Aldwinckle's astute development and deployment of this nuanced matrix of the interrelationship between history, experience, and interpretation contribute to the force and cogency of his Christological offering.

Less convincing is his championing of post-mortem evangelism. While understandably reducing the tension between particularism and pluralism, there are good grounds to be agnostic at best towards any affirmation of such a position. Significant evangelical voices have weighed in against the possibility. According to Al Mohler, for example, the problem with the position is that "Scripture teaches no such post-mortem opportunity. It is a figment of a theologian's imagination, and must be rejected."[73] Ronald Nash comes to a similar conclusion: "(The Bible) clearly say(s) that everyone will die and be judged (Heb. 9:27) and that each person's eternal destiny, either reward or condemnation, will be based on what was done in this life."[74]

Perhaps the most cautious response is agnosticism. Post-mortem salvation is clearly not explicitly taught in scripture. The case can be made that it is not denied and that it can be held in a manner consistent with the biblical witness. But neither should something so significant but not explicitly taught be the basis for proclamation of the church. Millard Erickson puts the matter succinctly:

> Could it be? Yes, most certainly that is a possibility. Is it the case, however? That is the question [...], but the scriptural evidence for postmortem encounter is not abundant. [...] Evangelicals are faced with whether to accept the notion of postmortem evangelism, a view for which there is no clear biblical teaching [...]. The burden of proof for a view such as

---

[72] Austin Farrer, *The Glass of Vision* (London: Dacre Press, 1958) 44.

[73] R. Albert Mohler, Jr., and Daniel L. Akin, "The Salvation of the 'Little Ones': Do Infants Who Die Go to Heaven?" online blog, Thursday, 16 July 2009, https://albertmohler.com/2009/07/16/the-salvation-of-the-little-ones-do-infants-who-die-go-to-heaven/.

[74] Ronald Nash, "Is There Salvation After Death?" *Christian Research Journal* 27/4 (2004): 32–40.

> this [...] rests on those who advance it. And here, one must conclude, the proof falls far short of demonstration.[75]

In this reviewer's opinion, the possibility of salvation after death is suggested by at least one biblical text (1 Pet.), and it is possible to read the view in harmony with the totality of the biblical witness. Nonetheless, because its support is so scant, the conclusion here is that it should be viewed with agnosticism at best and should not become part of the proclamation of the church or a component of the unambiguous announcement of the hope of the gospel.

Aldwinckle's work anticipates and addresses much of the theological conversation that will follow. Little of the ensuing discussion makes a contribution as lucid or lasting. Russell Aldwinckle's driving desire is to facilitate a contemporary hearing of the Christian faith and to guide Christian disciples in their experience and living of the Christian life.[76] Although Aldwinckle stresses the importance and role of history and event in and for Christian theology, his is preeminently a Christology from above. He prioritizes the role of faith in the perception of Christian truth. He crafted a Christology that advanced both the complete divinity of Jesus' person and the particularistic character of his work in a manner that was informed, uncompromising, and gracious. His Christology told the story of a God who entered time both to liberate and bind His people experientially to Himself. The work of Russell Aldwinckle offers a contemporary Christology that articulates in light of the most rigorous canons of reason and reflection a clear, coherent, and compelling picture of how and why Christian faith understands that Jesus of Nazareth is both more than man and strong to save.

---

[75] Millard Erickson, "Is There Opportunity for Salvation after Death?" *Bibliotheca Sacra* 152 (April/June 1995): 131–44, here: 143–44.

[76] Aldwinckle, *Jesus—A Savior or the Savior?*, 114.

SECTION 3

BAPTIST STUDIES

THOMAS LAMBE THE LINEN-DRAPER—SOME NEW EVIDENCE

Larry Kreitzer

The London linen-draper Thomas Lambe (1612–1686) has long been a subject of interest for students of seventeenth-century Baptist history, although the details of his life have been obscured in the past by scholars who have confused him with Thomas Lamb, the London soap-boiler (fl. 1629–1672).[1] The distinction between the two men has been noted within Professor Brackney's recent *The Early English General Baptists and Their Theological Formation* (2017), where they are given separate treatments.[2] Thomas Lamb the soap-boiler has perhaps received the lion's share of historical interest over the years, mostly due to his influential tracts *A Confutation of Infants Baptism* (1643) and *The Unlawfulnesse of Infants Baptism* (1645). That is not to suggest that Thomas Lambe the linen-draper[3] has failed to attract the interest of historians. His association with John Goodwin and the Leveller William Walwyn is noteworthy, and his relationship with the Presbyterian Richard Baxter has generated considerable attention, particularly as it sheds light on Lambe's eventual break with General Baptists and his eventual return to the Church of England.[4] Within this short study, I wish to call attention to two new sources that have hitherto not been discussed by historians considering Lambe's life.

---

[1] On the strength of the reference to a "Mr. Lamb, Bell-Alley Coleman-Street" contained in "A Collection of the Names of the Merchants Living in and about the City of London (1677)," Alexander Gordon asserted that Lambe carried on his business as a soapboiler in London well into the 1670s (*DNB* 32 [1892]: 4). This is incorrect and is driven by a conflation of the lives of Thomas Lamb the soapboiler († 1672) and Thomas Lambe the linen-draper († 1686) within the *DNB* article. Long ago, Thomas Crosby, in *The History of the English Baptists* (vol. 3 [London: np, 1740] 56–57), asserted that a distinction between the two was needed.

[2] Thomas Lambe, the soap-boiler on pages 189–206, and Thomas Lamb, the linen-draper on pages 206–209. Murray Tolmie, in his "Thomas Lambe, Soapboiler, and Thomas Lambe, Merchant, General Baptists" (*The Baptist Quarterly* 27 [1977–1978]: 4–13), was among the first to point out that the two men had been wrongly conflated.

[3] The common description of Thomas Lambe as a "linen-draper" is based on William Walwyn, *Walwyns Just Defence* (London: W. Larnar, 1649) 30. As far as I am aware, this is the only reference in contemporary literature describing him as a linen-draper (Walwyn says he was "a Linnen Draper in Cornhill").

[4] G.F. Nuttall, "Thomas Lambe, William Allen, and Richard Baxter: An Additional Note," *The Baptist Quarterly* 27 (1977–78): 139–40.

A. Thomas Lambe's Petition to London Authorities about Reforming

Ludgate Prison (c. 1675). Most discussions of Thomas Lambe the linen-draper note that following his abandonment of Baptist ideals and his return to the established church, one of the main focal points of his life was the plight of poor men and women jailed for their poverty. In Professor Brackney's words, "He spent the remainder of his life devoted to philanthropic projects particularly interested in the poor and prisoners, as illustrated in his Appeal to Parliament (1660) (Figure 1)."[5] This dimension of Lambe's life was something that was noted in the funeral sermon preached on 23 July 1686 by Richard Lucas (1648–1715), the vicar of St. Stephen's, Coleman Street.[6] Lucas spoke passionately of Lambe's abiding commitment to the idea of "Charity to men" as an essential expression of true Christian faith. He noted in particular how Lambe's involvement in prison reform exemplified this charity within his life:

> [H]e was not only a faithful Steward and dispenser of other mens Bounty, but also bountiful himself even to the diminution of his estate. To go on therefore to the point, several Hundreds of Prisoners were by him, with great travail and expence set free; Nay, Prisons themselves were set free from some oppressions and cheats that had obtain'd in them, and rendred more hospitable and tolerable to the miserable Inhabitants Fees being reduced to a Lower rate and Maintenance and Provision for Prisoners much better setled.[7]

Lucas' assessment is corroborated by a new primary source demonstrating Lambe's advocacy for prison reform that has not previously been published. I recently purchased from an autograph dealer a newly available document containing a petition written by Thomas Lambe. The document is a single folio page (360 x 480mm), folded in half and yielding four pages, with the petition written on the first page and a clerk's descriptive annotation written on page 4 (pages 2 and 3 are blank). This document offers a rare opportunity to add to what we know about the activities and interests of the erstwhile General Baptist leader Thomas

[5] William H. Brackney, *The Early English General Baptists and Their Theological Formation* (Oxford: Regent's Park College, Oxford, 2017) 205. The author of *An Appeal to the Parliament Concerning the Poor* (1660) is identified only by his initials, "T.L." The pamphlet is attributed to Thomas Lawson in EEBO.

[6] Richard Lucas, "A Sermon Preacht at the Funeral of Mr. Thomas Lamb, July 23, 1686." The sermon was reprinted in Richard Lucas, *Twelve Sermons Preached on Several Occasions* (London: Samuel Smith & B. Walford, 1699) 53–80.

[7] Richard Lucas, "A Sermon Preacht," 19–20. The pamphlet contains a dedication written by Lucas to Thomas Lambe's son John Lambe, who was the rector of Wheathampstead in Hertfordshire.

Lambe. We shall here discuss the contents of the petition, presenting a critical, line-by-line edition of the full text for the benefit of future scholarly investigations (Document 1). Most importantly, this petition serves as confirmation of what Brackney and others have sometimes suggested about Thomas Lambe's philanthropy.[8]

A few preliminary remarks about this petition are in order. First of all we note that Lambe identifies himself as a citizen of London and a member of the Leathersellers' Company of London, one of the ancient livery companies of the city with a royal charter dating back to 1444 (line 3). This alerts us to the way in which Lambe thought of himself professionally, and suggests we should perhaps stop describing him as a "linen-draper" (something Lambe himself never does)[9] and begin describing him as a "leather-seller."[10] Lambe was, in fact, a prominent member of the Leathersellers' Company and was made a freeman on 2 March 1637 after having served an apprenticeship to Henry Heald.[11] He himself took on at least seven apprentices within the Leathersellers' Company during the years 1637–1652. These seven apprenticeships were: Robert Tredway, son of Robert Tredway of Lough in Lincolnshire, on 20 March 1637; Francis Lambe, son of Robert Lambe of Longthorpe in Northamptonshire, on 28 January 1639; William Treavis, son of William Treavis of Morton Hillmarsh in Gloucestershire, on 17 March 1643; John Goodwin, son of John Goodwin of London, on 1 September 1644; Thomas Webb, son of William Webb of Longworth in Berkshire on 21 November 1647; Samuel Reynauld, son of James Reynauld of Kensington in Middlesex, on 2 March 1650; and Thomas Aynscombe, son of Michael Aynscombe of Reigate in Surrey, on 10 January 1652. The second apprentice, Francis Lambe, was Thomas Lambe's younger brother; the fourth apprentice was most likely the son of John Goodwin, the Independent minister in London with

[8] See R.L. Greaves, "Lamb (or Lambe), Thomas (d. 1686)," in *Biographical Dictionary of British Radicals in the Seventeenth Century*, vol. 2 (Brighton: The Harvester Press, 1983) 166–67; and Stephen Wright, "Lamb, Thomas (d. 1686)," in *ODNB* (Oxford: Oxford University Press, 2004; online ed., May 2008). Inexplicably, Tolmie, in "Thomas Lambe, Soapboiler, and Thomas Lambe, Merchant," fails to mention Lambe's concerns for the poor and imprisoned.

[9] Lambe describes himself as a "Merchant" on the title page of his *Truth Prevailing against the Fiercest Opposition* (London: G. Dawson, 1656).

[10] This means that the record to the leatherseller Thomas Lambe, who on 11 July 1642 pledged a horse and arms for the service of Parliament, is a reference to him. In part 4 of my *William Kiffen and His World* ([Regent's Park College, Oxford: Oxford, 2013] 22), I wrongly attributed this record (TNA, SP 28/131/part 3, folio 7 recto) to Thomas Lambe the soap-boiler.

[11] Lambe is named as living at Heald's near Gracechurch Street Conduit and paying the poll tax in July 1641 (TNA, E 179/251/22/29, folio 19 verso).

whom Lambe was closely connected.[12] Lambe rose through the administrative ranks of the company, serving as a second warden in 1666–1667 and as Master in 1673–1674.[13]

Returning to Lambe's petition, we note next that the petition is addressed to the Lord Mayor of London, the Aldermen of the city, and the Common Councillors of the the city (lines 1–2). Together these three addressees represented the civil administration of the city of London. London had twenty-six Aldermen, one from each of the constituent wards into which the city was geographically divided. The Common Council consisted of 236 members drawn from across the various wards. The most important civic authority was the Lord Mayor who was the king's representative in the city. The mayor served for one year and was annually elected on Michaelmas Day (29 September).

Determining who precisely the mayor of London was at the time Lambe submitted his petition is not an easy task, mainly because the petition itself is undated. However, it does contain a couple of passing references to events that took place in 1674 (in lines 4, 10, and 19), which indicates that a likely date for the petition is early 1675. This means that the mayor of London to whom Lambe addressed his petition would have been Sir Robert Vyner (1631–1688), a London goldsmith and influential banker within the city (Figure 2).[14] Vyner is perhaps best remembered as the goldsmith responsible for producing the crown and regalia used in the coronation of Charles II in 1660. Vyner lived in Swakeleys House in Ickenham in west London; it was a large property bought by Vyner from the wife of Sir James Harrington following Harrington's exile to France in 1660. The diarist Samuel Pepys (1633–1703) visited Vyner at Swakeleys on 7 September 1665 and related a horrible incident that reflects badly on Vyner's sensitivities to other people. Pepys says that Vyner showed him the body of a black servant boy who had died of consumption; after his death Vyner had the servant dried in an oven and placed in a box so that he could show his body to visitors.[15]

We turn now to consider the content of the petition. In lines 4–6 of the petition, Lambe explains that in July 1674 he had been employed by the Leathersellers' Company to ensure that the charitable bequests named within the will of the late George Humble were paid out in accordance with the wishes of the deceased. The details of these charities are not provided beyond the fact that they

[12] I am grateful to Jerome Farrell, the archivist for the Leathersellers' Company in London, for his assistance in these matters.

[13] He was thus following in the wake of another Baptist leader, William Kiffen (c. 1616–1701), who served as Master of the Leathersellers' Company in 1671–1672.

[14] G.E. Aylmer, "Vyner, Sir Robert, baronet (1631–1688)," in *ODNB* (Oxford: Oxford University Press, 2004; online ed., September 2014).

[15] https://www.pepysdiary.com/diary/1665/09/07/

were designed to assist in the release of freemen of the Leathersellers' Company who were being held in Ludgate prison as debtors.[16] Fortunately the will of George Humble has survived and it makes clear precisely what provision was intended for the incarcerated freemen.[17] It also explains Humble's interest in the matter: he, too, was a member of the Leathersellers' Company in London, eventually rising to serve as Master in 1628–1629. Humble († 1640) had a multifaceted career and distinguished himself in a number of fields, notably as a seller of prints and maps, which is where the bulk of his wealth came from.[18] A number of provisions were made within the will for the Leathersellers' Company, including the establishment of scholarships to both Oxford and Cambridge, and £500 to be lent to younger members of the company in need of assistance in establishing themselves in the trade.[19] Most significant for our concerns here is the provision that is made by Humble for helping unfortunate members of the company who had fallen into debt and found themselves imprisoned in the Ludgate prison. The will stipulates:

> Item: I give more unto the said Company of Leathersellers the some of Two hundred poundes in mony To be layd out & bestowed by them (w[i]th what convenient speede may be) in the purchasinge of so much freehold lands & tenements as farr as the same will extend To this intent and purpose That out of the Rents & profitts arising out of such lands and tenements so to be bought as aforesaid there may yerely and every yere for ever be acquited & Released out of the Prison of Ludgate London three fower or five poore men which shall lye in there for debt (those that bee free of the said Company of Leathersellers being p[re]ferred before others in this my Guifte).[20]

It is precisely this provision within Humble's will that Thomas Lambe attempts to address within his petition about prison reform.[21]

---

[16] An informative discussion of what life was like within the prison some years later is contained in *The Present State of the Prison of Ludgate* (London: A. Baldwin, 1725).

[17] Humble's 26-page will was signed on 28 September 1638 with a codicil added on 8 December 1640; the will was probated on 31 December 1640.

[18] Antony Griffiths, "Humble, George (d. 1640)," in *ODNB* (Oxford: Oxford University Press, 2004; online ed., January 2008).

[19] Humble's portrait still hangs in the hall of the Leathersellers' Company, and four silver goblets presented to the company as a legacy of his will are still used in ceremonial dinners. See Penelope Hunting, *The Leathersellers' Company, A History* (London: The Leathersellers' Company, 1994) 94–95.

[20] TNA, PROB 10/611, 21–22. A copy of the will is found in TNA, PROB 11/184, 369 verso-370 recto.

[21] A number of other benefactors also provided gifts and legacies for debtors imprisoned in Ludgate prison. See Marmaduke Johnson, *Ludgate—What It Is: Not What It Was* (London:

Lambe goes on to describe how the keeper of the prison was abusing prisoners and deceiving the prison's benefactors by demanding fees and rents from the prisoners, which were based on an illegal table of rates that violated the rules established by the Court of Aldermen (lines 6–9). He stated that on 6 October 1674 he made a complaint to the Court of Aldermen and requested that a committee be established to investigate the matter, which was granted (lines 10–11). Lambe claimed that at two subsequent meetings of the committee he proved the complaint, based on the cases of two prisoners who, according to the keeper's notes, owed him £16 16s 16d (lines 12–14). According to Lambe's investigations, this was £4 more than the keeper should have legally received (lines 14–16). In consequence the committee required the keeper to refund the overpayment (line 16). In addition, they ordered the keeper to withdraw a suit for £20, which he had brought against one of the prisoners, and to pay a fine of 8 shillings for unjustly arresting him (lines 16–18). Moreover, Lambe related that in December 1674 the sheriffs of London[22] came to Ludgate prison and informed the prisoners in the presence of the keeper of the prison that they were to pay one, two, or three pence per night (depending on the level of accommodation desired) instead of the two, four, and six pence per night that the keeper had been exacting from them (lines 19–22). The sheriffs also promised the prisoners that if they had any further difficulties in these matters, then upon complaint and proof of abuse, they would set things right (lines 23–24). The matter of an established rate for accommodation within the prison was a contentious one that had been addressed at several points over the years by the London civic authorities. For example, there was a complaint submitted by a group of Ludgate prisoners in 1663 to the Lord Mayor Sir Anthony Bateman, the Court of Aldermen, and the Common Council that similarly discussed the topic.[23] It was here recorded that a price differential was in place depending on the quality of the accommodation provided. Prisoners staying in the Long Ward and the Lumberies Ward were to be charged one pence per night; prisoners staying in the Horne Chamber, the Two Knights Wards, and the Portcullis Chambers were to be charged two pence per night; and prisoners staying in the Star Chamber, the New Chamber, the Carpenters Chamber, the Sun Chamber, and the Chequer Chamber were to be charged three pence per night.[24] It was claimed that the keeper of the prison at the time, Robert Nicholl, was overcharging for all of these accommodation costs. In addition Nicholl was

Thomas Johnson, 1659) 43–49, for details.

[22] The two sheriffs for London in 1675 were Sir Nathaniel Herne († 1679) and Sir John Lethieullier († 1719). There is record of them being sent by the Court of Aldermen on 12 March 1675 to Ludgate prison to review what repairs were needed there (Repertories of the Court of Aldermen, LMA, COL/CA/01/01/084, 3 November 1674–28 October 1675, 130).

[23] TNA, SP 29/88, 133–39.

[24] Also see Johnson, *Ludgate—What It Is,* 68–70.

accused of a number of other abuses, inluding overcharging for bedding, inflating the cost of beer and ale from the cellar, selling the prison bell for his own profit,[25] and deliberately destroying the prison's accounting books and the register of legacies, which were granted to the prisoners.

Lambe further reported to the mayor and the Court of Aldermen that when the keeper had been reproved for his faults, he tried to justify himself (lines 25–26). The keeper argued that he had paid a great deal of money to secure his position and questioned whether anyone had the right to prescribe rules to him (lines 26–27). It was suggested that by purchasing the place, the keepers reckoned that they had purchased freedom from all laws and had a dispensation to govern as they saw fit (lines 28–29).

Lambe next turns to address the issue of how the keeper of the prison was appointed and notes that, while a new keeper had recently been named, a corresponding table of legal fees had not been publicly posted (lines 30–31). He points out that the keeper's position had reportedly been sold by the city for a great deal of money, something that had never been done before (lines 31–33). He notes in passing that a previous keeper, identified as the son of "Old Nicolls," had "made merchandising" of the keeper's position, a move that was legally questionable and certainly was to the detriment of the poor freemen in the prison and the benefactions in place designed to help them (lines 33–38). It is unclear who the son of "Old Nicolls" was, but it is likely that this is a reference to Robert Nicholls, who inherited the position as Keeper of Ludgate from his father John Nicholls.

In light of these abuses of the system, Lambe requests that the Lord Mayor and the Court of Aldermen find some other way to ensure that the public positions of trust, such as the keepers of prisons, should not be sold but rather freely elected from amongst men of virtue so that these offices would always be put into the hands of worthy people (lines 39–44). He also asks that a committee be appointed to renew the previous act of Common Council agreed in 1606, which governed fees and chamber rents so that the current corrupt practices and disorder could be brought to an end (lines 44–47). Finally, Lamb requests that a new table of legal fees be set up as soon as possible so that the prisoners might know what they had to pay, and the keeper might know what he was allowed to demand and no more (lines 48–50).[26] Lambe concludes the petition with a pledge always to pray that the blessings of those willing to perish might come upon the mayor and the Court of Aldermen (lines 51–52).

---

[25] There is a receipt dated 27 August 1672 for £17 18s for the installation of a new bronze clock bell weighing over 200 pounds (LMA, CLA/033/01/018).

[26] "A Table of Fees for Lugdate Prison" agreed by the London civic authorities, dated 19 January 1687, is contained in book 3 of John Strype's *A Survey of the Cities of London and Westminster* (London: A. Churchill et al., 1720) 175–76; and in *The Present State of the Prison of Ludgate*, 9–10.

B. THOMAS LAMBE'S WILL (17 OCTOBER 1685)

The second new source of information about Thomas Lambe is his will, which has not hitherto been included in scholarly investigations of his life. Lambe signed his will on 17 October 1685; it was probated on 4 July 1686 (Document 2). Within the will Lambe named his wife Barbara, noting that she had recently deceased (lines 10–11).[27] He also stated that he lived in a house in Bartholomew Close and that he had previously agreed with his wife that the house should go to her family after his death (lines 11–12). Lambe mentions that he had some legacies that were to be paid out, although he does not specify what they are (line 14); it is possible that these included gifts in support of prisoners in places like Ludgate. Once these legacies had been paid out, and debts and funeral costs covered, the remainder of his estate Lambe left to his eldest son John and his son's family (lines 12–16). He also named John as the sole executor of the will (line 16); this is the John Lambe who was rector of the parish church at Wheathampstead and the person to whom Richard Lucas dedicated his funeral sermon (discussed above).

The Leathersellers' Company record relating to the apprenticehip between Thomas Lambe and his younger brother Francis (noted above) opens another avenue of investigation in that it specifically named Robert Lambe as their father. The will of Robert Lambe has survived and it provides further details of Thomas Lambe's family that were previously unknown. This will was signed on 14 April 1635 and probated on 11 June 1635.[28] From the will we learn that the family came from Northamptonshire, that Thomas' mother was named Sarah, and that he had at least four brothers (Robert, William, John, and Francis) and two sisters (Sarah and Waller). Some indication about the religious environment of the family can be seen by the fact that, within his will, Robert Lambe bequeathed his copies of Foxe's *Book of Martyrs* and John Calvin's *Institutes* to his sons Robert and John. Mere possession of such books (which were very expensive to buy!) is in itself an indication of the importance of religion within the household. Further investigation within Northamptonshire records reveals that Thomas Lambe's father Robert married Sarah Whiting on 7 July 1603.[29] This information also allows us to answer another question that has long eluded historians about

[27] Barbara is perhaps most famously remembered for her letter to Richard Baxter in which she provided details of her husband's theological struggles over infant baptism and the break with John Goodwin's church (see appendix iii of *Reliquiae Baxterianae* [London: T. Parkhurst, J. Robinson, F. Lawrence, and F. Dunton, 1696] 51–53). For more on this, follow the discussion in John Coffey, *John Goodwin and the Puritan Revolution: Religion and Intellectual Change in Seventeenth-Century England* (Woodbridge: The Boydell Press, 2006) 100, 249–52.

[28] TNA, PROB 10/539. A copy of the will is found in TNA, PROB 11/168, 152 verso-153 recto.

[29] Parish register of Elton, Northamptonshire, 1587–1737, unpaginated.

Thomas Lambe—namely, when and where he was born. We now can confidently state, through the invaluable gift to historians of an Elizabethan parish registry system, that Thomas was baptized on 20 September 1612 in Peterborough in Northamptonshire.[30]

SUMMARY

The place of Thomas Lambe the linen-draper as a significant leader among seventeenth-century General Baptists has long been recognized and has recently been reaffirmed within William Brackney's *The Early English General Baptists and Their Theological Formation* (2017). However, there are always new things to learn about such figures of the past. Knowledge about Thomas Lambe has been enlarged significantly by a number of fresh primary sources discussed within this study. Most important among these is the petition that Lambe submitted to the London civic authorities circa 1675 arguing for reform in Ludgate prison, a document which serves as a vivid illustration of Lambe's philanthropic ideals. Details about his association with the Leathersellers' Company in London also speak to his professionalism with that body as a master tradesman. The identification of Lambe's will (written in 1685) and that of his father Robert Lambe (written in 1635) provides further details of his family, and also contains the means to track down the record of Thomas Lambe's baptism in a Northamptonshire parish in 1612. In short, knowledge about the life of Thomas Lambe is thereby widened, and the value of him as a seventeenth-century figure worthy of contemporary consideration is asserted.

DOCUMENTS

1. Thomas Lambe's Prison Petition, c. 1675 (Private Collection of Larry Kreitzer).

[Page 1]

To the Right Honourable The Lord Maior, Aldermen and
Commons of the Citty of London, In Common Counsell Assembled

The Humble Petition of Tho[mas] Lambe Cittizen and Leatherseller of London
Humbly sheweth That being Imployed by my Company In July 1674 to apply the
[5] Charities of Georg Humble Esq deceased to the poor freemen In the prison of
Ludgate, for their Release according to his will, I found the keeper In demand-

[30] The parish register of St. John the Baptist, Peterborough, Northamptonshire, 1559–1644, unpaginated.

ing Fees, and Chamber Rent to have No Regard to the publike Rules of this Court, which was then shewed him, but made his demands by false Table of Illegall Fees to the greevous oppression of the freemen, and deceiving of all the benefactors

That upon the 6th of October 1674 I made my Complaint to the court of Aldermen and Requested A committee to Inspect this matter w[hi]ch was presently graunted

That at Two Meetings of the Committee, I effectually prooved the Matter of my Complaint, For that In Two Mens cases where the keeper by his Notes, made 16 16 16d due to him. I prooved that from the poor men themselves, and from the Charities for Releef hee had Received about Four Pounds More then was due to him by law, which the worthy Committee caused him to Refund, and ordered him to withdraw An Action of 20li which hee had entred against one of them, and pay 8 s[hilling]s for unjustly Arresting him.

That the Next week after being In December 1674 The sheriffs at that Time most worthily Repaired to the prison In person and told the prisoners before the keepers face that they had but A penny Two pence and Three pence per night to pay where he had for severall years exacted Two pence Four pence and Six pence besides divers Illegall Fees And promised that for the future if they Received Injury upon complaint and proof they would Right them

Lastly I would Informe your Lordship and this Court That the keeper when hee hath been Reprooved for his faults was wont to urge for himselfe That hee had paid A great Summe of Money for his place and what had any one to doe to prescribe Rules to him So that by purchasing the place they seem to Reckon they doe with that purchase freedome from all lawes And procure A dispensation to govern Arbitrarily

Now Forasmuch As that there Is A New keeper And No publike Table of Legall Fees set up In the house And that the place Is lately sold as Is Reported for a great Summe of Money Which I have heard was Never sold by the Citty before (though it was by Old Nicolls his Sonne to the late keeper And forasmuch as that Making Merchandise of this and the like places of Trust Is very New And the Legality questioned And that Experience prooveth An occasion of great Injury to the poor Freemen And Worthy benefactors)

My humble Request is That your Lordship And this Court would consider and find out some other way (If it may bee done conveniently) to ease the burthen of the government That this and the like places of Trust May Never bee sold More But that using

your freedome of choise Amongst Men of Vertue This and the like places may allwaies
bee put Into the hands of Men that are most worthy of them.
And that you would Appoint A Committee to Renew your old Act of Common counsell
In 1606 and to Reestablish the good lawes of it, Not onely for the Fees and Cham-
ber Rent, But for the government of the house, and Cellar, which the corruption
of Men and Times hath brought to great disorder
And withall Speed to Set up A New Table of Legall Fees In the house That the prison-
ers may know what they have to pay. And the keeper what hee hath to demand
upon his perill And your Petitioner Shall ever pray That the blessing of them that are
Ready to Perish May come upon you.
[Page 4]
Peti[ti]on Lamb
v[rsus]
Keep[er] Ludgate

2. The Will of Thomas Lamb, signed 17 October 1685, probated 4 July 1686; The Commissary Court of London: Registry of Wills, 1686–1687 (DL/C/B/004/MS09171/040, 150 verso).

October ye 17th 1685
In the name of God Amen
I Thomas Lamb of London Leatherseller being in good health
of body and perfect memory Doe make this my last Will and
Testament (Revokeing all former Wills in manner and forme
following Impri[m]is I bequeath my soule unto the hands of Allmighty
God My body to the Grave in hope of a Blessed Resurrection to
Eternall life through the meritts of my Deare Redeemer Jesus
Christ My Worldly Estate I dispose as followes First I Confirme
the settlement made by myselfe and my wife Barbarah Lamb
(lately Deceased) of my house in Bartholomew Close upon
her Heires after my Death as for all my other Estate both
Reall and personall my Debts and Funerall Charges
and Legacies being first paid I Give to my eldest sonne
John Lambe Rector of Whettamstead for the goods of himselfe
his wife and Children and make him my sole Executor
Thomas Lamb Signed Sealed and Delivered in
the presence of Thomas Day Mr Lavingtons man Dorothy
Upton Jane Lavington

Vicesimo Quarto die mensis Julii

Anno D[omi]ni Mill[es]imo sexcen[tes]imo Octoge[s]imo sexto Cor[am] Ven[erabi]li Viro D[omi]no Thoma Pinfold Milite et Legum D[octo]re Surro[gato] Ven[erabi]lis et Egregii Viri D[omi]ni Thome Exton Militis legum etiam D[octo]ris D[omi]ni Episcopi Lond[on] Com[missa]rii l[eg]itime constituti Juramento Johannis Lamb filii et unici Ex[ecuto]ris in d[ic]to Testamento no[m]i[n]at[i] Cui Com[m]issa fuit Ad[ministra]tio &c primitus de bene et fidelit[er] adm[ini]strand[o] Eadem ac de pleno &c Ac de pleno &c jurat &c salvo jure &c

[Translation of lines 20–28]

On the Twenty-Fourth day of the month of July In the Year of the Lord One thousand six hundred and eighty six Before the Venerable Gentleman Lord Thomas Pinfold Knight and Doctor of Laws Surrogate of the Venerable and worthy gentleman Lord Thomas Exton Knight also Doctor of laws, of the Lord Bishop of London the legitimately appointed Commissioner, On the Oath of John Lamb son and sole Executor named in the said Testament To Whom was Committed the Administration &c first concerning the good and faithful administration of the Same and concerning the full &c And concerning the full &c he having sworn &c with the right preserved &c

RHODE ISLAND AND PROVIDENCE PLANTATION: THE CRADLE OF BAPTISTS IN AMERICA

James Lemons

Nearly every Baptist historian knows that the first Baptist church in the New World was gathered in Rhode Island, but what is less well known and often forgotten is that the first three varieties of Baptists in America (four, if you count the Rogerenes) first appeared in that same colony. The first Baptist association in America formed in Rhode Island by 1692, fifteen years before the more famous Philadelphia Baptist Association in 1707. Some of the typical characteristics of American Baptists, namely associations and schisms, first manifested themselves among the Rhode Islanders. Not long after the English Baptists settled upon immersion as the proper form of baptism, Rhode Island Baptists adopted that manner of baptism before Baptist churches existed anywhere else in America. Until the eighteenth century, Rhode Island was the heartland of Baptists, dominated by a variety of Baptists (General Six Principle Baptists) that became extinct in the 1990s.[1] The "hive of heretics" was the bane of the rest of Puritan New England for nearly two centuries, and in 1764 it became the home of the first Baptist college in the New World.

The story of the beginning of a Baptist church by Roger Williams in Providence is familiar to most.[2] The court found him guilty of sedition and heresy and ordered his banishment from Massachusetts Bay Colony in October 1635 on pain of death if he were to return. Because Williams was ill, the execution of that order was stayed on condition that he ceased his agitation. When the authorities learned that he was meeting with a number of his followers in his home, they ordered his immediate arrest and deportation to England—where he probably would have

---

[1] Rather than see the Six Principle Baptist name and traditions disappear, in 2001 a number of Baptist ministers began organizing, and in July 2003 they were incorporated as the General Association of Six-Principle Baptist Churches, Inc. This organization is not exactly a denomination in that its membership includes churches, ministers, and individuals. See http://spbaptists.info/background.html.

[2] William H. Brackney, *The Baptists* (Westport: Praeger, 1994) 10; Edwin S. Gaustad, *Liberty of Conscience: Roger Williams in America* (Valley Forge: Judson Press, 1999) 90; Bill J. Leonard, *Baptist Ways: A History* (Valley Forge: Judson Press, 2003) 74–75; H. Leon McBeth, *The Baptist Heritage: Four Centuries of Baptist Witness* (Nashville: Broadman Press, 1987) 130–31; and John M. Barry, *Roger Williams and the Creation of the American Soul: Church, State, and the Birth of Liberty* (New York: Viking, 2012) 263. All of the many biographies of Williams have a version of the story.

died in prison after having his tongue bored through with a hot iron and his ears chopped off. Tipped off that the officers were coming for him, Williams fled in late February 1636 to the Narragansett Bay and spent the remainder of the winter with the Wampanoags.[3] In April he began his settlement of Providence on land acquired from the Narragansetts, where he was joined by a number of his parishioners from his church in Salem.[4] By 1637 he was holding frequent worship services in his home. In the following year, Williams continued his study of the scriptures and the requirements for a true church and concluded that believer's baptism was the basis of an authentic church. As a result, in late 1638 he baptized some twelve to twenty members of his congregation, starting the first Baptist church in America.

The evidence of this event is quite clear. Massachusetts Governor John Winthrop made an entry in his journal on 16 March 1639:

> At Providence things grew still worse; for a sister of Mrs. Hutchinson, the wife of one Scott, being infected with Anabaptistry, and going last year to live at Providence, Mr. Williams was taken (or rather emboldened) by her to make open profession thereof, and accordingly was rebaptized by one Holyman, a poor man, late of Salem. Then Mr. Williams rebaptized him and some ten more. They also denied the baptizing of infants, and would have no magistrates.[5]

He did not remain long with that church, but concluded that no existing church was a true church.[6] Like all Puritans, he believed that the "Great Apostasy" of the fourth century had totally corrupted the church. No authentic church existed, nor would there be until Christ sent a new apostle to recreate the

---

[3] Williams later maintained that John Winthrop himself warned him of his impending arrest. See "RW to Major John Mason and Governor Thomas Prence, 22 June 1670," in *The Correspondence of Roger Williams*, ed. Glenn W. LaFantasie, 2 vols. (Hanover: Brown University Press/University Press of New England, 1988) 2:610.

[4] Linda MacLachlan, "When Was Providence Founded?" *Rhode Island History* 71 (Winter/Spring 2013): 21–32.

[5] *The Journal of John Winthrop, 1630–1645*, ed. James S. Dunn, James Savage, and Laetitia Yeandle (Cambridge: The Belknap Press of the Harvard University Press, 1996) 286. Catherine Scott was the wife of Richard Scott and the sister of Anne Hutchinson. "Holyman" was Ezekiel Holliman, one of Williams' most devoted followers in Salem. "Having no magistrates" meant that civil authorities had no role in church affairs, which meant separation of church and state.

[6] In 1678, after Richard Scott, one of the founding members of the Providence church in 1638, had become a Quaker and severe critic of Williams, he wrote, "I had walked with him in the *Baptists* way for about 3 or 4 months [...] in which time he brake off from his *Society*, and declared at large the ground and *Reason* for it: that their baptism could not be right, because it was not *Administered* by an Apostle" (Scott, quoted in introduction to *Complete Writings of Roger Williams*, 7 vols. [New York: Russell & Russell, 1963] 5:li–liin).

church. Williams left his little congregation and became a "witness in sack cloth" for the rest of his life.[7] His church continues today as the First Baptist Church in America.

The second Baptist church in America was gathered by John Clarke in Newport. Clarke was one of the Antinomians, the followers of Anne Hutchinson who were exiled or departed to found Portsmouth on Aquidneck Island in 1638. Some accounts say that Clarke led some worship services at Portsmouth before the founding of Newport in May 1639. Again, Clarke led worship services for the Antinomian group in Newport until 1641 when that congregation fell apart. It is not clear what had happened, but he and William Coddington, the dominant figure in Newport, had a political and religious falling out. When the dust had settled by 1644, Clarke had gathered a half dozen into a congregation "in the Baptist way," which is to say that they adopted believer's baptism instead of infant baptism. The Antinomians were Congregationalists, practicing infant baptism. However, unlike the beginning of the Providence church, no evidence exists that Clarke baptized his original handful of members.[8] A few years later this church was the first in America to adopt immersion as the mode of baptism. Clarke's church continues today as the United Baptist Church of Newport (the John Clarke Memorial Church).

The practice of baptism by total immersion appears to have been brought to America by Mark Lucar, a member of John Spilsbury's Particular Baptist church in London. Lucar had been immersed by Richard Blunt in January 1642 and then immigrated to America.[9] He showed up on the membership list of Clarke's church in 1648,[10] and soon after, he and John Clarke were busy dipping people in the Seekonk section of Rehoboth in Plymouth Colony. Roger Williams testified to this when he wrote to his friend, John Winthrop, Jr., saying:

> At Secunck a great many have lately Concured with Mr Jo. Clarke and our Providence men about the point of a New Baptisme, and the manner

---

[7] J. Stanley Lemons, "Roger Williams, Not a Seeker, but a Witness in Sack Cloth," *New England Quarterly* 88 (December 2015): 693–714.

[8] Sydney V. James, *John Clarke and His Legacies: Religion and Law in Colonial Rhode Island, 1638–1750*, ed. Theodore Dwight Bozeman (University Park: Pennsylvania State University Press, 1999) 28.

[9] Some evidence indicates that Lucar was in Newport in 1644; see Paul Hanson, "By Word and Spirit: Baptist Identity in Newport, Rhode Island, 1638–1730" (doctoral dissertation, Gordon Conwell Theological Seminary, 2006) 90n, 91.

[10] The church consisted of twelve members in 1648: John Clarke and his wife, Nathaniel West and his wife, Mark Lucar, William Vaughn, John Thorndon, John Peckham, John and Joseph Clarke, William Weeden, and Mary Painter. See Edwin S. Gaustad, ed., with historical introduction, *Baptist Piety: The Last Will and Testimony of Obadiah Holmes* (Grand Rapids: Eerdmans Publishing Co., 1978) 106.

> by Dipping: and Mr Jo. Clarke had bene there later (and Mr Lucar) and hath dipped them. I believe their practice comes nearer the first practices of our great Founder Christ (Jesus) than other practices of Religion doe [...].[11]

As Williams noted, the new baptism was accepted by the Baptists in Providence and Newport, and dipping would be the practice of Baptists ever after.[12]

Probably the only issue about the beginning of the Baptist movement in the New World is that odd dispute about which came first: the church in Providence or the church in Newport? Did Roger Williams gather the first church or does the honor go to John Clarke? No one had ever raised this question until 1847 when the Newport church suddenly asserted that it had been founded in March 1638. If this were true, the date originally taken for the Providence church (based on an entry into Governor John Winthrop's journal of 16 March 1639) would clearly mean that John Clarke's church was the first.[13] The Newport church presented its case for priority to the Warren Association, and the association agreed that it was so. That provoked the champions of Providence, especially professors at Brown University, to come back with a strong rebuttal that largely demolished the Newport claim. The report from the Providence church recommended that the Warren Association not take a stand on the issue of who came first, and the Warren Association agreed and dropped the issue.[14] The

---

[11] "Roger Williams to John Winthrop, Jr., 10 November 1649," in *The Correspondence of Roger Williams*, 1:302.

[12] To the end of his life, Williams held that believer's baptism by immersion was the correct way. See Linford Fisher, J. Stanley Lemons, and Lucas Mason-Brown, *Roger Williams Decoded: The Lost Essay of Rhode Island's Founding Father* (Waco: Baylor University Press, 2014) 18–32.

[13] Samuel Adlam, *The First Church in Providence, Not the Oldest of the Baptists in America, Attempted to Be Shown* (Newport: Cranston & Norman's Power Press, 1850); Thomas W. Bicknell, *Story of Dr. John Clarke, The Founder of the First Free Commonwealth of the World on the Basis of "Full Liberty in Religious Concernments"* (Providence: published by the author, 1915); Thomas W. Bicknell, *History of the State of Rhode Island and Providence Plantations*, 5 vols. (New York: American Historical Press, 1920) 2:575–77; and Wilbur Nelson, *The Hero of Aquidneck: A Life of Dr. John Clarke*, 1998 ed. (NY: Fleming H. Revell Co., orig. 1938).

[14] "Minutes of the Eightieth Anniversary of the Warren Baptist Association Held with the First Baptist Church in Newport, on Wednesday 8 and Thursday 9, 1847" (Providence: H.H. Brown, 1847) 12; "Minutes of the Eighty-First Anniversary of the Warren Baptist Association Held with the Lippitt and Phenix Baptist Church, in Warwick, September 13 and 14, 1848" (Providence: H.H. Brown, 1848) 11; "Minutes of the Eighty-Second Anniversary of the Warren Baptist Association Held with the First Baptist Church, in Pawtucket on Wednesday and Thursday, September 12 and 13, 1849" (Providence: H.H. Brown, 1849) 13–15; James Granger, Alexis Caswell, and William Gammell, "A Review of a Report, Presented to the Warren Baptist Association at Its Meeting in 1849, on the Subject of the True Date of the First Baptist Church in Newport, R.I., Prepared by a Committee of the First Baptist Church

Newport church retreated from the 1638 date, agreeing that 1644 was correct for them, but then argued that the Providence church had disintegrated when Williams left and was embodied only in 1652 when it emerged as a General Six Principle church. Still later, Newport reverted to its claim of a March 1638 beginning and maintained that position into the twenty-first century. Today, except for Landmark Baptists and a few others, Baptist historians consider the case closed in favor of Roger Williams and the Providence church.

The principal flaw in the case for the Newport church was the fact that they had taken the Portsmouth Compact of 1638 as their foundation date. Not understanding that this was a civil compact to create a theocratic government for the new settlement for Anne Hutchinson and her Antinomian followers, the 1847 proponents assumed it had created a church. However, even if a church was started, it was a Congregational church, not a Baptist church. Moreover, there was no Newport until May 1839, when William Coddington and nine of his prominent friends (including Clarke) seceded from Portsmouth to found Newport. Despite efforts by partisans of John Clarke to assert that he was a Baptist when he arrived from England, no one has ever been able to discover when he became a Baptist, though it is evident that he was a Baptist by 1644. Nor has anyone been able to discover when or if he was ordained. He always identified himself as a "physician," a prestigious position in his era, and he never assumed any of the airs of the clergy found in Puritan New England.[15] It has been suggested that the first Baptist on Aquidneck Island (where Newport and Portsmouth are) was Ezekiel Holliman, the very person who baptized Roger Williams. He had come from Providence in 1640 in his quest to acquire land, and he might have been the person to introduce the Baptist infection to Aquidneck.[16] The eagle-eyed critics of the settlements at Portsmouth and Newport made no mention of "Anabaptists" until 1641, when Winthrop entered a note in his journal about

---

in Providence, and Read to the Warren Association September 12, 1850" (Providence: H.H. Brown, 1850); "Minutes of the Eighty-Third Anniversary of the Warren Baptist Association Held with the First Baptist Church in Providence, on Wednesday and Thursday, September 11 and 12, 1850" (Providence: H.H. Brown, 1850) 19.

[15] James, *John Clarke and His Legacies,* 22. He is not even called "Elder" in the Newport church in the seventeenth century, the usual title for a Baptist pastor.

[16] Sheila Skemp, "Freedom of Religion in Rhode Island: Aquidneck Island's Reluctant Revolutionaries, 1638–1660," *Rhode Island History* 44 (February 1985): 12–13. Robert Lenthal also arrived in Newport in 1640, associated himself with Clarke, and was hired to teach school, but he returned to England within a year. In 1638 Lenthal had been engaged to be the pastor of the church in Weymouth, Massachusetts, but he got into trouble with the authorities for his Antinomianism and for opposing infant baptism. He and several of his supporters were arraigned and punished by the General Court in Boston in March 1639.

heresies and Anabaptism in Portsmouth.[17]

The early Baptist churches in Rhode Island and Massachusetts encompassed different varieties of Baptists. Already the English Baptists came in Particular and General versions, and these were evolving into distinct denominations. The tiny Baptist churches in the little New England settlements originally contained any kind of Baptist. If one held to believer's baptism, he or she joined the only baptizing church in town without much regard to any of the other issues that might divide Baptists. Such was true of the first churches in Providence and Newport and of the first Baptist church in Plymouth Colony gathered by John Myles in 1663 in Swansea. All of these churches had mixed congregations and all experienced divisions in the course of the seventeenth century.

Roger Williams, John Clarke, and John Myles were all Calvinists, making them Particular Baptists, but General Baptists became part of their congregations. One historian has suggested that Gregory Dexter, the London printer of Roger Williams' most famous book, *The Bloudy Tenent*, was the one who brought the General Baptist doctrines when he returned with Williams to Providence in 1644.[18] Subsequently, General Baptist principles took hold with the result that in 1652 the Providence church split. The Calvinist minority seceded with Elder Thomas Olney while the General majority stayed with Elder William Wickenden. Olney pastored the breakaway Particular church until he died in 1682, whereupon his son, also named Thomas, became its elder. However, this splinter had dwindled away before the younger Thomas died in 1718. By that time, there was only one recognized Baptist church in the whole of Providence County, but it was already the center of a number of branch churches scattered across the county. As the people spread out, "meetings of convenience" were held in various places on a somewhat irregular basis, but all of the members of those scattered congregations were regarded as members of the church in Providence.[19] There is no way to know how many members the Providence church had in those circumstances, but soon elders from Providence went to the outlying congregations to lead them.[20]

By the 1650s, the General Baptists in Rhode Island had become General Six Principle Baptists, holding as their fundamental doctrines the six principles

[17] *The Journal of John Winthrop*, 362. This comment came nearly a year after Ezekiel Holliman had come to Portsmouth from Providence.

[18] James, *John Clarke and His Legacies*, 97.

[19] John A. Callender, *An Historical Discourse on the Civil and Religious Affairs of the Colony of Rhode-Island*, ed. Romeo Elton (Boston: Thomas H. Webb, 1843) 115.

[20] J. Stanley Lemons, *First: The First Baptist Church in America* (Providence: Charitable Baptist Society, 2001) 15; J. Stanley Lemons, *Baptists in Early North America: Volume II: First Baptist, Providence* (Macon GA: Mercer University Press, 2013) xx–xxi.

listed in Hebrews 6:1–2.[21] They elevated the laying-on of hands to equal importance to baptism, so that one could not become a member of the church or take Communion unless one had been baptized and gone under hands. In addition, the Six Principle Baptists came down against congregational singing, while the Particular Baptists in America generally sang psalms in church. They also allowed everyone, including women, to "prophesy" in church meetings and services and to vote in business meetings, unlike the Calvinist Baptists who excluded women from such privileges.

Soon John Clarke's church in Newport also suffered a split. In this instance the General Six Principle faction withdrew in 1656 to form the Second Baptist Church of Newport. The leaders of the break-away Six Principle Baptists went to Providence to go under hands, and then the Providence elders traveled to Newport to lay hands on the members of the new church there. They demanded that all believers go under hands, and they objected to congregational singing. Subsequently, the Second Baptist Church established a branch church in North Kingstown, and in 1664 Elder Thomas Baker went from Newport to lead that church.[22] Second Baptist soon exceeded the Newport First Baptist Church in size and in the eighteenth century became one of the largest Baptist churches in America.

John Myles, who had been a "Tryer" in Cromwell's national church, fled from England to escape the renewed persecution of dissenters after the restoration of the monarchy and the introduction of the Clarendon Code, which reestablished the Anglican Church. Coming to Plymouth Colony, in 1663 he gathered a mixed communion church in Swansea (near Rhode Island). This is the First Baptist Church of Swansea today. This church practiced both infant and believer's baptism until the second decade of the eighteenth century, when it clearly became a close communion Baptist church.[23] It also experienced a secession of General Six Principle Baptists in the 1680s. These people had the same objections to the principles and practices of the Swansea church as those in Newport.

The third variety of Baptists to appear first in America in Rhode Island was the Seventh Day Baptists. This denomination emerged in England in the 1650s,

---

[21] The six principles were repentance, faith in God, baptism, laying on of hands, resurrection, and eternal judgment.

[22] Richard Knight, *History of the General or Six Principle Baptists in Europe and America* (Providence: Smith and Parmenter, 1827) 265; and David Benedict, *A General History of the Baptist Denomination in America and Other Parts of the World*, 2 vols. (Boston: Lincoln & Edmands, 1813) 2:500.

[23] For a history of the Swansea church, see William H. Brackney and Charles K. Hartman, *Baptists in Early North America: Volume I: Swansea, Massachusetts* (Macon GA: Mercer University Press, 2013) xx–lxi.

and they held that the Ten Commandments required that the Sabbath be observed on the seventh day of week. The Seventh Day Baptists were cruelly persecuted after the restoration of the monarchy and some fled to America. One such person was Stephen Mumford, who followed John Clarke back to Newport in 1664.[24] While he did not join Clarke's church, he worshiped with them and soon influenced some of the church members to begin to hold worship services on Saturday. They remained within the church until 1671, when acrimony between the Seventh Day and First Day Baptists ended in a schism. Obadiah Holmes, the second pastor of John Clarke's church, said "the Sabbatarians had no more conscience than dogs."[25] After the Seventh Day Baptists had established a church in Newport, they soon spread west to what is present-day Hopkinton, Rhode Island. They built a meetinghouse in 1680 and organized a church, which today is the First Seventh Day Baptist Church of Hopkinton. This church became the center of the Seventh Day Baptist movement in the eighteenth century. By 1816, the Hopkinton church claimed to have 947 members worshiping in three meetinghouses, probably making it the largest Baptist church in America at that time.[26] As this denomination expanded in the nineteenth century, it grew up and left home—its center shifting to New Jersey and now to Wisconsin. Its original congregation in Newport died out in the nineteenth century, and its old meetinghouse is now part of the Newport Historical Society. The Seventh Day Baptists peaked in Rhode Island in the middle of the nineteenth century with eleven churches. Today, only two remain, and one of these has only about twenty participating members.

As mentioned in the beginning, one might count the Rogerenes, who were sometimes called the "Rogerene Baptists" or the "Rogerene Quakers," in that they began as Baptists and then mixed in Quaker ideas. This group lived in Connecticut, but they had connections to Rhode Island and the Seventh Day Baptists. Their leaders were John and James Rogers of New London, Connecticut, who engaged in coastal trade that took them to Westerly and Newport. Elder John Crandall baptized them in 1674 in Westerly, and then they were accepted as members of the Newport Seventh Day Church.[27] In the following year, several

---

[24] Don A. Sanford, *A Choosing People: The History of Seventh Day Baptists*, 2nd ed. (Macon GA: Mercer University Press, 2012) 86.

[25] James, *John Clarke and His Legacies*, 101; and Gaustad, ed., *Baptist Piety*, 55.

[26] Sanford, *A Choosing People*, 419.

[27] Ibid., 107–108. John Crandall was one of the three Baptists from Newport who were arrested and prosecuted in Massachusetts in 1651. The others were John Clarke and Obadiah Holmes, whose vicious whipping made him an early Baptist martyr. Crandall was never a Seventh Day Baptist, but he moved to Westerly in 1660 and ministered to the Seventh Day Baptists there. He baptized a number of people who became members of the Seventh Day church. At the same time, Crandall's wife "kept the seventh day."

more of the Rogers family were baptized, and the congregation in New London began worshiping on Saturdays. John Rogers assumed the role of elder, and the church grew to have several dozen members. In 1677, Rogers began mixing Quaker and Seventh Day Baptist ideas. While practicing baptism and the Lord's Supper, they also became pacifists, dressed in plain clothing, refused to take oaths, rejected a paid ministry, practiced faith healing and anointing with oil, believed in free will and perfectionism, and went back to holding services on Sunday.[28] When this happened, the Seventh Day Baptists ceased fellowship with them.[29] The Rogerenes became especially notorious in their desire to be martyrs, to suffer persecution. They flouted the blue laws of Connecticut by working and traveling on Sunday and by disrupting Sunday services and refusing to pay the ministerial taxes.[30] Compared to the Rogerenes, the Baptists and Quakers "appeared eminently sensible and praiseworthy."[31] Never numerous, the Rogerenes died out in the twentieth century.[32]

While divisions and schisms characterized the early Baptists, so did associationalism. The first Baptist association in America was formed by the General Six Principle Baptists in the seventeenth century. As early as 1670, elders and deacons of the three Six Principle churches (Providence, Newport, and North Kingstown) began meeting annually to recognize each other's leaders, to confer about doctrine and practices, and to fellowship with each other.[33] In 1692, the Second Baptist Church in Swansea was officially recognized and joined the association. The number of Six Principle churches grew in the early eighteenth century so that, by June 1728, the meeting at East Greenwich had thirteen churches and thirty messengers.[34] At the yearly meeting in September 1729 at

---

[28] See John R. Bolles and Anna B. Williams, *The Rogerenes* (Boston: Stanhope Press, 1904) 12–13; Ellen Starr Brinton, "The Rogerenes," *New England Quarterly* 16 (March 1943): 8; and David D. Hall, *Worlds of Wonder, Days of Judgment: Popular Religious Belief in Early New England* (New York: Alfred A. Knopf, 1989) 142.

[29] William G. McLoughlin, *New England Dissent, 1630–1833: The Baptists and Separation of Church and State*, 2 vols. (Cambridge: Harvard University Press, 1971) 1:250–51. The Newport Seventh Day Baptist church officially excommunicated John Rogers in 1685.

[30] In *The Rogerenes*, Bolles and Williams catalogue a long tale of punishments meted out to the Rogerenes. John Rogers spent a total of fifteen years in prison for opposing the established church. Also see McLoughlin, *New England Dissent*, 1:252.

[31] McLoughlin, *New England Dissent*, 1:250.

[32] Patricia M. Schafer, "The Rogerenes Leave Their Mark on Connecticut Society," http://connecticuthistory.org/the-rogerenes-leave-their-mark-on-connecticut-society

[33] Robert G. Torbet, *A History of the Baptists* (Philadelphia: Judson Press, 1950) 273; and McLoughlin, *New England Dissent*, 1:281.

[34] John Comer wrote that this gathering "is supposed to be ye largest Convention y^t ever hath been" (*Diary of John Comer*, ed. Edwin Burrows, vol. 8 in *Collections of the Rhode Island Historical Society* (Providence: Rhode Island Historical Society, 1893) 66. (This meeting included a church each from Massachusetts and Connecticut.)

North Kingstown, they adopted a petition to the Connecticut authorities supporting the Baptist protest against the religious taxes.[35] Even by the end of the eighteenth century, in Rhode Island the Six Principle Baptist churches outnumbered any other variety. However, by then, they were being rapidly surpassed by the Regular (Calvinist) Baptists. The original Six Principle Baptist Association had been mortally wounded by then by the defection of their three largest churches (First in Providence, Second in Newport, and Second in Swansea) to the Regular Baptists. Most of their churches were insular, close-knit congregations in which everyone knew everyone. They opposed anything that smacked of high-church ecclesiasticism and pretension, including music, written sermons, liturgy, and paid, educated clergy.

Outside of Rhode Island, the Six Principle Baptists were totally overwhelmed by the flood of Calvinistic Baptist churches. Only minimally inspired by the revivalism of the Great Awakening, the Six Principle Baptists were swiftly surpassed by the Calvinist varieties of Baptists who soon outnumbered them in churches and members all over New England. While the Six Principle Baptists did organize an association and hold a yearly meeting, they did not develop any other instrumentalities. They failed to create the missionary, educational, and benevolent societies that characterized most other Baptist denominations. They had no educational institutions, no publishing house, or distinctive literature. They generally scorned educated ministers, and when some churches desired greater respectability (or even church music), they defected to other denominations, especially to the Freewill Baptists in the nineteenth century. By 1852 only thirteen Six Principle Baptist churches were left in New England, along with three more in New York and Pennsylvania. Only six of these churches had more than fifty members, and all of them were in rural towns.[36] By 1850 the Regular and Freewill Baptists in Rhode Island each outnumbered the national total of Six Principle Baptists. The last original General Six Principle Church, the Stony Lane Baptist Church in North Kingstown, adopted a Calvinist confession in the 1990s and then became non-denominational.[37]

As noted above, the General Six Principle Baptists in Rhode Island formed the first Baptist association in America. Then in the 1750s and 1760s, a dozen

---

[35] Comer, *Diary of John Comer*, 79–80.

[36] "Annual Report of the Old General Baptists Yearly Conference of Rhode-Island and Massachusetts Held at the Wood River Meeting House in Richmond, R.I., On the 10th, 11th, and 12th of September, 1852" (Pawtucket: A.W. Pearce, Printer, 1852) 4–5 [author's collection]. Three of the churches had fewer than thirty members and appeared to be without an elder.

[37] Interview of John Wheeler, pastor of Stony Lane Church, 17 January 2017. About the adoption of a Calvinist confession, see *The Roots and History of the Stony Lane Six Principle Baptist Church, Founded 1665* (North Kingstown: Stony Lane Baptist Church, 1995) 10.

Separate Baptist churches along the backcountry borders of Rhode Island, Massachusetts, and Connecticut formed an association of *Calvinist* Six Principle Baptist churches. This was the first Calvinist Baptist association in New England, but it was soon superseded by the Warren Association, which was founded in 1767. After Isaac Backus became part of the Warren Association, he played a major role in the dissolution of the Calvinist Six Principle Baptists by persuading a number of their churches to join the Warren Association.[38]

The coming of the Warren Association and the establishment of a Baptist college in Rhode Island were clear indicators that Rhode Island's peculiar place in Baptist history was coming to an end. Both of these major developments were the work of the Philadelphia Baptist Association, which by the 1760s had become the closest thing to a general denomination of Baptists in America. Begun in 1707, the PBA first included churches in Pennsylvania, New Jersey, and Delaware. In due course, it came to include churches in New York, Connecticut, Maryland, and Virginia.[39] In reaction to the turmoil and enthusiasm of the revivalism of the Great Awakening in the 1740s, the PBA felt a need for more discipline and definition. They adopted the Philadelphia Confession of Faith in 1742 and produced the Short Treatise of Church-Discipline in 1743.[40] The PBA sent agents and missionaries to the South and to Nova Scotia and was the initiator in 1764 of Rhode Island College (now Brown University).

The Philadelphia Association chose Rhode Island for the location of a college for at least four important reasons. First, the colony lacked a college so that no competitor stood in the way. Second, no established church existed that could block the creation of a Baptist institution. Third, Rhode Island was home to many Baptists (albeit in at least five varieties) and some of them were wealthy and might be expected to support an institution of higher education.[41] The vast majority of Baptists in America were of the lower classes, but in Rhode Island, some of the wealthiest and most powerful people were Baptists. Finally, the dramatic growth of the number of Baptists and churches in all of New England made Rhode Island a convenient site from which to organize and utilize this new strength for the

---

[38] William H. McLoughlin, "Arminian and Calvinist Baptists," in *Soul Liberty: The Baptists' Struggle in New England, 1630–1833* (Hanover: University Press of New England, 1991) 124–33.

[39] Winthrop S. Hudson, *Religion in America* (New York: Charles Scribner's Sons, 1956) 44.

[40] The Philadelphia Confession was a modest revision of the Second London Confession of 1689.

[41] I.e., Five Principle Regular, General Six Principle, Calvinist Six Principle, Separate, and Seventh Day Baptists. When the college was created, major figures from the Regular, General Six Principle, and Seventh Day Baptists were included on the board of trustees in order to elicit their support. This cooperation was part of the transformation of several of the major Six Principle churches who subsequently joined the Warren Association.

denomination.

The influence of the Philadelphia Baptist Association spread over Rhode Island and New England with the arrival of the college in 1764–1765; the formation of the Warren Baptist Association in 1767, which was patterned on the Philadelphia association; and the coming of the so-called "Western men" from Pennsylvania, New Jersey, and New York. These men assumed many of the leadership positions in New England. These included James Manning, Hezekiah Smith, Samuel Stillman, John Davis, Charles Thompson, William Williams, David Howell, Benjamin Stelle, and later Stephen Gano. These, along with men such as Isaac Backus, solidified the Baptists in New England and brought respectability and stability to the denomination.

By the nineteenth century, Rhode Island's dominant Baptists were now part of the Baptist mainstream, and the Baptist denomination itself was part of the new Protestant establishment in America. Unfortunately, this all came at a cost to a fundamental principle Roger Williams had held most dear. Now, the Baptist establishment believed that the United States was—or ought to be—a Christian nation, and that a "sweet harmony" (to quote Isaac Backus) should exist between church and state. Williams had regarded the idea of a Christian nation to be a blasphemous notion, and the early Baptists in Rhode Island had believed in a rigid separation of church and state. By the nineteenth century, the new Baptist establishment wanted religious liberty for itself, but not for Shakers, Universalists, Unitarians, Deists, Roman Catholics, Jews, or even for Freewill Baptists and Methodists.

BAPTIST POVERTY INITIATIVES IN CONFESSIONS, COVENANTS, AND DEACON WRITINGS

Charles W. Deweese

Poverty is a major global problem. "Nearly 1/2 of the world's population—more than 3 billion people—live on less than $2.50 a day. More than 1.3 billion live in extreme poverty—less than $1.25 a day."[1] Poverty denies people of housing, food, clothing, healthcare, education, protection, and opportunity.

In August–September 2015, my wife and I spent five weeks in and around Gulu, Uganda, while visiting a missionary family, Julie and Kristopher Mobbs; our daughter; son-in-law; and our three grandchildren, Chase, Cooper, and Zoe. They are there through the sponsorship of Four Corners Ministry, headquartered in Opelika, Alabama. Most of the board members and executive leaders of Four Corners are Baptists, but the organization has an ecumenical thrust to it.

Through meeting the people for whom Julie and Kristopher and other Four Corners missionaries provide ministry, we saw what poverty is really like. The Acholi people live in small, round, one-room, thatch-roofed huts with dirt floors. They spend much of their day searching for water and firewood, and they constantly fight off malaria. They struggle to get education in antiquated buildings where teachers sometimes do not show up. Recent wars have contributed to rampant unemployment, political instability, a large-scale absence of economic infrastructures, an impoverished state of medical and dental care, and many abused women and children.

Four Corners provides many Acholi people with work and educational opportunities, food and water, clothing, solar Bibles, limited dental care, and other signs of hope. Work opportunities offered include construction, farming, jewelry-making, cooking, maintenance, and security. Most of all, Four Corners provides Sunday school and worship as 250 or more Acholi people meet every Sunday morning at Abaana's Hope, the center of Four Corners' ministry. These people worship with enthusiasm through dancing, singing, praying, and preaching. We even witnessed the baptisms of about twenty-five people, including that of our grandson, Cooper.

But the Acholis' poverty never goes away. Neither does the poverty of tens of millions of other people worldwide, including the poor in the United States.

---

[1] "Eleven Facts about Global Poverty," https://www.dosomething.org/facts/11-facts-about-global-poverty (accessed 20 April 2015).

In sharp contrast, a prosperity gospel dominates far too much American religion today. In fact, it is totally out of place in any expression of faith. A classic example was the March 2015 announcement of Pastor Creflo Dollar of the World Changers Church International in College Park, Georgia, that he and other church leaders wanted to raise $65 million, by asking for $300 each from donors, to purchase a luxury jet, a Gulfstream G650, to carry God's word and thousands of pounds of food and supplies to the church's mission points around the world. Public reaction was quick and negative. Careful investigative reporting by various news media, coupled with critical letters to editors, prompted a major Atlanta newspaper to publish the article, "Creflo Dollar's Call for $65M Jet Never Gets off Runway."[2] The next day, just prior to Easter, that newspaper printed a political cartoon by Mike Luckovich that pictured a drawing of Creflo Dollar with a poster behind him showing a dollar mark and the words "Give More," while Dollar, with outstretched arms, shouted, "Hallelujah, Price Has Risen!"[3] Heavily focused on itself, the prosperity gospel cares little for the poor.

Insidiously, the prosperity gospel can gradually but certainly affect the giving attitudes of Baptists at large. Self-indulgence can silently superimpose itself over the biblical requirement to assist brothers and sisters in need. Fortunately, however, secular and religious advocates for the poor do exist. Recent examples include the comments of Jeanine Grant Lister, of Corinth, Kentucky, who wrote "Poverty in America: Why We So Hate Poor People";[4] and Dana Milbank, of the *Washington Post*, who wrote "Punishing Our Poor."[5] NBC's "Red Nose Day" TV special on 21 May 2015 was designed to raise a large amount of money to fight childhood poverty.[6] In September 2015, the United Nations adopted the goal to end poverty and hunger on a global basis.[7]

Baptists at large take actions to eliminate poverty, especially hunger. The Baptist World Alliance observes World Hunger Awareness Month in October. It has supported many valuable projects designed to alleviate both poverty and hunger. The Southern Baptist Convention sponsors an annual Global Hunger Sunday in October to collect funds for its Global Hunger Relief program. In

---

[2] "Creflo Dollar's Call for $65M Jet Never Gets off Runway," *The Atlanta Journal-Constitution*, 24 March 2015, B1, B8.

[3] Mike Luckovich, political cartoon, *The Atlanta Journal-Constitution*, 25 March 2015, A18.

[4] Jeanine Grant Lister, "Poverty in America: Why We So Hate Poor People," *Waco* (TX) *Tribune-Herald*, 3 April 2015, 6A.

[5] Dana Milbank, "Punishing Our Poor," *Waco* (TX) *Tribune-Herald*, 9 April 2015, 4A.

[6] Frazier Moore, "'Red Nose Day' TV Special Is Comedy for Good Cause," *The Atlanta-Journal Constitution*, 20 May 2015, D5.

[7] Mark G. Shrime and John G. Meara, "Surgery Can Fight Poverty," *International New York Times*, 28 September 2015, 7.

September 2015, Suzii Paynter, executive coordinator of the Cooperative Baptist Fellowship, met in Washington, D.C., with more than one hundred religious faith leaders who affirmed a statement calling on the country to commit to ending hunger by 2030. Baptists often mobilize their resources to assist persons suffering from natural disasters and other desperate situations that could lead to poverty.

Baptists have adopted hunger resolutions; issued denominational statements regarding poverty; collected offerings for the poor and hungry; supported global, national, regional, and local hunger initiatives; launched dental and medical clinics; participated in disease-eradication efforts; financed water discovery and conservation projects; provided clothes closets; elected benevolence committees; constructed houses for the poor; coordinated disaster relief efforts; provided overnight housing for the homeless; and fed the hungry and taught them how to grow their own food.

But not everyone has been impressed with Baptist contributions toward helping the poor. Thomas Wolfe, the famous American novelist of the early 1900s, commented on a Baptist school that he called Pine Rock College. Even though the graduates of this institution were young idealists willing to die on behalf of "monogamy, matrimony, pure sweet women, children, the Baptist church, the Constitution, and the splendid ideals of the Democratic and Republican parties," most of them would go out to die in defense of "child labor, cotton mills, tenant farmers, poverty, misery, squalor, damnation, death, and all the rest of it [...]."[8]

More recently, a significant Baptist dictionary asserted in an indicting claim that "a good deal of traditional, Western theology has been biased in favour of the powerful. By concentrating on spiritual aspects of salvation, it has often sidestepped issues of justice and social change and in so doing has upheld the status quo and the interests of those who benefit from it."[9] By implication, the poor have often gotten left out.

And what about the comments of David Platt, president of the Southern Baptist Convention's International Mission Board, who included a chapter in his 2015 book *Counter Culture* entitled "Where Rich and Poor Collide: The Gospel and Poverty"? He claimed that many of us

> have insulated and isolated ourselves from the massive material poverty that surrounds us in the world. We have filled our lives and our churches with more comforts for us, all while turning a blind eye and a deaf ear to abject poverty in others. We have a gaping hole in the way we see the

---

[8] Thomas Wolfe, *The Web and the Rock* (New York: Harper and Brothers, 1939) 196–97.

[9] Michael H. Taylor, "Preferential Option for the Poor," *A Dictionary of European Baptist Life and Thought*, Studies in Baptist History and Thought, vol. 33, ed. John H.Y. Briggs (Eugene OR: Wipf & Stock, 2009) 403.

> world, and we need new insight. We need our eyes opened to the implications of the gospel for how we live.[10]

So how is a Baptist Christian supposed to interpret the preceding kinds of information? This essay will attempt to answer that question by focusing on the poor in the Bible and by demonstrating how Baptists, across their entire four-century history, have incorporated support for ministry to the poor into such key representative documents as confessions of faith, church covenants, and deacon writings.

The Poor in Scripture

To start with, Holy Scripture presents powerful incentives for Judeo-Christian communities to consider the needs of the poor. The traditional biblical books of poetry offer key insights. Because of God's righteousness, "the poor have hope, and injustice shuts its mouth" (Job 5:16);[11] and those who have "crushed and abandoned the poor" (Job 20:19) will be punished. The Psalmist affirms that the Lord takes thought for the poor and needy and offers a beatitude: "Happy are those who consider the poor" (Psalm 40:17–41:1). The writer of Proverbs declares: "If you close your ear to the cry of the poor, you will cry out and not be heard" (Prov. 21:13); further, "Whoever gives to the poor will lack nothing, but one who turns a blind eye will get many a curse" (Prov. 28:27).

The prophetic literature does not mince words. Isaiah praises God because he has been a refuge to the poor and needy (Isa. 25:4). Amos declares God's judgment on Israel for selling "the needy for a pair of sandals" and trampling "the head of the poor into the dust" (Amos 2:6–7); for oppressing the poor and crushing the needy (Amos 4:1); and, again, for trampling on the poor and taking levies of grain from them (Amos 5:11).

Jesus, who applies various meanings to the word "poor," often focuses on the poor. In Matthew, in addition to offering a blessing on the poor in spirit (Matt. 5:3), he encourages messengers to go tell John the Baptist that "the poor have good news brought to them" (Matt. 11:5); and he tells the rich young man that, in order to be perfect, he must sell his possessions and give his money to the poor (Matt. 19:21).

In Luke, Jesus offers further thoughts. Claiming that the Spirit of the Lord "has anointed me to bring good news to the poor" (Luke 4:18), he puts forth an exciting blessing: "Blessed are you who are poor, for yours is the kingdom of God" (Luke 6:20). Jesus encourages those who give a luncheon or dinner to "invite the

---

[10] David Platt, *Counter Culture* (Carol Stream IL: Tyndale House Publishers, Inc., 2015) 25.

[11] The New Revised Standard Version serves as the basis for all biblical citations in this essay.

poor" (Luke 14:13). He tells the story of the sickness, death, and heavenly rewards "of a poor man named Lazarus" to emphasize the dangers of converting riches into a god (Luke 16:19–31). Jesus tries to convince a rich ruler that he will have treasure in heaven if he will sell all that he has and "distribute the money to the poor" and come and follow him (Luke 18:22). Jesus offers salvation to Zachaeus after he commits to sell half his possessions, give them to the poor, and pay back fourfold to anyone whom he has defrauded (Luke 19:8–9). Toward the end of his earthly ministry, just prior to foretelling the destruction of the Temple, Jesus commends a "poor widow," who contributes two small copper coins into the treasury: "she out of her poverty has put in all she had to live on" (Luke 21:2–4).

Upon the urging of the Twelve Disciples, the early church selected six men, who were either deacons or precursors to deacons, "to wait on tables," including the special request of the Hellenists to minister to the "widows [who were] being neglected in the daily distribution of food" (Acts 6:1–3). This represented a formal ministry to the poor. Other portions of the New Testament provide further guidelines for understanding and relating to the poor. The apostle Paul compliments the churches of Macedonia who out of their "extreme poverty...overflowed in a wealth of generosity" during a time of great affliction (2 Cor. 1–2). He puts forth the model of the Lord Jesus Christ who, though rich, "became poor, so that by his poverty you might become rich" (2 Cor. 8:9). First Timothy urges the rich not "to set their hopes on the uncertainty of riches, but on God" (1 Tim. 6:17). James defines pure and undefiled religion as that which cares for orphans and widows (James 1:27), and he warns rich oppressors who have defrauded laborers of their wages (James 5:4). He also encourages readers to minister to "a brother or sister [who] is naked and lacks daily food" as a way to ensure the vitality of their faith (James 2:14–17). First John asks, "How does God's love abide in anyone who has the world's goods and sees a brother or sister in need and yet refuses to help?" (1 John 3:17).

Throughout their history, Baptists have obviously read biblical teachings about the poor and have incorporated them into many of their own writings and practices. Baptists' confessions of faith, church covenants, and deacon writings have captured much of their denominational and local-church thought regarding the poor for 400-plus years.

The Poor in Anabaptist and Baptist Confessions of Faith

Anabaptist and General Baptist confessions stressed ministry to the poor in more detail than did the English Separatist and Calvinist confessions. The former tended to place more emphasis on practical aspects of church and Christian duties, while the latter focused more heavily on theological statements. Anabaptist confessions, particularly those of the Mennonites, asserted support for the poor as a critical component of ministry. The first-generation Anabaptist confession "Discipline of the Church: How a Christian Ought to Live," dated 1527, devoted two of its twelve articles to the poor. Articles 4–5 affirmed that all in the brotherhood are "to hold in common all gifts received of God," to "contribute to the common need so that brethren and sisters will always be helped," that "needy members shall receive from the brotherhood as among the Christians at the time of the apostles," and that the elders and preachers are to "look after the needs of the poor."[12] The Moravian Anabaptist confession, "Account of Our Religion, Teaching, and Faith," prepared by Peter Ridemann about 1540, also taught a "community of goods."[13]

The 1580 Mennonite Waterland Confession listed "care of the poor" in its article on ministries that the church should exercise.[14] The 1632 Dordrecht Confession, described as "the most influential of all Mennonite confessions," provided more detail on how the church should do its ministry to the poor. Deacons "should have the care and oversight of the poor," should "receive gifts and alms," and should "distribute them among the poor saints." And widows chosen as deaconesses should "visit, comfort, and take care of the poor, the weak, afflicted, and the needy" and "visit, comfort, and take care of the widows and orphans."[15]

The earliest English General Baptist confessions assigned to ministers and deacons the task of caring for the poor. John Smyth's 1609 "Short Confession of Faith in 20 Articles" claimed that "deacons, men, and widows" should "attend to the affairs of the poor and sick brethren."[16] Then Smyth's 1610 "Short Confession of Faith" gave "oversight of the poor" to ordained ministers.[17] Thomas Helwys' 1611 "Declaration of Faith of English People" appointed deacons, male and female, to the office of relieving "the necessities off the poor and impotent brethren concerning their bodies."[18] The Smyth party's 1612–1614 "Propositions and Conclusions Concerning True Christian Religion" defined the ministry of "[d]eacons, men, and women" as the need "to serve tables and wash the saints' feet" (table-serving includes the table of the poor). Further, "all things are to be common" in "the necessities of the church, and poor brethren."[19]

---

[12] William L. Lumpkin, ed., *Baptist Confessions of Faith,* rev. ed. (Valley Forge: Judson Press, 1969) 33.

[13] W.J. McGlothlin, *Baptist Confessions of Faith* (Philadelphia: American Baptist Publication Society, 1911) 14.

[14] Ibid., 40.

[15] Lumpkin, ed., *Baptist Confessions,* 66, 73.

[16] Ibid., 101.

[17] McGlothlin, *Baptist Confessions,* 60.

[18] Ibid., 90–91.

[19] Ibid., 80, 83.

Four additional English General Baptist confessions of the 1600s also revealed concern for the poor: the 1651 "Faith and Practice of Thirty Congregations," the 1654 "True Gospel Faith," the 1660 "Standard Confession," and the 1679 "Orthodox Creed." The 1651 confession noted that the church should make contributions "for the relief of those that cannot help themselves with food and rayment," particularly those who belong to the household of faith and those who are willing to work but cannot because of "sickness or weakness of body." The confession urged that the church should set apart some "men," likely deacons, to ensure that the needs of the poor were met. Further, if a church could not meet its poor members' needs, it should inform "other Churches or saints of God" to secure their assistance in meeting those needs.[20] The 1654 confession simply stated that believers "ought to relieve the poor."[21] The 1660 confession provided more detail, claiming that poor church members should be "sufficiently provided for by the Churches, that they neither want food or rayment, and that by a free and voluntary contribution...and this through the free and voluntary help of the Deacons (called Overseers of the Poor)."[22]

The 1679 "Orthodox Creed" included a lengthy article titled "Of Communion of Saints, and Giving to the Poor." Because the church is a community of believers, this article asserted that all members should have

> an interest in each other's goods and possessions [...] and tho' no equality, or property, be pleaded for; yet the works of charity and mercy, must be minded as a duty to lend to the Lord, and pity and relieve the Lord's poor, weekly laying out for them, as God hath prospered us, according to our ability in freedom, liberality, and charity, according to our brethrens' necessity, whether sick, or in prison, to visit and relieve them, and not only within the church, but to all as we have opportunity, and ability to be doing good.[23]

The English Separatist "True Confession" of 1596; the highly influential Calvinist Baptist "London Confession" of 1644, which depended heavily on the "True Confession"; and the famous Second London Confession of 1677 and 1689, upon which the Philadelphia Confession of 1742 heavily depended, said little about ministry to the poor, except by general implication.

The closest the "True Confession" came to ministry to the poor was its assertion that God has placed in office "special men" who are to "govern, oversee, visit, watch, &c.," while all church members possess the duty "to watch one over

---

[20] Ibid., 105–106.
[21] Lumpkin, ed., *Baptist Confessions,* 194.
[22] McGlothlin, *Baptist Confessions,* 117–18.
[23] Ibid., 150–51.

another."[24] The "London Confession" gave the "special men" and church members the identical duties.[25] According to the "Second London Confession," the saints of the church must tend to "relieving each other in outward things according to their several abilities, and necessities."[26] The "Philadelphia Confession" used the same wording as the "Second London Confession."[27]

The English "Somerset Confession" of 1656, which combined Calvinist and Arminian elements, included the following in a list of commandments: "ADMINISTERING one to another according to the gift received, whether it be in spirituals, or temporals." Also, the ministry, when necessary, should "labor and work with their hands" so that they may be able to support the weak.[28]

In 1756, the Backus Memorial Baptist Church in North Middleboro, Massachusetts, a noted Separate Baptist church pastored by the famous Isaac Backus, adopted a confession of faith. This confession urged that deacons should serve the Lord's table, care for the poor, and oversee the church's secular affairs.[29]

In the United States two important confessions emerged in the 1830s. The 1833 "New Hampshire Confession" simply stated that deacons should carry out their duties as "defined in the Epistles to Timothy and Titus."[30] The 1834 "Treatise on the Faith of the Freewill Baptists" assigned duties relating to the poor to deacons and the church. Clearly, "deacons should attend to the temporal wants of the poor members of the church," and the church should sponsor the ministry of "administering to the necessities of the poor and afflicted."[31]

In 1925, the Southern Baptist Convention adopted the "Baptist Faith and Message," revised in 1963, 1998, and 2000. The 1925 statement contained an article titled "Social Service" that included the Christian obligation "to provide for the orphaned, the aged, the helpless, and the sick."[32] The 1963 revision claimed (as did the 1998 revision), in an article titled "The Christian and the Social Order," that Christians "should work to provide for the orphaned, the needy, the aged, the helpless, and the sick."[33] The 2000 revision stated, "We should work to provide for the orphaned, the needy, the abused, the aged, the helpless, and the sick."[34]

---

[24] Lumpkin, ed., *Baptist Confessions,* 90.

[25] McGlothlin, *Baptist Confessions,* 186.

[26] Ibid., 269.

[27] Ibid., 297.

[28] Ibid., 209, 211.

[29] Minutes, Backus Memorial Baptist Church, 16 January 1756.

[30] McGlothlin, *Baptist Confessions,* 306.

[31] Ibid., 325, 327.

[32] Annual, Southern Baptist Convention (SBC), 1925, 74.

[33] Annual, SBC, 1963, 280.

[34] "The 2000 Baptist Faith and Message," Southern Baptist Convention, http://www.sbc.net/bfm2000/bfm2000.asp (accessed 27 March 2015).

In 2005 the General Board of the American Baptist Churches USA adopted an "Identity Statement," based on previous confessions. The statement affirmed that "God through Jesus Christ calls us to be [...] a caring people who care for the needy, the weak, and the oppressed."[35]

In 2009, the North American Baptist Conference adopted a statement titled "Our Beliefs," an update of a 1982 statement. After confessing the belief that "Christians, individually and collectively, are salt and light in society," the statement stated that "in a Christlike spirit, they [...] aid the needy and preserve the dignity of people of all races and conditions."[36]

Baptists in other countries have also incorporated statements regarding the poor into their confessions in the larger context of social order, social justice, and social responsibility, as well as in general and specific statements about meeting human need, with special focus on deacons' roles. About 1948, Yugoslavian Baptists adopted a "Confession of Faith of the Yugoslavian Baptist Churches." It stated that "Baptists are committed to the principle of social justice. Every inhabitant of this country has the right to earn a livelihood with just payment to meet life's necessities. The work of no person should be exploited in favor of those who do not work." Further, the community of the church "is responsible for social justice, striving to improve social conditions first of all among its members."[37]

Baptists in Spain, Portugal, Greece, and the European Baptist Convention have adopted, at different times, the precise wording of the Southern Baptist Convention's 1963 "Baptist Faith and Message," including its article on "The Christian and the Social Order."[38] In 1974, the first International Congress on World Evangelization, with participants from more than 150 nations, including many Baptists, adopted the "Lausanne Covenant." In an article titled "Christian Social Responsibility," the covenant confessed that Christians should share God's "concern for justice and [...] for the liberation of men from every kind of oppression." Further, "[t]he message of salvation implies also a message of judgment upon every form of alienation, oppression, and discrimination, and we should not be afraid to denounce evil and injustice wherever they exist."[39]

Confessions of Baptists in France, Germany, Poland, and Romania contain pertinent, although general, information. In 1879, the Union of the Baptist Churches of France adopted a "Confession of Faith and Ecclesiastical Principles."

---

[35] "Identity Statement," American Baptist Churches USA, http://www.abc-usa.org/what_we_believe/identity/ (accessed 27 March 2015).

[36] "Our Beliefs," North American Baptist Conference, www.nabconference.org/about-us/our-beliefs (accessed 3 March 2015).

[37] G. Keith Parker, *Baptists in Europe: History & Confessions of Faith* (Nashville: Broadman Press, 1982) 206, 211–12.

[38] Ibid., 243, 253–54.

[39] Ibid., 269–70.

It put forward the view that deacons and deaconesses should carry out scriptural requirements, including a special focus on meeting "the material wants of the assembly."[40] In 1895, the Federation of French Baptist Churches in France claimed in its "Confession of Faith of the Federation of French Baptist Churches" that deacons' service to the church should make them particularly "responsible for all the material needs of the congregation."[41] The "Confession of Faith and Ecclesiastical Principles of the Evangelical Association of French-Speaking Baptist Churches," a modification of a similar 1979 confession, placed on deacons and deaconesses "special responsibility for everything that relates to the material interests of the congregation."[42]

Confessions arose in Russia and the broader Soviet Union. The "Russian Baptist Confession" of 1884 and the twentieth-century "Confession of Faith of the Evangelical-Christian Baptists" in the Union of Soviet Socialist Republics both simply indicated that deacons and other church servants should carry out the duties assigned to them in scripture,[43] which, of course, included ministry to the poor.

The 1908 German Baptist "Confession of Faith and Constitution of the Churches of Baptized Christians Commonly Called Baptists" committed to deacons "the temporal affairs of the church," and to all church members "the bodily welfare of all."[44] The 1930 "Confession of the Baptist Churches in Poland" identified as a duty of church members the need to "procure spiritual and physical well-being for all."[45] The 1974 "Confession of Faith of the Romanian Baptist Churches" placed in the hands of deacons responsibility "for assisting the pastor in managing the material affairs of the church" and "for cultivating financial giving and for calling for philanthropic actions." It also asserted that church members have an obligation "to help poor orphans and widows."[46]

The Poor in Baptist Church Covenants

Many Baptist church covenants of the 1600s–1900s included affirmations relating to the poor. Since these covenants constituted basic commitments that church members made to God and one another, their contents reflect church ideals and ethics, all allegedly based on scripture. So, historically, what agreements have churches made in their covenantal statements regarding ministry to the

---

40 McGlothlin, *Baptist Confessions,* 362.
41 Parker, *Baptists in Europe,* 131.
42 Ibid., 143.
43 Lumpkin, ed., *Baptist Confessions,* 428; Parker, *Baptists in Europe,* 156.
44 McGlothlin, *Baptist Confessions,* 344–45.
45 Parker, *Baptists in Europe,* 180.
46 Ibid., 223, 227.

poor?

Essentially three traditions (or wordings) have manifested themselves in Baptist covenants in regards to ministry to the poor. In one tradition, covenants have included promises to provide support or relief for the poor. A second pattern has emphasized bearing one another's burdens. And a third has implied ministry to the poor within general pledges regarding social justice.

Examples of the first tradition have included covenants among various types of Baptists: the 1771 covenant (revised in 1826) of the Separate Baptist Kiokee Baptist Church, Kiokee, Georgia, in which members pledged to contribute to the "poor of the flock"; the 1870s covenantal commitment of the Bethany Swedish Baptist Church in Moline, Illinois, to "help the poor in any way we can"; and the pledge of the 1895 covenant printed in the *Church Book Alphabetically Arranged and Record Book* (probably written by the Landmark Baptist leader J.R. Graves) to "aid the poor and needy."[47]

The 1833 "Covenant of the New Hampshire Baptist Convention" set in motion a decided preference for language highlighting "support of the poor." In this covenant, church members promised to "cheerfully contribute of our property for the support of the poor." "Support of the poor" also appeared in the 1859 model covenant printed in Edward T. Hiscox's "The Baptist Church Directory."[48]

Then a similar pledge to provide "relief of the poor" appeared in numerous covenants. Examples included the 1841 "Covenant of Kennebec (Maine) Baptist Association"; the widely used 1853 covenant in J. Newton Brown's "The Baptist Church Manual"; the 1868 covenant of Citadel Square Baptist Church in Charleston, South Carolina, which more specifically referred to "relief of the poor in the church"; and the 1871 covenant included in "The Baptist Praise Book: For Congregational Singing." The 1987 covenant of the First Baptist Church of Lodi, California (a church of the North American Baptist Conference), varied the wording to "relief of the needy."[49]

In the 1900s, this tradition also manifested itself in the 1935 agreement of the model covenant printed in England's *The Baptist Quarterly,* in which church members specifically committed to remember "the material need of the poor and the sick"; and in the 1945 covenantal affirmation of the Primitive Baptist Conference of New Brunswick, Maine, and Nova Scotia "to be benevolent to the needy, and especially to the poor of our own church."[50]

In a second tradition covenants focused on the more general promise "to

[47] Charles W. Deweese, *Baptist Church Covenants* (Nashville: Broadman Press, 1990) 143, 167, 170.

[48] Ibid., 157, 164.

[49] Ibid., 160, 161, 165, 166, 180.

[50] Ibid., 131, 187.

bear one another's burdens" or "each other's burdens," which, by implication, included ministry to the poor. While Baptist covenants in America during the 1600s and early 1700s did not tend to include elements relating to the poor,[51] those in England did. Four such covenants included the 1697 covenant printed in separate publications by the Baptist leaders Benjamin and Elias Keach; the 1699 covenant of Great Ellingham Baptist Church, Norfolk, England; the 1719–1720 covenant of the Baptist Church at Bourton on the Water; and the 1790 covenant of the Baptist Church in Horse Fair, Stony Stratford, Bucks, England.[52]

Other examples of this second tradition include covenants dating from 1780 to 1986 in Canada, the United States, and Australia: the 1780 covenant of the Freewill Baptist New Durham Baptist Church, New Durham, New Hampshire; the 1798 covenant of the Calvinist Philadelphia Baptist Association; the 1827 covenant of the Halifax (Nova Scotia) Baptist Church; the 1846 covenant adopted by the Maine Baptist Convention; the 1847 covenant printed in William Crowell's "The Church Member's Manual"; the 1858 covenant printed in "A Treatise on the Faith of the Freewill Baptists"; the 1889 covenant included in the *Free Baptist Cyclopaedia: Historical and Biographical*; the 1948 covenant approved by the Baptist Union of Victoria (Australia); and the 1986 pledge of the New Covenant Baptist Church in Winnipeg, Manitoba.[53]

The third tradition has used various wording, often within the larger context of emphasizing social justice. Examples include the 1972 commitment of the Baptist Church of the Covenant in Birmingham, Alabama, to support "an innovative church—one that is warmly evangelical and socially concerned"; the 1954 covenantal pledge of the Baptist Convention of the Republic of Cameroon to "help the old, the sick, and the troubled in our Church and in the Town"; and the 1976 covenantal promise of the First Baptist Church of Decatur, Georgia, to engage in "ministry that addresses itself to the needs of the total person."[54]

Like Baptist confessions of faith, church covenants have incorporated language relating to ministry to the poor. Although that language is always brief, does not appear in all covenants, and seems highly derivative and imitative, concern for the poor, nevertheless, runs through several centuries of Baptist covenantal thought on a global basis.

THE POOR IN BAPTIST DEACON WRITINGS

In the earliest centuries of church history, "the deacons were charged with ongoing responsibility for the poor beyond the private almsgiving of individual

---

51 For the texts of nine such covenants dating from 1663 to 1756, see ibid., 132–40.

52 Deweese, *Baptist Church Covenants,* 120, 122, 123, 129.

53 Ibid., 146, 151, 160, 161, 163, 169, 184, 188, 194, 234.

54 Ibid., 177, 178, 187, 196.

Christians"[55]— see, for example, the Shepherd of Hermas (c. 96) and the Pseudo-Clementines (c. 200).[56] Further, "together with the bishop, they [deacons] also provided an organizational framework for charity to maximize coverage."[57] Deacons then became subordinate to presbyters and deaconesses to deacons in the fourth and fifth centuries. Eventually, deaconesses were absorbed into the monastic movement, and the "male diaconate became a stepping-stone to the priesthood."[58] The Protestant Reformation recovered some of the New Testament spirit of service for deacons by again involving them "in social welfare and the care of the poor."[59] Anabaptists gave deacons financial and pastoral duties.

Many English Baptist writers of the 1600s discussed deacons and the poor. In 1654, Thomas Collier described the service of deacons as ministering to the tables of the Lord, the minister, and the poor.[60] In 1681, N. Cox stated in a deacon ordination service that "yea the poor Members of Christ, which are dear to him as the Apple of his Eye, are committed to your Care," and that you cannot "relieve the Necessities of the poor Saints" unless you "do by a gracious Sympathy, as it were, put your selves in their stead."[61] In what may be the earliest detailed list of deaconess duties in Baptist literature, the Broadmead Baptist Church in Bristol, England, listed five duties, all of which focus on visiting the sick. Duty number three stated: "Not only to take care of their sick bodies, of the brethren and sisters, but that their wants may be supplied; and therefore to make reports back of their condition, to the elders and deacons of the congregation."[62]

Although published in London in 1697, Elias Keach's *The Glory and Ornament of a True Gospel-Constituted Church* achieved prominence in America, where Keach had served as a Baptist pastor in the late 1600s. It contained a significant statement on deacons and the poor: "The Work of Deacons is to serve Tables, viz. to see to provide for the Lord's Table, the Minister's Table, and the Poor's Table." Deacons were to see that "each Member do give weekly to the Poor, as God has blessed them [...]. Also visit the Poor, and know their Condition as

[55] Jeannine E. Olson, *One Ministry, Many Roles: Deacons and Deaconesses through the Centuries* (St. Louis: Concordia Publishing House, 1992) 36.

[56] James Monroe Barnett, *The Diaconate: A Full and Equal Order*, rev. ed. (Valley Forge: Trinity Press International, 1995) 46–47, 57–58.

[57] Olson, *One Ministry, Many Roles*, 36.

[58] Barnett, *The Diaconate*, 82.

[59] Ibid., 134.

[60] Thomas Collier, *The Right Constitution and True Subjects of the Visible Church of Christ* (London: Henry Hills, 1654) 30–31.

[61] N. Cox, a sermon preached at the ordination of an elder and deacons in a baptized congregation in London, printed for Thomas Fabian, 1681, 12–14.

[62] Edward Bean Underhill, ed., *The Records of a Church of Christ, Meeting in Broadmead, Bristol, 1640–1687* (London: Hanserd Knollys Society, 1847) 397–98.

much as in them lies; that none, especially the aged Widows, be neglected."[63]

In 1743, the Philadelphia Baptist Association printed a treatise on church discipline, which it attached to the Philadelphia Baptist Confession, adopted in 1742. This treatise emphasized the table service of deacons, asserting that deacons "are to be intrusted with the stock of the church, out of which stock they are to assist the poor members of the church" and that they "should see that all the members of the church do contribute toward the proper uses of the church," including the poor "so that none be neglected."[64] A detailed description of a deacon ordination at the First Baptist Church of Philadelphia in 1763 resorted to the three-fold ministry of deacon table service.[65]

Morgan Edwards, the first historian of Baptists in America, wrote in 1774 of deacons, deaconesses, and the poor, and included an ordination hymn about deacons, whose second stanza focused on the poor. After noting that "caring for the poor" was a key deacon duty, he wrote that the office of deaconess "is chiefly limited to the care of the sick, miserable, and distressed poor," and "like that of the deacons, hath the poor and helpless for its objects, but is chiefly confined to those things wherefor men are less fit. The helpless poor must be kept clean, and fed."[66] Stanza two of the deacon hymn reads as follows: "The poor behold their father's care / To find them daily bread; / For them the caring deacons are / Both food and raiment to prepare; / And where to lay their head."[67]

Also in 1774, David Thomas, an important Regular (Calvinistic) Baptist in Virginia, discussed the role of deacons in a book he wrote. He claimed that "the place of a deacon is to take care of the secular concerns of a church," including seeing "that the necessities of the poor and indigent are supplied."[68]

Further in 1774, the Charleston Baptist Association adopted *A Summary of Church Discipline*, which highlighted the table service of deacons. In addition to collecting from church members "for the poor," they "are to serve the poor's table; to whom they are to distribute of the church's stock, with all impartiality, simplicity, chearfulness, and sympathy."[69]

In 1796, the Warwick Baptist Association in New York published a circular

---

[63] Elias Keach, *The Glory and Ornament of a True Gospel-Constituted Church* (London: n.n., 1697) 10–11.

[64] "A Short Treatise of Church Discipline," in *A Confession of Faith Adopted by the Baptist Association, Met at Philadelphia, September 25, 1742* (Philadelphia: Anderson and Meehan, 1818) 83.

[65] Minutes, First Baptist Church of Philadelphia, 20 December 1763.

[66] Morgan Edwards, *The Customs of Primitive Churches* (n.p.: n.n., 1774) 42–43.

[67] Ibid., 40–41.

[68] David Thomas, *The Virginian Baptist* (Baltimore: Enoch Story, 1774) 27–28.

[69] Charleston Baptist Association, *A Summary of Church Discipline*, 2nd ed. (Charleston SC: Markland, M'Iver & Co., 1794) 10–11.

letter on "The Character and Office of a Deacon." Although it reiterated the table-service motif of many earlier writings, it gave more attention to the table of the poor than most. A key paragraph read:

> "The Poor's Table; for the poor ye have always with you. In this, distinction is to be made between the negligent and the necessitous; the former to be exhorted in industry; the latter to be supplied with all affection, as far as the ability of the Church may extend. In order to [do] this, Deacons must not only husband the Church's stock in hand, but exhort the members to contribute for this benevolent design. 1 Cor. xvi. 2. That "the laws of our country make provision for the poor,' is a poor, though too common excuse from this duty by cold, narrow-hearted professors. Shall the laws of our country exhibit more compassion than the friends of Jesus? If you see your brother hath need, and shuteth up your bowels of compassion towards him, how dwelleth the love of God in you? Widows, who are widows indeed, are the particular objects of the Deacon's attention: that such might not be neglected, Deacons are appointed. Acts vi.1.[70]

In what Bill Brackney has described as "the first Baptist church manual printed in America,"[71] Samuel Jones, in 1798, wrote "A Treatise of Church Discipline and a Directory" at the appointment of the Philadelphia Baptist Association. This manual further emphasized the table service of deacons, including ministry to the poor.[72]

In the 1800s the production of church manuals proliferated among Baptists in America. Published between 1845 and 1867, hundreds of thousands of copies of just four manuals by William Crowell, J. Newton Brown, Edward T. Hiscox, and J.M. Pendleton have been distributed. One of the general duties assigned to deacons in these manuals was to take the alms of the church to poor members.[73] The same was true in numerous associational circular letters published during these years.[74] Admittedly, emphasis on helping the poor diminished in many of these manuals as they placed more responsibility on deacons for "managing" church affairs. Other terms began to creep into Baptist literature to describe the functions of deacons, such as boards, and assessors, collectors, and disbursers of

---

[70] Minutes, Warwick Baptist Association, 31 May–1 June 1796, 7–8.

[71] William Brackney, ed., *Baptist Life and Thought, 1600–1980: A Source Book* (Valley Forge: Judson Press, 1983) 126.

[72] Samuel Jones, "A Treatise of Church Discipline and a Directory" (Philadelphia: S.C. Ustick, 1798) 15.

[73] See Charles W. Deweese, *The Emerging Role of Deacons* (Nashville: Broadman Press, 1979) 43–44, for more detailed descriptions of these manuals.

[74] Ibid. See a list of eight such letters published between 1804 and 1850.

church funds. By assigning deacons more business, administrative, and management duties, churches obviously weakened their involvements in ministries to the poor.

In the 1890s, Walter Rauschenbusch, pastor of the Second German Baptist Church in New York City, and leader of the Social Gospel Movement, published a sixteen-page leaflet titled "To the Deacons of Our Churches." He admonished deacons:

> My dear, my brethren, is that you have been faithful to the letter of your office, but not to its spirit [...]. In some cases you have even lost sight of the essence of your office altogether, thinking more of serving at the Lord's Supper and in the worship of the church, and of making your influence felt in the management of the church than of the lowly work of service which might be so dear to your master.[75]

He suggested that deacons, in contrast, "ought no longer to confine your work to the poor of your own church [...]. The deacons of today ought to grapple with the problems of poverty in the world [...and] ought not to be content with healing physical misery after it has come, but ought to prevent it before it comes." Because of deacons' strong influence in church life, he further suggested that they expose themselves to "specialists" who could teach them how to use their power to deal with the causes of poverty.[76] In response to his own concerns, Rauschenbusch helped to create a deaconess sisterhood in New York City. Its purpose was to meet the social and spiritual needs created by modern industrialization, urbanization, and immigration.

In the 1900s, particularly in Southern Baptist life, church assignments given to deacons tended to move their functions away from serving the table of the poor. A Southern Baptist encyclopedia claimed in 1958: "Although Baptist polity permits a wide latitude of form and practice, the deacon usually renders an administrative and officiating ministry."[77] Then the release of various books by American and Southern Baptists began to encourage deacons to move toward more servant ministries: Robert E. Naylor's *The Baptist Deacon* (1955), Harold Nichols' *The Work of the Deacon and Deaconess* (1964), Howard B. Foshee's *The Ministry of the Deacon* (1968), Donald F. Thomas' *The Deacon in a Changing Church* (1969), and Henry Webb's *Deacons: Servant Models in the Church* (1980).

Today, not much has changed. Deacons in most Baptist churches continue to do administrative and officiating ministries; therefore, ministries to the poor

---

[75] Walter Rauschenbusch, "To the Deacons of Our Churches" (New York: Samuel Batten, n.d.) 11, 14.

[76] Ibid.

[77] J.B. McMinn, "Deacon," in *Encyclopedia of Southern Baptists,* vol. 1 (Nashville: Broadman Press, 1958) 352.

receive little attention. In some churches, however, deacons resort to creative ministries to assist those dealing with poverty. A good example was the Deacon Economic Assistance Committee created in 1975 by the Hominy Baptist Church in Candler, North Carolina, to assist church members suffering from economic problems.[78]

CONCLUSION

Three slices of Baptist history (confessions of faith, church covenants, and deacon writings) plainly show that Baptists, for more than four centuries, have viewed caring for the poor as a basic ideal. They have affirmed the need to inject biblical mandates regarding poverty into their theological ideals, their commitments to God and one another, and the duties of deacons. Clearly, they have expressed concern for the poor through many other means. Holy Scripture mandates the need to convert statements of faith into practical action:

> What good is it, my brothers and sisters, if you say you have faith but do not have works? Can faith save you? If a brother or sister is naked and lacks daily food, and one of you says to them, "Go in peace, keep warm and eat your fill," and yet you do not supply their bodily needs, what is the good of that? So faith by itself, if it has not works, is dead. (James 2:14–17)

Baptists have not always agreed on how they should minister to the poor. The 1774 Charleston Baptist Association's *A Summary of Church Discipline* claimed that deacons should "serve the poor's table...with all impartiality,"[79] while the 1796 circular letter of the Warwick Baptist Association in New York urged deacons to make a distinction "between the negligent and the necessitous; the former to be exhorted in industry; the latter to be supplied with all affection."[80] Regardless of *how* such ministry should be done, Baptists have stated for four hundred years that such ministry *should* be done.

Because ministry to the poor is a key component of Baptists' historical and theological DNA, such ministry could appropriately become a permanent fixture of the total Baptist experience. Every church, association, convention, fellowship, federation, alliance, and union could consider injecting such ministry into its reason for being and into its annual budget to support specific programs and staff to implement the ministry. Rather than approach ministry to the poor through occasional, and sometimes haphazard, projects that offer some help but primarily ameliorate the Baptist conscience, why not integrate such ministry into the

---

[78] Toby Druin, "Asheville," *Home Missions* 46 (June–July 1975): 29.

[79] *A Summary of Church Discipline*, 10–11.

[80] Minutes, Warwick Baptist Association, 31 May–1 June 1796, 7–8.

church's essential function? Baptist covenants, confessions, and deacon writings suggest that this is the right thing to do. Rauschenbush's encouragement "to grapple with the problems of poverty in the world," both to prevent and attack poverty, applies to all Baptists. My recent trip to Africa has forever convinced me to relate more compassionately to the poor by digging deeper into my wallet to support Four Corners Ministry.

LETTERS OF ENQUIRY
THE CORRESPONDENCE FILE OF THE MARITIME BAPTIST CONVENTION CHAPLAIN SERVICE COMMITTEE 1939–1941

Roger H. Prentice

INTRODUCTION

Acadia University, Wolfville, Nova Scotia, maintains the archives of the United Baptist Convention of the Atlantic Provinces, a treasure trove for a researcher in this field of study. It contains an archival box that was not catalogued so that it did not appear in the past archival records.[1] The recent discovery of this box was almost accidental. Research was taking place concerning a prominent Maritime Baptist Minister, Dr. John Howard MacDonald, and one of his positions was, from 1917 to 1919, Deputy Director of the Canadian Armed Forces Chaplaincy Service overseas during World War I (1914–1918). Since the collection indicated that the contents concerned "Chaplaincy" in World War II, it was logical to give the contents a thorough inspection.

One of the first acts of the Maritime Baptists at the outbreak of World War II in 1939 was to create a committee to recommend willing clergy of the Baptist Convention to the Canadian Department of National Defence as chaplains to the armed forces. It was hoped by these Baptist leaders that the committee serving the chaplaincy needs of the new world war would consult Dr. MacDonald because of his earlier invaluable experience. Although in his mid-seventies by the time World War II broke out for Canada on 10 September 1939, he played a significant but "silent" role for the Maritime Baptist committee. In other words, he was an unofficial advisor to both the committee and the applicants.

This collection contains the file of correspondence of the Maritime United Baptist Convention Chaplain Service Committee from 1939 to 1941. These letters are very interesting for several reasons. They are the only record known of this vital committee to Baptist history. The letters shed important light upon the members of this committee who were also important leaders within the denomination. We also discover the personalities and motivations of clergy who applied or who were selected to be chaplains in the Canadian Armed Forces. Finally, they

---

[1] The original catalogue number was Y380. C55A6 Since the recent discovery of this material, it has been catalogued as cat. No. D900.823.

give previously unknown information about the relationship of the denomination to the authorities appointed by the Armed Forces to govern the armed forces' chaplaincies.

These letters also exhibit some of the dynamics of the Baptist denominations in Canada, their divisions, fraternal relationships, and how the government of the day perceived them through the chaplaincy and the principal chaplain. Part of this involves two of the three Ministers of National Defence who were themselves well-known and respected members of one Maritime Baptist congregation, First Baptist Church, Amherst, Nova Scotia.

The reader needs to know that with such a vast country with a population of only 11,000,000 at the time, the Baptists did not have a "national" organization (this would come in 1944), but rather three regionally independent denominations separated by geography: the United Baptist Convention of the Maritime Provinces, the Baptist Convention of Ontario and Quebec, and the Baptist Union of Western Canada. The oldest and largest was the Maritime Baptist Convention.

Provenance

It is unknown when this significant box of letters was accessed to the archival collection at Acadia University. Obviously, it began as a file in the hands of the Reverend L.E. Ackland, Secretary of the Maritime Baptist Chaplain Service Committee, and the letters began with the committee's formation in September 1939.[2] Ackland gave up his position as secretary two years later, in September 1941, when he moved to a new congregation in Shelburne, Nova Scotia, a significant distance from other members of the committee. It is at this point that the collection ends.

It is unknown whether he transferred this file to the Baptist Convention Office in Saint John, New Brunswick, when he moved to Shelburne, or if his estate did after his untimely death. The university did not receive it until the mid- or latter 1950s, detected by the handwriting on the box spine and initial letter. The handwriting was clearly that of Mrs. Isobel Horton, University Librarian, and the archaic catalogue number indicates this. Not only that, a published catalogue of the archival holdings at Acadia University, published in 1955, does not indicate the letters' presence.[3]

---

[2] Reverend Lemuel Ernest Ackland was born 15 February 1881, graduated from Acadia University with a Bachelor of Arts in 1908, and a Bachelor of Divinity from Newton Theological Seminary in 1911. At the time of this correspondence he was the minister of Union Street United Baptist Church, St. Stephen, New Brunswick. Ackland was also the Secretary of the United Baptist Convention as a whole during this time.

[3] George E. Levy, ed., *A Catalogue for the Maritime Baptist Collection in the Library of*

The collection itself is not arranged in chronological order. Various groupings of the letters have been clipped together but it is unknown by whom or why this sorting was done, although it was likely arranged by Mrs. Horton herself. In a loose way, the groupings reflect identifiable subjects or issues that involve several recognizable authors and subjects. As far as it is known, this is the first time this collection has been examined by a researcher. The chronological order of the letters is greatly disrupted since a specific issue might span some significant time.

To identify individual letters in this study, they are numbered in the order in which they appear in the collection without disturbing the order. A chronological order in which they were written has been constructed to facilitate this paper along with an alphabetic index of authors.

The Maritime Baptist Chaplain Service Committee

When war was declared by Canada on 10 September 1939,[4] there was no organization to support any Canadian Armed Forces chaplaincy programme. It was the Privy Council of Canada that ordered, on 13 June 1921, the dissolution of the Chaplain Service that had been established for World War I (Order No. 2002).[5] The Canadian churches were a part of this unpreparedness. Post World War I, all the Protestant churches were eager to proclaim the need for ongoing peace.[6] The Great Depression, particularly in the Maritime Provinces and the Canadian West, captured the attention of the churches' leadership. It was a complete readjustment for them to consider the outbreak of another world war. In Canada, at that time, there was considered to exist a "big four" collection of Protestant denominations: the United Church of Canada (a union in 1925 of the Methodist, Congregational, and a majority of Presbyterian churches), the Presbyterian Church in Canada, the Church of England in Canada (later to be named

---

Acadia University (Kentville, Nova Scotia: Kentville Publishing Company Ltd., 1955).

[4] Canada declared war one week after Great Britain to enable members of Parliament to reach Ottawa from the far west and north. It also made the point that Canada was independent from Mother Britain.

[5] Thomas James Hamilton, "'Padres Under Fire': A Study of the Canadian Chaplain Services (Protestant and Roman Catholic) in the Second World War" (unpublished thesis submitted for the degree of Doctor of Philosophy, Graduate Department of History, University of Toronto, 2003) 63.

[6] W.T. Whitley, ed., *Fourth Baptist World Congress (Toronto, Canada, 23–29 June 1928): Record of Proceedings* (Toronto and London: Stewart Printing Service, Kingsgate Press, 1928) 266–69. Dr. MacDonald gave a significant address to the Baptist World Alliance on "Militarism." In it he said, "Peace is not a negative state, the mere cessation of war; it is active participation in the things which go to make up a new heaven and a new earth in which righteousness shall dwell" (268).

the Anglican Church of Canada), and the Baptist churches in Canada. The leaders of all these major denominations had to adjust quickly their distaste for war and, thus, soundly backed the Mackenzie King Government in its response to Nazi Germany's attack on Poland.[7]

Overall, in Canada, the Baptists were and are the smallest of the "big four" Protestant denominations. In itself, it is also divided into the three separate and independent denominations named "conventions." There were and still are the Maritime Provinces, Ontario and Quebec, and the Western Union[8] as natural boundaries. This separate denominational governance, which is in principle voluntary, is distinct from the more centralized denominations with an Episcopacy or Presbyteries. Nevertheless, the three conventions of that day were fraternally connected and cooperated on such projects as the publication of a hymnbook, Sunday-school curricula, overseas missions, and youth-group programmes.

The United Baptist Convention of the Maritime Provinces exists in the smallest territory of Canada—Nova Scotia, New Brunswick, and Prince Edward Island—but was the largest convention in numbers of the three. It was also the oldest in establishment.[9] This independence will play a role in some of the tensions that are revealed through these letters.

In 1937 and 1939 the Anglican, United Church, and the Baptist of Ontario and Quebec sent delegates to the ecumenical gatherings held at Oxford and Edinburgh, introducing them to the awaking desire for ecumenical dialogue and cooperation.[10] The Maritimers did not attend. Being an older organization, the Maritime Baptists tend to be somewhat more "conservative" than the Ontario/Quebec convention, so in some parts of the Maritimes this elicits some suspicions, notably in New Brunswick and Prince Edward Island, of "liberal" and ecumenical theology. It is understandable that the denominations that attended the broadening Oxford and Edinburgh conferences would easily take initiatives to address their unpreparedness and consult the government and Armed Forces to see what would be required of them when war became a reality.

This is important because the Roman Catholic bishops of Ontario met quickly, on 12 September, and nominated the Bishop of Pembroke (Ontario),

---

[7] This would harken back to the British Empire's declaration of war in 1914 (which included Canada automatically) when Germany invaded Belgium unannounced.

[8] Newfoundland remained a British colony and did not become a province of Canada until 1949. The Maritime Baptist Convention would later become the United Baptist Convention of the Atlantic Provinces to include Newfoundland.

[9] George Edward Levy, *The Baptists of the Maritime Provinces 1753–1946* (Saint John, New Brunswick: Barnes-Hopkins, Limited, Printers and Publishers, 1946). This is the latest and most comprehensive history of the convention.

[10] Hamilton, "'Padres Under Fire,'" 49.

Monseigneur C. Leo Nelligan, as the person they would have as principal chaplain for the Roman Catholic Church in Canada. By 23 September, they had Vatican approval and were ready to present this news to the authorities in Ottawa.[11] Nelligan met with the Minister of Defence, the Honorable Norman McLeod Rogers, on 3 October 1939 and was officially appointed principal chaplain (RC) on 21 October.

The Protestants had to catch up. The Anglican archbishop of Ottawa, John Charles Roper, contacted the then Minister of Defence, the Honorable Ian Alistair MacKenzie, on 8 October. The Reverend J.R. Mutchmore of the United Church also had begun some informal contact and visited officialdom, which seemed equally unprepared.[12] It was this activity that resulted in a memorandum from the Minister of Defence to the offices of the United, Anglican, Presbyterian, and Baptist denominations, soliciting their support for a combined chaplaincy with the overseas forces.

It was out of this muddle that the Ontario/Quebec Baptist Convention, which was the only Baptist convention contacted by the Ottawa authorities because of all this unpreparedness, and their own unawareness of Baptist governance that would cause stress with the Maritime Convention. It was just assumed by both officialdom and the Ontario/Quebec Convention that all communication with Baptists would go through that Central Canada Convention. The Western Baptists capitulated from the beginning but the East was distinctly uncomfortable with this arrangement.[13]

In fact, the Ontario/Quebec committee did not meet for the first time until 24 October, but before that time, on 15 October, the Anglican bishop of the Cariboo diocese, George Anderson Wells, had been appointed principal chaplain for the Protestants.[14] From 15 October to, at least, January 1941, Wells governed all three services: Army, Navy, and Air Force. The Ontario/Quebec Baptists formed their chaplain service committee on 24 October and, like in the Maritimes, already had applicants for a chaplaincy position. This assumed the delicate presumption that they would be the conduit for all Canadian Baptist recommendations to the principal chaplain. This belief would soon cause wonderment and a growing dubiousness amongst the Maritimers, as will be seen below.

---

[11] Ibid., 66.

[12] Ibid., 71.

[13] Ibid. Hamilton succumbed to this understanding throughout his thesis since he had not seen the letters at Acadia. He writes, "The [Baptist] Chaplain Service Committee [of Ontario and Quebec] was formed, with the Rev'd H.H. Bingham serving as chairman. This chaplaincy committee coordinated the Baptist chaplains on behalf of the other Baptist denominations in Canada" (73).

[14] A copy of the minutes of the Baptist meeting in Toronto on 24 October 1939 was sent to the Maritimes and is found in this collection. Letter no. 97.

Protocol for Appointment

As might be expected during the first months of the war, there was some confusion concerning the procedure for applying to be a chaplain within the Canadian armed services, both amongst the committees and the applicants. For the clergy to apply for a chaplaincy position, they required a recommendation from one such a committee, named the "chaplain service committee" of their specific denomination. If the applicant received this, his name would be sent on to the office of the principal chaplain Brigadier General Wells. He would also interview the candidate and decide whether the person was appropriate and met the qualifications. If so, he would recommend the candidate to the armed forces that were requiring a chaplain.

This was a simple system but, remarkably, candidates often were confused, or tried to manipulate the system to their advantage.[15] Even Wells was confused at times about the use of his own authority.[16] Wells could not get it out of his mind that the Ontario/Quebec committee did not speak for all the Baptists in Canada but for just those two provinces, as much as the Upper Canadians desired to do so.[17]

When war was declared, the Maritime United Baptist Convention had just concluded their annual meetings, this time in Woodstock, New Brunswick. The executive committee of the convention decided that something had to be done immediately about chaplaincy and so formed what they termed, "the emergency committee." Like the First World War, no one had any idea of how long the war would last, so it is likely they did not anticipate a five-and-a-half-year conflict. Indeed, the first eight months were termed "the phony war," for the lack of any battle on the Western Front. This ended on 10 May 1940 with the invasion of the Low Countries and concluded with Dunkirk. It became obvious to all that it was not just an "emergency" and the committee conformed with the accepted title, "chaplain service committee."

The executive committee of the Maritime Convention, the president being the Reverend Dr. H.R. Boyer of First Baptist Church, Moncton, New Brunswick,[18] seems to have formed this subcommittee with little consultation outside their own executive ranks. Dr. Boyer accepted the chair of this committee, and

[15] For example, letter no. 242.

[16] For example, letter no. 228.

[17] When Maritimers wish to disparage those in Ontario, they often call them "Upper Canadians." It stems from Ontario originally being named "Upper Canada" before the Confederation in 1867, but the local inference is that they tend to seem "uppity."

[18] Dr. Henry Rosebrook Boyer was highly esteemed by Maritime Baptists. He was granted an honorary Doctor of Divinity degree by Acadia University in 1927. Previously he had been secretary of the convention for many years.

the secretary of convention became its secretary, the Reverend Lemuel Ernest Ackland.[19] They also assumed that the revered Reverend Dr. John Howard MacDonald would accept a position on the committee and, without argument, he would have been extremely helpful. Unfortunately, this was a surprise to him and he had to decline due to his health and age. Not only that, he had become editor of the denominational weekly newspaper, *The Maritime Baptist*, after retiring from his professorship at Acadia University in 1936. He was 76 years of age.[20]

To replace the reluctant MacDonald, Ackland suggested to Dr. Boyer the name of the Reverend Dr. Sheldon Samuel Poole,[21] minister of the prestigious Germain Street United Baptist Church in Saint John, New Brunswick. He had been minister there since 1916, and would remain until his death in January 1950.[22] Boyer agreed.

Much of the committee's business was carried on through the postal service rather than by formal meetings. There were times when other meetings brought the committee members together and so could consult in person. For instance, Dr. Poole, Mr. Ackland, James Layton Ralston (Minister of Defence), and the Reverend E.S. Mason (Superintendent of the Convention Home Mission Board) were all members of the Acadia University Board of Governors at the same time. The Board of Home Mission included Dr. Mason, Dr. Poole, the Reverend L.E. Ackland, the Reverend J. Murray Armstrong (an applicant who was appointed), the Reverend J.B. Wilson (another applicant approved), the Reverend G.W. Guiou (another candidate but failed the medical test), the Reverend E.A. Kinley (enquirer about chaplaincy), and the Reverend S.D. Trites (applicant)—all were well known to each other.

---

[19] Lemuel Ernest Ackland, sometimes called "Lem," but mostly "L.E.," was the "work-horse" of the committee, attending to all the official correspondence of their work (see footnote 2).

[20] See Roger H. Prentice, *The Cardinal,* no. 3 (Wolfville: Acadia Centre for Baptist and Anabaptist Studies, 2016).

[21] Letter no. 124. A manuscript note added by Ackland to a letter by MacDonald sent to Ackland and being forwarded to Boyer on 5 October 1939: "Shall we carry on alone or ask Dr. Poole to join us, and then when we do make our final selection [of candidates] submit the appointees to Dr. MacDonald for his O.K. (*sic*)."

[22] Poole was a Maritimer, born in Yarmouth, Nova Scotia, on 31 December 1874, who was awarded a Bachelor of Arts degree by Acadia University in 1900 and an honorary Doctor of Divinity degree in 1922. He was president of the convention during 1936–1937. See Watson Kirkconnell, *The Acadia Record 1838–1953* (Wolfville, Nova Scotia: Acadia University, 1953) 497; and C.E. Rockingham, ed., *The United Baptist Year Book of the Maritime Provinces of Canada 1937* (Truro, Nova Scotia: News Publishing Co., Ltd., 1937) 8.

Expectations and Qualifications of Chaplains

Chaplains entering the Armed Forces were expected to be of good health, relatively young, and with three years' experience as an ordained minister in a parish. Bishop Wells wrote that "religious," "natural," and "physical" were three characteristics he expected in applicants.[23] The "religious characteristic" was defined as providing "for the spiritual needs of his fellows" so that the army would be strong in faith in God. The "natural characteristic" meant that a chaplain should communicate and relate well with those around, "comrade to all," so they might easily relate. For the "physical characteristic," Wells required candidates to be between the ages of 30 and 50 years, meet the army medical tests like any other officer, and be "cheerful and willing to share the dangers that soldiers are expected to meet."[24] In due course, an application form was devised and circulated with these qualifications stated.[25]

These qualifications would loosen as the demands of the war progressed and the need for more chaplains became obvious. Some were accepted a year or so under 30 years of age and with less than three years of ministerial experience. Bishop Wells informed the Ontario/Quebec committee that home appointments (i.e., within Canada) of senior chaplains might extend to five or six years beyond the age of 50.[26]

At the early stage of recommendations, the committee itself seemed unaware of the age requirement. For example, the Reverend Max DeWolfe was one of the first "chosen" by the committee to approach and invite his application, and his name appears on their next list of "Approved for Recommendation,"[27] but DeWolfe was only 23 years of age, graduated from Acadia in 1939 and ordained in 1940. As it happened, DeWolfe himself declined their invitation. It was 30 April 1941 when DeWolfe decided, at 25, to join either the chaplaincy, if acceptable, or to enlist in the Royal Canadian Air Force (RCAF).[28] He had tired of seeing mothers in his congregations with sons already in the services and knew he had to do something for "King and Country." He received unanimous approval from the committee. Hamilton interviewed an elderly Max DeWolfe on 31 October 1991 and reported that "[...] although too young for the chaplaincy, he volunteered as a civilian worker in the YMCA War Services until he met the age

---

[23] Hamilton, "'Padres Under Fire,'" 86, quoting from Wells' war diary.

[24] Letter no. 172. Ackland wrote to the Reverend L.B. Estabrooks on 8 July 1940 that the committee would make a decision on the qualifications of a chaplain and "[...] whose judgment would take into consideration your age, physique, training, disposition, fitness in many ways [...]." Estabrooks withdrew his application on 11 July 1940 (letter no. 174).

[25] Letter no. 111.

[26] Letter no. 220 (13 February 1940).

[27] Letter no. 53.

[28] Letter no. 29.

qualifications for chaplaincy."[29]

Other applicants had already passed the age termination of 50 years and were not recommended as a result. One minister in Cape Breton was almost desperate to enter as residential chaplain to the famous Cape Breton Highlanders. Stuart Ivison, the secretary to the Ontario/Quebec committee, reported on 8 July 1940, "[...] the department has said that his age would prohibit his going overseas."[30] Several failed the medical test.

Pathetically, there were some students who, probably inspired by thoughts of adventure, also applied, oblivious of the need to be ordained and with three years' ministerial experience. One letter was from a student in Yarmouth County who only had his Grade XII certificate but "[...] was prepared to enter Acadia as a second-year student this fall."[31] Another dear soul from Pubnico, Yarmouth County, Nova Scotia, applied at the age of 61.[32]

Wells also might have held one or two hidden qualifications, as indicated by the application of one Maritime minister who did not pass his approbation. Ivison, as usual, on 2 January 1940, almost gleefully reported to Ackland, "In confidence, I may tell you that Bishop Wells was not at all enthusiastic with [the recommended candidate]; in fact, he told us that he would prefer that we did not recommend [this] appointment."[33] The die, however, was already cast before Ivison could report it. Dr. Poole had already written to Ackland on 13 December 1939, "[The candidate] is the only [Maritime] Committee recommendation [for the position] but [Major] Bland reported: '[...] that [the candidate] has been before the officials and found unacceptable.'"[34]

THE LETTERS

There are 246 letters, notes, and telegrams included in this collection in spite of the archival box reporting 150. Most are one-page long, although a few contain

---

[29] Hamilton, "'Padres Under Fire,'" 118.

[30] Letter no. 176 and 219. Ivison to Ackland (8 July 1940) and Johnston to Ackland (15 February 1940), respectively.

[31] Letter no. 79 (5 October 1939).

[32] Letter no. 82. He enlisted in March 1916 for World War I and proudly reported that he had been in charge of recreation and a reading room at Bramshott Army Camp, England.

[33] Letter no. 143. The candidate was notoriously "conservative" and "evangelical," but the Maritime committee, probably naively, could well have recommended him so no particular theological bias would be detected of the committee by those similar to the candidate's theological stripes. The Maritime Convention had an active right-wing element, especially in New Brunswick.

[34] Letter no. 75. Poole elaborated that chaplaincy applicants need "[...] to be physically, mentally, and morally O.K." He added, "In the last war some were not." Note that Poole neglected the need to be spiritually fit, a cornerstone of Wells' criteria.

more. Some are annotated with handwritten notes: comments or reminders from one member of the committee to another to whom the letter has been circulated. The first letter that appears in the collection was written by the Reverend William Alton White to Mr. Ackland from Middle Sackville, New Brunswick, on 16 December 1939. There is no obvious reason why it appears on top of the others. It is actually the seventieth in chronological order. The first in chronological order was written by the Reverend Robert A. Snelling on 13 September 1939, three days after Canada's declaration of war was signed by King George VI.[35]

Other letters appealing for chaplaincy positions came from clergy situated close to new airfields constructed for the Commonwealth Air Training Plan, such as Penfield, Salisbury and Moncton, New Brunswick, Summerside, Prince Edward Island, and Debert, Nova Scotia. It was the one from the Salisbury area where the applicant suddenly felt called to this particular ministry, so contacted his member of Parliament to twist the arms of the committee members.[36]

Most of the letters do concern applications for a chaplaincy position, and the reasons for doing so vary greatly from the admirable to the tawdry. Others concern administration, a touchy relationship with the Ontario/Quebec committee, and several unique communications. Together, they make up a mosaic of purposes and business of the chaplain service committee.

The letters of enquiry were usually very simple in nature, asking how to apply or suggesting that they would be ready "to serve King and Country."[37] The Reverend A.P. Hunt, serving at the Debert, Nova Scotia, Army Camp, wished to be transferred to the chaplaincy.[38] Interestingly, Hunt wrote his application letters on Knights of Columbus stationery, perhaps a hint of how ecumenical the service chaplains would become. Hunt must have been persuasive, for his colleague, the Reverend J.B. Messenger, also working at the No. 7 Hospital (RCAMC) at the Debert Camp, wrote to say that Hunt, "his associate," informed him that he was

[35] Letter no. 112. Reverend Robert A. Snelling was, at this time, minister at Wilson's Beach, Campobello Island, and was ordained in 1938, which would have made him lacking in ministerial experience. Max DeWolfe, on Grand Manan Island, also in southwestern New Brunswick, mentions in his letter of 13 May 1941 gratitude to the committee for their confidence and recommendation and that Snelling had joined him in "evangelistic work" at North Road, Grand Manan, and, "We are having a good time there." Letter no. 68.

[36] See letter no. 17, 18, and 19.

[37] King George VI and his wife, Queen Elizabeth, made an exceptionally successful tour of Canada in May and June 1939, which bonded the people of Canada even more firmly to the monarch.

[38] Alberne Porter Hunt was born in Nova Scotia in 1910 and was the minister in Guysborough, Nova Scotia, until 1940. His letters were written in January 1941 when he was a corporal in the Royal Canadian Army Medical Corps (RCAMC). He left the medical corps in 1943 to become the minister of the Yarmouth North Baptist Church. After 1945 he became a social worker for Yarmouth County.

applying for a position as a chaplain in the forces, so he thought he would do the same. He esteemed Hunt greatly.[39] Messenger received the coveted position by May.[40]

In the beginning, the committee had selected "the chosen few" to invite their application for a chaplaincy position. One more of these was the Reverend Harry Knight Grimmer, who was highly esteemed by the leaders of the convention. He was a veteran, having served in the Canadian Army Artillery (1916–1919), born in St. Stephen, New Brunswick (where Ackland was serving at the time of the committee), graduated from Acadia in 1923, ordained in 1924, attended Newton Theological Seminary (1923–1924), and was, in 1939, minister of the church in Campbellton, New Brunswick.[41] He replied to the committee's invitation on 7 February 1940 by simply saying, "I feel that I can render a real service in the army and especially since I have already served in the ranks."[42] Grimmer was the ideal candidate with previous war experience, good pastoral service, and often called "a man's man." Newly elected convention president, Dr. R.S. Longley,[43] wrote to Ackland on 29 November 1940 that "[…] even though our ideal Chaplain may be a big man with experience—like Grimmer, if the Lord does not make candidates of that size in all cases, we must use the smaller ones."[44] Writing about a recent committee recommendation, the perceptive Dr. Poole wrote from Saint John on 16 February 1940 about another applicant, "I don't think he would make nearly as good a Chaplain as Harry Grimmer […]."[45]

Some other enquiries were far more demanding on the committee's patience. They even reached the stage of being impolite. An extraordinarily rude series of letters emerged from a minister in rural New Brunswick.[46] An acidic comment was finally made by Dr. Poole: "This urge for a position as Chaplain [from the above candidate] seems to me is becoming something of a Racket! I may be uncharitable but I fear that the salary attached to it has something to do with the

[39] Letter no. 64 (8 January 1941).

[40] Letter no. 65 (Bishop Wells to Rev. L.E. Ackland, 19 May 1941).

[41] Kirkconnell, *The Acadia Record 1838–1953,* 149.

[42] Letter no. 138.

[43] Ronald Stewart Longley, born at Paradise, Nova Scotia, in 1896, graduated with a B.A. from Acadia in 1921; received his Master's and Ph.D. from Harvard in 1924 and 1934, respectively; and became a distinguished professor at Acadia and administrator (Kirkconnell, *The Acadia Record 1838–1953,* 139). Longley was elected president of the convention in August 1940.

[44] Letter no. 166.

[45] Letter no. 169. It might be added that Dr. Grimmer presented the author for ordination in 1969.

[46] See letter no. 61, 81, 169, 176, 199, 200, 201, 202, 203, 204, 206, 209, 210, 220, and 225.

desires of some."[47]

Another vulgar communication came from Cape Breton. The supplicant had heard that the Presbyterian resident chaplain to the Cape Breton Highlanders had retired. He demanded immediate appointment to that position.[48] So anxious to receive this posting, he first applied immediately to the Minister of Defence, the Honorable Norman McLeod Rogers.[49] Rogers only referred him to the principal chaplain, who properly referred him to the Maritime Baptist committee. Ackland replied to the applicant on 16 January 1940.[50] Ackland's tone was cool: "Of course, that order of events [first applying to the Minister of Defence] is hardly the courteous one, but the committee does not hold that little matter against you." Ackland went on to explain that the armed services used "proportional representation" in terms of the numbers of each denomination selected as chaplains, and caustically observed that Cape Breton had few Baptists. Nor did the committee's recommendation guarantee an appointment by the Armed Forces.

In the above fray, the Reverend John A. Johnston, president of the Ontario/Quebec Convention and a member of their similar committee, to whom the applicant had also written, advised him to write to Ackland but added that he would "[...] place your name on file in Ottawa [regardless of the Maritime committee] so that no time will be lost." Undoubtedly, trying to be helpful, Johnston only "stirred the pot" in their relationship with the Maritimers. The applicant, with this letter in hand, immediately sent the Maritime committee a request to forward his own recommendation, as if it were just a formality. The result was that the principal chaplain determined the applicant was too old for appointment. This was confirmed by the ever-alert Ivison on 8 July 1940: "In January, I also received a word from [the applicant] [...] that he has been approved by your committee and consequently his name has been placed with Bishop Wells, though the Department has said his age would prohibit him going overseas."[51] The Maritime committee was far more reticent. Dr. Poole wrote in his usual charming manner:

> I have good reason to think that [the applicant] has no use for me except when he wishes me to use any little influence I may have in his interests [...]. My first impression on reading his letter was that this would be an

[47] Letter no. 7.

[48] Letter no. 212.

[49] Rogers was a Baptist from Amherst, a graduate of Acadia (1919), a Rhodes Scholar, and a professor at Acadia (1922–1927). Many Maritime Baptist ministers, with personal acquaintance, looked to him for favourable consideration. He always passed their appeals to the principal chaplain.

[50] Letter no. 216.

[51] Letter no. 176.

> opportunity to relieve [the applicant's] church on (*sic*) their Minister which I am led to think would not be at all displeasing to them. [...] In your letter to the Minister of Defence I am sure you can write so diplomatically that he will be able to read between the lines.[52]

These letters were beginning to take their toll, at least on Dr. Poole. Upon the reverse of this letter, Poole wrote whimsically, "If this Chaplaincy business gives us such a headache what must be the condition of the men who have to assume REAL responsibility with regard to the war? Poole."

Other applicants attempted to use the name of the Reverend John Howard MacDonald to support their claim. The Reverend J.B. Wilson, one of "the chosen," was one who was not so manipulative.[53] He had spoken to MacDonald about the chaplaincy and assumed that was all he had to do. The Reverend Stuart Trites of Tryon, Prince Edward Island, admitted to doing the same in a note to Ackland.[54] The Reverend G. Wilfred Fletcher also wrote to MacDonald enquiring about qualifications for the chaplaincy service.[55]

Why the Reverend Dr. (Lieut. Col.) John Howard MacDonald, F.R.G.S., C.B.E., was so often canvassed for his approval was because of the high respect he had attained among so many Maritime Baptists and beyond. He was, at that time, editor of the denominational weekly newspaper, *The Maritime Baptist*, an office that he held twice (1914–1917; 1936–1942). He had been minister of large and influential congregations in Nova Scotia and New Brunswick, president of the Baptist Convention (1920–1921), deputy director of the Canadian Armed Forces Chaplaincy in London (1917–1919),[56] and professor of Church History at Acadia University (1923–1936).[57] It is no wonder that former students, colleagues, and acquaintances sought his approval and that the convention executive wanted him on their chaplaincy committee.[58]

On the other hand, as Poole noted in one letter, other motives were worldlier. One poor clergyman from rural Pictou County, Nova Scotia, wrote at length of the illness of his wife for over a year, spending many months in the hospital

---

[52] Letter no. 214.

[53] Letter no. 44.

[54] Letter no. 89. "As a matter of fact I wrote Dr. MacDonald the day after war was declared asking his advice [...]."

[55] Letter no. 110. Fletcher was a graduate of Acadia in 1933, so undoubtedly knew MacDonald personally, but had been ministering for a number of years in Readsboro, Vermont, at the time. The Maritime committee stuck strictly to those living in the three Maritime Provinces for their selections.

[56] MacDonald stayed on into 1919 to assist with demobilization.

[57] Prentice, *The Cardinal.*

[58] In this collection of correspondence, thirty-one either were written by MacDonald or mentioned by others.

and unable to do her housework, preventing him from his Gospel ministry. His salary was so low that they could not afford "a girl" to help out, and he sought a chaplaincy position to relieve him of his financial burden. He pleaded, "I hope you will give your cooperation in this matter because I am desperately in need."[59]

The Reverend Arlington Edgar Wry of Newcastle, New Brunswick, was another who was willing to enter the chaplaincy of either the Army, Navy, or Air Force, "either overseas or home duty."[60] It was no wonder why so many, particularly rural clergy, wished a position. The Great Depression was plaguing them all through the 1930s. Salaries were abysmal for ministers of Baptist churches, and often the naively ideal hopes of former theological student life turned out to be a mirage in the face of the hard treatment they received from troubled congregations.

Finally, there were some applicants who could not decide whether the chaplaincy was suitable to their ministry. Max DeWolfe was one, who first declined the invitation of the committee, and a year later changed his mind and let his name stand.[61] The committee enthusiastically endorsed him. On 6 May 1941 Dr. Longley, then chair of the committee (and president of the convention) wrote that he agreed with Ackland and Poole that DeWolfe should be recommended without hesitation, "[...] provided his age and experience were clearly stated."[62]

Another indecisive person, another of "the chosen," wrote before 19 October 1939, when he was invited to submit an application, stating that he could not decide. He even summoned a meeting of his important men in the congregation to discuss it. He did not want to be seen as a coward, but the work in his congregation was just beginning to be successful and he was not certain he should leave them.[63]

The Upper Canada Affair

One of the more interesting glimpses that these letters reveal is a growing tension between the committees of the Maritimes and the Ontario/Quebec Convention during these first two years of the war. Understanding that the Maritime Baptist Convention is the oldest of the three (at that time) Canadian Baptist conventions, and the oldest part, historically, in the country, it was also the largest

[59] Letter no. 23. Apparently the applicant had written directly to the Minister of Defence (James Layton Ralston) and it had been passed on to the principal chaplain. His office had replied to him on 5 March 1941, mentioning the applicant's letter of 20 February.

[60] Letter no. 27.

[61] Letter no. 29, 33, and 68.

[62] Letter no. 108. By this time, DeWolfe was 25 with two years of pastoral experience.

[63] Letter no. 93. Oddly, not long after, this man accepted the call of a large, prestigious congregation elsewhere in the Maritimes.

group of churches in a "convention." Also, it should be remembered that Acadia University is the oldest Baptist institution of higher learning in Canada. This long story of existence, size, and academic prowess has allowed the Maritime Baptists a sense of religious security and acceptance within their society.

Another important note of understanding is the fact that, during the two years over which these letters span, there were two ministers of national defence under which the chaplain service served: Norman McLeod Rogers and James Layton Ralston.[64] It is a historical oddity that both of these men grew up in Amherst, Nova Scotia, and were members of First Baptist Church. Incidentally, they knew well Dr. John Howard MacDonald, who was a minister at their church as an assistant (1892–1893) and then minister (1896–1899). Later, MacDonald was minister of Wolfville Baptist Church (1919–1923) and a member of the Board of Governors of Acadia University when Norman McLeod Rogers was a student at Acadia and James Layton Ralston was a member of the board. Both Rogers and MacDonald were on the faculty of Acadia in the 1920s. This connection should not be forgotten.

This is the situation when the "emergency committee," later known as the Chaplain Service Committee of the Maritime Baptists, began to receive epistles from their parallel committee in Ontario and Quebec. The most persistent letters were penned by the Reverend Stuart Ivison, the secretary of the Ontario/Quebec committee.[65] Through their letters it became clear that the Ontario/Quebec clergy assumed they possessed a special mission for all Canadian Baptists regarding the Armed Forces' chaplaincy services. Their correspondence via Mr. Ivison seemed to radiate this opinion. One such example is when Ivison reported "[…] on the work we have been doing on your behalf here at Ottawa." In the same letter, he lectures the Maritimers on how appointments should be made, offers critical comments about one of the Maritime recommendations, and urges that they should "[…] look further among your ministers for a man whom might fill a senior post."[66]

In all, there are nineteen letters that either Ivison wrote to the committee, the committee wrote to Ivison (rare), or where he was mentioned in a text. It might not be unfair to describe Ivison's letter to the East as ingratiating and, to some, almost imperialistic. On one occasion, in a letter dated 14 October 1940, Dr. Poole mentions that Dr. Ernest S. Mason, who would succeed Dr. Longley

---

[64] At the outbreak of the war on 10 September 1939, the Minister of National Defence was the Honorable Ian Alistair MacKenzie, but he was moved to another department almost immediately, replaced by Rogers. Upon his untimely death, Rogers was succeeded by Ralston.

[65] Ivison was also the minister of the august First Baptist Church, Ottawa, the nation's capital. This geographical position would offer a presumed importance to the Ontario/Quebec committee.

[66] Letter no. 143.

as convention president, had received a letter from Stuart Ivison (Ottawa), and "[...] he practically refused to meet us on Friday night of last week."[67]

This situation with the Ontario/Quebec committee came about because of the unpreparedness of Canada and the churches for another war. The "war to end all war" didn't. It was a former Methodist minister, J.S. Woodsworth, who cast the sole vote in the Canadian Parliament against the declaration of war in 1939. Others did an about-face from their interwar pacifist positions, including the Baptists.

In his dismay over a new war, the Presbyterian moderator, Dr. Stuart C. Parker, began thinking about a restoration of the Armed Forces' chaplaincies.[68] The Roman Catholics were not far behind. Bishop Leo C. Nelligan, of Pembroke, Ontario, was selected by the Ontario bishops to be their leader.[69] Finally, the "Big Four" Protestant denominations met together at the instigation of the United Church.[70]

Hamilton, in his 2003 thesis, is wrong when he cites that the Baptists were very late in organizing for such a chaplaincy for the Armed Forces. In fact, the Maritime Convention Executive quickly established an "emergency committee" to initiate discussions about such a project. On 26 September 1939, Dr. MacDonald, the former deputy director, wrote to Dr. Boyer, the convention president, to say that the convention "pursued a wise course" in forming the "emergency committee."[71]

Hamilton fell into the trap by believing that the Ontario/Quebec group represented all Canadian Baptists: "Because [...] of Baptist congregational policy, it is not surprising that the [Baptist] Chaplain Service Committee failed to meet until 24 October." His reference is to the Baptist Convention of Ontario and Quebec (BCOQ) yearbook.[72] Unaware that the Maritime committee's correspondence lurked deep within the archives of Acadia University, Hamilton could not know of the letter written on 25 September 1939 by the Reverend Dr. J.A. Johnston, President of the Baptist Convention of Ontario and Quebec, to the Reverend Dr. H.R. Boyer, then president of the United Baptist Convention of the Maritime Provinces, raising the question of united cooperation of their two committees.[73]

Johnston's letter also informs Boyer that he had written to former Minister

---

[67] Letter no. 137. In this same letter, Poole informs Ackland that Harry Grimmer was going overseas with the First Division, "[...] a very great honour."

[68] Hamilton, "'Padres Under Fire,'" 58.

[69] Ibid., 65–66.

[70] Ibid. See especially, chapter 2, "Creating the Service," 38–79.

[71] Letter no. 113.

[72] Hamilton, "'Padres Under Fire,'" 74–75.

[73] Letter no. 118.

of Defence Ian Alistair MacKenzie regarding a possible chaplaincy programme for the Armed Forces and that he had names of clergy willing to volunteer. He also asked Boyer if the Maritimers had taken any action about this matter. Johnston then made a proposition that hid behind his question: "Would it be wise for us to make united representation? [...] I think it would be a fine thing if we attended to this matter unitedly (*sic*). Such united action would put us on a level with the other major denominations."

This letter was circulated among the Maritime committee, notably including J.H. MacDonald. It did not take long for MacDonald to respond. On 2 October 1939, he wrote to Dr. Boyer, "[...] I think the idea of linking us with Ontario and Quebec a good one for it may help the Baptists of Canada to be fairly represented so far as numbers are concerned in the chaplain services. In the last War we were not represented in proportion to our population and to the number of troops we sent to the field."[74]

A second letter arrived from Dr. Johnston, written on 19 October 1939, which was prior to the Ontario/Quebec Baptists' first committee meeting on 24 October.[75] In it he described how Bishop Wells was appointed "Senior Chaplain" for "Protestant bodies." He went on to relate how the Ontario and Quebec Convention was "[...] consulted with regards to this appointment and on your behalf as well on that of the Baptist Union of Western Canada, approved it most heartily. As soon as the first meeting with the Chaplain General is over, I shall write or wire you so that you will be fully conversant with what is required." It is difficult not to recognize the tone of condescension in Johnston's words, intended or not.

Without a doubt, this would not have been the type of cooperation that MacDonald expected. The Maritime committee was not slow in acting and soon directed their list of approved names for chaplaincy positions directly to the Honorable Norman McLeod Rogers on 26 October. The minister replied directly to Mr. Ackland on 30 October 1939, "In reply to your kind letter of October 26th, in which you forward certain names [...]," and informed Ackland of the protocols for recommending candidates through the newly appointed principal chaplain, Wells.[76] Significantly, no mention was made of the Ontario/Quebec committee.

Along with this, the Maritimers had to consider another epistle from Mr. Ivison of the 20th.[77] Ivison apparently saw himself as organizing the Baptists across Canada. He requested a Maritime Baptist yearbook, "[...] giving names and addresses of all your ministers." He went on to say that he had met with the

---

[74] Letter no. 114.

[75] Letter no. 91.

[76] Letter no. 54.

[77] Letter no. 40.

"Protestant Chaplain Services Director General," adding that he was able to provide Bishop Wells with the yearbooks of the Ontario/Quebec Convention and the Baptist Union of Western Canada, adding somewhat caustically that he was unable to supply "[…] him with the yearbook of the maritime provinces (*sic*). I would suggest that you send him a copy of your latest edition as soon as possible." Likely, the receivers—reading this rather sly, commanding tone—would have noted the lack of capitalization for "maritime provinces," a customary politeness. One can imagine the raised Maritime eyebrows.

At least, the local New Brunswick Command Chaplain in Saint John, Major H. Stanley Bland, was getting the point as mentioned by Dr. Poole to Mr. Ackland on 26 November 1940: "[Bland] makes this request [of an applicant], recognizing fully that our Committee is quite independent of the Committee in Ontario, but he has difficulty in making Wells understand that." He goes on, in careful Maritime style, in suggesting that Ackland concede the point and let the authorities consult the Ontario/Quebec people about their recommendation, "[…] but if it will get quick action we can afford to be generous in this case."[78]

Another letter arrived from Mr. Ivison on 13 December 1940 describing Baptist appointments of Maritime ministers almost in terms as if the Maritimers did not know their own men. For instance, Ivison reported that the Reverend Harvey Denton "[…] has declined the opportunity to serve with the Naval Forces, due to his having recently accepted a call to First [Baptist] Church, Halifax." The Maritimers were well acquainted with Denton and his decision. Ivison goes on to other possible appointees, where they live and their situations. All of them had been in previous close contact with the Maritime committee.[79]

The New Year arrived with yet another correspondence from Ivison. Written on 2 January 1940, Ivison reported to the Maritimers of the work "we have been doing on your behalf here in Ottawa." He went on, "We hope that a senior chaplaincy would go to Mr. Guiou of Nova Scotia[80] but he was not able to pass the physical test. This meant that a man from Ontario has been placed with the Second [Army] Division." No doubt more Maritime eyebrows were raised. Ivison continued his very free advising of the Maritimers about whom their next recom-

---

[78] Letter no. 158.

[79] Letter no. 60. Ivison mentions Denton, Armstrong, and Baker. Harvey Denton, eminent minister at Charlottetown, was one of the candidates asked by the committee to submit his name as a candidate, one of "the chosen." J. Murray Armstrong was another selected by the committee and asked to apply. Lorne Baker of Annapolis Royal had been in continuous contact with the committee about joining the RCAF, the chaplaincy or otherwise.

[80] Letter no. 143. In fact, Gerald Wallace Guiou was born on 3 August 1894 at Ottawa, his family prominent members of McPhail Baptist Church. MacDonald, once minister there (1913–1914), was a family friend.

mendation should be, and that, in confidence, was another Maritime recommendation found wanting by Bishop Wells. The committee already knew.

It continued. On 10 July 1940, Dr. Poole wrote to Ackland relating, "Was talking with Major Bland on Sunday and he has told me that Bishop Wells still thinks that recommendations must come from the Committee of which Bingham is Chairman and Ivison Secretary. He has written to the Bishop that that Committee has nothing to do with Maritime Baptists."[81]

More was to come from the typewriter of Mr. Ivison.

The Maritime committee, by happenstance, was having a difficult time with a Baptist minister at Sydney, Nova Scotia. This minister desperately wanted to become a resident part-time chaplain to the Cape Breton Highlanders, an elite regiment.[82] The minister did not seem to recognize that the regiment would be transferred overseas in the not too distant future and taking their chaplains with them. There was much writing to and fro but it became obvious that the minister was trying unethical tactics to get his own way. He attempted to "pull strings," bypass authority, and use rude arguments and accusations.[83]

Unfortunately, it was this case that erupted into a quarrel with the principal chaplain and C.E. Rockingham, Command Chaplain of the RCAF in Halifax, and a "prize appointment" of the Maritime Baptist committee, and exasperated the situation with the Ontario/Quebec committee. To solve the problem with the Sydney minister, Rockingham wrote directly to the Minister of National Defence, Norman McLeod Rogers. Rogers, of course, was well known to Rockingham through the Baptist community in the Maritimes. Quite rightly, Rogers immediately passed Rockingham's letter on to Bishop Wells. In effect, Rockingham had passed over the head of the principal chaplain, who considered this action "insubordination." This prompted Mr. Ivison to write a scolding letter to the Sydney applicant. It was an indiscreet letter that chastised the applicant's tactics, but added:

> [...] but I do know that Squadron Leader Rockingham made the fatal mistake of writing directly to the minister about the part time position you mention, and went so far to say that he did not consider himself

---

[81] Letter 173. Commenting about a stalling of another Maritime recommendation, Harry Grimmer, Poole comments, "Certainly we have never been consulted about it."

[82] The 48th Highland Regiment. It moved to Toronto on 8 October 1939 and left Halifax for overseas in the latter part of December. *Dileas gu brath* is its Gaelic motto: "Faithful Forever."

[83] Letter no. 33: Dr. Poole wrote to Mr. Ackland (3 May 1941), "[The minister] of Sydney tries to stir up something in Convention, over not receiving the chaplaincy position." Letter no. 35: Command Chaplain of Nova Scotia, C.E. Rockingham (a Baptist) wrote on 28 April 1941, "I am more and more convinced that [the applicant] is showing himself unworthy of any consideration in this respect, and must resist any effort on his part to force my hand."

> responsible to the Principal Chaplain. As this amounts to insubordination it will be a wonder if he will be able to hold his commission as a result. I would not tolerate for a moment such action as Mr. Rockingham followed, and if I were the Principal Chaplain, I would dismiss him at once. [...] I fear our man down there has let the whole denomination down.[84]

This appalling lack of discretion on the part of Ivison could result only in a breakdown of mutual trust between the two committees. Sparing no pains in saying what he thought should happen to Rockingham, who was an appointment from the Maritimes and not Central Canada, to another applicant in the East (the difficult Sydney minister), is almost unpardonable. It certainly caused confusion within the Maritime committee's ranks. It also elicited a long, confidential letter from Rockingham explaining the situation to his friend, Ackland. He found himself in what he termed, "a mess."[85]

Rockingham reported that it was not as serious as it seemed in the beginning. It all revolved around the subject of whether Bishop Wells had, at that point, any jurisdiction over the RCAF once a chaplain was appointed. When he reported for duty, Rockingham was told that he was responsible to the Air Officer Commanding alone and reported only to that officer. Since Rockingham's Officer Commanding sought clarification from the Department of National Defence and no answer had been given, this was the cause of the confusion. It was at this point that the applicant in Sydney showed Rockingham a letter from Norman McLeod Rogers stating that the General Office Commanding had the power to appoint part-time chaplains (which the Sydney applicant gleefully wished). Rockingham, still desiring confirmation, " [...] wrote to Norman Rogers as a Baptist and friend, asking if the Air Officer Commanding had the same authority. Just at that time, Mr. [Charles Gavan ("Chubby")] Power was appointed Minister of National Defence for Air, and my letter was passed on to him, and he passed it to Bishop Wells." That is when the fur began to fly. Bishop Wells was eventually chastised for writing directly to Rockingham on a matter of procedure and discipline, for Wells should have directed his letter of admonishment to the Adjutant Officer Commanding. As it turned out, the RCAF Adjutant in Halifax saw all the correspondence and heard the whole story from Rockingham and approved Rockingham's correspondence to Bishop Wells. Rockingham concluded his letter to Ackland by saying, "In his last letter to me, Bishop Wells has considerably softened in his attitude to me." Rockingham was off the hook.

Ivison's letter to the Sydney applicant was totally out of order. Not only that,

---

[84] Letter no. 38. Ivison continued to contribute more of his thoughts: "We are taking pains to see that the various Baptist groups from coast to coast are represented."

[85] Letter no. 208.

on 20 June 1940 Ivison wrote Ackland a long letter, the second part about the Rockingham situation. Ivison began to slip any responsibility onto the Maritime committee's shoulders when beginning, "[...] a difficulty has arisen regarding Honorary Squadron Leader the Reverend C.E. Rockingham, who was recommended by you for the Command Chaplaincy in the Air Force at Halifax."[86] He continued, "He has aroused the anger of the Principal Chaplain, and I am bound to admit, justifiably, by writing directly to the Minister regarding his work, instead of Bishop Wells." Then came the real point: "This has caused us a great deal of concern, as we worked hard to secure this senior appointment for a Maritime representative [...]." Then, the sermon:

> You can do your man a service by impressing upon them (*sic*) very strongly that Lieutenant Colonel Wells is Principal Chaplain of the Protestant section of the *Army*, the *Navy*, and *Air Force*, that he was placed in this present position with the approval of all the Denominations in Canada at the beginning of the war, and that any man writing to the Department regarding Chaplaincy business is making a grave mistake to write to anyone else.

Of course, the Maritime Baptists, an independent denomination, were not consulted in giving Bishop Wells the position he held.

The letters end in September 1941 when Mr. Ackland moves to Shelburne, but it would be interesting to know how the relationship with the Upper Canadians continued to the end of the war. Rockingham, for one, is transferred overseas.[87]

The Sidey Affair

A serious crisis occurred in the 1930s for the Maritime Baptist Convention. English-born fundamentalist preacher, the Reverend J.J. Sidey, challenged the convention on testy theological issues and caused a major disturbance in the Maritime theological teapot. He had many followers, but when it came to stepping out of the convention, a number of his supporters could not follow in his direction. In the end, Sidey pulled several congregations away from the convention in a dispute that eventually landed in the Nova Scotia courts. It came to a head in 1933. Sidey eventually established a Bible school in Kingston, Nova Scotia, but it did not grow as he expected. Nonetheless, Mr. Sidey, probably looking for

[86] Letter no. 244. He made no reference to the Ontario/Quebec committee, which also approved Rockingham.

[87] Rev. L.H. Crandall, ed., *United Baptist Year Book of the Maritime Provinces 1943* (St. John, New Brunswick: Barnes & Co., Ltd., Printers and Publishers, 1943) 305.

recognition by someone, began approaches to any who would accredit his ministers, more importantly including himself, so they would be acceptable as Armed Forces' chaplains. This, too, wound its way to the Ontario/Quebec committee and became a cause for confusion.

John J. Sidey first wrote to the Ontario/Quebec committee requesting recommendations to the chaplaincy programme, obviously attempting to avoid his recent protagonists.[88] Ivison was totally ignorant of the Sidey issues with the Maritime Convention, which is definitely curious because of all the publicity given to the court cases by the Baptist and secular media, and the rapid Baptist world of "word-of-mouth" information delivery. This prompted Ivison to write a letter to Ackland about the whole issue. Ivison connected Sidey's minor schism with their own major split of their convention over a dispute with Dr. T.T. Shields.[89] He thus asked Ackland his opinion " [...] as to whether we would be justified in sending in this man's name as a properly accredited Baptist nominee." There is no record of Ackland's response to this particularly distasteful proposition.

The first direct contact the Maritimers received of Sidey's desires was a letter Mr. Ackland received from Sidey himself, written on 15 October 1940.[90] An indication of the tactics manipulated by Mr. Sidey was immediately revealed. Sidey approached the Ontario/Quebec committee first. They were quick to refer him to the Maritime committee, no doubt to his chagrin. The Upper Canadians went on to inform him, he said, "[...] that in this matter of the approving of men for appointment to the Chaplain's (*sic*) Corps the Chaplaincy Service Committee in the Maritime Convention is supposed to have a working arrangement with the Regular Baptists and the Independent Baptists, following the precedent of the Baptist Convention of Ontario and Quebec." The eyes of the Maritime committee must have popped at this news.

Sidey had no intention of being held up by his former foes. "As Convenor of the Committee on this matter for the Independent Baptists of Nova Scotia, I am writing you for information re the position of your Committee and asking what arrangements you suggest for the proper accrediting of our men desiring to serve as Chaplains." Poole was quick to send this missal to Ackland, adding a typed note that it required "careful consideration. [...] If one followed his inclinations he would tell the gentleman to 'go to blazes.' We certainly can't put our imprimatur on any of his men."[91]

Ackland was not slow in acknowledging Sidey's letter and wrote to him on

---

[88] Letter no. 244.

[89] Leslie K. Tarr, *Shields of Canada: T.T. Shields (1873–1955)* (Grand Rapids MI: Barker House, 1967).

[90] Letter no. 144.

[91] Letter no. 144. A typed annotation appears at the bottom of the letter by Poole.

17 October. It was diplomatic in the extreme.

> There is no desire on the part of our Committee to exclude any man of any religious body from any form of service he may be able to render to the British Empire or the Kingdom of God; but as the Independent Baptists and the International Christian Mission are an organized body, we feel that we are no more in a position to pass judgment on the fitness of the Ministers of the United Church, the Anglican Church, or any other body. To do so would undoubtedly give rise to complaints that authority has been assumed where none exists.[92]

One wonders what Ivison would have thought about this answer.

There is a hint in Ivison's reply to Sidey, written on 30 October 1940.[93] After saying that none would be recommended unless they had the approbation of their local groups, he went on in a self-satisfied way, "Here in Ontario and Quebec, our Convention Committee has made a very satisfactory arrangement with the Independent Baptists and the Regular Baptists led by Dr. Shields, so that all Baptists work together." Ivison goes on recommending that Sidey work out an agreement with the Maritime committee, "[...] and the work would thus be unified." He obviously was unaware of the critical issues and rupture between Sidey and the Maritime Convention.

Ackland replied to Sidey in his letter of 30 October that terminated the discussion. Ackland's final comment was, "Your own personal application for a chaplaincy as evident from that correspondence was made thro Mr. Ivison not thro our Committee."[94] Ackland's continual responses to Sidey may have been "polite" but might indicate a note of insecurity in dealing with Sidey's brashness.[95]

It was Ivison's turn to make a final comment on 12 December 1940.[96] Apparently Mr. Sidey had sent the whole file of correspondence to Ivison and he brought it to the whole Ontario/Quebec committee. "I laid everything before the Committee, and they answered No!" This was the Maritimers' answer as well, so Mr. Sidey remained at home, but it illustrates the beginning of some stress between the committees—and especially how unaware the Ontario/Quebec committee was of the Maritime situation and society.[97]

---

[92] Letter 146. In regards to Ackland's letter to Sidey, Dr. R.S. Longley wrote to Ackland on 20 October 1940, saying that he spoke to both Dr. MacDonald and Dr. H.T. ("Toddy") DeWolfe and all agreed that Ackland's letter was appropriate and that the Independent Baptists were indeed a separate body.

[93] Letter no. 147.

[94] Letter no. 149.

[95] Letter no. 148. Longley would have preferred to answer Sidey with silence.

[96] Letter no. 161.

[97] George Levy's exhaustive history of the Maritime Convention completely omits any reference to the Sidey controversy.

EVALUATION OF THE COLLECTION

Evaluating the letters of this collection unfolds a number of issues that faced the Baptist denomination in the Maritime Provinces of Canada. It is obvious that the Baptists were not prepared for the eventuality of another world war. It seems that they had been asleep, at least ecclesiastically, to what was happening in the world for the past number of years. Mussolini was in power in Italy and there was the Ethiopian crisis. Hitler had gained power and there was the occupation of the Rhineland, the Munich debacle and the occupation of Czechoslovakia. Then came Poland.

It is true that Canada was living in its own "bubble" with the Great Depression taking much of the nation's energy and attention. Nonetheless, one might expect that the thoughtful Christians would have had an eye to the East and quietly started some preparations "just in case." The letters show that no previous thought had been given to the need for chaplains during an approaching and dangerous conflict. The letters indicate that no consideration had been given to which clergy in their Baptist ranks could make good chaplains. In its selections, the chaplain service committee was only partially successful: some were accepted, some were unsuccessful, some withdrew, and some took up other causes. They were not prepared, either, for the rush of unsuitable clergy who lacked the personal insight for such a ministry. One would have thought that their experience during the Great War would have shown the need for training to meet serious conflict situations.

Not only was the leadership of the denomination's chaplain service committee unprepared, but it also was amateurish in their first two years, at least, in seeking suitable clergy as chaplains. Their organization, so quickly formed after the declaration of war on 10 September 1939, showed great inefficiencies. One of the members they thought to appoint to the committee, Dr. MacDonald, was added without consulting him even though he was 76 years of age and with declining health. For much of the time, the committee was made up only of New Brunswick clergy. As a result, their focus was often on Saint John, Fredericton, Moncton, and New Brunswick clergy, the latter who were the source of much of the committee's correspondence. This was efficient but it narrowed their focus.

Early letters show that there was a lack of communication and publicity with the churches and potential applicants. As a result, many did not know where they should apply or guessed wrong portals for their applications. Some applied to the Minister of National Defence himself, others to commanding officers, the principal chaplain, or to other denominational leaders. There was no Baptist consultative office, so many sought advice from their only known source, Dr. J.H. MacDonald. It could be wondered why there were no advertisements in *The Maritime Baptist* or even provincial secular papers.

There was no infrastructure for the committee: a paid secretary, for instance. The convention could have easily afforded this to ease the workload of the members of the committee who were all volunteers with their other full-time duties to perform. L.E. Ackland, for example, was the minister of the Union Street United Baptist Church in St. Stephen, New Brunswick. It is no wonder that communication was sometimes very meagre. No doubt Ackland did not have the time or, perhaps, the energy to deal with so much correspondence and its consequences. For example, the Reverend J.B. Wilson wrote on 9 November 1939 that he had not heard a word since his offer to the committee. In fact, he wondered why he had been "passed by."[98] He wasn't. Wilson was one of the select clergy of the committee in the beginning, and he should have had regular contact with their decisions regarding his application that they had sponsored. It is understandable how taxing it was for the members of the committee to meet the needs of their own congregation as well as maintain all the meetings and correspondence of the committee and the convention. Then there were the demanding situations such as that of the Sydney minister, the Rockingham difficulty, the Sidey application, and the overshadowing by the Ontario/Quebec committee.

The relationship with the Ontario and Quebec committee was particularly delicate. There was every reason for not having a schism with the Baptists of that area of the country. As the letters indicate, there was a willingness to cooperate but, more and more, the imperialistic attitude of the Upper Canada committee, notably expressed by its unfortunate secretary, the Maritimer hearts and minds were hardened into the direction of declaring "independence." On the other side of the same coin, the Maritimers had a struggle to convey to an Anglican bishop who was the principal chaplain that there were three main and independent bodies of Baptists in Canada. They were used to acting independently, but fraternally, but not with one of them dominant. To complicate matters, it almost seemed as if the Ontario/Quebec crowd wished to be the controlling committee for all Baptists of Canada.

These letters show how close the Maritime Convention was among its member clergy. Most knew many, if not all, of those in their clergy ranks. The Maritime Convention had not split asunder with Sidey, as the Ontario/Quebec Convention did with T.T. Shields in 1927. In fact, the Maritime Convention was a union of two Baptist denominations, the Regular (Calvinistic) Baptists and the Free Will (Armenian) Baptists, that took place over 1905/1906. When Ivison was declaring that their committee was also including the Regular Baptists of Ontario, it could be argued that the Maritimes already had the Regular Baptists under their convention umbrella.[99]

---

[98] Letter no. 44.
[99] Letter no. 244.

Acadia University was another unifying force where most of the Maritime clergy received part, if not all, of their education. The professors were often Baptist clergy themselves and the atmosphere of Acadia was well known for its intimate and friendly nature between student and faculty. All presidents up to that time were Baptist ministers. In 1939, the president was the long-serving and much-beloved Reverend Dr. F.W. Patterson (president from 1923–1948). The convention was well organized so that the annual meetings were more like a family reunion than a conference meeting. This close fellowship, not without its theological disagreements but with a greater loyalty to the convention itself, maintained their inheritance of the joyous union in 1905/1906. This can be seen by the diplomatic and sensitive replies that the committee sent to their most cantankerous or devious correspondents.

On the other hand, these letters show the variety of clergy who were serving the convention churches at that time. There were those who had served as regular troops in World War I—some decorated for bravery and service. When applying, these men were well aware of the dangers and stresses involved by serving overseas and on the battlefield. Other applicants were a generous and even an idealistic lot who offered to serve in any possible way. Some of them were very young or even Licentiates just out of high school.[100] There were other motivations, too, sometimes blatantly obvious. There were applicants who were self-serving, like the man at Sydney, or self-interested, such as the applicant from Albert County, New Brunswick.[101] Pathetic cases revealed the nasty part of ministry where one is so poorly paid that illness can bankrupt a family, such as the one in River John, Nova Scotia. Finally, it may be surprising to discover clergy who could be very rude not only to the committee but also to the principal chaplain.[102]

The Maritime Baptists had one "ace up their sleeve," and that was the Reverend Dr. John Howard MacDonald. MacDonald was modest but adept, intelligent and compassionate, able and generous. He wielded power with an articulate pen but was always kind and gracious. His experiences enabled him, through his pastoral ministry, to know many members of the congregations of the convention. He had immense battle experience in the trenches of World War I and rose to become deputy director of the whole chaplaincy overseas. He became friends as well as a mentor to hosts of students when a professor at Acadia. This also meant that he had fresh knowledge of students of that era who were just at the right age to enlist into the chaplaincy by 1939. His help was subtle but of great assistance to the committee at strategic occasions. One can also imagine that many private conversations were held with Dr. MacDonald that were not recorded, as well.

---

[100] For example, letter no. 79.

[101] Letter no. 61, 81, 169, 176, 199, 200, 201, 202, 203, 204, 206, 209, 210, 220, and 225.

[102] See comments in letter no. 239 and 240.

Sadly, this collection contains only the first twenty-four months of the committee's deliberations and action. Nonetheless, it offers the reader of these letters a glimpse of their mandate and considerations at their formative stage of the chaplaincy organization. One can identify the beginning of the maturing of their outlook, which reveals the working machinery that the committee developed in the process of forwarding recommendations to the armed services of people who might become chaplains.

CONCLUSIONS

The chaplain service committee became an influential part of Baptist life at the outbreak of World War II. Its importance lay in the committee's role of placing clergy within the services to minister to the Armed Forces personnel under extremely difficult situations: away from their homes and loved ones; living in new cultures and surroundings, absent from normal social conditions in a completely male environment; entering battle conditions on land, air, and sea; suffering unexpected and traumatic wounds; under strict discipline abnormal from their usual lives at home; and encountering others with extreme injuries and death. There was a lot of room for chaplains to serve faithfully and imaginatively in their special ministry.

The committee members had their own concerns. They were ministers serving large congregations at home. This meant that they faced and comforted families whose young were leaving to join the forces, experiencing the anxiety of realizing that their young people were sometimes in action against a determined enemy. They had to go to the homes of the bereaved to offer comfort when the dreaded telegram arrived at a parent's front door. This, along with their normal functions of ministry, filled each moment of their day and meant that their duties on the committee could only bring more stress,[103] sometimes-unearned abuse, as they struggled to find competent candidates for a difficult chaplaincy beyond the Atlantic shores. Each one also had an even larger responsibility with the executive of the convention itself, another daunting responsibility. They should be admired for their tenacity, wisdom, and tact in governing this committee for the Armed Forces' chaplains. It is remarkable that the members of the committee were able to maintain their sensibilities and even humour during this period of national emergency.

These extraordinary letters the committee received demonstrate that denominations should plan ahead for national eventualities. The Canadian armed forces abolished the regular full-time chaplaincy in 1921. It would have been much more wise for the authorities of church and state to evaluate the competence and use of chaplains in World War I, maintain even a "skeleton chaplaincy" so

[103] For example, letter no. 206 of 6 March 1940. Poole reacted in letter no. 207.

that both the armed forces and the churches would not have to begin from scratch once more in 1939, using up important time and enduring the initial confusion.

When the new war began, all the church denominations, including the Baptists, were unprepared and did not understand the demands that were to be placed on them, especially identifying, recruiting, and recommending adequate clergy for the needs of the Armed Forces.

The letters also reveal the need for quick and reliable information.[104] Applicants, after their initial contact, sometimes felt a lack of information about how their application was being received, how appointments were being made,[105] and who the committee was recommending. There were enquiries sent to the committee about how one applied for a position, or from those who had previously, out of ignorance, applied in the wrong place. There was administrative confusion because the Ontario/Quebec Convention acted on its own without consultation, especially without the largest convention located in the Maritimes.

There was the lack of a secure line of communication among the Baptists themselves and also with the principal chaplain's office. This was partly due to the short-circuiting of the communication by the Ontario group and partly by a lack of understanding by the principal chaplain of Baptist congregationalism.

The committee itself might have resolved some of these difficulties with regular reports in the denominational newspaper, *The Maritime Baptist*,[106] and other media. Regular press releases would have conveyed the current situation, but the clergy involved on the committee were obviously not accustomed to releasing news and information publicly to newspapers or advertising their interests and offers.

The Maritime Baptist Convention, if it anticipated the call for clergy to enter the chaplaincy, should have prepared their congregations for this drain of leadership. Some of the clergy selected were the best they had (and badly needed) in their larger churches, and many were from small rural congregations who could ill afford a loss of their minister, no matter how important the need elsewhere. This emptying of pulpits was a surprise consequence to the committee. The convention could well have established a lay school of Theology at Acadia and else-

[104] Letter no. 173. Poole wonders about Harry Grimmer's appointment being held up.

[105] For example, one of the greatest misunderstandings among those outside the services was the rule of proportional representation where the number of chaplains from one denomination appointed reflected the number of soldiers, sailors, or airmen from that denomination within the separate divisions. Maritime Baptists often wrote about a perceived underrepresentation within the chaplaincy ranks when that was not the case.

[106] Letter no. 119. Editor MacDonald wrote on 26 September 1939 thanking Mr. Ackland for his story submitted to *The Maritime Baptist* concerning the convention's plan for selecting chaplains for recommendation to the armed forces.

where for training some of their layfolk to step in and supply congregational ministries while their clergy were acting as chaplains.

These letters also open the door to some of the personalities of the clergy of that time. They reveal various kinds of people who believed they were called into the ministry. Some were very practical, some prompted by ideals and spiritual sensitivities, and some were patriotic and saw a need that was required to be filled. Others indicated that the chaplaincy was an escape from difficult situations, lack of adequate salary,[107] or offering status and a deeply desired superior social position.[108]

The value of this collection is in what the letters reveal both intentionally and unintentionally. They are a glimpse into a denomination attempting to deal with a national crisis—learning the needs of the soldiers, sailors, and pilots—and the people who wished to take part in a ministry of this special nature. On a larger scale, the letters reveal the need for denominations to think in the long term and for unexpected eventualities. Studies should be made of what special training would be needed for the clergy in such situations. Conversations should take place with peacetime armed forces to become aware of new ministries, notably post-traumatic stress disorder (PTSD), peace-keeping operations, cultural differences, and other new considerations that armed forces are required to encounter.

Also of value is the revelation that such committees need infrastructure to support their specialized work, members acquainted with the issues involved, and more financial resources to reinforce the training that should be required of any person thinking of joining the chaplaincy. Denominations should also consider what training their theological seminaries teach to promote ingenuity, creative thinking, wisdom, clinical pastoral training, innovative ministry, issue-solving, and current-affairs awareness.

In the long run, it could be hoped that reevaluating these letters might move clergy and denominational leaders in the direction of informed action during national emergency situations and to be ready to minister in some way for the establishment of the Kingdom of God, and specifically to encourage peaceful reconciliation as part of the solution.[109]

---

[107] Letter no. 170.

[108] See letter no. 212 and 214.

[109] The author is deeply grateful for the assistance of Acadia University Archivist Pat Townsend, along with Wendy Robicheau, Catherine Fancy, Emily Clark, and the unwitting inspiration given to us by Dr. William H. Brackney.

IS TODAY'S SOUTHERN BAPTIST CONVENTION A "BAPTIST" BODY?

Erich Geldbach

INTRODUCTION

The headline of this article is not a rhetorical but a real question. The inquiry may be of help to determine the identity of Baptists. For decades now, William Brackney has tackled the question of Baptist identity, and a close look at the Southern Baptist Convention (henceforth: SBC) by someone who is not a United States citizen may perhaps be helpful for the discussion on Baptist identity. The main body of this article will attempt a comparison between some Baptist distinctives as they have evolved in the course of history, and "The Baptist Faith and Message" (henceforth: BF&M) as revised in 2000 by a committee that had been appointed in 1999 by then SBC President Paige Patterson.

Paige Patterson together with former Texas Judge Paul Pressler and others—the "PPPP coalition"—ran a "get out the vote" campaign in 1979 to defeat "moderates." Messengers were provided buses so that there was a large voter turnout at the annual convention, and quite a number of them left after the vote for president had been taken. None other than the chair of the 1999/2000 BF&M committee, fundamentalist pastor Adrian Rogers, was elected president of the SBC. This was what Paul Pressler referred to as the "engineering" of the takeover of the SBC. The simple strategy was to have like-minded men elected in successive years as presidents of the SBC because the president has the power to appoint members to various committees, boards, and agencies. Through appointments over the next ten years, fundamentalists gained total control of strategically important boards so that the SBC was fundamentally changed. Proponents called it the "conservative resurgence," whereas opponents spoke of a "hostile fundamentalist takeover."

In a brochure, "Meet Southern Baptists," the convention states basic beliefs that are summarized in the BF&M. The first item is the belief that the Bible is God's revelation of himself to mankind. It is noteworthy that the word "man"kind instead of humankind is being used. This is not a minor point, but is symptomatic for the language used. One would have thought that when the BF&M was revised, the language would have also been changed to reflect current usage. The failure to do so is especially noticeable in the section on "man," which reads in part:

> [...] In the beginning *man* was innocent of sin [...]. By *his* free choice *man* sinned against God and brought sin into the human race. [...] *man* transgressed the command of God, and fell from *his* original innocence whereby *his* posterity inherit a nature [...] inclined toward sin. [...]. Only the grace of God can bring *man* into His holy fellowship and enable *man* to fulfill the creative purpose of God.

When a female student read this passage, she exclaimed: "I'm surely glad I am not a man!"[1]

More significant is the statement that Southern Baptists are not a "creedal" people, but a "confessional" people. What is the difference between a creed and a confession? According to the brochure, a "creedal church" requires of churches or individuals "to embrace a standardized set of beliefs." However, this is exactly what happened within the SBC during the last three decades. For Southern Baptists the BF&M as revised in 2000 represents the "confessional consensus" of "certain definite doctrines that Baptists believe, cherish, and with which they have been and are now closely identified." All ministers, missionaries, official representatives, and employees of the SBC and its organizations, as well as all seminary teachers, must sign the "confessional consensus." In other words, the BF&M functions as a binding creed for all officials. This recent move represents a stark deviation from the Baptist tradition, which never knew a creed that bound the conscience of the believers. From the beginning, Baptists drafted various confessions to make known to anyone who they were. At other times they were requested or compelled by state officials to present their beliefs, but they always made sure that their confessional statements were open to future revisions according to new light that the Holy Spirit might grant them. Therefore, creeds or confessions served a certain function in the historic process.

As the Bible is the benchmark of all beliefs and practices of the SBC, it is necessary that the articles of the BF&M will not only be compared with historic Baptist distinctives, but also with the Bible itself. Are Southern Baptists, as they claim, "people of the book," or do other sources or a selective reading feed the BF&M?

The brochure "Meet Southern Baptists" states that the first five articles of the BF&M "affirm historical, orthodox, evangelical beliefs." This statement asserts that there are beliefs that go back in history and that there is a continuity from the "historical" setting to today's BF&M. It is unclear, however, to which part of history this statement refers. Is it the early church and the traditional

[1] Reported by Curtis Freeman, research professor of theology and Baptist studies and director of the Baptist House of Studies at Duke Divinity School, on his Facebook account, https://www.facebook.com/curtis.freeman.777/posts/10156178332823103 (accessed 28 December 2017).

creeds, or is it the time of the Reformation and the confessions of various Protestant churches? Is it the time when creeds were developed in conjunction with revival movements, or does this statement refer to the original BF&M of 1925 or its revision of 1963? If this were the case, "historical" would cover a very short period of time.

In addition, the BF&M beliefs are supposed to be "orthodox," which is not meant pertaining to the Eastern Orthodox Churches, but being not heterodox or heretical. Finally, these beliefs are presented as "evangelical," but there is no agreed-upon explanation as to what this term encompasses. The three adjectives, "historical," "orthodox," and "evangelical," are wide-open to interpretation, which is especially true for the last one. It must clearly be asserted that there is no one creed or confession to which the BF&M can go back; hence, the articles in question that are being "affirmed" seem to come from different sources and seem to be assembled eclectically.

Baptist Distinctives

The Baptist movement grew out of English Puritanism of the early seventeenth century and developed into one of the major worldwide Christian communities, and thus it must have certain features that distinguish it from other Christian communities.[2] The German Baptist minister Dietmar Lütz and I developed a grid almost simultaneously in order to help understand the distinguishing features, and we used the word "Baptist" as an acronym[3] so that the letter "B" stands for the first Baptist distinctive, which is the rite of baptism.

Baptism

Early Baptists had to refute the notion that they were violent revolutionaries who were determined to overthrow the existing church and social order. Because of their rite of baptism, they were identified with the Anabaptists of the previous century. The polemical literature had never made a distinction between the peaceful Baptizers and the instigators who forcefully established the Anabaptist Kingdom in the city of Münster. As the early Baptists insisted to follow the Scriptures and, accordingly, baptized only believers, this act seemed to be proof enough that such people must be revolutionaries who deserved to be tried for heresy.

Indeed, believers' baptism was a radical diversion from tradition. Both the Roman Catholic Church and the established churches that developed as a result of the Reformation—Lutheranism, Reformed-Presbyterianism, Anglicanism—

---

[2] For a historical overview, see David W. Bebbington, *Baptists Through the Centuries: A History of a Global People* (Waco TX: Baylor University Press, 2010).

[3] See Dietmar Lütz, *Wir sind noch nicht am Ziel* (Berlin: WDL Verlag, 2002) 24ff.

practiced infant baptism. By doing so, these churches were able to enlist the entire population of a country or territory as members. Baptism has always been interpreted in Christian history as the "door" to the church regardless of the age a person was baptized. When infants were admitted to the church, they grew up as members, and the result was a "Christian nation," a "Christian state," or a "Christian territory." The total identity of church and society was thus achieved without much of a commitment on the part of the church members. Against this background, the Baptist break with tradition is truly revolutionary and radical: It is radical because Baptists went back to the roots—"radical" is derived from the Latin *radix* = root—and found no infant baptism in the Scriptures. It is also revolutionary as the identity of church and society cannot be upheld when only believers are baptized. Church and society are "revolved" and given separate identities. As in a nutshell, the change from infant to believers' baptism indicates a totally new approach to church polity and body politics. It is not so much the mode of baptism as, rather, the person to be baptized that signifies the radical deviation from tradition. In fact, the early Baptists at Amsterdam followed the normal practice of pouring water over the candidate's head as a valid mode of baptism. When later the mode was changed to immersion, baptism turned out to be a powerful means to signify the believer's dying and rising with Christ. Baptism presents many distinguishing characteristics of Baptists:

- it points to the priority of the Scriptures as the sole authority for faith and practice, which led to the break with the long-held tradition of infant baptism;
- it emphasizes that each individual must come to the saving knowledge of Christ;
- it incorporates the baptized into the *corpus Christi*;
- it stresses that Christ is the focal point of the Christian experience;
- it leads a person into a covenant relationship with the head of the church;
- it also unites a believer with fellow believers within the community of the faithful;
- it turns the church into a believers' church;
- it underscores the voluntary aspect of becoming a member of Christ's body;
- it may never be forced upon a person such as an infant;
- it underlines that faith has an experiential dimension; and
- it accentuates the double meaning of the water: it is at the same time life-threatening ("buried with Him through baptism into death") and life-giving ("certainly we also shall be in the likeness of his resurrection") and life-sustaining ("even so we also should walk in newness of life"; see Rom. 6:4–5).

Baptismal initiation is the voluntary answer on part of the believer to God's call to faith and fellowship. Thus, the voluntary principle is not rooted in the notion of free will, but in the voluntary response on the part of the believer to God's own initiative.[4] From the very beginning, Baptists have always held what the Lima convergence document of the Faith and Order Commission of the World Council of Churches of 1982 says in § 8: "Baptism is both God's gift and our human response to that gift."[5] An infant is incapable of responding to a gift. William Brackney sums up what he thinks of the baptismal rite and Baptist identity: "More than any other characteristic of the Baptist tradition, then, believers' baptism by immersion was the functional essence of historic Baptist identity." Unlike the magisterial reformers of the sixteenth century who did not want to constitute a new church, but to reform the existing church, Baptists followed the theory of the total fall of the church and the inevitableness of the reconstruction of the original early church according to the New Testament pattern. For this reason Brackney goes on the say, "For those [Baptists] who claimed to reconstitute primitive Christianity, the ordinance [= believers' baptism by immersion] spoke literally from the New Testament of the salient issues in the gospel, and of a voluntary personal relationship with Jesus Christ."[6]

What is the "confessional consensus" on this vital issue of baptism as expressed in the BF&M? Baptism is, first of all, an "act of obedience." The emphasis is totally on the human person and not on God's initiative. Hence, secondly, baptism is degraded to a mere symbol. The act of baptism is said to symbolize "the believer's faith," "the believer's death to sin," and "a testimony to the believer's faith in the final resurrection." A symbolic understanding of baptism, however, remains on the surface. The shift from a God-centered view of baptism to a believer-centered understanding ends up in mere symbolism. Worse yet because totally unscriptural, the act of baptism itself is irrelevant as it merely "testifies" to something that happened before when a person "accepts Christ as his/her personal Lord and Savior," or when the Holy Spirit calls the human person to the Savior, effects regeneration, and at this moment "baptizes every believer into the Body of Christ."[7] The symbolic understanding ends up in a baptism without one drop of water.

Likewise, the Lord's Supper "is a symbolic act of obedience whereby mem-

---

[4] For a discussion of voluntarism, see William Brackney, *Christian Voluntarism: Theology and Praxis* (Grand Rapids: Wm. B. Eerdmans Publishing Co.) 1997.

[5] "Baptism, Eucharist, and Ministry," F & O paper no. 111, Geneva, World Council of Churches, 1982.

[6] William H. Brackney, "'Commonly, (Though Falsely) Called…': Reflections on the Search for Baptist Identity," *Perspectives in Religious Studies* 13 (Fall 1986): 67–82, here: 80.

[7] BF&M article 2C on God, the Holy Spirit.

bers [...] memorialize the death of the Redeemer and anticipate His second coming." As with baptism, the emphasis is on the "members" and their "obedience," which is why the Lord's Supper is only a "symbolic" act. The partakers look back ("memorialize") and into the future ("His second coming"), but the most important aspect is left out, i.e., the presence of the Lord and the proclamation of his saving death by the very act of celebrating (1 Cor. 11:26).

The richness of the biblical tradition of both baptism and the Lord's Supper is reduced to mere acts of obedience. Nowhere in the New Testament is baptism or the Supper associated with obedience. The encounter of God and the human person is not based on a "command-and-obedience" structure, but on God's unconditional grace and love. God's initiative is communicated through a language of love that is aimed at eliciting a consent on the part of those to whom God speaks through his Spirit in human language. To associate baptism and the Supper with obedience has wide-ranging repercussions for the behavior of Christians: There is, first of all, the danger of perceiving God as an authoritarian person. The BF&M says of God that he "is all powerful, all knowing, all loving, and all wise," and that he "is Father" and is "fatherly in His attitude toward all men." To be sure, biblical verses could be found for each claim, which can also be said for the use of the Bible by Jehovah's Witnesses. What the BF&M conveys sounds like an extension of a male father to be an all-domineering superman. What does it mean that in the Bible God is also presented as a mother when, in Isaiah 66:13, God proclaims, "As a mother comforts her child, so will I comfort you"? What does it mean that God as a comforter and savior forfeits all his glory and power and takes on human flesh?

Second, when at baptism as the "door" to the congregation and the beginning of the Christian pilgrimage, "obedience" is demanded, and when "obedience" is reinforced at every celebration of the Supper, there is the danger that conformity to someone's or the congregation's opinions becomes the behavioral norm. This behavior is further implemented by what the BF&M affirms about the person of Christ: "He honored the divine law by His personal obedience." The believer is to follow Christ, and if the life of Christ is characterized by his obedience, how much more must believers follow the standard that Christ represents?

Third, this normative pattern of behavior may also help explain why, in contrast to Baptist beginnings, few, if any, initiatives of civil disobedience come from the ranks of Southern Baptists.

Fourth, the emphasis on obedience may also be a decisive factor why so many very young people, often kindergarten toddlers, are being "baptized." This act of "obediential" baptism is more likely than not the result of parents' or Sunday-school teachers' pressure and mimicry on the part of the child. It is less the result of a "mature" decision to answer God's call.[8]

Finally, one can point to the all-male language when speaking of God and baptism, which results in a distorted view of women or wives to be "submissive."

In sum: There can be little doubt that the understanding of baptism and the Lord's Supper does not reflect Baptist history, nor does it meet the rich biblical testimonies.

Autonomy

In the Baptist tradition, the letter "A" stands for the autonomy of the local church. This concept also constitutes a break with tradition. The notion of autonomy was closely tied to the context in which it arose. According to King James I, the relationship of church and crown is established by the fact that the bishop anoints the king at the crowning ceremony so that the crown rights of the king are divinely bestowed upon the ruler: "No bishop—no king." It follows that the church must have a bishop to perform the rite so that the church order must be Episcopalian; as Archbishop William Laud (1573–1645) said, "No bishop—no church." Baptists have neither bishops nor a pope, neither a church council nor a single church leader who with authority can speak for or govern the entire church. Baptists also have no person in history to whom they can turn for guidance as Luther for Lutherans, Calvin for Reformed-Presbyterianism, or John Wesley for Methodism. The church in Baptist tradition is not a structure top down, but bottom up, and therefore, the Baptist church structure is referred to as a congregational order: Each local congregation comes together and, through Bible studies, prayers, and careful deliberations, discerns the mind of Christ for a particular situation or an important decision. This approach is possible as, on the one hand, the local congregation lacks nothing to be wholly the church of Christ, but, on the other hand, each congregation is not the whole church. Thus, shortly after congregations began to be organized and incorporated, regional associations of different local congregations were also formed, sometimes for practical purposes, but generally as an expression of belonging together both spiritually and materially. At the same time, Baptists could declare that God's children are dispersed throughout the world and can be found not only in their own congregations, but also beyond. The autonomy of the local church does not prevent its members from recognizing other Baptists or other Christians as God's precious children. This is true even though Baptists held the conviction that baptism is the "door" to the church, and if a person uses the wrong door, he or she will end up in a "false" church. Nevertheless, true Christians may be found even in a false church. In the modern era, not all Baptists, but a substantial number participate in the ecumenical movement as an expression to find common ground and to advance

[8] See below on "transformation."

Christian unity in diversity.

The BF&M states in article VI that "a New Testament church of the Lord Jesus Christ is an autonomous local congregation of baptized believers [...]," and that "each congregation operates under the Lordship of Christ through democratic processes." It is surprising that, at the beginning of the twenty-first century, the autonomy of the local church can be stated in this way. The Baptist tradition clearly points to the notion of autonomy, but modern society and the operation of the church demand more than the focus on the local congregation. To assume that "a New Testament church" operates "through democratic processes" is to project modern democratic ideas, which are doubtless practiced in Baptist congregations, back into the time of the New Testament. Mentioning the New Testament clearly has the function to give credence to the statement. However, there never was such an entity as "*a* New Testament church," because the congregations that are noticeable in the New Testament are very different. The church in Jerusalem differed decisively from, say, the churches in Corinth or Rome. The statement would have been much more convincing had this fact been pointed out, as it speaks for, not against, the idea of autonomy. However, the principle of autonomy does not mean that individual congregations live in isolation. During the time of the New Testament, there existed the feeling of togetherness as the Apostle Paul demonstrated: He traveled to Jerusalem for consultations, and he again took to the road to deliver financial help he had diligently collected in congregations of mostly non-Jewish ethnicity in Corinth and Macadonia for the poor brethren in Jerusalem. According to 2 Corinthians 8:14, the believers in Corinth have enough to help their co-believers in Jerusalem. However, the situation may change in the future so that, perhaps, the congregation in Jerusalem is called upon to assist others. "The goal is equality." The Apostle goes on to say: "This service that you perform is not only supplying the needs of the Lord's people but is also overflowing in many expressions of thanks to God" (2 Cor. 9:12–13, New International Version). Paul wants the aid to be mutual as the occasion requires to achieve equality, and he interprets this service as a bond of unity among the churches of very different backgrounds and as a confession of the gospel. This clearly goes beyond the autonomy of the local church.

The article on the church also says that "its scriptural officers are pastors and deacons." This is definitely not in accordance with the Scriptures. As an example, one may turn to 1 Corinthians 12, where Paul discusses different kinds of gifts (*charismata*), services (*diakonia*), and workings (*energemata*) that the Spirit gives to different people. It is obvious that all these talents cannot be bestowed in "a pastor" or "a deacon." Paul sums up his deliberations by saying that "God has placed in the church first of all apostles, second prophets, third teachers, then miracles, then gifts of healing, of helping, of guidance, and of different kinds of tongues," all of which indicate that the "scriptural officers" are more numerous than in the BF&M. Besides, the office of a pastor as we know it today was unknown during the time of the New Testament. Also, the vote of the Home Mission Board in 1987 and later of the Foreign Mission Board to forbid appointments to persons who speak in tongues is clearly unbiblical. It is also surprising that various other offices, such as elders or widows, are not mentioned at all.

One assertion of the BF&M drew wide attention in both religious and secular media: "While both men and women are gifted for service in the church, the office of pastor is limited to men as qualified by Scripture." Such a statement negates the autonomy of the local church and is not in accordance with the New Testament. It is sometimes said that autonomous local congregations are not required to accept this position. However, when, after careful deliberations "under the Lordship of Christ," churches reach a different conclusion and ordain women or call a female pastor, they are not only criticized, but excluded from fellowship within the SBC. In mid-November 2017, First Baptist Church in Jefferson City, Tennessee, was no longer considered a "cooperating church" because it had called Ellen Di Giosia to be its minister. The Tennessee Baptist Convention had officially embraced the BF&M in 2006 over objections that it would be used as a "creed" to exclude local churches, which is exactly what happened now. In 2009 the Georgia Baptist Convention took similar actions when First Baptist Church in Decatur was excluded for calling Nancy Sehested as its pastor. These examples demonstrate that the BF&M functions as a "creedal" test to determine the fidelity of a supposedly "autonomous" church. A creed that binds the consciences of church members has always been refuted in Baptist tradition until the "conservative resurgence."

The restriction of the pastorate to men is proof-texted by certain sections in the pastoral letters, which are among the younger writings of the New Testament, when the Christian churches had somehow adjusted to the prevailing culture and thus treated women differently than had been the case a few decades earlier. In the last chapter of Paul's letter to the Roman church, he lists a number of persons and adds some qualifying remarks. Thus, he begins in verse 1: "I commend to you our sister Phoebe"; she was a businesswoman who was about to travel to Rome and was possibly carrying Paul's letter to the church in the capital of the empire. This woman was "a deacon (*diákonon*) of the church in Cenchreae." It is the same word that Paul uses for Christ (Rom. 15:8), for himself and Apollo (1 Cor. 3:5), and again for himself (2 Cor. 3:6; 6:4). Romans 16:3f says: "Greet Priscilla and Aquila, my co-workers (*synergoi*) in Christ Jesus.[9] They risked their lives for me." This erstwhile Jewish couple had been ousted from Rome together with the entire Jewish community during Emperor Nero's reign, had settled in Corinth where Paul worked for them, and had resettled in Rome. All churches of the Gentiles,

[9] The title "co-worker" is used by Paul in reference to Titus in 2 Corinthians 8:23.

Paul says, are grateful to them, and a church met in their home. Priscilla is mentioned before her husband, which indicates that she is on equal terms with him in the congregation. Verse 6f states, "Greet Mary, who worked very hard for you. Greet Andronicus and Junia, my fellow Jews who have been in prison with me. They are outstanding among the apostles." It is not known what the "hard work" was that Mary is remembered for, but it was certainly more than preparing a bowl of soup or homemaking. Most importantly, however, Paul refers to a couple who, he says, were both "outstanding among the apostles." Surely, if a woman could hold the most authoritative office in the early church, the apostleship, women would be eligible for all offices. In verse 12, Paul continues to mention women: "Greet Tryphena and Tryphosa, those women who work hard in the Lord. Greet my dear friend Persis, another woman who has worked very hard in the Lord." Again, Paul remembers the "hard work" of the three women "in the Lord." The mother of Rufus is cited in verse 13, of whom the Apostle says that she had been a mother to him as well. Julia and Nereus' sister and some unnamed sisters are mentioned in passing. The list indicates that women in the early church were treated in the same way as men, and that a Jewish female convert could become an apostle. This would be an impossibility in today's SBC.

Another passage that is often quoted to limit the office of pastor to men is 1 Corinthians 14:34–36. The NRSV puts these verses in parentheses to indicate that they interrupt Paul's thought. Without them verse 37 would follow directly verse 33, which makes sense. In addition, verses 34–36 contradict what Paul wrote earlier in the same letter when, in 11:4–5, he speaks of "any man" or "any woman who prays or prophecies." The Greek *propheteuo* means "to proclaim God's revelation." The office of proclaiming, which today is one of the main functions of a pastor, is undoubtedly not restricted to men, but open to women as well if one follows the Apostle Paul.

The argument that equality, which the SBC claims it supports for women, does not mean sameness, which the SBC in the case of female pastors does not support, is very shallow and is based upon so-called complementarianism, i.e., the view that God created men and women for different, but complementary roles. This view is a perfect reminder of the separate-but-equal doctrine. Nancy Hastings Sehested writes from her experience in Decatur: "A religion that justifies the subjugation of women and the superiority of men through sacred texts is a religion that creates the dynamic for the abuse of power."[10] The limitation of the pastorate to men had far-reaching consequences: It was one of the reasons why members that now belong to the Cooperative Baptist Fellowship broke from the SBC in 1991 and established the separate Fellowship.

---

[10] "God Speaks through Donkeys, Burning Bushes, Rocks—and Women Ministers," *Baptist News Global*, 22 November 2017.

In sum: The autonomy of the local church must take the historical context into consideration when it was developed. As the context today is very different, this notion must be improved without losing its original meaning. The restriction of the church offices to pastors and deacons and the exclusion of women are clearly not supported by Holy Scripture.

Priesthood of All Believers

The letter "P" represents the priesthood of all believers or, as the early Baptists also put it, the "soul competency" of every believer. First Peter 2:5 is the main passage: "You [...] are being built up as a spiritual house, to be a holy priesthood [...]." Priests had the function to offer various kinds of sacrifices for the sins, but in the New Testament that tradition had come to an end as "Christ had offered *for all time* a single sacrifice for sins"; Christ is the "great High priest" through whom all believers have direct access to God. A mediating priest is not required (Heb. 4:16). The priesthood of all believers can only mean that every believer may make himself or herself available to a fellow believer or some other person as a "priestly instrument" for spiritual counseling, consolation, help, prayer, assistance, or any other comfort that a person may require.

Another aspect of the priesthood of all believers is the egalitarian principle. There may be ordained people in leadership positions, but they are all on equal footing with the entire membership before the Lord of the church. Every believer is through the in-dwelling of the Holy Spirit competent to make his or her voice known in theological and ethical deliberations in congregational meetings, and every believer has one vote when a decision is taken. The early Baptist expression "soul competency" is probably more adequate than "priesthood." The egalitarianism entails a third aspect: Every person is competent to read the Scriptures and to follow its instructions, and every believer has a right to his or her judgment in the interpretation of the Bible. This competency is based upon the freedom that God provides for human beings and applies to all, not just to the powerful and rich or to kings and magistrates or to politicians and bishops.

It is noteworthy that BF&M makes no mention of the priesthood of all believers. This may be the case because there are powerful forces within the SBC that call for a privileged position of a male pastor and for the congregation to follow unconditionally his leadership. In light of Baptist history, the tendency toward authoritarian pastors that clearly exists within the SBC can only be deplored.

Transformation

The letter "T" stands for transformation or conversion. According to early Baptist thinking, which has run practically throughout the history of Baptists, every human person stands in need of the experience of transformation, but no one is able to bring forth such an experience at his or her own volition. It takes God's gracious intervention to accomplish a change of the human heart. This is achieved through the preaching of the word and through the power of the Holy Spirit. The experience of transformation has direct consequences for baptism, church membership, and ethical behavior. As has been pointed out above, many Southern Baptist Churches "baptize" children at a very early age. This is done so much more as the simple phrase, "to accept Jesus as personal Lord and Savior," is very often used to indicate someone's readiness to be baptized. However, can young children—or some adults, for that matter—realize that by repeating this phrase they are making a political statement? In the early church this confession meant that Jesus was Lord and Savior, not the emperor in Rome who claimed both titles for himself.

Baptists have been known throughout their history as "missionary people," as they tried to present the good news and effect a change of the human heart. A person must be transformed from self-centeredness to a lifestyle that attempts to fulfill God's calling for the good of the congregation and for the common good. The center of the preaching exercise is Jesus Christ. People are called to trust Christ as their Savior so that this experiential act of transformation underlines that faith or trust in Christ is a spiritual experience, and that Christ is the focal point of that experience.

Individualism

The letter "I" may further emphasize that the process of transformation concerns every individual. However, the individualism thus signified is not the "rugged individualism" often associated with that term. The individual, rather, finds himself or herself within a congregational setting, where faith originates through preaching and where it is lived within the community of the faithful. Baptist life is ideally a communal lifestyle, and thus, Baptists are within the believers' church tradition. There exists a similarity between an individual believer and an individual congregation. Just as one congregation is not an isolated entity, but a community bound together in mutual aid and council with other congregations, so is the individual not separated, but integrated in a community of faithful people. The purpose of integrating is for the person to develop fully his or her potential and become a mature Christian individual. Baptist individualism may also mean that every believer has a right to read and interpret the Bible. Baptist individualism expresses the Christian view of the worth and dignity of every human person regardless of nationality, ethnicity, religion, gender, color, sexual or political orientation, age, status, wealth, education, or any cultural or other factors that might separate human beings from each other.

In the areas of transformation and individualism, the BF&M is straightforward in so far as it states that salvation can be attained exclusively by personal faith in Christ. It speaks of a "change of heart" and of "turning from sin toward God" and maintains that repentance and faith are inseparable experiences of God's grace.

SEPARATION

The most far-reaching contribution of the early Baptists that helped change Western societies is the call for a separation of government from religion. Baptists insisted that neither king nor parliament nor bishops may by fire or sword constrain "peoples to receive that one true religion of the gospel." As no king or bishop can command the wind, so is neither the representative of the government nor the proponent of an established church "able to command faith; *That is the gift of God, who worketh in us both the will and the deed of his own good pleasure.*" Persecution does not gain any soul unto God, but only unto the devil.[11] At a time when religious persecution was the norm in European Catholic, Protestant, Anglican, and Orthodox countries, Baptists pleaded for uncoerced religion, for freedom of conscience and religious liberty. Thus, Thomas Helwys concluded: "For mens religion to God, is betwixt God and themselves; the King shall not answer for it, neither may the King be judg betwene God and man. Let them be heretikes, Turks, Jewes, or whatever, it apperteynes not to the earthly power to punish them in the least measure."[12] To ensure individual liberty, religion must be held separate from the government.

A dissident from Puritan New England, Roger Williams (circa 1603–1683) became the founder of the Baptist tradition in the New World. For Williams, the *providentia Dei*—the providence of God—had watched over him when he was forced to flee from Salem southward and survived the harsh winter of 1636 because Native Americans provided food and shelter. Hence, he called his new home Providence Plantation, and in 1638 he was baptized and helped start the first Baptist church on American soil. He soon left the Baptist congregation, but kept his dissenting spirit. Together with Baptist pastor and physician John Clarke (1609–1676), Williams organized the colony on the basis of separating "the garden of the church" from the "wilderness of the world" by a "hedge or wall of separation." In addition, the two organizers promoted a democratic form of government so that this experiment is the first attempt of democratic government in

---

[11] Leonard Busher, "Religion's Peace: Or a Plea for Liberty of Conscience" (1614), in H. Leon McBeth, *A Sourcebook for Baptist Heritage* (Nashville TN: Broadman Press 1990) 73. Italics in the original.

[12] Thomas Helwys, "A Short Declaration of the Mystery of Iniquity" (1612), in McBeth, *A Sourcebook*, 72.

the modern Western world on the basis of liberty of conscience and religion. This is so much more astounding as democracy at that time carried no positive connotation; it was "a nasty word": "democracy was really bad news," even for the founders of the American Republic and Constitution.[13]

Although the colony of Rhode Island was small, this dissident venture, nonetheless, points way into the future. In Europe, by comparison, it took a century and a half before the enlightenment brought forth similar ideas, albeit in many cases in the guise of anti-church tolerance rather than liberty. Williams was familiar with the writings of early English Baptists on religious liberty, and he was appalled by the Thirty Years' War on the European continent and the English civil war. At the time of his arrival in Boston in 1631, he declared that the Bay Colony's government could concern itself only with matters of the civil order, but not interfere in religious beliefs of its citizens. To force people to a religious faith constituted a "rape of the soul" or a "ravishment of the conscience." Williams forthrightly affirmed, "Forced worship stinks in God's nostrils," and in refutation of the attempt to reach religious uniformity, he wrote that "the sword may make a whole nation hypocrites, but it cannot bring a single soul in genuine conversion to Christ."[14] This is why the "hedge or wall of separation" is an absolute necessity to ensure liberty. Edwin Gaustad summarized Clarke's and Williams' efforts in a simple sentence: "Religious liberty created Rhode Island."[15]

Baptists acted as watchmen of the hedge or wall from the time of Williams and Clarke, but when the Baptist movement grew, especially in the South, it developed more and more to what might be called a form of "Baptist Culturalism"; it was no longer a dissident counterculture, but changed into the main religious pillar of society. The watchmen no longer made sure the wall was in place, but helped to open it, and the wall, finally, "came tumblin' down." The first gap in the wall came when Baptist preachers in the South found ways to interpret the Bible as endorsing slavery. Slaves were to obey their masters, and even ministers owned slaves. In some congregations, blacks were admitted as members, but the white leadership made sure they were seated separately from the white folks.

In 1814 the General Missionary Convention of the Baptist Denomination

---

[13] Charles Taylor, "Democratic Degeneration: Three Easy Paths to Regression," edited transcript of the 2017 Fritz Stern Lecture, delivered on 16 November 2017 at the American Academy Berlin, *The Berlin Journal*, on the academy's website, www.americanacademy.de (accessed 22 December 2017).

[14] Quoted in Chana B. Cox, *Liberty: God's Gift to Humanity* (Lanham MD: Lexington Books, The Rowman & Littlefield Publishing Group, 2006) 26.

[15] *The Baptist Tradition of Religious Liberty in America*, two lectures by Edwin Scott Gaustad, J.M. Dawson Institute of Church-State Studies (Waco TX: Baylor University, n.y.) 4.

in the United States of America for Foreign Missions was organized. It was usually referred to as the Triennial Convention because it met every three years. When a conflict erupted over the issue of whether or not a slave owner may be charged with missionary duties, almost 300 Baptist leaders from the South came together in May 1845 at the First Baptist Church in Augusta, Georgia, and decided that a separate Baptist body for missionary work was necessary to avoid the slavery issue to interfere with appointments of missionaries. This was the birth of the SBC. From the beginning, the convention suffered from the serious birth defect of racism and discrimination against Afro-Americans. In addition, slaveholders were permitted to become missionaries both within the United States and abroad.

Discrimination of Afro-Americans was widespread in the South and was expressed in Jim Crow laws. Segregation was until the Civil Rights movement, and possibly decades beyond, a way of life, and the churches were the bastions of discriminatory behavior. The BF&M finally came somewhat to terms with this issue and stated in article 15 that "Christians should oppose racism." The question immediately arises whether "opposing" racism is enough. Should not "eradicating" racism be the proper term? In addition, racism is, in this article, just one example of others that follow: "every form of greed, selfishness, and vice, and all forms of sexual immorality, including adultery, homosexuality, and pornography." One can argue that this list contains another prejudice, as homosexuality is included. Why is the SBC so "soft" on racism and so "strict" on matters of sexual behavior? Ever since the United States Supreme Court ruled in *Roe v. Wade* on 22 January 1973 that women have the right to an abortion during the first twenty-four weeks of pregnancy, free of interference by the State, there has been an uproar in the SBC, its leadership, and in other Baptist circles.

Separate Baptist Jerry Falwell organized his Moral Majority and aggressively argued against the Supreme Court's ruling. He had been conspicuously silent during the Civil Rights struggle when he argued that preachers ought to stay out of the political debate. In the SBC, it was Richard Land who in 1987 began to work for Texas Republican Governor Bill Clements as adviser on church-state relations and anti-abortion legislation. He was a close friend of the engineers of the "conservative resurgence" Paige Patterson and Paul Pressler, and later became president of the influential Ethics and Religious Liberty Commission (ERLC) of the SBC. The scope of responsibilities of the ERLC was greatly enlarged so that the SBC would not have to cooperate with the Washington-based lobby organization, the Baptist Joint Committee on Public Affairs, which the SBC defunded. While Land worked for the governor, he met the political operative Karl Rove, through whom he was introduced to George W. Bush. Land stayed on very friendly terms with Bush after the latter became President of the United States. This friendship had far-reaching repercussions as far as the issue of separation of church and state is concerned.

Two areas can be singled out where the "wall" of separation was not only cracked, but totally destroyed. One has been the still ongoing fight to reverse the *Roe v. Wade* decision, and the other is the issue of war and peace. The first issue is based on the often-repeated sentence that life begins at conception and that, therefore, an abortion is murder.[16] The BF&M defines marriage as "the uniting of one man and one woman in covenant commitment for a lifetime" (article XVIII). Both statements are assertions within a moral or religious framework. In a pluralistic society it is to be expected that people with a different moral or religious outlook or with no religion at all might differ from these statements. It is the obligation of the State to ensure that all people are treated equal. This represents a core value of the Baptist tradition. SBC leaders, in violation of this principle, ran a campaign to add a marriage amendment to the "God-less" United States Constitution to reflect their definition of marriage.[17] Richard Land was the SBC's chief lobbyist during the anti-abortion and marriage amendment crusades. He cooperated well with President George W. Bush and Karl Rove, and they landed a partial success: When in 2003 President Bush signed the Partial-Birth Abortion Ban Act into law, Richard Land, Jerry Falwell, and other ministers were guests in the Oval Office. The aim of this politicking was to make their religious and/or moral belief the law of the land and, thus, the attempt to impose a possible, but nevertheless religious and sectarian outlook, upon the entire country.

When George W. Bush, Dick Cheney, Donald Rumsfeld, and others prepared a "preemptive" strike against Iraqi dictator Saddam Hussein, Land was among few religious leaders to defend the actions unequivocally. He even made a trip to Berlin, Germany, to convince German church leaders that it was now time to go to war.[18] Article XVI of the BF&M on War and Peace states: "It is the duty of Christians to seek peace with all men on principles of righteousness. In accordance with the spirit and teachings of Christ they should do all in their power to put an end to war." Land and the SBC leaders acted against this article as they

---

[16] The BF&M says in section XVIII on the family: "Children, from the moment of conception, are a blessing and heritage from the Lord."

[17] In a church with several million adherents, it is realistically to be expected that not all marriages are commitments for a lifetime. Quite a number will end in a divorce, for which the SBC makes no provisions.

[18] Traugott Jähnichen, "'Gerechte Kriege' gegen den Terror? Friedensethische Traditionen und Perspektiven angesichts von Terror und 'neuen Kriegen,'" in Lena Lybaek, Konrad Raiser, Stefanie Schardien, eds., *Gemeinschaft der Kirchen und gesellschaftliche Veantwortung. Die Würde des Anderen und das Recht anders zu denken. Festschrift für Erich Geldbach* (Münster: LIT Verlag, 2004) 239–50. Neither church nor political leaders in Germany found the political, military, or religious reasons convincing, so Germany stayed out of the military conflict.

did not "do all in their power" to end a war, but, on the contrary, worked tirelessly to start a war. For all with eyes to see, the Iraq conflict was from the very beginning based on pretenses and lies and was against international law. The atrocities committed by American troops and Blackwater mercenaries[19] as well as the abduction and torture programs were inexcusable by any standards, most of all by "the spirit of Christ." When President Bush prematurely declared "Mission Accomplished" on deck of a United States warship, Baptists, as a "mission people," should have unambiguously objected to the term "mission" as applied to an illegal military adventure.

Article XVI also affirms: "The true remedy for the war spirit is the gospel of our Lord." By not resisting the "war spirit" of the United States government, the SBC leadership betrayed, in their own words, the very gospel. They even asked the government to send the troops from Iraq further into Iran for a regime change in that country. Article XVI continues: "The supreme need of the world is the acceptance of His teachings in all the affairs of men and nations, and the practical application of His law of love." How can the SBC make such an assertion and how can they expect the "world" to accept Christ's teachings in *all* the affairs of men and nations when its own leaders are not abiding by these standards? It is very obvious that the wall of separation no longer exists for the SBC. The demonstration of being part of political power rather than raising a prophetic voice was more important than the traditional Baptist distinctive of separation. Richard Land, meanwhile, enjoys the mingling with the powers that be, as he is part of the unofficial evangelical advisory committee to President Trump.[20] Roger Williams was right when he declared, "When they have opened a gap in the hedge or wall [...], God hath ever broke down the wall itself, removed the candlestick, and made His garden a wilderness, as at this day."[21]

In order to protect their churches from becoming a "wilderness," the Baptist Convention in Virginia and the Baptist General Convention of Texas refused to cooperate with the SBC. Both applied for membership in the Baptist World Alliance and were admitted. The same is true of the Cooperative Baptist Fellowship. Meanwhile, in Virginia and Texas rival groups were organized: Southern Baptist Conservatives of Virginia in 1996 and Southern Baptists of Texas in 1998. In the same year, fundamentalist Moral Majority leader Jerry Falwell began attending the SBC's annual conventions and voiced his conviction that the six SBC's seminaries, after they had been thoroughly purged from so-called "liberal"

---

[19] The founder of Blackwater, the former United States Navy Seal Erik Dean Prince, is the brother of President Trump's controversial Secretary of Education, Betsy DeVos.

[20] This is so much more astounding, as article 15 of the BF&M seems to apply verbally to Trump: "every form of greed, selfishness, and vice, and all forms of sexual immorality, including adultery [...]."

[21] Quoted in "Roger Williams," on Wikipedia, accessed 1 December 2017.

seminary presidents and professors, could be recommended again as sound institutions. This was a key statement as it proves that Falwell, who approvingly characterized himself as a "fundamentalist," did not move in the direction of the SBC, but that the SBC moved in the direction of Falwell and must therefore be recognized as being "fundamentalist." The "Falwellianization" of the SBC was a departure from the Baptist community into a separate entity.

Another fundamentalist culture warrior was Wallie Amos Criswell (1909–2002), who pastored the First Baptist Church of Dallas, Texas, from 1944 to the end of his life and was able to turn the church into one of America's first megachurches with well over 20,000 members. From Criswell College, which he founded and which began in 1971, both Richard Land and Paige Patterson emerged as leaders of the "conservative resurgence"; Patterson even moved up to be president of the college in 1975. Curtis Freeman has convincingly proved that Criswell throughout his life had never changed his mind with regard to defending racial segregation.[22] Criswell succeeded George W. Truett (1867–1944), who had served this church from 1897 until his death, and who in 1920 eloquently defended religious liberty and the separation of church and state as "everlasting" Baptist and American principles on the steps of the United States Capitol. One must keep this in mind in order to notice the radical change in the SBC. Both Falwell and Criswell were esteemed guests at Republican National Conventions, and in 1984 Criswell, whom the journal *Christianity Today* in March 2002 called "the Baptist Pope," spoke at the convention, where he said: "I believe this notion of the separation of church and state was the figment of some infidel's imagination."[23] This is the worst sentence a Baptist ever voiced on the church/state issue. The logical end of this betrayal of a time-honored Baptist principle was achieved when the SBC left the Baptist World Alliance in 2004, which made it crystal-clear that the SBC had given up traditional Baptist values.

In sum: To keep the realm of government and religion separated was a radical idea through which the persecuted small band of Baptists tried to ensure liberty for all people in a given land. The state was not to be used for religious ends, nor any religion exploited for political gains. The government had to make sure that religion was not to be narrowed to a personal piety in seclusion, but that each religious faith had the right to free and secure exercise of religion in public. The early Baptists were convinced that these goals could be attained only by keeping a hedge or wall between the two realms. When Baptists gained power in the South by their sheer numbers and acted as a pillar of Southern culture, they went on a rampage to have their own convictions made the law of the land. The SBC

---

[22] Curtis W. Freeman, "'Never Had I Been So Blind': W.A. Criswell's 'Change' on Racial Segregation," *Journal of Southern Religion* 10 (2007): 1–12.

[23] Quoted in Richard V. Pierard, "Religion and the 1984 Election Campaign," *Review of Religious Research* 27 (December 1985): 104–105.

turned into a "culture-based Baptist church," which is a *contradictio in adjecto.*[24]

THE HOLY SCRIPTURES

The letter "S" must be represented twice and refers, secondly, to the Scriptures. From the very beginning of the "conservative resurgence," the view of Holy Scripture was crucial, and here the belief that the Bible is inerrant was identified as the key to success. In fact, the "conservatives" are known to this day as "inerrantists." Therefore, the BF&M's first article is on the Scriptures. The Bible is said to be God's revelation and to have been "written by men divinely inspired." The Scriptures are "the supreme standard" by which all conduct and opinions "should be tried." This can be said because the Bible "has God for its author" and, hence, is pure truth "without any mixture of error"; "all Scripture is totally true and trustworthy." Even though the term "inerrancy" did not find its way into the revised BF&M, the idea is conveyed in no uncertain terms. The committee that revised the BF&M responded to the question as to why it had changed the language in article 1 with these words:

> Events in recent years have demonstrated that we needed to clarify that the Bible is not merely the record of God's revelation, but is itself God's revealed Word in written form. With Christians throughout the ages, most Southern Baptists believe in verbal inspiration. The Bible itself teaches that every word of Scripture was inspired by God, and is therefore completely true and trustworthy (2 Tim. 3:16). The Bible is inerrant, infallible, and is our sole authority for faith and practice in the Church.

In this section all the important words are assembled: verbal inspiration, inerrant, infallible, sole authority. The Bible is a divine dictum, and every story or passage, even every word, is looked upon as on the same level because it is God who speaks. Distinctions within texts cannot be made as it would mean to differentiate between inerrant, and therefore non-negotiable, texts.

One thing is certain, however. The proof-text 2 Timothy 3:16—"All Scripture (*pasa graphe*) is God-breathed (*theopneustos*) and is useful for teaching, rebuking, correcting, and training in righteousness"—does not say what the committee seems to imply. What does the author mean by "every writing"? In the preceding two verses the writer addresses the recipient of the letter: "continue in what you have learned [...] and how from childhood you have known the sacred writings (*hiera grammata*) [...]." Apparently the addressee was brought up in the Jewish tradition and was familiarized with the sacred texts. The writer was certainly not referring to New Testament texts or to his own letter. Consequently,

---

[24] A contradiction between parts of an argument. A Baptist church can never be culture-based or dependent upon the prevailing culture.

the Bible nowhere teaches "that every word of Scripture was inspired by God" because the Bible did not exist at the time 2 Timothy 3:16 was written. As this is the only verse in the entire Bible that addresses the issue of "inspiration," the SBC's contention rests on very shallow ground.

Nevertheless, representatives of the SBC refer to their constituencies as "a people of the book" and their understanding of Scripture as a "high view." This claim is made because the Bible, in their opinion, is "inerrant," "infallible," "completely true." and "trustworthy." By contrast, it must be inferred that theologians or laypeople who do not subscribe to this perspective uphold a "low view." In Baptist history it has always been maintained that every individual believer has a right to his or her interpretation of Holy Scriptures so that the SBC standpoint, irrational as it is, represents one possibility. What is wrong, however, is the official categorizing by the denomination that theirs is a "high" view, and all others are "low." One must argue that those who follow the "low" concept are deeply convinced that their theological discourse is no less based upon the Scriptures. Their position reflects the biblical tradition even closer than the SBC's because they read the Bible not with dogmatic assumptions of seventeenth-century Protestant scholasticism, with its emphasis on verbal inspiration, or with philosophical suppositions of nineteenth-century Scottish Common Sense philosophy. Nowhere in the Bible can be found anything that resembles the idea of inerrancy or infallibility.

The latter word was used in the fourth chapter of the Dogmatic Constitution on the Church, *Pastor aeternus*, by the Roman-Catholic First Vatican Council in 1870. The council defined as a divinely revealed dogma that the Roman pontiff, when he speaks *ex cathedra* on matters of faith and morals, is possessed of infallibility and that his definitions "are of themselves and not from the consent of the Church irreformable" (Denziger § 1839). Whereas papal infallibility was defined in 1870, less than a decade later a number of conservative evangelicals in the United States began to meet at the Niagara Bible Conferences (1878–1897) and applied the term to the Bible. Papal and scriptural authority were in both cases defiant assertions against a perceived threat: With unification of Italy, the Papal States were seized by the Italian Kingdom, and Pope Pius IX, one of the longest-reigning popes (1846–1878) and by all accounts one of the most conservative in history, referred to himself as "the prisoner in the Vatican."[25] Through the decision of the First Vatican Council, he created the last absolutist State in Europe as an ecclesiastical-monarchical regime to be a bulwark against liberal and democratic ideas.

The emerging fundamentalist movement acted likewise against the crisis of

---

[25] What came to be known as the "Roman Question" was the status of the Pope in Rome, which was finally resolved in 1929 when the Lateran Treaty was signed.

authority, presumably brought forth by liberal modernism. The highest authority in the Roman-Catholic Church was by the decision of the council invested in a person, the bishop of Rome. As in seventeenth-century Protestant scholasticism, the rising fundamentalist movement in America at the end of the nineteenth century responded by creating an infallible "paper pope," which is what the SBC reiterated in the BF&M. In both cases, Luther's concept of *sola scriptura,* the Scripture alone, was misrepresented. Luther proclaimed that the Bible alone rules: *solam scripturam regnare*; it alone is the source of authority and the sole criterion of Christian theology. He thus refuted the Catholic notion that the authority is based upon a combination of the Bible, Holy Tradition, and the teaching *magisterium* of bishops and the pope. The question presented itself who, if not the Roman pontiff, had the final authority to interpret Scripture. According to Luther, that authority is inherent in the Bible itself; the Bible is "through itself most trustworthy, perspicuous, and its own interpreter" (*per se certissima, apertissima, sui ipsius interpres*). The Bible, however, should not be "divinized" or "sacralized," but the living word of the gospel (*viva vox evangelii*) must constantly be proclaimed to human beings. Humans must receive God's word passively; God and likewise His Word are not at the disposal of any human person, be he or she pastor, bishop, president of a seminary, pope, or any other church functionary or layperson.

As God's word is not a human property, it must be safeguarded against any sort of arbitrary interpretation. There is also no doubt that the Bible needs to be interpreted; otherwise, any preaching would be worthless. In fact, if the doctrine of verbal inspiration were true, the only way to use the Bible responsibly in a worship service would be simply to read portions of Scripture. Any kind of comment or any attempt to clarify a text would have to be considered a human encroachment upon the very Word of God. If the Holy Scriptures need interpretation, there can be little doubt that in order to interpret a biblical text, the interpreter needs to have a criterion for the art of interpretation. According to Luther, the only protection against capricious interpretation must be derived from the Bible itself as it is its own interpreter. For Luther, there is a "center of Scripture" (*Mitte der Schrift*), which is the "Christ-message." This message is the only valid criterion because it is inherently part of the Bible. Any other criterion would be a human measure from outside the Scriptures. With this standard, Luther was in a position to criticize decisions of church councils, the popes, bishops, and even parts of Scripture itself. The letter of James is a case in point. It stated, contrary to Luther's understanding of Paul, that good deeds were necessary for salvation: "What good is it if someone claims to have faith but has no deeds? Can such faith save them? [...] You see that a person is considered righteous by what they do and not by faith alone" (James 2:14.24, NIV). For Luther, righteousness was granted by God for free to the believer on behalf of Christ, and he saw James' letter as teaching differently. For this reason, he called the letter "straw," i.e., the fruit had been threshed. This metaphor underlines that Luther, despite of *sola scriptura*, took the liberty to criticize a passage of Scripture when he saw the Christ-message and, as in this case, justification by faith alone, endangered. The principle *sola scriptura* must not be singled out, but must be seen in relation to three other "alones": *solus Christus, sola gratia, sola fide* = by Christ alone, by grace alone, by faith alone.

The BF&M does not follow the Reformation principle. Adrian Rogers as chair of the committee stated, "We have removed the statement that identified Jesus Christ as 'the criterion by which the Bible is to be interpreted,' because it has been subject to misunderstanding." Rogers, however, contributes much to misunderstanding when he writes, "We must not claim a knowledge of Christ that is independent of Scripture or in any way in opposition to Scripture."[26] Who makes such a claim? Who can be a Christian theologian and "invent" extra-scriptural or even scripture-opposing christological assumptions? This is clearly a misrepresentation of theological discourses beyond the limited scope of Southern Baptist theology. Whoever is outside the latter's "bubble" cannot be recognized as a Christian who is also "committed to historic Christianity," as Albert Mohler once wrote. Mohler, president of Southern Baptist Seminary, also stated that whoever embraces the historical critical analysis of Holy Scripture does so to "undermine" biblical truth. This is absolutely not the case; the historical analysis is done to differentiate between human language and the Word of God.[27] The criterion, for Luther, was whether or not Christ is "driven" (*Christum treyben*), i.e., the Christ-message is spread. If Christ is not the criterion by which to interpret the Bible, extra-biblical criteria such as verbal inspiration, inerrancy, or infallibility are the lenses through which the Bible is read without taking any historical or sociological facts into consideration. This very low view of Scripture readily lends itself to abandon historic Baptist distinctives or to introduce topics that traditionally never had a place in a confession.[28]

When in 2017 the Tennessee State Convention voted to oust First Baptist Church in Jefferson City from its ranks, Kelly Moreland Jones concluded that the only rationale

> was a vague proof-text reference to what I presume was 1 Timothy 2:12, "I permit no woman to teach or to have authority over a man; she is to keep silent." It might be interesting to consider other verses that appear

---

[26] Quotes are taken from www.sbc.net/bfm2000/bfmchairman.asp.

[27] Colin Harris, "Divide-and-Conquer Strategy Weakens Christian Unity," *EthicsDaily.com* (posted 6 January 2015).

[28] An example is the section on the family.

> in the same chapter: "I desire, [...] that the women should dress themselves modestly and decently in suitable clothing, not with their hair braided, or with gold, pearls, or expensive clothes" (1 Tim. 2:8–9). If we are to accept these verses as literal instructions from God for worship, then my congregation should get kicked to the curb also. I see designer clothes, pearls, and gold every Sunday and often a woman will pray publicly.

Her closing remark is as simple as it is convincing: "Proof-texting as means of biblical interpretation does not work. It is a disrespectful, inappropriate use of the holy text to cherry-pick verses and selfishly use them to control and undermine people."[29]

In sum: There is no proof-text that the Bible is verbally inspired, inerrant, or infallible. These categories are applied to the Bible from "outside" the biblical tradition. The Bible must be historically analyzed to avoid a fundamentalist misreading or cherry-picking verses. It is not a textbook with "instructions" for a culture war.

TRINITY

The last letter "T" could stand for trinity, even though this is not a particular Baptist distinctive, but a concept that unites Baptists with the entire Christian community. It is true, however, that some Baptists in the eighteenth century yielded to the unitarian movement and rejected the trinity, but the majority of Baptists never did. Accordingly, the BF&M presents as its second article on "God" three sub-articles on Father, Son, and Spirit. There are two marks Baptists emphasized, but which are not mentioned in the BF&M. In connection with the Lordship of Christ, Baptists have often referred to "the crown rights of the redeemer" as opposed to the crown rights of a king. The first General Secretary of the Baptist World Alliance, James Henry Rushbrooke (1870–1947), in his opening address at the fifth Congress in 1934 in Berlin, Germany, spoke of a higher loyalty that transcended political, national, or economic programs and urged his hearers "to resist any invasion of the Crown Rights of the Redeemer."[30] It seems that this expression goes beyond "crucicentrism" as the Easter event, and not the cross, is at the center of this metaphor. The second mark early Baptists emphasized and which seems to have been mostly forgotten concerns the third person of the trinity. The Holy Spirit is, after Christ ascended into heaven, sent down to

---

[29] Kelly Moreland Jones, "Three Lessons from TN Baptists' Decision to Oust Church," *EthicsDaily.com* (posted 17 November 2017).

[30] Quoted in *Baptists Together in Christ 1905–2005: A Hundred-Year History of the Baptist World Alliance* (Falls Church VA: BWA; and Birmingham AL: Samford University Press, 2005) 84.

his saints as the true comforter. The spirit now takes the place of Christ on earth; the spirit and not the pope or any other human is Christ's deputy on earth, and hence, the spirit is a "public" spirit: "That is a private spirit that is not of God, though it be in multitudes; but the Spirit of God, though but in one saint is not private. God's spirit is not private, for it is not comprehended only within one place, person, or time, as man's is, but it is universal and eternal."[31]

Conclusion

Almost all of the Baptist distinctives under discussion are in the area of ecclesiology: the structures of the church in conjunction with believers' baptism, its congregational polity, its membership, its voluntary principle, and its role in public as a community that is filled by the public Spirit of God and cries out for liberty of conscience and religion in a century of religious persecution and military strife. If another and outstanding Baptist contribution would be added, the idea of liberty would be further underlined: It is the tremendously important gift that the black Baptist tradition contributed to Baptist life. In the midst of slavery and, later, Jim Crow laws and segregation, black Baptist ministers and laypeople never forgot that God is on the side of the oppressed and disinherited, and that He eventually will lead his people out of slavery into the promised land of freedom: "free at last."

If one would have to compile a list of the distinctives in the order of their theological importance, ecclesiology or freedom would not occupy the first place. Neither would the Bible be in this position. As the church is not a human organization, but the church of Christ, and as the Holy Scriptures bear witness to Christ, it is the Lordship of Christ that is theologically the center of all thinking and practice of faithful Baptists. The *sola scriptura* principle also entails the centrality of Christ: *solus Christus*. It also needs to be pointed out that the trinitarian approach comes into focus: Baptists try to discern and do the will of *God* in the name of the Lord *Jesus Christ* and in the power of the *Holy Spirit.*

The Authority of the Bible

When reviewing some Baptist distinctives in light of Baptist tradition, scriptural evidence, and modern developments, and when comparing these factors with what the SBC holds in its BF&M, it must be concluded that almost all of the important Baptist distinctives are no longer held by the SBC. This is also true

[31] "A Most Humble Supplication of Many of the King's Majesty's Loyal Subjects, Ready to Testify All Civil Obedience by the Oath of Allegiance, or Otherwise, and that of Conscience; Who Are Persecuted (Only for Differing in Religion) Contrary to Divine and Human Testimonies" (1620), repr. in Edward Bean Underhill, *Tracts on Liberty of Conscience and Persecution 1614–1661* (London: Hanserd Knollys Society, 1846) 200.

for the authority of the Bible. When the historic-critical analysis of Holy Writ and Darwin's evolutionary biology made their way into academic discourses, conservative sections of American Protestantism felt they had to safeguard the Bible against "modernist" intrusions. They went back to Protestant scholasticism of the seventeenth century, which had advanced the idea of verbal inspiration. Additionally, the views of infallibility and inerrancy were applied to the Scriptures, and the Bible was interpreted by methodological tools as advanced by Scottish Common Sense philosophy. These safeguards have not prevented the SBC or leading figures to come to absurd conclusions. A few examples may suffice: One is the 1982 resolution of the convention that called for the teaching of "scientific creationism" in the public schools. In recent discussions on gun control, both Southern Baptist ordained ministers Tony Perkins (Family Research Council) and Russell Moore (president of ERLC) found nothing in Scripture that only "vaguely" supports gun control or that is "clearly revealed in Scriptures."[32] The president of Southwestern Baptist Theological Seminary, Paige Patterson, gives away guns to attract "unchurched men" at "second amendment rallies" and tells his audience that every boy should have "a dog, a dad, and a gun."[33] How can any clear-thinking person expect a "revelation" on "gun control" in the Bible? Why would a theologian resort to the second amendment and to a ridiculous "pedagogic trinity"? The epidemic of mass shootings in America is not only caused by the astronomical number of guns in private hands, but also by pro-gun Baptist theologians who claim "second amendment freedom."[34] Why do "Bible-believing" Southern Baptist inerrantists not recall the simple and clear commandment, "Thou shalt not kill"?

THE CHRISTIAN RIGHT

The SBC and its leading figures are part of what is called the Christian Right. It has been carrying on an assault on liberalism and the cultural changes that are part of an "open" and "free" society. The paradox is that this anti-liberal movement can thrive only in a liberal (= free) society, but that the liberality would give way to illiberality or authoritarianism at the very moment the Christian Right would succeed to establish its norms and values as the law of the land. It must be pointed out that liberal ideas are not an alien tradition that had as its aim the

---

[32] Sara Palliam Bayley, "A Sin Issue or a Gun Issue? Why Evangelicals Are Deeply Skeptical of Gun-Control Laws," *Washington Post*, 6 November 2017.

[33] "Bob Allen's Report," in *Baptist News Global*, 10 November 2017. Patterson emphasized that he did not mean a toy gun.

[34] The Second Amendment right to keep and bear arms was for members of a state militia before there was any United States military service. Besides, this "freedom" was especially used against Native Americans.

destruction of Christianity.

Baptists should always remember that their forefathers in colonial America, contrary to evangelicals for example, were political allies of James Madison, Thomas Jefferson, and other enlightened deists in their fight for religious liberty. Contrary to the myth that the Christian Right propagandizes, the founding fathers of the American Republic and the framers of the Constitution were not evangelical Christians whose aim had been to establish a "Christian America." The United States Constitution does not invoke God;[35] the "Godlessness" of the Constitution was to give every denomination and religion a chance to flourish in public, which actually happened.[36] A few years after the Constitution was ratified, the Bill of Rights amended this fundamental law with the blessings of Baptist leaders. The first amendment concerns freedom of religion, to be followed by the freedom of speech, of the press, of demonstrations, and to petition the government. Religious freedom was the door to political freedoms, including the freedom of the press, which today is in jeopardy because of media concentration in the hands of a few. In addition, there is the infotainment industry and, in recent months, the relentless attack by President Trump on the press and other media for spreading "fake news," whereas he is, in fact, twittering countless lies and misinformation. To be true to the Baptist tradition of freedom would mean today to stand up for truth in the media and government, to combat white supremacy and all other powerful forces that try to undermine individual and social human rights.

Human Sexuality and American Exceptionalism

It is striking how much the discussion in the United States is concentrated on issues related to human sexuality. Sex, sex education in public schools, birth control, contraceptives, abortion, reproductive healthcare, pro-choice, pro-life, homosexuality, same-sex marriage, the LGBT community, obscenity, and censorship laws are examples. They lead to grotesque consequences: Should censorship laws extend to museums and the removal of pieces of art, as they are considered pornography? Can the constitutionality of the Affordable Care Act be upheld, as it would provide money for contraceptives? Why do lawmakers in many states make it difficult for women to obtain an abortion by not allocating money for hospitals that perform a termination of unwanted pregnancies? Will lawmakers intentionally increase back-alley abortions of poor women or trips

---

[35] Religion is referred to only in article VI, section 3, which prohibits a test of religious affiliation as qualification for public office, as was the case in England.

[36] See the illuminating book by Roger Finke and Rodney Stark, *The Churching of America 1776–2005: Winners and Losers in our Religious Economy* (New Brunswick NJ: Rutgers University Press, 2005).

abroad of the rich to acquire the desired end? Why is public funding for organizations such as Planned Parenthood refused? Why is the sale of a wedding cake an expression of religious liberty? This list could go on so that the question must be addressed why human sexuality is such a cardinal issue, which seems to border on an obsession.

In large part, perhaps exclusively, the answer has to do with gender roles and the desire to conserve traditional norms that are sometimes referred to as "American," sometimes as "Christian" values. To use the words of the BF&M, in the traditional home the husband is the "servant-leader" and his wife is "graciously submissive" to his leadership. The relationship is thus clearly defined in favor of male dominance. Any changes would mean to empower women and to upset the value system of the "American-Christian" family. As this system is supposedly based on biblical teaching, the underlying theory is that "modernist" changes would result in a total break-up of the structure of American society and would, thus, result in the downturn of America as God's chosen nation. In the final analysis, the issue of sexuality has to do with American exceptionalism as a nation that is especially chosen by God to be a "city upon a hill" (Matt. 5:14) among the nations of the world.[37]

In this connection, it is disturbing that two high-profile public figures of the SBC made headlines late in 2017 because of alleged sexual misconduct. One is retired Alabama judge Roy Moore, who, with the endorsement of President Trump, ran unsuccessfully for the United States Senate on the platform of family values and to secure America's standing as a "Christian nation." He was accused by several women of sexual harassment when the judge was in his early thirties and the women were teenagers. At the time of these alleged incidents, the judge was denied entrance to a shopping mall where he is supposed to have chased the girls.

The other figure is former justice on the Texas 14th Court of Appeals, Paul Pressler. In this case, a now 55-year-old man accused Pressler of sexual misconduct for decades. The news of this case must be seen as a bombshell because Pressler was the prime architect of the "conservative resurgence" that radically changed the entire SBC. It goes without saying that both men denied the charges. Pressler invoked the statute of limitation. Whatever verdict the courts will reach in either case, it is noteworthy that the SBC leadership was conspicuously silent when the news broke, but there is little doubt that these incidents further deteriorated the SBC's public reputation as "America's largest Protestant denomination."

American exceptionalism, however, has very little to do with religion, but

---

[37] See Andrew J. Bacevich, *The Limits of Power: The End of American Exceptionalism* (New York: Holt Paperbacks, 2009).

much more with the military-industrial complex. Not the good, benevolent, friendly, helpful, church- and synagogue-attending American people are known throughout the world as a "city upon a hill," but large-scale military adventures, lately known as the "global war on terror," and arm sales including those to dictators and other authoritarian potentates.[38] Other areas where America as a city upon a hill is widely visible include the financial power of Wall Street and its enslaving global impact on nations, or the turning a blind eye on global warming and other forms of pollution, as President Trump demonstrated for all the world to see when he withdrew the United States from the Paris climate accord. The expansion of the American Empire has only recently been visualized on a world map showing "no less than 76 countries, 39 percent of those on the planet, as involved in that global conflict."

The map, prepared by the Costs of War Project at Brown University's Watson Institute for International and Public Affairs, "offers an astounding vision of Washington's counterterror wars across the globe." By November 2017 the cost had reached "an astronomical $5.6 trillion."[39] If one adds the human suffering that these prolonged military conflicts cause, one wonders why the Global Church does not cry out more loudly and why the Christian Right in the United States is more interested in "making America great" and in spending millions of dollars in the fight for the unborn than in defending and saving the lives of the born and in keeping the military-industrial complex "somewhat" under control.

It is unbelievable how much power military people have assumed in the Trumpian White House: Retired General James ("Mad Dog") Mattis is Secretary of Defense, Lieutenant General H.R. McMaster was appointed to the role of national security adviser, retired General James Kelly acts as the White House chief-of-staff, and Lieutenant General Mark Inch is the director of the Bureau of Prisons. The latter spent his career running military prisons, including the secret ones where crimes against humanity were committed. It used to be that civilians controlled the military. Trump, however, relies on former generals, despite a five-year ban on such service, which in these cases was waived. This seems to be a dangerous development for American democracy, as these men are used to thinking in military rather than political terms, which will further stabilize the notion that American exceptionalism means its military might.[40] If one adds to

[38] Even though the United States is the largest supplier of weapons in today's world, other Western countries like Germany, France, or Great Britain are guilty of the same "business" undertaking.

[39] For this valuable information, see Tom Engelhardt, "Mapping a World from Hell: 76 Countries Are Now Involved in Washington's War on Terror," *TomDispatch,* 5 January 2018.

[40] Tom Engelhardt, "Creating an Empire of Graveyards? At the Circus with Donald Trump," www.tomdispatch.com/post/176377.

this list Secretary of State Rex Tillerson, who is totally inexperienced as a diplomat and, instead, headed one of the world's gigantic polluters, it is little surprising that career diplomats are leaving the department and thereby diminishing the reputation of the United States even further.[41]

Make America Great Again

When Southern Baptist leader and pastor of First Baptist Church in Dallas, Robert Jeffress, had his church choir sing a special musical piece with the words "Make America Great Again," the first word as sung in a sanctuary during a worship service can only be understood as a supplication for God's gracious assistance to restore America to its former grandeur.[42] For both President Trump and Baptist pastor Jeffress, America's greatness is its extraordinary—some would call it "terrifying"—military might. When Trump announced on 6 December 2017 that the United States embassy would be moved from Tel Aviv to Jerusalem, Jeffress commented: "President Trump is not only on the right side of history; he is on the right side of God."[43] This statement is closely tied to American exceptionalism, as the idea behind it is that God will bless the United States if it blesses Israel and curse America if it does not. To invoke God to ensure America's military power also means to maintain its ability to help Israel within a geopolitical frame. Thus, "Make America Great Again" involves traditional "family values" with the husband as servant leader; American exceptionalism that is, first of all, its military strength; and the protection and support of Israel, not for the sake of the Jewish State, but for America to enjoy God's continued blessing.[44] All of this is blasphemy and heresy.

The same can be said of the Values Voter Summit organized by Southern Baptist minister Tony Perkins of the "Family Research Council" in mid-October 2017, when both President Trump and Steve Bannon showed up. One need not have a "research" council to know that the United States President is two times divorced and married for the third time with a "model." Why does the president's marital status represent "Christian" or "family values"? Why is his sexual behavior

---

[41] This essay was completed at the end of February 2018. In the meantime, persons who are mentioned here are no longer in their positions, but have withdrawn or were fired by the chief executive (August 2018).

[42] If "make" is grammatically the imperative singular or plural, it would be an appeal to a voter or voters.

[43] See "Bob Allen's Report," in *Baptist News Global*, 19 December 2017.

[44] To ensure God's blessing for the United States, thus, has anti-Jewish overtones. If certain views of the end-time as held by many fundamentalists would be added, the anti-Jewish attitude would be even more apparent.

with a porn star and a playboy model not an embarrassment for the Values Voters?[45] Why is there such a confusion among SBC leaders?

Another document underlines this confusion: At the end of August 2017, an "evangelical coalition statement on biblical sexuality" was released in Nashville. Almost identical with the BF&M article on the family, the "Nashville Statement" defines marriage as a "lifelong union of one man and one woman" and denies justification for any "sexual intercourse before or outside marriage." Russell Moore who heads the SBC's ERLC called the statement, which was signed by the six seminary presidents of the SBC, "an urgently needed moment of gospel clarity." President Trump is obviously exempt from this "clarity." Why are the Values Voters and the SBC leadership making these public statements only to turn around and compromise their convictions in order to support a man whose lifestyle is the opposite of what they present to the public? The credibility crisis that such statements cause in the public eye is damaging for the entire Christian community, not just for the "Christian Right." It is hypocrisy, and its falseness turns the Christian faith into an ideology.[46] That the "Christian Right" and white "evangelical" voters supported Trump by more than 80 percent will probably have long-lasting effects as far as the next generation and its views of Christianity are concerned. Evangelicalism lost its integrity by being power-hungry and by acting as a "state and culture church."

"Make America Great Again" is also an expression of crude social Darwinism. It takes the fittest to survive, which is also true for nations. To make America great means it proves to be the fittest for its survival at the expense of any other nation. This, needless to say, is a totally un-Christian attitude.

---

[45] When the "Access Hollywood" tape surfaced with Trump bragging about grabbing women "by the pussy," many observers thought that Trump was unelectable, especially by women. Nonetheless, 53 percent of women voted for him.

[46] It is astounding that President Trump's behavior does not cause "evangelical" leaders to withdraw their endorsement. His twitter messages reveal that he has no respect for truth. His insistence on total non-facts as facts or the expressions "fake news" and "alternative facts" speak for themselves. Telling the truth has always been a Christian virtue and may not be sacrificed at the altar of narcissistic self-glorification, which has always been looked at as a vice. Trump's attitude on race is another point. He has widened the racial divide in the United States and was a "birther." His assertions that Nigerians live in huts, all Haitians have AIDS, all Mexicans are drug smugglers, Mexican judges do not know the law, and many immigrants come from "shithole" countries are further indications of his racial biases and his contempt for others. This is most certainly an un-Christian attitude. The gospel—good news—is betrayed when a white tribalist and divisive mysoginist is given standing ovations by Christian "values voters."

Closing Remarks

Christianity has proven itself very flexible when in the past it encountered other religious or cultural traditions. Missiologists speak of a process of contextualization for Christianity to take roots. Famous German church historian Adolf von Harnack (1851–1930) spoke of a "Hellinization," a "Romanization," and a "Germanization" of Christianity. By the same token, one may speak of an "Americanization," i.e., a blending of religion and culture. The most important factors in defining the Americanization developed over a rather long span of time and certainly include a democratic culture and the notion of religious liberty, as well as individual and social human rights. How different religions would live peacefully side by side was of prime importance. It concerned first the various Christian denominations, to be joined later by non-Christian religions as well. The hedge or wall of separation proved to be the most convincing answer so that diverse religious communities enjoyed the free display of their convictions in the public square, while the government made sure that every individual had the freedom to exercise his or her religion or stay away from any religion. At the same time, religious communities had the liberty to function as independent centers of free, informed, and public debates and would, therefore, have the responsibility to raise their prophetic voices in the interest of the common good to call the attention of government officials and members of Congress to certain negative developments, such as breaches or denials of human rights, racial inequality, poverty, unemployment and huge gaps of income, injustices, militarization of society, war, and other deficiencies.

This ideal would last only as long as one religion would not attempt to dominate the body politic. However, should that happen, the blending of Christianity and culture would be carried to an extreme that would have to be referred to as an effort to establish a "theocracy" of sorts. There can be little doubt that the tendency to such an extreme is inherent in American fundamentalism. According to this outlook, the moral crisis in American society can best be substantiated by looking at the deviations of gender roles and sexual behavior. These deviations must be overcome by a supposedly Bible-centered religiosity that entails patriarchic authority in the church and patriarchal control of women in order to go back to and advance the traditional American family. As the modern pluralistic state does not help in this effort, it must be taken over in order to come to a "religiously and morally integrated society."[47] This explains why leading Southern Baptists

---

[47] Martin Riesebrodt, *Fundamentalismus als patriarchalische Protestbewegung: amerikanische Protestanten (1910–1928) und iranische Schiiten (1961–1979) im Vergleich* (Tübingen: J.C.B. Mohr, 1990) Engl. trans. as *Pious Passion: The Emergence of Modern Fundamentalism in the United States and Iran*, trans. Don Reneau (Berkeley CA: University of California Press, 1993) 208.

try to get close to the powers that be to promote their cause. This kind of Americanization, however, is not a legitimate blending of religion and culture, but an intrusion of ideological religion into the gospel and into the culture and public policy.

In sum: The theological deviation from traditional Baptist distinctives, the fundamentalist approach to the Bible, and the extreme political ambitions make the Southern Baptist Convention a denomination that carries the name "Baptist," but is actually a Southern fundamentalist culture religion. It is more than symbolic that the SBC isolated itself from the rest of world Baptists when, in 2004, it withdrew from the Baptist World Alliance, which SBC leaders had worked hard to get started in 1904/1905.

SECTION 4

HISTORICAL STUDIES

THE REFORMATION ACCORDING TO ALBERT HENRY NEWMAN[1]

Chris Chun

Albert Henry Newman (1852–1933) was one of the first historians to cast a positive light on sixteenth-century Anabaptists. This was done before the patron saint of the Reformation, Roland Bainton (1894–1984), tagged the movement as the "left wing" of the Reformation,[2] before Harvard's George Huntston Williams (1914–2000) dubbed them as the "radicals" of the Reformation,[3] and even ahead of Southwestern's William Estep (1920–2000) stripping the negative stigma of Anabaptist caricatures.[4]

A.H. Newman was born in the Edgefield District of South Carolina on 25 August 1852, and died on 4 June 1933. From his early years as a child prodigy into adulthood and his professional career as a church historian, he exhibited remarkable intellectual capacity. Newman bypassed two academic grades when he entered Mercer University and graduated at the top of his class in 1871. After graduating from Rochester Baptist Theological Seminary, Newman wanted to further his studies in Germany with the intention of becoming a scholar. However, Crawford Toy, cognizant of Newman's exceptional abilities in Old Testament exegesis and linguistics, recruited Newman to study with him at the Southern Baptist Theological Seminary. In addition to Toy, he was mentored in New Testament and Patristics from none other than John Broadus.[5] After his

---

[1] On Wednesday, 15 November 2017, an earlier version of this paper was delivered at the 69th Annual Meeting of the Evangelical Theological Society held in Providence, Rhode Island. To commemorate the 500th-anniversary Protestant Reformation, the theme in the Baptist study group was "Baptist Historians and the Reformation." In this venue, Professor William Brackney presented his paper, "Interpreting the Reformation from within German Dissent: August and Walter Rauschenbusch," from 9 until 9:40 A.M. It was indeed a great honor for me to give my paper on A.H. Newman immediately following Brackney's presentation.

[2] Roland H. Bainton, "The Left Wing of the Reformation," *The Journal of Religion* 21/2 (April 1941): 124–34; see also, Roland H. Bainton, *Studies on the Reformation* (Boston: Beacon Press, 1963) 119–207.

[3] George Huntston Williams, *The Radical Reformation* (Philadelphia: The Westminster Press, 1962).

[4] William R. Estep, *The Anabaptist Story* (Grand Rapids: Eerdmans, 1975); and also, William R. Estep, "A.H. Newman and Southwestern's First Faculty," *The Southwestern Journal of Theology* 21 (Fall 1978): 83–98.

[5] For his year at the Southern Seminary, see Frederick Eby, *Newman the Church Historian*

formal education, Newman's academic appointments as a church historian in Baptist institutions were wide-ranging. He taught for four years at the Rochester Theological Seminary (1877–1881), ten years at Toronto Baptist College (1881–1891),[6] twelve years at McMaster University (1891–1901, 1927–1929),[7] six years at Baylor University (1901–1907), and six years at Mercer University (1921–1927). He also was a visiting professor at the University of Chicago during an era when the institution's Baptist roots could still be felt in 1906. He was one of the founding faculty members when the Southwestern Baptist Theological Seminary relocated near Fort Worth in 1910. Given his academic background, it is no surprise that Newman published hundreds of articles. Two of his most substantial works were *A History of Anti-Paedobaptism: From the Rise of Paedobaptism to A.D. 1609* (1897)[8] and *A History of the Baptist Churches in the United States* (1894).[9]

At this point, I noticed a striking parallel between Newman and William Brackney. Both esteemed Baptist historians have intricate connections to McMaster University, Canada, and the Radical Reformation—*um nur einige Beispiele zu nennen*, to mention only a few examples. Brackney currently is Millard R. Cherry Distinguished Professor of Christian Thought and Ethics, Emeritus, at Acadia Divinity College in Wolfville, Nova Scotia. He is the director of Acadia Centre for Baptist and Anabaptist Studies, and the Fellow at Institut für Baptismusstudien des Theologischen Seminars, Elstal, Germany. Brackney also is the chairman of the board of governors and president of the Canadian Bible Society; moreover, he is the general editor for both Baptists in the Early North America Project as well as the Walter Rauschenbusch Project. In one of his personal e-mails addressed to me, Brackney recollects a time when A.H. Newman became his role model:

> Arguably, Newman's greatest literary achievement was his *History of the Baptist Churches in the United States*, a volume in the American Church History Series, published between 1893 and 1897. Among several contemporary Baptists, Newman was chosen, probably because of his chair in a university. Newman's recognition in a wider readership was evident.

(Nashville: Broadman Press, 1946) 28–29.

[6] Ibid., 36–40.

[7] For Newman's service to McMaster and Canada, see ibid., 40–47.

[8] A.H. Newman, *A History of Anti-Paedobaptism: From the Rise of Paedobaptism to A.D. 1609* (Philadelphia: The American Baptist Publication Society, 1897).

[9] A.H. Newman, *A History of the Baptist Churches in the United States* (New York: The Christian Literature Co., 1894). The revision of this book can be found in a series called "Denominations in America"; it was authored by Professor Brackney. See William H. Brackney, *The Baptists,* Denominations in America series (Westport CT: Greenwood Press, 1994). I am gratefully indebted to Erich Geldbach, who brought this point to my attention.

> Henry Warner Bowden at Rutgers University and Greenwood Press introduced a successor to the American Church History Series, the Denominations in America Series, envisioning a reworking of the original concept. The editorial committee, with the support of Robert T. Handy, nominated an emerging scholar at Eastern Baptist Seminary, soon to be at McMaster University, to do the Baptist volume in the new series. I was overwhelmingly honored to accept the assignment. Once at McMaster, I became very familiar with Newman's career and he became a role model for me.[10]

In spite of Newman's scholarly achievements, this almost forgotten historian[11] escaped my attention until Michael Haykin repeatedly touted Newman as someone who said that Andrew Fuller's "influence on American Baptists has been incalculable."[12] Newman published this statement in a 1909 encyclopedia article on Andrew Fuller in *The New Schaff-Herzog*, a venue where he was a regular contributor as well as one of its editors. Newman's commendation of Fuller caught my attention since I, too, share his assessment of Fuller's significant impact on Baptist life and doctrines in America. This led me to pick up Newman's two-volume magnum opus, *A Manual of Church History* (1900–1903),[13] which was a widely used textbook for church-history courses in many Baptist universities. It is to that tome we turn our attention.

---

[10] William Brackney, e-mail message to author, 5 December 2017. Needless to say, I did not receive a permission to quote this e-mail from Professor Brackney. Both of our ETS papers on Rauschenbusch and Newman were requested to be submitted for publication in the same journal, but I respectfully turned down the request, which Brackney is unaware of the latter. It is in that context, I asked Brackney if I may pick his brain about Newman. Given our relationship, previous conversations, and my admiration for his scholarly knowledge, it is likely that I could direct such a question. Unbeknown to him, I asked because I wanted his thoughts on Newman to be included in this *Festschrift* piece.

[11] One of the main theses of Jonas is that Newman's work was largely outdated in the twentieth century due to failure to "incorporate new development in the field" and "inability to identify with scientific church historiography." See William Glenn Jonas, Jr., "A Critical Evaluation of Albert Henry Newman, Church Historian" (Ph.D. diss., Baylor University, 1990) iv–v.

[12] A.H. Newman, "Fuller, Andrew," in *The New Schaff-Herzog Encyclopedia of Religious Knowledge* (New York and London: Funk & Wagnalls Company, 1909) 4:409. See also, Anthony Chute, Nathan Finn, and Michael Haykin, *The Baptist Story: From English Sect to Global Movement* (Nashville TN: Broadman & Holman, 2015) 101. Michael Haykin quotes, "A.H. Newman said that 'his influence on American Baptists' was 'incalculable.'"

[13] A.H. Newman, *A Manual of Church History*, vol. 1, *Ancient and Mediaeval Church History (to A.D. 1517)* (Philadelphia: American Baptist Publication Society, 1901); and A.H. Newman, *A Manual of Church History*, vol. 2, *Modern Church History (A.D. 1517–1903)* (Philadelphia: American Baptist Publication Society, 1903). Henceforth, *Manual.*

REFORMATION ACCORDING TO NEWMAN IN *A MANUAL OF CHURCH HISTORY*

In the first volume of *A Manual of Church History*, Newman laid out his methodology for engaging in the work of a historian. He did not hesitate to use providentialist language in the opening chapter of his classic. Newman stated, "Sacred history is the setting forth of his known facts of man's development as it has been affected by the providential, inspiriting, and self-revealing presence of God."[14] Having firmly established his commitment to narrating the history of "the kingdom of Christ on earth,"[15] Newman was not timid in displaying his confessional colors or baptistic convictions in print. That said, he also argued for employing a critical and scientific approach to historiography: "The aim of the church historian should be to ascertain and to represent the exact facts in their relations." Newman also stated that the historian should deal with the investigation as "impartially with his materials as does the chemist with his specimens."[16] George Williams, therefore, saw the principles found in the manual as mediating a position between "older sectarian concern" (i.e., providentialist), and yet "within the framework of German ecclesiastical historiography."[17]

Newman sought to stay away from partisan or denominational interest, with the goal instead of pursuing objectivity as a church historian. His principle of critical and scientific versus traditional Baptistic commitments was tested in his lifetime when he was unwittingly drawn into the Whitsitt controversy.[18] Newman agreed with William Whitsitt's basic historical conclusion while keeping Whitsitt at arm's length in the dispute. In fact, there was a side of Newman wanting to believe in the Baptist successionist view as someone who was in sympathy with "spiritual kinship," but his critical method would not allow him to locate the Baptist church prior to the seventeenth century. Hence, if push came to shove, he was willing to go wherever the historical evidence took him. This, of course, led to his reliance on sources.

Newman wrote at great length about the use of primary sources and its employment in his manual. He underscored the need for original language and stated that historians must be able to distinguish between the "genuine and the spurious." On the controversial issues, he highlighted the necessity of examining

---

[14] Newman, *Manual*, 1:4.

[15] Ibid.

[16] Ibid., 1:5.

[17] George Huntston Williams, "Church History: From Historical Theology to the Theology of History," in *Protestant Thought in the Twentieth Century*, ed. Arnold S. Nash (New York: The MacMillan Company, 1951) 151–52.

[18] Jonas gave a fascinating account of why both sides of the debate appealed to Newman for his support. See Jonas, Jr., "A Critical Evaluation of Albert Henry Newman," 201–202.

both sides and reading "prejudiced" writers critically when "they make grave accusations against opponents."[19] In that sense, he relied on primary sources in the spirit of German historiography, although he neither studied in Germany nor was in conformity with their critical method's conclusion.[20]

There is no doubt that Newman was a historian in the Baptist tradition; in fact, Newman produced many pieces to advance Baptist heritage. It is interesting to observe that Newman's biographer, Frederick Eby, titled his book, *Newman: The Church Historian* (1946).[21] This was because, as Charles Deweese observed, "Newman believed that an effective handling of Baptist history presupposed a thorough familiarity with general church history."[22] This, along with his critical methodology, makes his take on reformation so telling. In volume two of the manual, as a general church historian, Newman devoted 346 pages[23] to the sixteenth-century Protestant Reformation. The fact that he dedicated bountiful words suggests the significance of the Reformation in Newman's mind.

In the second volume of the manual, right from the opening chapter, Newman corrected a popular misconception by stating, "The Reformation was not inaugurated by Martin Luther,"[24] then laying out a complex and nuanced survey of various reformatory forces of the later middle ages, such as economic, social, and political conditions that favored what he often referred to as the "Protestant Revolution." Newman next moved into the role humanism played in this milieu, and how the notion that any literate person had the ability to study the scripture in its original language revolutionized the concept of authority. He addressed the Lutheran Reformation meticulously. He also highlighted Luther's peasant background, attributing Luther's direct and rough speech with winning

---

[19] Newman, *Manual*, 1:5.

[20] No wonder Baptist theologian par excellence A.H. Strong referred to Newman's *Manual* as "the most thorough, minutes, and trustworthy account that has ever been given of the American Baptists." For full commendation, see "A.H. Strong's Letter to Newman," in Eby, *Newman the Church Historian*, 74–75.

[21] I was delighted to see that this particular hardback in my possession had a signature of the late Morgan Patterson (1925–2010), a retired dean of what is now Gateway Seminary (formerly, Golden Gate Baptist Theological Seminary). When Patterson passed, he donated his extensive personal library of nearly 5,000 Baptist history and theology books to Gateway Seminary's "Patterson Collection." There were two figures who were instrumental in this acquisition: one was Patterson's widow, Ernestine Patterson, and the other was a longtime family friend, William Brackney.

[22] Charles William Deweese, "The Contributions of Albert Henry Newman to Baptist Historiography," *Baptist History and Heritage* 7 (January 1972): 6.

[23] Newman, *Manual*, 2:3–349. The number would be 387 pages if Catholics' Counter Reformation were counted.

[24] Ibid., 2:3.

favors with German peasantry, who made him their champion over "foreign exploitation and oppression."[25] One of the chief foreign exploitations that Luther reacted against was the abuse of indulgences, of which Newman wrote, "The pope was to have one-half of the proceeds for the building of St. Peter's Cathedral and the payment of his debts."[26] The patriotism of what it meant to be a citizen of Germany and foreign financial corruption were at the root of the Protestant Revolution, according to Newman.

Newman did not hesitate to acknowledge heroic aspects of Luther; nonetheless, he was also critical of Luther and the magisterial reformers: "The preaching and writings of Luther were destructive, rather than constructive. He could, by these denunciations, undermine papal authority, and bring the doctrine of salvation by works into utmost contempt; but he failed signally to develop an apostolical in the place of this monkish piety in his followers."[27]

Indeed, a former Augustinian monk "taught against opera operata (works performed for merits)," but Newman criticized him for being inconsistent. In quoting Luther, Newman roared across the pages of the manual: "Yes, justification by faith alone. No outward rite, apart from faith, has any efficacy...yet baptism must be administered to infants," because "infant baptism has always gone hand in hand with State churches."[28] Paedobaptism is the medium in which the mainline reformers maintained a religious establishment and the state church. The idea that two different forms of Christianity could co-exist in any given state seemed as preposterous to Luther as it did to Catharine de Medici. In that sense, Newman asserted, Reformers were hypocritical, especially as they related to Anabaptists, in that although they themselves were "schismatic," they had a "horror of schism almost as decided as that of the Romanists."[29] As a consequence of their sanctimonious attitudes, magisterial reformers persecuted the Anabaptists in gruesome fashion. "The Reformers were, for the most part, intolerant," according to Newman.[30]

Newman's perception of the Zwinglian Reformation was a mixture of commendation and condemnation. Similar to his exposition of the Lutheran Reformation, he began with the survey of political, social, and economic conditions in Switzerland, though the Swiss were different from their German counterparts because Zwinglians had a more "civil and moral" overtone to it. Furthermore, Zwinglian Reformation was quieter than that of the Lutherans because "[n]o man

[25] Ibid., 2:42.

[26] Ibid., 2:53.

[27] Ibid., 2:117–18.

[28] Ibid., 2:120.

[29] Ibid., 2:121.

[30] A.H. Newman, "The Reformation from a Baptist Point of View," in *Baptist Quarterly Review* 6 (1884): 60.

arose in Switzerland of Luther's vehemence and zeal."[31] Having said that, as a military chaplain, "Zwingli was far more militant than Luther." For instance, when Zwinglian preacher Jacob Kaiser was burned at the stake in 1529 after being pronounced guilty of "evangelizing in Catholic territory," the Protestants immediately took military action "under Zwingli's leadership."[32] Nevertheless, Newman, as a Baptist historian, wrote positively of both reformers when dealing with scriptural authority. Still, this is not without a significant caveat. In one of his many journal articles that were intended for Baptist readers, Newman addressed the subject of Reformation from a Baptist perspective, perhaps more candidly than in the manual:

> Luther and Zwingli had professed to make the Bible the supreme and all-sufficient guide. These men demanded something more than outward profession. They recognized the principle as true, and they demanded that it be unconditionally adhered to. If the Bible is the standard, they argued, why retain papal forms which have no action in the Bible; why allow the unregenerate and evidently irreligious to partake of the ordinances of the Church side by side with the truly regenerate? Why baptize infants, seeing that there is no Scriptural authority for it, and that it is utterly antagonistic to pure Church membership?[33]

This, of course, brought the Zwingli and Anabaptist conundrum into focus. The manual asserted that, according to both Balthasar Hubmaier and Conrad Grebel in their "private conversation," Zwingli had expressed his view "against infant baptism." In critiquing Zwingli's fickle attitudes, Newman reminded that in the early church, "the baptism of infants was not so common as at present, but those to be baptized were instructed as catechumens" and "only baptized after they had firm faith in the heart, and had confessed with the mouth."[34] However, by 1530, "Zwingli denied that anyone had ever heard him say anything against infant baptism."[35] For Newman, the necessity of maintaining infant baptism in Zwingli's thoughts rose out of a need to preserve a "State-Church system." As

---

[31] Newman, *Manual*, 2:126.

[32] Ibid., 2:142.

[33] Newman, "The Reformation from a Baptist Point of View," 65–66.

[34] Newman, *Manual*, 2:152. Zwingli wrote: "Although I know, as the Fathers show, that infants have been baptised occasionally from the earliest times, still it was not so universal a custom as it is now, but the common practice was as soon as they arrived at the age of reason to form them into classes for instruction in the Word of Salvation (hence they were called catechumens, i.e., persons under instruction). And after a firm faith had been implanted in their hearts and they had confessed the same with their mouth, then they were baptised" (Zwingli, as quoted in Samuel Macauley Jackson, *Huldreich Zwingli: The Reformer of German Switzerland (1484–1531)* [New York and London: The Knickerbocker Press, 1901] 243).

[35] Newman, *Manual*, 2:152.

such, Zwingli did not "hesitate to counsel rigorous persecuting measures."[36] Zwingli and other Reformers allowed their political expediency to override their "clear scriptural authorization."[37]

Similar to that of Lutheranism, Newman's treatment of Calvinistic Reformation was detail-oriented, especially for a general church-history survey textbook.[38] The manual designated the Calvinistic Reformation as a "continuation of Zwinglianism," yet had the tendency to mediate between Lutheranism and Zwinglianism, and to that end, was able to consolidate the Protestant forces.[39] Even though John Calvin built the Reformed tradition upon "Zwinglian foundations," Calvin was far from being a Zwinglian, as he had "little esteem" for Zwingli, not nearly as much as for Luther. This was because Zwingli was "liberalistic, humanistic, Erasmic" and "not Augustinian," while on the contrary, Calvin was thoroughly Augustinian. Whereas Zwingli carried out his reformation in subservience to the civil authorities, Calvin more or less "rejected such subserviency." According to Newman, Calvin espoused theocracy where "the church must not only not be dependent on the State, it must rule the State."[40]

In addressing the English Reformation, Newman spelled out religious and political preconditions for Reformation in England—first with Henry VIII, and then followed by the reign of Elizabeth when the "Protestant party had become strong in numbers and in influence," but there was a "constant struggle between the Romanizing and the Protestant parties." The Romanizing party ruled until the time of Charles I, and then the "Protestant (Puritan) party" manifested its power in the execution of the king, thereby overthrowing the "Episcopal system," and "forming of an alliance with the Scottish Presbyterians." In spite of this alliance, Newman criticized the "most characteristic feature of English Protestantism," which was none other than "half-hearted, compromising disposition." He, of course, qualified that Puritans do not fit the characterization of being "half-hearted." Nevertheless, according to Newman, people with "convictions and of conscience were, accordingly, excluded from leadership" in England.[41]

Newman's View of the Anabaptists

The apex of sixteenth-century reformation was the rise of the Anabaptists, according to Newman. He was convinced that this movement best represented the Apostolic Christianity where all the magisterial reformers had failed. While

[36] Ibid., 2:153.
[37] Ibid.
[38] The coverage is from Switzerland, France, Scotland, the Netherlands, and to England.
[39] Newman, *Manual*, 2:201.
[40] Ibid.
[41] Ibid., 2:252.

there were "many varieties of Anabaptist, each leader in having their own 'idiosyncrasies,'" there were also common principles that united them.[42] Such characteristics were (1) regenerate church membership, (2) rejection of infant baptism, (3) repudiation of the connection between church and state, (4) denial of the right to exercise magistracy, (5) prohibition on taking oaths (as pacifists, even in self-defense or defense of country), (6) refusal of capital punishment, and (7) opposition to the Augustinian system of doctrine (i.e., the Lutheran and Calvinistic understanding of free will).[43] What is more, by dividing the Anabaptists into five distinct groups, Newman was one of the first historians to offer a nuanced slant to the stigma that was traditionally associated with this radical reformation.[44]

The first group Newman mentioned were what he called "Chiliastic Anabaptists," the sometimes violent and fanatical faction associated with Thomas Müntzer and the Peasants' War. In the subcategories of Chiliastic Anabaptists, he included Hans Hut, Melchior Rinck, Melchior Hofmann, Jan Matthys, and others. His discussion on the fanaticism feud by the millenarianism of Münster Kingdom was quickly condemned, yet at the same time, Newman displayed significant concerns: "The opinion was almost universal that the Münster fanaticism was the logical outcome of the Anabaptist position."[45] Guilt by association mattered: "In England and America the opponents of the Baptist movement long persisted in holding up the Münster Kingdom as a sample of what might be expected when it should have an opportunity to show its colors."[46] The nonconformist's practice of separation of church and state meant that English Baptists were susceptible to similar accusations.

Immediately after his discussion on Chiliastic Anabaptists, Newman proceeded with the second category, called "The Soundly Biblical Anabaptists." In using this descriptor, Newman carefully qualified that he was not arguing that these people were "wholly free from error in doctrine and in practice," but their teachings were "comfortable" with the "best type of medieval evangelical thought."[47] He wrote,

> Their adherence to the Scriptures, especially the New Testament, as the only sufficient rule of faith and practice, their use of reasonably sound methods of Scripture interpretation, their freedom from chiliastic enthusiasm, their intense zeal for the spread of the gospel, and their readiness

---

[42] Ibid., 2:153.
[43] Ibid., 2:154.
[44] Ibid., 2:156ff.
[45] Ibid., 2:168.
[46] Ibid.
[47] Ibid.

to suffer even unto death for their faith, commend them to us as worthy of admiration.[48]

In the subcategories, examples of Soundly Biblical Anabaptists were early Swiss Brethren such as Balthasar Hubmaier, George Blaurock, Conrad Grebel, and Felix Manz. Another subgroup was "Moravian Anabaptists," including figures like Jacob Hutter, Leonhard Schiemer, and Hans Mandl. Next, the Soundly Biblical Anabaptists were Menno Simons and the Mennonites. Newman wrote, "Menno and his associates were so horrified by atrocities of Münster that they earnestly disclaimed not only any sympathy with the Anabaptists who had taken in the fanaticism but any historical connection of their anti-paedobaptist party with that of Hofmann and Matthys." Instead, Mennonites often emphasized their connection to Waldenses as they, like Waldenses, championed the "principle of non-resistance, rejection of oaths, magistracy, warfare, capital punishment, etc."[49]

The third sect was what Newman called "Mystical Anabaptists." Under that label, he had individuals like Hans Denck, Ludwig Haetzer, and Caspar Schwenckfeld. "The Pantheistic Anabaptists" were the fourth group that he addressed, referring to folks like David Joris and Henry Nicholis, perhaps less familiar names in church history; writing details about lesser-known historical figures could be seen as a consistent characteristic of Newman's work.

The fifth group was the "Anti-Trinitarian Anabaptists" such as Faustus Socinus[50] and Michael Servetus.[51] In discussing the latter, Newman underscored Servetus' correspondences with John Calvin. In the years between 1546–1553, during the course of their literary frays, at one point Servetus severely criticized Calvin's view. Consequently, Calvin sent his *Institutes* to Servetus as a full representation of his views. However, Servetus returned *Institutes* with annotations of the "most ill-natured criticism," of which Newman reported that Calvin said, "[T]here is hardly a page that is not defiled by [Servetus'] vomit."[52] By no means did Newman agree with Servetus; in fact, he described Servetus as an "abominated author" with pertinacious, "erratic views," especially on Anti-Trinitarianism. That said, he also had critical words for Calvin for possessing "theocratic ideas" and being "intolerant on principle," which led to Servetus' "arrest, condemnation, and execution." However, unlike many critics of Calvin, Newman still did not single out this particularly infamous act by also stating that the "leading Reformers of Germany and Switzerland heartily commended Calvin and the Genevan

[48] Ibid., 2:168–69.
[49] Ibid., 2:178.
[50] Ibid., 2:199–200.
[51] Ibid., 2:191–95.
[52] Ibid., 2:193–94.

Council for ridding the world of one who was regarded as an arch-enemy of the truth."[53]

A prominent Mennonite scholar, Harold Bender, argued that Newman was the first historian writing in the English language whose work was "free of doctrinaire distortion"[54] in narrating Anabaptist tradition. By and large, this accuracy was possible because Newman was able to discern their characteristics among different types of radicals. Even though these movements shared distinctive elements like regenerate church memberships and rejection of paedobaptism, he labored to make certain that these classifications were highlighted rather than written off as stereotypical fanaticism.[55]

In conclusion, for good or ill, Newman wore his Baptist convictions on his sleeve. Be that as it may, due to lack of historical evidence, he did not endorse the Baptist secessionist view in an era when it may have been politically advantageous to hold such a view, vis-à-vis the idea of an unbroken lineage of succession from the apostolic era to seventeenth-century English separatists. However, as William Jonas, Jr., has convincingly argued, Newman held "spiritual kinship" with sixteenth-century Anabaptists and believed that they were spiritual forerunners to Baptist beginnings.[56] For Newman, the Reformation that magisterial reformers brought forth was a compromised version, an enormous letdown for what could have been the best of medieval evangelicalism. The magistrates arrived at a settlement by making concessions, by keeping paedobaptism alive, and not fully embracing regenerate church membership—albeit it was only the courageous Anabaptists, called "Soundly Biblical Anabaptists," who finished the incomplete reformation that mainline reformers had simply commenced.

---

[53] Ibid., 2:195.

[54] Harold S. Bender, "Newman, Albert Henry," in *The Mennonite Encyclopedia: A Comprehensive Reference Work on the Anabaptist-Mennonite Movement*, vol. 3 (Scottdale PA: The Mennonite Publishing House, 1957) 866.

[55] In fact, he devotes a book-length treatment; see Newman, *A History of Anti-Paedobaptism*.

[56] Jonas, Jr., "A Critical Evaluation of Albert Henry Newman," 141.

"ECCLESIA SEMPER REFORMANDA"? THE PLURALIZATION OF PROTESTANTISM AND THE ANNIVERSARY OF THE REFORMATION 2017

Andrea Strübind

To begin my contribution, I would like to present some autobiographical details that I hope will demonstrate why this topic of pluralization of Protestantism holds particular significance for me and to set the scene for the following explanations. I am a Baptist and, furthermore, a Baptist of the fifth generation in my family, which is quite unusual in Germany. Typically, the Baptists are classified as one of the traditional Free Churches in Germany, congregations that initially emerged in the early nineteenth century as a result of repressive political relationships and the consequences of the era of Confessionalization.[1] My great-great-grandmother spent time in jail as a child because her mother had converted to the Baptists and was consequently sentenced to imprisonment. In 1991, I was ordained as a pastor in the Union of Evangelical Free Churches. I worked as a minister in the fields of preaching and pastoral care for many years in a number of congregations, prior to my appointment as a professor in Oldenburg.

In the light of this biography, it was important for me to research the history of the so-called Free Churches, which have consistently remained in the ranks of minority churches since they first emerged in Germany. In my post-doctoral thesis, I focused on Anabaptism during the Reformation period, which receives scant attention in the traditional Church History curriculum within academic education. I graduated from the Kirchliche Hochschule ("Protestant School of Theology") in Berlin, and was awarded the Venia legendi (authorization to teach at tertiary level) at the Theologicum in Heidelberg. From the beginning of my studies I was very involved in ecumenical activities. Ongoing dialogue with teachers

---

[1] Erich Geldbach, *Freikirchen: Erbe, Gestalt, und Wirkung*, Bensheimer Hefte 70 (Göttingen: Vandenhoeck & Ruprecht, 2005); Herbert Strahm, *Dissentertum im Deutschland des 19. Jahrhunderts: Freikirchen und religiöse Sondergemeinschaften im Beziehungs- und Spannungsfeld von Staat und protestantischen Landeskirchen* (Stuttgart: Kohlhammer Verlag, 2016); Karl-Heinz Voigt, *Freikirchen in Deutschland* (19.-20. Jahrhundert), Kirchengeschichte in Einzeldarstellungen vol. 3/6 (Leipzig: Evangelische Verlagsanst alt, 2004); and Wolfgang E. Heinrichs, *Freikirchen - eine moderne Kirchenform. Entstehung und Entwicklung von fünf Freikirchen im Wuppertal* (Gießen: Brunnen-Verlag, 1989).

and with students from other churches and denominations, as well as subsequent interaction with colleagues in the local ecumenical movement in Berlin, had a strong, formative influence on me. As a church historian, I undertake research and teach from a clearly ecumenical perspective, which also illustrates the unique profile of the institute at the university where I teach. Currently, I am the only member of a Free Church who is teaching at a department of Protestant Theology in the role of professor. Therefore, when I contemplate the pluralization of Protestantism, it is easy to recognize that it is not only an integral component of my research interests, but also an inherent part of my personal biography.

1. The Pluralization of Protestantism

1.1 Pluralization As an Interpretive Approach. In the 500th anniversary year of Luther's 95 theses, Protestantism cannot be understood in its inherent diversity without first considering the sixteenth century, which is typically referred to as the "Age of the Reformation."[2] However, even with this designation as an era, which was introduced into the study of history by Leopold von Ranke,[3] a preliminary decision is taken regarding the understanding of Protestantism. Following Ranke, the notion has dominated the German cultural memory that the Reformation marks the end of the Middle Ages and the beginning of the modern era. Within the framework of this historiographical approach, Martin Luther has generally been portrayed as the first person of modern times. Nowadays, however, these historical interpretations are being challenged as to whether, in fact, it was the fifteenth or the sixteenth century that heralded the modern era, given that such ascriptions are easily exposed as ideological constructs. Increasingly, the identification of the Reformation as a watershed or a historical turning point between the Middle Ages and the modern era is also being repudiated.

It cannot be disputed that, continuing the reform movements of the late Middle Ages, the Reformation deepened and intensified a process of inner-religious pluralization that had long since begun to take root, and which began to spread globally from various central points in Europe and, later, from North America. This led to a long process whereby a multitude of independent, mostly antagonistic confessions or denominations were established, which also clearly distanced themselves from the Western church. Through the theologically motivated movement for radical change, which had implications for all spheres of social and cultural life in the early modern period, religious-cultural differentiation

[2] Berndt Hamm, "Abschied vom Epochendenken in der Reformationsforschung. Ein Plädoyer," in *ZHF* 39/3 (2012): 373–411.

[3] Leopold von Ranke, *Deutsche Geschichte im Zeitalter der Reformation* (Berlin: Duncker & Humblot, 1839–1847) (digitalised ed. in German Text Archive: http://www.deutschestextarchiv.de).

and pluralization[4] became a sustained signature for Europe and the Western world. Moreover, it should be noted that these churches and denominations have never been homogeneous. On the contrary, as a group they should be looked at as being fundamentally and diversely differentiated.

The perspective of "religious pluralization"[5] has over recent years led to a reassessment of the context of Reformation events and of its cultural and social consequences in the study of history and also, to some extent, in church historiography. Within this perspective, the "Reformation" is understood as a correlation of events, communication, conflict, and meaning, which was accompanied by a pluralization of religious interpretation and options for interpretation. This theory of pluralization—which was taken up in the study of history, originating from the more recent sociology of religion—presented an ongoing challenge to established "teleological" concepts,[6] such as modernization, rationalization, secularization, and confessionalization. In particular, cultural-scientific investigative horizons were added to the established research of confessionalization by means of the reception of the pluralization theory, focusing on the replication of experiences, of faith and cognitive processes, norms and traditions, as well as on their implementation in everyday life and experiences in the early modern era. In this perspective, pluralization processes, which can be determined in social transformations of class affiliation and economic systems, as well as in the sciences, become the hallmark of this epoch. In this respect, however, it should be noted that the different pluralization processes in the early modern era were not perceived as a positive value. On the contrary, the processes were, in fact, essentially approached and dealt with through strategies for their containment.

1.2 The Self-Image of Protestantism. In order to outline the pluralization of Protestantism, it is imperative to be aware that, to the present day, the extensive worldwide branches of Protestantism continuously see themselves as being in the process of acquiring and mastering the Reformation message, albeit in differing contexts, regions, and at different times. Therefore, according to their self-un-

---

[4] Pluralization is understood here as a concept of process and movement. See Cornel Zwierlein, "Pluralisierung und Autorität. Tentative Überlegungen zur Herkunft des Ansatzes und zum Vergleich mit gängigen Großerzählungen," in Jan-Dirk Müller, Wulf Oesterreicher, and Friedrich Vollhardt, eds., *Pluralisierungen. Konzepte zur Erfassung der Frühen Neuzeit*, vol. 21 (Berlin/New York: Pluralisierung und Autorität, 2010) 3–30.

[5] Detlef Pollack, *Religion und gesellschaftliche Differenzierung. Studien zum religiösen Wandel in Europa und den USA*, vol. 3 (Tübingen: Mohr Siebeck, 2016) 159ff. For pluralization as a concept for interpretation in the early modern era, see http://www.sfb-frueheneuzeit.uni-muenchen.de/; and Martin Mulsow, "Pluralisierung," in Anette Völker-Rasor, ed., *Oldenbourg Geschichte Lehrbuch: Frühe Neuzeit* (München: Oldenburg, 2000) 303–307.

[6] Mulsow, "Pluralisierung," 303.

derstanding, the churches and communities that stem from the Anabaptist spectrum of the 16th century, or from the heterogeneous movements of Puritanism of the seventeenth century, also belong to the "Churches of the Reformation."[7] My observation is, however, that the concept of "Churches of the Reformation" is primarily used in ecumenical debates in Germany to strengthen a position that is clearly differentiated from the Roman Catholic Church, which is perceived as pursuing an authoritative approach. In a most instructive introduction, Friedrich Wilhelm Graf, accordingly, presents the definition that "'Protestantism' is a collective singular for all those Christian churches, groups, and movements that arose from the Reformation in the sixteenth century, and which see themselves as heirs of the Reformation protests."[8] As a result, and in line with a whole range of researchers, Graf no longer refers to a Reformation, but to Reformations, and he likewise does not use the singular term of Protestantism, choosing instead to discuss Protestantisms.

In addition to Lutheranism and the Reformed tradition, a search in any dictionary or encyclopaedia of Ecumenism and Confessional Studies using the keyword "Protestantism" will invariably list so-called pre-Reformation movements, such as the Waldensians and the Bohemian Brethren, that emerged from Jan Hus' Reform initiative, as well as the traditional Free Churches (e.g., Methodists and Baptists), Pentecostal Churches, and the Anglican Church.[9] In this way, Protestantism no longer comprises simply the initial Reformatory configurations, but also the various forms following reception of the Reformation.

1.3 The Pluralization of Protestantism and the Anniversary of the Reformation 2017. This inclusive view of Protestantism is certainly typical around the world, and yet German church-history research still finds it difficult to grasp. Ever since the age of confessionalization, the bi-denominational nature of the two main churches—the Roman Catholic Church and the churches coming under the umbrella of the Evangelical Church in Germany (EKD)—has dominated the understanding of Church and church structures among the general public in this country. The EKD's official announcements regarding the anniversary of the Reformation could be seen here as a revealing example, as they still do not take account of the pluralistic understanding of Protestantism and, thus, ultimately

[7] Andrea Strübind, "Die Kirche der Freien," Der Kongregationalismus als Kirchenreformmodell, 400 Jahre Baptismus, in *Materialdienst des Konfessionskundlichen Instituts* (MD) 60 (2009) 103–109.

[8] Friedrich Wilhelm Graf, *Der Protestantismus. Geschichte und Gegenwart* (München: C.H. Beck Verlag, 2006) 7.

[9] Reinhard Frieling, "Protestantismus," in Wolfgang Thönissen, Michael Hardt, Peter Lüning, Burkhard Neumann, Johannes Oeldemann, eds., *Lexikon der Ökumene und Konfessionskunde* (Freiburg, Br.: Herder Verlag, 2007) 1099–1100.

disregard the real events surrounding the Reformation.[10] In fact, the traditional picture of the "actual" Reformation (Lutheranism and Reformed) can thus be established, which differs from other movements that are classified as "existing on the margins," whereby the provincial-denominational limitations of this viewpoint are revealed. The traditional historical picture of the main streams of the Reformation is served once again, albeit indirectly, where the Reformation also encompasses the aberrations of an alleged initial and fundamental agreement.

It is not the historical pluralization of religion that is understood as the paradigm here, but the traditional notions of a denominational writing of history with supposed references to unequivocal identities. Yet again, the Baptists', Dissidents', and Non-conformists' Reformation movements are listed in various statements, if at all, as "enthusiasts" or "proliferations" or "outsiders" of the Reformation. Clearly, this should provoke some reflection in light of the fact that denominations that evolved from pluralistic Anabaptism and, in particular, from the denominationally separatist (divergent) Puritanism or Congregationalism in England (including the Baptists), now encompass large sections of Christianity in the United States and—on a global scale—the majority of Protestant Christians.

Even though the EKD's 2016 theme for the year was "Reformation and the One World" during the "Luther-decade," declared by the EKD in 2008, and even though the world has been invited "to the village" Wittenberg, not far from Berlin, for a world exhibition in this anniversary year, the inherent diversity of worldwide Protestantism, to some extent, has not yet been fully acknowledged. It is not reflected in the organization of this anniversary year, and especially not in the church's standpoint and various statements, with potentially frightening consequences. Even the EKD's core theological text for the anniversary, "Rechtfertigung und Freiheit: 500 Jahre Reformation" ("Justification and Freedom: 500 Years of Reformation"),[11] which was presented in 2014, contains a selective understanding of the Reformation and Protestantism. Churches and denominations that have arisen from the traditions of Anabaptism and Puritanism appear not to belong, and are effectively not even mentioned.[12]

A very recent illustration of this typically German, denominational-provin-

[10] Andrea Strübind, and Erbe und Ärgernis, "Was gibt es für Kirchen aus der täuferischen und nonkonformistischen Traditionen anlässlich des Reformationsjubiläums 2017 zu feiern?" in Volker Spangenberg, ed., *Luther und die Reformation aus freikirchlicher Sicht* (Göttingen: Vandenhoeck & Ruprecht, 2013) 71–89.

[11] Rechtfertigung und Freiheit, https://www.ekd.de/2014_rechtfertigung_und_freiheit.htm.

[12] Erich Geldbach, "Rechtfertigung und Freiheit. Die langen Schatten des Reformationsjubiläums 2017," *ZThG* 19 (2014): 15–31.

cial interpretation of history and of the traditional "Protestant" self-understanding can be seen in the document "Erinnerung heilen—Jesus Christus bezeugen" ("Healing of Memory—Witnessing to Jesus Christ"), which was presented at the German Bishops' Conference and the EKD in September 2016.[13] Time and again in this text, Protestants and Catholics are presented as the key players in historical events, and alluded to as being responsible for the reconciliation process, from which the claim can logically be derived that the EKD represents all of Protestantism in Germany. It is obvious that other Protestant denominations were not invited to cooperate in this project or even offered an opportunity for consultation in the process.[14]

Moreover, it is all the more surprising that a text that focuses on the history of conflict and violence in denominational disputes since the sixteenth century, and that promotes "healing," should not include a single word about the repressive treatment of religious minorities. These are groups that have consistently been excluded from all peace agreements undertaken by the two mainstream churches, and in religious legislation up to 1918. The choice of problematic "memorial sites" and descriptions of religious wars and the serious consequences of confessionalization are completely and entirely focused on the two mainstream churches. The internal differentiation within Protestantism and the co-presence of religious minorities simply do not even appear on the horizon with regard to the Confessional Age, nor with respect to the consequences that last to the present day.[15] It is only with reference to the topic of "Unity and Diversity" that a single sentence addresses denominational pluralism and, even then, the content of the statement is noticeably vague: "A history of differentiation between Christian creeds and traditions begins in the West with the age of the Reformation, and the origins of this differentiation should not be placed solely at the feet of the theological disputes."[16] The characteristic style of this text clearly implies a negative assessment of this pluralization, which can be traced back to vested political and national interests. Ultimately, this negative connotation culminates in the statement, "In the context of missionary endeavors, especially in the nineteenth century, religious denominations that invoke the Reformation as the source of their identity

---

[13] https://www.ekd.de/download/erinnerung_heilen_gt24.pdf.

[14] It comes across as extremely embarrassing when the only reference to the Anabaptist tradition associated with looking back to successful cases of the healing of memory uses the pejorative term of "Re-baptizing," a concept that is denominationally charged and contradicts the self-understanding of the identified individual. See "Erinnerung heilen," 12.

[15] Interestingly, this also applies to the Reformed tradition, which is likewise not mentioned. The respective controversial religious debates are solely outlined with references to Luther's works.

[16] "Erinnerung heilen," 54.

have contributed to a worldwide pluralization of religious conditions and circumstances."[17] This development apparently makes it very difficult for the "World Federations" to maintain "unity in the understanding of the Gospel."

Thus, it remains to be said that this document, which undoubtedly holds considerable significance within church politics, simply does not acknowledge the pluralist character of the Reformation movements in the sixteenth century and only to a very limited extent takes the diversity of Protestantism into account. Furthermore, denominational pluralism is ultimately classified as an ecumenical problem and a historical burden.

It is my opinion that a dogmatically and denominationally narrow-minded, not to mention historically inaccurate, concept of the Reformation is thus also being continuously perpetuated. I am very concerned that there is insufficient clarification or consideration of the fact that this understanding of the Reformation, maintained and communicated in this manner, is simply a denominational construct that is exclusively oriented towards the benchmark of Luther's theology, even with its cheap emphasis on the diversity of the Reformed. At any rate, it leads to a certainly justifiable suspicion that the events of the Reformation are once again being manipulated and, in the process, exploited to the benefit of specific denominations or church politics.[18]

A further consequence, as well as a desideratum for the German memorial culture, therefore, involves an inclusive expansion of the understanding of the Reformation, incorporating the diverse movements of Anabaptism and non-conformism. Primarily, the Reformation should really be understood as religious pluralization, incorporating the many and varied movements, socializations, and, ultimately, denominational institutionalizations that have arisen from it and that evoke the Reformation as their source and roots. In doing so, it is important that any exclusive appropriation of the Reformation in the German (and partially European) context by means of anachronistic memorial configurations from the mainstream churches is finally overcome.

1.4 The Pluralization of Protestantism as a Process. However, the "pluraliza-

---

[17] Ibid.

[18] Keep in mind the current dispute over the role of academic theology with respect to the anniversary of the Reformation, which is being waged between the Vice President of the Church Office of the EKD, Thies Gundlach, and representatives of Theology faculties, and by the church historian Thomas Kaufmann in particular. See Thies Gundlach, "Perspektiven vermisst. Die akademische Theologie verstolpert das Reformationsjubiläum," in *zz* (March 2017): http://www.zeitzeichen.net/religion-kirche/kritiker-der-reformationsjubilaeums. See also, the response by Thomas Kaufmann and Martin Laube in "So nicht! Die EKD hat die Reformation theologisch entkernt," in *zz* (April 2017): http://www.zeitzeichen.net/religion-kirche/ekd-und-reformationsjubilaeum_17203/.

tion of Protestantism" should not only be traced back to the age of the Reformation, but should be seen instead as a continuous and constant process. It is not simply a case of the pluralist beginning and the nature of the Reformation: on the contrary, there is a clear and obvious dynamism residing within Protestantism in its many shapes and forms, upon which new denominations are able to draw, and through which established denominations are constantly transformed in revival movements, periodic "awakenings," and new starts (such as Pietism and Pentecostalism). In this way, it could be said that alternative forms of Christian piety continuously emerge under the Protestant banner, each finding their individual expression in independent communities, denominations, and confessions, especially in the Pentecostal context.

The following section will consider what it is within Protestantism that causes these dynamics of pluralization to unfold.

2. The Talk about Ecclesia Semper Reformanda

2.1 The Church's Enduring Need to Reform. The search for clues essentially leads back to what is possibly one of the most frequently quoted slogans that has long been associated with the Reformation era: The Church is "*ecclesia semper reformanda*," and therefore must be reformed and renewed time and again, and led back to its beginnings. And yet this well-known formula does not originate from Luther or any other contemporary Reformer, but is attributed to Jodocus van Lodenstein (1620–1670), a Pietist from the Netherlands.[19] Furthermore, numerous references can be named that suggest the concept of the Church's ongoing need for reform is to be found in various council texts dating back to the Middle Ages and in even earlier sources.[20]

Further movements that take up these concepts of the Church's continual need to reform can be found in sixteenth-century Anabaptism, in Pietism, and also in the nineteenth-century revivalist movement. At the same time, a demand that the Reformation be resumed or that a significant reshaping of the unfinished Reformation be undertaken in the areas of sanctification or leading a moral life frequently came to the forefront.

In Anabaptist writings, criticism of the incomplete Reformation, or that it had even been entirely reversed, can frequently be identified in historical reviews

---

[19] Martin Abraham, *Evangelium und Kirchengestalt. Reformatorisches Kirchenverständnis heute*, Theologische Bibliothek Töpelmann, vol. 140 (Berlin/New York: Walter de Gruyter, 2007) 511; and Theodor Mahlmann, "*Ecclesia semper reformanda*: Eine historische Aufklärung," new ed., in Torbjörn Johansson, Robert Kolb, and Johann-Anselm Steiger, eds., *Hermeneutica Sacra. Studien zur Auslegung der Heiligen Schrift im 16. und 17. Jahrhundert* (Berlin/New York: Walter de Gruyter, 2010) 381–442.

[20] Abraham, *Evangelium*, 513.

where the entire church history is construed as a history of decay.[21] In this context, the reformers are even accused of teaching a faith that justifies, without also demanding the ethical consequences ("fruits of faith").[22] Likewise, the lack of implementation of scriptural reforms with respect to the Blessed Sacrament and in the liturgy was roundly criticized. A further example of the classification of the Reformers in a degenerative view of history can be found with Bernhard Rothmann, the so-called "Keeper of the word" and theologian of the Anabaptist Kingdom of Münster.[23] In Rothmann's apocalyptic view of history, Martin Luther's Reformation was interpreted as the beginning of this last restitution of God:

> Und eigentlich, so wir es nur recht verstehen wollen, hat Gott der Allmächtige die Restitution recht angefangen, da er Martinus Luther erweckt hat, als derselbe durch Gottes Gnade (wiewohl er nun leider nicht weiter will, sondern in seinem eigenen Stolz und Dreck liegen bleibt) so hat er doch das Kind des Verderbens, den rechten Antichristen aufgezeigt und das rechte Evangelium einzuführen begonnen.[24]

In the oldest chronicle of the Hutterites, an Anabaptist movement, origin of which is to be found in Moravia, the fundamental criticism directed against the Reformists is summarized succinctly:

> Dise beede / Luther und Zwingel / haben alle tück vnd Bueberej der Bäbstlichen heiligkeit eröffnet vnd an tag herfür gebracht / gleich alls wenn sies mit Donnderschlegen alles zu boden wolten schlagen. / Aber dargegen kein bessers auffgericht / sond alsbalt sie sich an den weltlichen gwalt gehencket / auff menschen hilff vertröstet / Ist es mit Inen nit anderst gwesen / als ob einer ainen alten kessel flicket / das loch nur erger wirt / Vnd haben ein gantz frech volck zu sündigen erzogen / vnnd hinder Inen glassen.[25]

---

[21] Andrea Strübind, *"Eifriger als Zwingli." Die frühe Täuferbewegung in der Schweiz* (Berlin: Duncker & Humblot, 2003) 216ff.

[22] See explanations regarding the Müntzer letter, *QGTS* 1/14: 13.

[23] Regarding Rothmann, see Martin Brecht, "Die Theologie Bernhard Rothmanns," *JWKG* 78 (1985): 49–82.

[24] Bernhard Rothmann, *Restitution nach der Übersetzung von Richard van Dülmen, Das Täuferreich zu Münster 1534–1535* (München: Deutscher Taschenbuch Verlag, 1974) 197, 219. Translation: "[A]nd in fact, as we simply and truly want to understand it, God the Almighty truly began the restitution, in that he awakened Martinus Luther, as the same through God's grace (even though he regrettably does not want to continue, but to remain lying in his own pride and filth), thus he showed up this child of decay, the true Anti-Christ, and began to implement the true Gospel."

[25] Andreas Johannes Friedrich Zieglschmid, ed., *Die älteste Chronik der Hutterischen Brüder* (Ithaca/New York: The Cayuga Press, 1943) 42f. Translation: "These two, Luther and Zwingel / have opened up all the deceit and adornment of the papal holiness and unveiled these

The Puritans also understood things in this same manner. Their works are freely described as a "second Reformation," as they sought to implement a fundamental change in church relationships in the sense of a continental reform movement.[26] Other voices campaigned that there not be a second Reformation, but that the norms and principles of the original Reformation merely be developed further. What interconnects these demands, either for a "continuation" of the Reformation or for its consistent application, is the observation that it is the teachings, but not the life itself, that have been reformed.

Even though the abiding need for reform of the Church was accordingly picked up historically in various Protestant revivalist movements time and again, the formula of *ecclesia semper reformanda* principally shaped church developments in the twentieth century, and developed at this time into a fundamental principle of Protestant ecclesiology.[27] It was Paul Tillich who effectively raised the permanent criticism of the existing state to a Protestant principle.[28]

The Church's principle need for reform arises especially in the various social and political upheavals of the "century of extremes" (Eric Hobsbawm) and, in addition, plays an increasingly important role today in the agenda of all Christian denominations in the Western world in light of dwindling material resources, waves of secularization, and the erosion of church membership. As a consequence, it is only reasonable also to describe the twentieth century, in comparison to previous eras, as the "century of church reform par excellence" (Traugott Jähnichen).

The shape and composition of the church, as well as its defining relations to changing social systems, were and are elemental starting points for every demand for reforms. Not only economic constraints and secularization, but also theological conflicts, trigger criticism of the established church social form and hasten the push for change. The range of content of church-reforming demands and concepts, together with the respective leaders, proves to be extremely diverse and complex in the various phases of contemporary church history, as well as in the individual European countries. Calls for reform came to the fore in the face of

/ as if they would strike these down to the ground with thunderbolts. But they have not erected anything better in its place / instead as soon as they have latched onto the secular world / trusted in men's help / it is no different with them / it is as if someone tinkered an old cauldron / the hole only becomes bigger / and they have nurtured an entire people to be sinners / and left them behind as such."

[26] Klaus Deppermann, "Der Englische Puritanismus," in Martin Brecht, ed., *Der Pietismus vom siebzehnten bis zum frühen achtzehnten Jahrhundert, Geschichte des Pietismus,* vol. 1 (Göttingen: Vandenhoeck & Ruprecht, 1993) 11ff.

[27] See Volker Leppin and Dorothea Sattler, eds., *Reformation 1517–2017. Ökumenische Perspektiven* (Freiburg/Göttingen: Herder/Vandenhoeck & Ruprecht, 2014) 55.

[28] See also, Abraham, *Evangelium,* 513ff.

crises, as well as in the processes of social transformation to which the church was reacting, so long as these did not belong themselves to the forces initiating political upheaval.

Momentous times in the twentieth century, when calls for reform of the churches were expressed particularly vehemently, included the immediate post-war eras, the 1960s, and the period of transformation after the political turnaround of 1989/1990. The new millennium, the horrifying impact of the terror attacks on 11 September 2001, the economic downturn, debates about integration, and national identity in the course of European unification, as well as the global financial crisis, are clearly further factors that have once again significantly shaped the question of the future form of the church in the twenty-first century. Furthermore, both the mainstream churches in Germany have initiated comprehensive reform agendas and processes over recent years, with the aim of responding to the course of social change with consequent, appropriate, and essential structural changes.

The Community of Protestant Churches in Europe (CPCE, in German: Gemeinschaft Evangelischer Kirchen in Europa/GEKE) held its seventh general assembly in 2012 with the central theme of "Church Reform" in European churches. In the process, the assembly evaluated the results of the consultation process, "*Ecclesia Semper Reformanda*: Ecclesiological Reflections in Regard to the Renewal of the Protestant Churches in Europe" (2009–2011), in which thirty young ecumenists had participated.[29]

In a study prepared by the "Ecumenical Working Group of Protestant and Catholic Theologians," it was stated, moreover, that the Church's constant need for renewal and the "continuous reform" was being picked up by the Roman Catholic Church through the Second Vatican Council. "The renewal of the Church in the spirit of the Gospel is no longer a sole specific characteristic of the churches of the Reformation. Christ's call for 'continuous reform' is no longer bound to the boundaries of particular denominations."[30]

2.2 The Potential for Vitalization of the Scriptural Principle. It could be said that a further starting point for the momentum of renewal in Protestantism is founded in the Reformation scriptural principle of "sola scriptura," which urges that there be continual openness with regard to the testimony of the Holy Scripture.[31] Hence, it was maintained time and again in the confessional writings and

---

[29] http://www.leuenberg.net/sites/default/files/basic-page/11_ecclesia_semper_reformanda_d.pdf.

[30] Leppin and Sattler, eds., *Reformation*, 55.

[31] Bernd Oberdorfer, "Das reformatorische Schriftprinzip. Historische und gegenwärtige Perspektiven," in Wilhelm Damberg, Ute Gause, Isolde Kahle, and Thomas Söding, eds., *Gottes Wort in der Geschichte, Reformation und Reform in der Kirche* (Freiburg/Basel/Wien: Herder, 2015) 70–82.

creeds, especially in the reformed traditions, that one should adhere to the formulated faith or belief, so long as there is no other contradictory specification in the prescribed text. All knowledge is temporary and can be revised by a rereading of the scriptural text or by the application of Scripture as its hermeneutical key.

An important function of the scriptural principle, which is universally accepted in the churches of the Reformation, is that the Bible has a critical function as "norma normans" with respect to the church and believers. The Holy Scripture, however, has more than simply a critical function with respect to the church, but it also has a strongly creative function, in that the Protestant understanding prescribes that the church is "creatura verbi"—created by the Word. Thus, the church is the object of interpretation, not its subject.[32] In this way, the "sola scriptura" of the Reformation has been taken up as a critical-constructive principle of church reform in Protestantism.

3. Congregationalism—The "Church in Progress"

In recourse to the historical contextualization of the formula *ecclesia semper reformanda*, I have previously referred to the call for further development, or more specifically, the consistent continuation or resumption of the Reformation—especially with regard to the ethical way of life. I have also suggested that the scriptural principle could also be understood as a potential starting point for initiating the momentum of reform. The Congregational ecclesiology can also be deduced from this, which developed as a reformist understanding of the church, and which should consequently be surveyed with regard to its reform dynamics.

The emergence of the Congregational church model can be traced back to Puritanism, which represented the dominant crusade for religious piety and church reform movement in England between 1560 and 1660. Working as an inner-church revivalist movement within the framework of Puritanism, a separatist movement arose as a result of an extended prior history. After many development stages of a conventicle and associated membership, this separatist movement ultimately pushed for complete secession, or separation, from the Anglican church, the Church of England, and the creation of independent congregations, which was ultimately achieved, emerging ecclesiologically as Congregationalism.[33] Members were often persecuted and forced into hiding, and yet the community implemented a covenant, or local covenants, as its founding act, with which it set the seal on its community, on the one hand, and on the other hand,

---

[32] Ulrich H.J. Körtner, *Reformatorische Theologie im 21. Jahrhundert* (Zürich: Theologischer Verlag Zrich, 2010) 77.

[33] Andrea Strübind, "Die Kirche der Freien," Der Kongregationalismus als Kirchenreformmodell, 400 Jahre Baptismus, in *Materialdienst des Konfessionskundlichen Instituts* (MD) 60 (2009) 103–109.

ensured members' mutual solidarity, thereby gradually creating an ecclesial identity for the community.

The amalgamation of like-minded people simultaneously signified the Congregationalists' radical abandonment of the Anglican Church, and their structure's territorial and episcopal composition.[34] The covenant, which denoted believers' voluntary contractual agreement, developed into a typical guiding principle for Puritan separatism.[35] It emancipated the church from the nationally designated unity of the Church of England and, at the same time, created a form of religious association that could be implemented locally, independent of parochial structures.

The principle of the autonomous local community is part and parcel of the Congregational ecclesiology. Each individual congregation lives and functions in spiritual self-responsibility, but with collective and intercongregational solidarity at the same time. The rigorously implemented "universal priesthood," which is designed and construed on the basis of spiritual equality for all members, is intended to shape life within the congregation. This concedes expertise in matters of interpretation and evaluation of doctrine to all members of the community.[36] According to the ideal, the ecclesiological model constitutes an interdependent community and community of service for all members, who will organize and govern themselves in a form of consensus democracy. In this way, the Congregational understanding of the church is based on the fundamentally visible, sacred community of faithful believers. This basic ecclesiological concept leads to intensive community life that is shaped by personal belief and a "binding piety" among individual members.

If one reflects on Congregationalism's traditional Covenant-theology from a modern-day perspective, then the process character of Christian life and belief quickly becomes apparent, which comes to the fore through the dynamism inherent in the concept of association.[37] In the first instance, denominations structured

---

[34] Alan P.F. Sell, "Varieties of English Separatist and Dissenting Writings," in Roger D. Sell and Anthony W. Johnson, eds., *Writing and Religion in England 1558–1689* (Farnham: Ashgate, 2009) 25–46, here: 28ff.

[35] Stephen Brachlow, *The Communion of Saints: Radical Puritan and Separatist Ecclesiology 1570–1625* (Oxford: Oxford University Press, 1988) 34f; John Huxtable, "Kongregationalismus," in *TRE* 19 (Berlin/New York: Walter de Gruyter, 1990) 452; Jason K. Lee, *The Theology of John Smyth: Puritan, Separatist, Baptist, Mennonite* (Macon GA: Mercer University Press, 2003) 128ff; and William Henry Brackney, *The Baptists* (Westport: Praeger, 1988) 44f. For a history of the consequences of covenant ecclesiology, see Harald Beutel, *Die Sozialtheologie Thomas Chalmers und ihre Bedeutung für die Freikirchen* (Göttingen: Vandenhoeck & Ruprecht, 2007).

[36] See 1 Corinthians 14:29.

[37] Paul S. Fiddes, "'Walking Together': The Place of the Covenant Theology in Baptist

on the concept of Congregationalism do not place themselves in the historical, and therefore enduring, shape of the church, but inquire anew about the contextual realization and implementation of the church—analogous to their contingent ecclesiological structure, which is ultimately dependent on the commitment of the entire membership. The Congregational understanding of the church is equipped per se with a vitality that constantly accommodates new times, places, and constellations. A distinguishing characteristic of Congregationalism is, thus, its high level of adaptability to various cultural and social circumstances. And yet, at the same time, it incorporates an accompanying lack of indistinguishability in the form of clear and constant signature marks that repose in the certainty of a tradition that explores the present time.

In his renowned works on the relationship between Protestantism and the modern era, Max Weber addresses the Congregational community model in depth. In the course of his study, he concentrates on the characteristics of Congregational denominations, which he describes with respect to their core voluntary structure and the associated criteria for admission, whereby the requirements in particular of the lifestyle for individual members held specific significance in his analysis.[38] He contrasted this extremely demanding form of church membership with those churches in which fellowship is simply gained by birth and infant baptism. In his terminology, he differentiates between the church as an "institution of grace and mercy," and "sects" as a voluntary assembly of the "religiously qualified."[39] Described in this way, the creation of "sects" (in the strictly sociological sense) and their assurance of high ethical quality ("methodology of life") formed the foundation of modern individualism in Weber's view.

Congregational denominations, such as the Baptists, are transformed time and again through religious revivals and awakenings. In addition, their origins are intimately linked with revivalist and reform movements that lie outside their immediate sphere. Markus Matthias' interpretation of Pietism points out, therefore, the ecclesiological difficulty found in Congregationalism. In his opinion, Pietism developed into

> a utopian movement that essentially never reaches its goal given that, on the one hand, it wants to achieve a universal (and enduring) reform

---

Life Yesterday and Today," in *Tracks and Traces: Baptist Identity and Theology* (Carlisle, Cumbria; Waynesboro GA: Paternoster Press, 2003) 21–47, here: 40.

[38] As in passages in *Protestantische Ethik* ("Protestant Ethic"), Weber in his *Die protestantischen Sekten und der Geist des Kapitalismus* ("The Protestant Sects and the Spirit of Capitalism") describes the historical development of Protestant denominations, the Baptists and Quakers in particular, where he attempts to demonstrate the connection between church membership and trustworthiness, as well as social recognition. See Max Weber, *Gesamtausgabe,* ed. Wolfgang Schluchter, sect. 1, vol. 18 (Tübingen: Mohr Siebeck, 2016) 493–548, here: 510ff.

[39] Weber, *Gesamtausgabe,* 517.

> through the transformation (conversion and rebirth) of individuals, while, on the other hand, every level of Christianization becomes the occasion once again for a new "more resolute" Christianity and has to be utilized for the purpose of creating Christian identity.[40]

There is also evidence of similar phenomena in worldwide Congregationalism, such as the Baptist Church and especially the very diverse configurations of Pentecostal-charismatic transformational churches.

Is *ecclesia semper reformanda* a "movement that essentially never reaches its goal"? The congregational church model repeatedly inculturates itself worldwide in new spaces and social circumstances, whereby its flexibility and capacity for integration are constantly proven. Thus, it creates a flexible framework that can establish or moderate completely different forms of expressions, practices, and interpretations of Christianity from within.[41] In the final analysis, it is the church reform model that, in my view, consistently drives the process of pluralization of Protestantism. What is problematic for this "church in progress" is, admittedly, the constant further differentiation and the frequent disagreements and divisions by newly prominent divergences, and especially also their latent openness to revivalist and fundamentalist transformations.

4. Conclusion

In the course of this paper, the question has been pursued as to whether the potential and the dynamics exist within the many forms of Protestantism to express and convey the church's perpetual need for reform—an *ecclesia semper reformanda*—and, therefore, to push for an ecclesiological restructuring and transformation. Using the example of the congregational church polity, a movement that emerged from the Reformation, the intention has been to explain and clarify this fundamental attitude for constant reform and renewal. In my view, further consideration is needed with respect to other Protestant denominations (such as the Methodist Church) that—similar to Pietism—understood sanctification as a lifelong process of spirit-inspired transformation.[42] The procedural occurrence of

[40] Markus Matthias, "Bekehrung und Wiedergeburt," in Hartmut Lehmann and Ruth Albrecht, eds., *Glaubenswelt und Lebenswelten. Geschichte des Pietismus*, vol. 4 (Göttingen: Vandenhoeck & Ruprecht, 2004) 49–82, here: 50f.

[41] In connection with historian Martin Marty, William Brackney even refers to a process of "Baptification" that is currently taking place in many other church traditions, which are gradually opening up to the local structural principle of community. See William Brackney, "Die baptistische Geschichte. Rückblick und Vorschau," in *ZThG* 15 (2010): 172–84, here: 182.

[42] Theodor Runyon, *Die neue Schöpfung. John Wesleys Theologie heute* (Göttingen: Vandenhoeck & Ruprecht, 2005).

sanctification for every Christian, which is closely interconnected with social involvement, offers a frank resonance space for reforms and renewing inspiration.[43] In this way, the churches with a tradition of sanctification as the root of the Pentecostal movement can be understood, in particular churches that, at the beginning of the twenty-first century, remained largely under the radar in our part of the world, and yet quantitatively developed into the second largest denominational family worldwide. The pluralization of Protestantism is a far-reaching process. It remains to be seen whether this process might also offer an opportunity to make the Gospel audible and comprehensible to our modern-day pluralist and globalized world.[44]

[43] Christoph Raedel, "Gotteserfahrung im Widerstreit? Zwischen methodistischer Identität und charismatischer Erneuerung," in Christoph Raedel, ed., *Methodismus und charismatische Bewegung. Historische, theologische und hymnologische Beiträge* (Göttingen: Edition Ruprecht, 2007).

[44] Is it possible that a part of this Reformation dynamism is to be found in the "emerging churches," which increasingly view the church as being a decentralized network, and thereby also *ecclesia semper reformanda*?

WILLIAM HENRY ANGAS ENCOUNTERS THE MENNONITES: HOW NINETEENTH-CENTURY PALATINE MENNONITES BECAME PROTESTANT

John D. Roth

In early July 1824, Johannes Risser, pastor of a small Mennonite congregation in the Palatine village of Friedelsheim, invited his fellow Mennonite pastors to participate in an unusual conference. An itinerant Baptist preacher, William Henry Angas had recently appeared in the community and was eager to speak with Mennonite church leaders. Commissioned by the Baptist Missionary Society in London, Angas had been visiting Mennonite communities throughout Europe for the past fourteen months in an attempt to stimulate spiritual renewal and generate financial support for the society's overseas mission effort. Following extended visits with Mennonites in the Netherlands, Prussia, and Switzerland, his journey now led him to the Palatinate, where Angas found a welcome reception in Risser's home.

Although Mennonite ministers in the Palatinate had long enjoyed informal fellowship with each other, only rarely—usually in times of crisis—did they gather for formal meetings. Two decades earlier, in 1803, Mennonite church leaders in the region had convened in the nearby village of Ibersheim to address the moral, spiritual, and political cataclysm unleashed by the French Revolution and the subsequent French occupation of the Rhineland. At the forefront of their concerns at Ibersheim in 1803, and in a subsequent conference of 1805, were a host of distinctive Mennonite practices that seemed suddenly to be imperiled: traditional practices of church discipline and in-group marriage, for example, or the doctrines of nonresistance, simplicity in dress, and humility.[1]

But the forces of change introduced by the French Revolution persisted, even after the French occupation came to an end in 1815. In sharp contrast to the experience of a previous generation, early nineteenth-century Mennonites in the region were no longer merely tolerated as religious sectarians; instead, they were full citizens equal under the law—free to worship as they pleased, to build churches, and to proselytize without fear of legal consequences. But this era of newfound liberation was also a time of great uncertainty and tension within the

[1] Paul Schowalter, "Die Ibersheimer Beschlüße von 1803 und 1805," *Mennonitische Geschichtsblätter* 20 (1963): 29–48.

Mennonite community.

More than he could have imagined, Angas' presence became a catalyst for transformation among the Mennonite congregations in the Palatinate. The meeting hosted by Johannes Risser at the Spitalhof on 13 July 1824—in which Angas was the featured speaker—set in motion a series of events that resulted in renewed interest in missions, new expressions of ecumenism, and a profound shift in theology and practices that marked a shift among Mennonites from a sect to a denomination. To put it another way, William Henry Angas and the Baptist connections he promoted enabled Mennonites in the Palatinate to adopt a new identity as "Protestants."

Palatine Mennonite Identity Prior to the French Reformation

Virtually all the Mennonites living along the upper Rhine River during the last half of the eighteenth century were descendants of Swiss Brethren emigrants—religious refugees for the most part—who had been driven out of their native cantons of Zrich and Bern during the various waves of persecution that swept through those regions in the 1640s, the 1660s, and again in the first decade of the 1700s. Along with other religious minorities, these Swiss Brethren—or Mennonites, as they became known in the Palatinate—found a measure of toleration among the feudal princes and territorial lords of southwest Germany, who were seeking farmers to resettle their lands following the devastating depopulation of the Thirty Years' War.

By the middle of the eighteenth century, there were approximately thirty Mennonite congregations in the region, which included some 3,500 people. None of these congregations had more than 150 members and they were geographically scattered, some separated from their closest neighbor by as much as five hours of travel. Yet despite geographical distance and the absence of any formal organizational structure, Mennonites continued to maintain a distinctive religious identity.

In part, this identity was imposed on them from the outside by a host of idiosyncratic legal restrictions and civil disabilities. Thus, most Mennonites in the region were forced to pay an annual "toleration" tax; their population could not exceed a fixed number; they were not permitted to join guilds or practice any profession apart from those related to agriculture; they could not build distinctive meetinghouses; and they were strongly forbidden to engage in any sort of religious proselytizing. Symbolic of their tenuous legal status was the so-called "law of retraction"—imposed by the Palatine Elector on Mennonite landowners in 1726—which gave any person who sold land to a Mennonite the right to buy it back at any time for the original sale price.[2] To be sure, not all of these laws were strictly enforced. But a significant element of Mennonite identity in the eighteenth century was forged in the delicate balance between the paternalistic goodwill of the feudal lord, their reputation as progressive farmers, and the various legal, social, and economic restrictions they endured as a tolerated religious minority.

At the same time, the distinctive character of the Mennonite community was reinforced from within by a cluster of theological convictions and practices that clearly separated them from their Catholic, Reformed, and Lutheran neighbors. Mennonites, for example, did not baptize their infants; they refused to swear oaths, carry the sword, or participate in civil governance. At baptism, Mennonites not only promised to follow the commandments of Christ, but they also explicitly vowed to abide by the congregational regulations (*Ordnung*) and to submit to church discipline if they failed to comply. All baptizands promised to marry only within the church, and male members also agreed at baptism that they would accept the call to serve in ministerial offices—unpaid and without formal training—if the lot should happen to fall on them.

The style of Mennonite worship further set them apart from their neighbors. Mennonites met for worship in private homes or in meetinghouses built to look like homes. Their hymns, comprised mainly of martyr ballads, which they sang slowly and in unison, came from the *Ausbund,* a Swiss German hymnbook dating back to the sixteenth century. And their ministers—often barely literate farmers—preached without notes, drawing heavily on Scripture passages that they had committed to memory with a strong emphasis on simplicity, humility, and the suffering Christians could expect to endure at the hands of an unregenerate world.

This internal sense of group identity was further strengthened by a complex network of family ties, by shared memories of persecution and suffering, and by the energetic efforts of a few itinerant ministers whose informal authority in matters related to church *Ordnung* transcended their particular congregation.

Despite their eccentricities, at the eve of the French Revolution, Mennonites had come to enjoy a widespread reputation as hardworking, productive farmers who could be counted on to pay their rents and taxes. In the eyes of most contemporary observers, they were models of industry, neatness, and moral rectitude. An official report in 1763 noted that "no more industrious, efficient, or peaceful subjects are to be found."[3] And another report to the privy council of the Electoral Palatinate twenty years later, having established that Mennonites do

---

[2] Christian Neff, "Das Auslösungsrecht gegen die Mennoniten in der Kurpfalz," *Christlicher Gemeinde-Kalendar* (1912): 120–34.

[3] Quoted in Fritz Hege, "Beruf und Berufung die Mennoniten in der Kurpfalz," *Christlicher Gemeinde-Kalendar* (1954): 65.

not lie, cheat, steal, quarrel, or beg, concluded "in short, they are a peaceful, orderly, God-fearing people whose conduct puts many other Christians to shame."[4] Indeed, some Mennonites, such as David Möllinger of Monsheim, were famous throughout the region for their progressive innovations in agricultural reform.[5]

But there were also signs of religious tensions and uncertainty within the Mennonite communities during the last half of the eighteenth century. In 1757, for example, Peter Weber—a young, newly ordained minister at Höningen—began holding private meetings for Bible study and devotion that included people from outside the Mennonite church. At these meetings, Weber reportedly was critical of the church's emphasis on tradition and external form. By contrast, he preached "redemption through faith in Christ and His sacrifice, and [...] salvation in that faith alone."[6] Though deeply moved by the Anabaptist model of costly discipleship and martyrdom, Weber's hunger for spiritual nourishment led him and his colleagues to look beyond the boundaries of the Mennonite community. His library included the complete works of Pietist leaders like Gerhard Tersteegen and Friedrich Oetinger. Weber avidly read August Herman Franck's *Glaubensweg* and Johann Heinrich Reitz's *Historia der Wiedergeborenen*; and he carried on an extensive correspondence with the famous South German Pietist, novelist, and physician, Heinrich Jung-Stilling.

Weber was removed from his office and only reinstated in 1763 when he—along with a cohort of younger ministers—promised to conduct himself in "stillness and quiet." But his critique of Mennonite spirituality and his search for sources of renewal beyond the Anabaptist theological tradition point toward tensions latent within the Mennonite community that would find fuller expression in the years following the French Revolution.[7]

---

[4] Quoted in "Eine Bekehrungsgeschichte: Aus den Akten des Karlsruhe General-Landesarchiv," *Christlicher Gemeinde-Kalendar* (1906): 67.

[5] Möllinger was praised throughout the region for introducing crop rotation, new forms of fertilizers, and new breeds of cattle, and is still identified in textbooks such as *The Father of Palatine Agriculture*. For more on Möllinger and other examples of Mennonite agrarian success, see Ernst Correll, *Das schweizerische Täufermennonitum* (Tübingen: J.C.B. Mohr, 1925) 125ff; as well as the contemporary account of Johann Nepomuk Hubert Schwerz, *Beobachtungen über den Ackerbau der Pfälzer* (Berlin: Verlag G. Reimer, 1816) 21ff. Frank Kornersmann has transcribed and edited Möllinger's diary, *Das Gästebuch der mennonitischen Bauernfamilie David Möllinger Senior 1781–1817. Eine historisch-kritische Edition* (Alzey: Rheinhessische Druckwerkstätte, 2009).

[6] Quoted in Christian Neff, "Peter Weber, ein mennonitischer Pietist aus dem 18. Jahrhundert," *Christlicher Gemeinde-Kalender* 39 (1930): 72.

[7] For a fuller account of Weber's story, see John D. Roth, "Pietism and the Anabaptist Soul," in Stephen L. Longenecker, *The Dilemma of Anabaptist Piety: Strengthening or Straining the Bonds of Community* (Bridgewater VA: Bridgewater College Forum for Religious Studies, 1997) 27–33.

IMPACT OF THE FRENCH REFORMS

In 1792 the Mennonite communities of the Palatinate—along with all of the territories in southwest Germany—collided with the modern world in the form of the French Revolution. In October 1792, the revolutionary French army under the command of General Custin conquered Speyer, Worms, and Mainz in quick succession, planting liberty trees in villages throughout the Rhineland, while calling on German subjects to join in the revolution.

Like their neighbors, Mennonites experienced the initial consequences of the French occupation not in the lofty abstractions of revolutionary rhetoric, but in the tangible realities of sequestered grain, forced lodging of soldiers, and the raw fear that accompanied each passing wave of troops. Along with their Catholic and Protestant neighbors, Mennonite families either endured the interruptions of warfare or, like Christian Dettweiler of Kindenheim, they fled "the *Schrecknissen* (horrors) of the French Revolution" to the comparative safety of friends and relatives in Baden or Bavaria.[8] Adam Krehbiel, an aged Mennonite minister who chose to stay, watched in despair as French soldiers turned his meetinghouse at the Weierhof into a temporary barracks and then a granary.[9] A Mennonite farmer from Spitalhof kept track of the numerous requisitions for wood, hay, and straw demanded by the French; and he remembered with special clarity the *Republiksonntag* of 1794 when French Commissars Gibois and Gro planted a liberty tree and held a celebration "amidst gluttony and drunkenness, dancing and music" for their high-ranking officers.[10] Martin Möllinger, a Mennonite pastor in Monsheim, wrote to Johannes Weber in 1795 that Prussian officers in the Imperial army had plundered his possessions to the tune of 5,000 florins. Three years later Weber recalled his own experiences with the French: "It was a common saying then," he wrote, "that the French never left anything behind except two eyes for crying."[11]

In later years, leaders were quick to blame the general decline in the nineteenth-century Mennonite church on the chaos, upheaval, and anti-ecclesiastical rhetoric of the French occupation. "Beginning with the French," wrote Hermann Reeder, a minister at the Weierhof, "a relaxed, frivolous spirit spread through the Palatinate [...] which had a destructive influence on the churches."[12] David Kägy

---

[8] Chr. Dettweiler, 77.

[9] Gary Waltner, "Aus der Pfalz nach Nordamerika," *Mennonitische Geschichtsblätter* (1976): 15.

[10] H.S., "Überlieferungen eines Bauern des Spitalhofes aus der Franzosenzeit," *Christlicher Gemeinde-Kalendar* 46 (1937): 106.

[11] Martin Möllinger to Johannes Weber (1795), Hist. Mss. 1-536, Weber Collection, Archives of the Mennonite Church USA (hereafter cited as AMC); and Johannes Weber to Martin Möllinger, 17 May 1798, Hist. Mss. 1-536, AMC.

[12] Hermann Reeder, *Predigten zu Festtagen und bei besonderen Veranlaßungen* (Leipzig:

of Offstein blamed the baneful influence of French atheism for the collapse of moral standards he observed among Mennonites. "For a while there were no church services held in our whole region," he reflected in 1842. "[T]hey were despised [...] and Sunday was not to be recognized at all. For these reasons the sensuous and worldly people among us walked freely down the broad road of lust and temptation."[13]

When a large group of Mennonite ministers gathered at Ibersheim in 1803 and again in 1805 to address matters of common concern, they readily admitted that the church was approaching a crisis. According to minutes from these meetings, members selected by the lot to serve as ministers were routinely refusing to accept their call; it had become commonplace for Mennonites to marry non-Mennonites; baptism was increasingly an empty symbol, formulaic and routine; church discipline was practiced only rarely; and many Mennonites had taken up with "worldly amusements" such as dancing, drinking, and card-playing. Perhaps most painful of all was the recognition that the principle of pacifism had been endangered by the "voluntary taking up of weapons."[14]

The impact of the French occupation, however, also had more complicated political consequences for Mennonites. Between 1797 and 1814, a white-collar army of French-speaking bureaucrats, recruited on the basis of education and talent, replaced the notables and court society of German dukes and princes. At the same time, a new, highly rationalized system of municipal administration supplanted the fragmented and idiosyncratic jurisdictions of the ancien regime. Religious institutions—Catholic, Protestant, and Jewish alike—came firmly under the tutelage of the state, a secular state that guaranteed the freedom of individual religious conscience to everyone, including the Mennonites.

The anchor of these reforms—equality under the law, individual rights, religious liberty, and a secular state—was the Code Napoleon, or the French Civil Code of 1804. Lucid, simple, unencumbered with casuistry or abstractions, the civil code embodied a modern society established on the principles of reason rather than the habits of tradition. Despite complaints about legal fees and *Vielregelei* (red tape), the civil code became firmly established in the Rhineland in the first decade of the nineteenth century, penetrating the consciousness of people at all levels of society. "Every illiterate farmer in the Pfalz," wrote folk historian Wilhelm Heinrich Riehl, "became a born professor, a true doctrinaire," brandishing the code at every breach of trust and arguing vigorously over its principles.[15]

Karl Tauchnitz, 1843) ix.

[13] David Kägy to John Lapp, 22 May 1842, 1-536, AMC.

[14] Schowalter, "Die Ibersheimer Beschlüße von 1803 und 1805," 38.

[15] Wilhelm Heinrich Riehl, *Die Pfälzer: Ein rheinische Volksbild* (Stuttgart: Cotta, 1846)

By the time allied German armies reconquered the western bank of the Rhine early in 1814, most of the reforms introduced by the French were deeply rooted. In 1815, attempts by the allied military government to roll back these administrative reforms met with fierce local resistance. Even the conservative Bavarian monarchy, which absorbed the Palatinate as a province in 1818, left the civil code virtually untouched—freedom of religion continued to prevail, and the basic outlines of the French constitution persisted intact through the conservative reaction of the 1820s and 1830s.[16]

Post-Revolution Tensions

On the surface, the initial consequences of these reforms were overwhelmingly positive for Mennonites. For three full centuries, Mennonites had always been wary of civil government, regarding it both as a divinely ordained source of order as well as a potential threat to their very existence. Now, suddenly, the state turned out to be their friend and protector—the guarantor of civil liberties, religious freedom, and legal equality. No longer merely "tolerated" by the arbitrary whim of their feudal lords, Mennonites now enjoyed every individual right and liberty afforded by their status as "citizens." In the free market of religious opinion that now prevailed, Mennonites could worship as they pleased, build public meetinghouses to rival those of their neighbors, and proselytize without fear. They were now free to leave their isolated estates, purchase land without restrictions, pursue university education, and enter any profession or occupation that they might choose.

Yet, paradoxically, the new age of freedom ushered in by the French political reforms also marked an era of profound uncertainty within the South German Mennonite church. By the early 1820s a cluster of five conservative congregations, led by Johannes Galle of Monzernheim and David Kägy of Offstein, had formed a *Bund* or conference in opposition to the energetic new projects being initiated by such progressive leaders as Johannes Risser of Friedelsheim and Leonhard Weydman of Monsheim.[17]

When William Henry Angas appeared in Palatinate in summer 1824, he had no understanding of these complex cross-currents within the small Mennonite congregations of the region. His sights were set primarily on the emerging

261; see also Max Springer, *Die Franzosenherrschaft in der Pfalz 1792–1814* (Stuttgart: Deutsche Verlags-Anstalt, 1926) 333ff.

[16] Adam Sahrmann, *Pfalz oder Salzburg? Geschichte des territorialen Ausgleichs zwischen Bayern und Österreich von 1813 bis 1819* (München: R. Oldenbourg, 1921).

[17] The best overview of this scarcely noted conservative movement can be found in Christian Neff, "David Kaegy von Offstein," *Christlicher Gemeinde-Kalendar* (1925): 39–63.

Baptist mission fields in India, Java, and Jamaica. But during his prolonged sojourn in Europe, Angas had also come to regard the Mennonite communities he visited as themselves mission fields—a tradition that was clearly prospering economically, but ignorant of the lost souls in heathen nations far from home and badly in need of spiritual revival.

William Henry Angas (1781–1832)

William Henry Angas was born in Newcastle, England, in 1781 and raised in a pious home. As a young boy he apprenticed as a sailor on several lengthy voyages, and then studied navigation and served as a captain's apprentice.[18] At the age of 19, he took command of a ship belonging to his father. According to his memoir, exposure to the coarse morality of sailors, encounters with distant cultures, and several harrowing experiences while at sea—including his capture and imprisonment by French privateers—gradually nurtured in him a desire to devote his life to Christian ministry. In 1817, after a year of study at Edinburgh, Angas was ordained as a Baptist minister. Soon thereafter he moved to Brussels for intensive language instruction in French and Flemish. Seven months later, he relocated to Rotterdam, where he lived with a Moravian family while learning Dutch; at some point, he also became fluent in German.[19]

In 1820, the Baptist Missionary Society in England asked Angas to accompany William Ward, a pioneer Baptist missionary to India, on a visit to the Netherlands with the express purpose of raising funds among Mennonite churches there for the Baptist mission effort. Although Ward soon returned to England, Angas remained for several additional months and reported positively on his initial encounters with Dutch Mennonites. By December he had "visited all the principal Mennonite churches in Holland and in the lower provinces of the Rhine." His encounters, he thought, "had a very favourable effect," which was "likely to lay the foundation of a large and lasting good to the Mission." Nevertheless, he also noted that even though Mennonites were "the most wealthy people in Holland," their actual contributions to the mission effort fell far short of their capacity.[20]

At the time, members of the Baptist Missionary Society seem to have had

---

[18] Much of the biographical information that follows is taken from Francis Augustus Cox and William Henry Angas, *Memoirs of the Rev. William Henry Angas Ordained a "Missionary to Seafaring Men," May 11, 1822* (London: Thomas Ward & Co., 1834). Also useful is the brief overview by James R. Hertzler, "English Baptists Interpret Continental Mennonites in the Early Nineteenth Century," *Mennonite Quarterly Review* 54 (January 1980) 42–52.

[19] Cox and Angas, *Memoirs*, 42. For a short time, Angas served with the British and Foreign Seaman's Friend Society as a missionary to seafaring men.

[20] Ibid., 55–56.

only a vague understanding of the Mennonites.[21] The society's annual report in 1821, for example, mentioned "the Mennonite, or Baptist Churches" in the Netherlands, suggesting that the editors regarded Mennonites as their continental cousins.[22] Angas' initial encounter with Mennonites encouraged him to learn more about them. "During my tour in Holland," he wrote,

> I received information of an immense number of Baptist [i.e., Mennonite] churches in different parts of the continent of Europe [...]. Now all these being, for the most part, very well able, as I learn, to aid in the spread of the gospel in India, I intend, in a year or two more, to be among them all, for the purpose of forming them into a solid union, for the good cause of Him who bled and died for us. [...] I intend to seek all these brethren out; and yoke them in different sections to the great care of the gospel, that they may cooperate with us in England, in every work of faith and labour of love.[23]

In 1823, the society reported that Angas was "making known, by personal communication, the nature and objects of our institution among the Mennonites in the North of Europe."[24]

That spring Angas had launched an expedition, at his own expense, to acquaint himself with the Mennonite presence in Europe. After another renewing his contacts with Dutch Mennonite ministers, he set out for the large Mennonite community in the Vistula Delta of Prussian Poland, where he sojourned for four months.[25] Again he reported mixed results. "Nothing could surpass the kindness and hospitality" with which he was received, "and yet the temperature of feeling toward missions was lukewarm." Following a detailed description of a worship service at the Mennonite congregation in Brenkenhofswalde, Angas noted that the Mennonites he encountered there had heard of the Baptists, "but they thought the English Baptists were only a better sort of Roman Catholics!"[26]

While in Danzig, Angas published an open letter "To the Elders, Ministers,

---

[21] Shortly thereafter the Dutch Mennonites created an auxiliary breach of the British mission society (*Engelse Baptisten-Zendingsgenootschap, Nederlandse Afdeling*), which led to several decades of modest financial support to the Baptist Missionary Society. The organization continued until 1847 when the Dutch Mennonites formed their own missionary society. See Hertzler, "English Baptists Interpret Continental Mennonites," 44.

[22] See also C.C. Tauchnitz, "The Mennonite Baptists," *The Baptist Magazine* (London) 22 (1830): 393–94.

[23] Cox and Angas, *Memoirs*, 58.

[24] *The Annual Report of the Baptist Missionary Society* (London: printed by order of the General Meeting, 1823) 29.

[25] Cox and Angas, *Memoirs*, 78.

[26] Ibid., 81.

and Members of All Mennonite Congregations in West Prussia,"[27] in which he described in great detail the missionary efforts of the English Baptists in India and closed with the confident claim that if "the faithful and pious Menno" was still alive, he "would rejoice deeply and be the first to offer his hand in support of our efforts."[28]

By December 1823 Angas had arrived in Switzerland, where his travels led first to the "Swiss Baptists" of Basel, then to the French-speaking "Anabaptistes" in Moutier, and finally to the "Baptists" of Bern. His lengthy letters included detailed descriptions of their dress, doctrine, history, and practices. Swiss Baptists, he claimed, were "gentle and peaceful in their dispositions," though they "mingle no more with other denominations than their secular business requires, and are consequently shy of strangers, arising chiefly from a fear of innovation."[29] Their style of preaching was "very confused," consisting of "pure quotations from the scriptures, though brought forward with scarcely any order. The Bible is the only book they read, excepting a sort of Baptist Martyrology [...]."[30] They wore distinctive dress (with hats "not unlike our Quakers of the old school"), refused to bear arms or join the military, and refrained from dancing, alcohol, smoking, and snuff. "For the rest," Angas concluded, "their doctrines are soundly evangelical, and differ from us only in their not touching on Predestination and Election."[31] Again, it was difficult for him to assess his impact:

> After a good deal of work, I got the ice broken at last, and have kept it open ever since. My main argument was, that I had come a great many hundred miles to see them; and that my message was no other than love to them, and to the cause of Him, whose example was love; and though I differed with them in outside, they might not find, perhaps, so great a difference [...][32]

By April 1824 he reached out to the French "Baptists" in Upper Alsace, whom he described as "richer for this than for yonder world." Although he had enjoyed their hospitality, Alsatian Mennonites responded with "little curiosity." In general, Angas concluded, they are "engrossed with the world, and ignorant of the nature of vital religion." Indeed, the visit prompted a reflection on the dangers

---

[27] Consciously signaling a fraternal connection between the English Baptists and the continental Mennonites (*Taufgesinnten*), Angas signed the document "In the name of the Baptism-Minded [*Taufgesinnten*] British Mission Society and as a member of the Committee who directs their affairs in London."

[28] William Henry Angas, *An die Aeltesten, Lehrer und Mitglieder der sämmtlichen Mennoniten-Gemeinen in Westpreußen* (Danzig: np, 1823) 23.

[29] Cox and Angas, *Memoirs*, 86.

[30] Ibid., 88–89.

[31] Ibid., 87.

[32] Ibid., 88.

of wealth, with a final admonition that "every professing Christian be cautious of the fascinations of wealth and glory."[33]

By the time Angas reached the Palatinate, he undoubtedly had a deeper, more nuanced understanding of the Mennonite tradition—ranging from the culturally sophisticated merchants in Amsterdam to rustic farmers in the Swiss Alps. It is highly unlikely, however, that he fully understood the catalytic role he was to play within the Mennonite community in southwest Germany.

ANGAS' ENCOUNTER WITH MENNONITES IN THE PALATINATE, 1824

During the four weeks that he spent in the Palatinate, Angas visited all of the Mennonite churches. On 13 July 1824, thanks largely to the initiative of Johannes Risser, his efforts were rewarded in the form of a gathering of some fifteen ministers from eight Mennonite congregations at the Mennonite meetinghouse at Spitalhof. According to the published minutes of the meeting, the purpose for the gathering was to determine "whether, and how, we should initiate a means by which our congregations could also assist in the spread and advance of the Gospel among the poor heathen."[34] Following an opening hymn, a "heartful prayer" by Angas, and a short sermon on the Great Commission by Mennonite minister Heinrich Ellenburger, the group turned to Angas.

In his sermon, Angas noted he had learned a great deal about Mennonites in the course of his travels, but his efforts to promote missions had thus far resulted in only marginal success. The key to spiritual revival, he continued, would have to start with a transformation of the hearts of Mennonite leaders. His visit was not primarily about raising money from the wealthy; indeed, in England the most generous supporters of mission were often the poor, who gave what they had. Everyone, regardless of wealth, could support missions in prayer; and prayer for those who were sharing the gospel in distant mission fields, Angas concluded, would create a generous heart.[35]

At the end of the meeting the ministers addressed several church-related concerns, particularly related to the distribution of alms. For Risser, however, who served as secretary of the gathering, Angas was clearly the high point of the conference. Taking the liberty of his role as recorder, Johannes Risser added another six-page defense of Angas' character and integrity. "It pains me," he wrote, "to have to defend him against the least suspicion. Even the necessity of writing this tries my patience." Risser continued, "I was in his presence daily for three weeks, during which time I had more than 100 conversations with [Angas],

---

[33] Ibid., 98–99.

[34] *Guttbefinden einer kleinen Kirchenversammlung der Mennoniten-Gemeinen. Gehalten auf dem Spitalhof, am 13 Julius 1824* (n.p.: 1824).

[35] Ibid., 8–12.

which all testified to his character as an alert and thoughtful Christian."[36] Moreover, "his noble heart, the compassion of his character, and his warm love of the brethren" had earned Angas a positive reputation with Leonard Weydmann, the Mennonite pastor from Monsheim; and the Dutch Mennonites had supported the Baptist mission efforts for at least four years. Citing reports from a periodical issued by the mission institute in Basel, Risser insisted that "what is now happening has not happened since the time of the Apostles. Not only are our Mennonite brothers being drawn into the field against the Lord of Darkness, but from all religious parties the sword of the spirit is being drawn...and success is being witnessed everywhere."[37] Risser ended with an apology for moving from the "student's bench" into the "teaching stool" and begged his readers to interpret his zealous words with charity. But he could not refrain from a final appeal that compared the sacrifice "of our ancestors who were beheaded in the fierce persecution" with the comparatively simple offering of the "widow's mite" in support of the mission program. "How sad it would be," he wrote, "for us if the Lord should return and find us sleeping." He closed the report with a warm invitation to all people—"the more distant from us, the more welcome" (*je fremder, je willkommener*)—to attend the next conference in May 1825.[38]

In the years that followed, Angas' work among the Mennonites in the Palatinate clearly bore fruit. He had arrived in the region at a critical moment, when Mennonites were still struggling to understand their identity as citizens in a new context of legal, economic, and religious freedoms. His charismatic presence, and particularly his invitation to participate more fully in the larger overseas mission movement, played a significant part in a deeper transformation taking play among Mennonites. Fraught with tensions, that transformation found expression in the following years in a new interest in missions, a new posture of ecumenism, and new expressions of faith and practice that borrowed heavily from their Protestant neighbors. In short, Angas helped formerly sectarian Mennonites in the Palatinate enter fully into the mainstream of Protestant Christianity.

Palatinate Mennonites in Transition

1. Missions. The most obvious long-term consequence of Angas' visit was a renewed interest in mission. For several years, both Johannes Risser and Leonard Weymann had attempted to persuade Mennonites in the region to support the emerging mission initiative among the Dutch Mennonites. In January 1824, Weydmann, who had been educated at the Dutch Mennonite Seminary in Amsterdam, translated and circulated a leaflet published by the Dutch Mennonite

---

[36] Ibid., 17–18.

[37] Ibid., 19.

[38] Ibid., 22–23.

Missionary Aid Society that invited other Mennonites to support their work and the larger vision of the Baptist Missionary Society.[39] But few ministers in the Palatinate expressed any interest in the initiative.

Angas' visit in July 1824, by contrast, provided both a persuasive theological rationale and a ready-made framework for Palatine Mennonites to engage the cause of overseas mission. Before the day was over, the ministers gathered at Spitalhof agreed to several specific actions. On the first Sunday of each month, pastors agreed to read aloud a mission report to their congregations, based on a regular summary of information that Angas would supply in German. The ministers also committed themselves to pray "for faith and repentance, as always [...] but especially for the power and outpouring of the Holy Spirit on the poor heathen." And every participating congregation agreed to create a special collection box for missions, located next to the alms chest by the meetinghouse door so that "friends of missions" would have the opportunity to make a financial contribution to the Baptist Mission Society in London.[40] The proceeds would be pooled at the next meeting, set for May 1825, and forwarded to Angas. Finally, Angas also agreed to send two young Mennonite men, at his own expense, to the Teachers' Training Seminar for the Poor *(Armenschullehreranstalt)* at Beuggen/Basel, to prepare them for leadership to become teachers in the Mennonite community.

No archival records remain from the 1825 conference, but an extensive printed report of a conference of sixteen ministers who gathered in Friedelsheim on 7 May 1826 noted that some 119 florins had been raised "for the spread of the gospel among the heathen and sent to the Baptist Mission, our brothers, in England."[41] According to the alms book of the Weierhof congregation, donations to the society continued regularly until the founding of the Dutch Mennonite Missionary Society in 1847.

In 1829, Angas returned to Germany where he met with Karl C. Tauchnitz, son of the well-known Leipzig bookseller and printer Christian Bernhard von Tauchnitz, "to engage his services for the revival and diffusion of religion among the Mennonites." In July 1830, Tauchnitz was ordained in the Camberwell Baptist Church in London specifically "to do the work of an evangelist to the Mennonite churches on the continent of Europe."[42] Six months later, Tauchnitz reported that he was planning to settle in Mannheim as the base for his visits to Mennonite churches in the region, where he intended to promote the cause of

[39] Ibid., 17.

[40] *Guttbefinden* (1824), 13. This collection canister can still be seen at the Mennonitische Forschungsstelle, Weierhof, Germany.

[41] Leonhard Weydmann, *Nachricht von den Verhandlungen der dritten Jahres- und Kirchenversammlung der Menonitten-Gemeinden. Gehalten in Friedelsheim, bei Dürkheim a. d. Haardt, den 7ten Mai 1826* (Worms: Johann Andreas Krnzbhler, 1826) 7.

[42] Cox and Angas, *Memoirs*, 130, 155.

missions. In 1833 Tauchnitz helped to co-found the Pilgrim Missionary Society in Basel. Although he eventually came to realize that Baptists and Mennonites were not as closely aligned as Angas had assumed, his influence on the Palatinate Mennonite community continued long after he returned to Leipzig in 1836 to take over his father's publishing house.

Though resistance would continue among some Mennonite pastors, many Mennonites in the Palatinate enthusiastically participated in the broader Protestant mission movement, inspired by the direct appeal from William Henry Angas. In the decades that followed, progressive congregations in Sembach, Friedelsheim, Monsheim, and the Weierhof aggressively pursued their interest in missions, holding periodic mission rallies, collecting funds, circulating translations of the Baptist Missionary Society newsletter, and supporting scholarships to the mission schools at Beuggen and Basel.

2. New Forms of Ecumenism. In a closely related way, collaboration with the Baptists in missions opened the door for Mennonites to adopt other practices from neighboring Protestant churches that signaled a fundamental shift away from their identity as a separatist minority. Confession identities ran deep in the Palatinate prior to the French occupation. The local archives are filled with reports of bitter disputes between Lutheran and Reformed villagers over access to cemeteries, ringing of church bells, issues related to mixed marriages, and even the proper language for the Lord's Prayer: the Lutherans began the prayer with the words "*Vater Unser*," whereas the Reformed version began with "*Unser Vater*."

But the shared trauma of the French Revolutionary armies, along with the political reforms enacted during the twenty-year occupation that followed, put these confessional antagonisms in a new perspective. From 1801 to 1816 ecclesiastical administration of all churches in the Palatinate had come under the firm oversight of the French state. Under the French, confessional identity no longer conferred political benefits or liabilities. Greater freedom of mobility led to a noticeable increase in mixed Lutheran-Reformed marriages. And Lutherans and Reformed villagers found common cause in their fears when the Congress of Vienna determined in 1816 that the Palatinate would be incorporated as a province of Catholic Bavaria.

The celebration of the 300th anniversary of the Reformation in 1817 turned these concerns into a concrete program of action. In August 1817 Lutheran and Reformed members of the General Consistory in Speyer began holding regular meetings to discuss details of a possible Protestant Union, leading to the publication of a joint Lutheran/Reformed songbook. Between November 1817 and February 1818, at least twenty-five communities in the Palatinate—including communities with significant numbers of Mennonites, such as Kirchheimbolanden, Marnheim, and Göllheim—arranged local church mergers on their own initiative.[43] When the General Consistory put the matter to a vote in spring 1818, popular support was overwhelmingly in favor of a merger (98.6%). In August 1818, the Lutheran and Reformed churches formally joined to create the Union Church of the Palatinate.

Although Mennonites were not formally invited to participate in the Union, they clearly took note of the new ecumenical spirit. Indeed, welcoming Angas and joining in the mission movement were only the first expressions of a new openness to the broader Protestant world that would flourish in the course of the next two decades. In the late 1820s, for example, Abraham Hunzinger, a young Mennonite from across the Rhine in Baden, enlisted a group of subscribers to finance an analytical study of the German Mennonite church, which he titled *The Religious, Ecclesiological and Educational Conditions of the Mennonites or Baptism-Minded*. Published in 1830, the book was a blend of history, theology, criticism, and polemic. The first section began in a descriptive mode, listing South German Mennonite and Amish religious doctrines and then slipping into a lengthy harangue against the Mennonite practice of church discipline and their rejection of scientific study. In the second half of the book Hunzinger offered his solution to halt the church's decline. In somewhat pompous tones, he called for dramatic changes in the Mennonite position on non-resistance, endogamous marriage, divorce, and their attitudes toward government. The salvation of the Mennonite church, according to Hunzinger, depended on restructuring its polity along the lines of the state churches. Thus, he argued in favor of a salaried church council, the introduction of church synods, the use of graded Sunday-school material for religious instruction through the age of 18, and an endowment raised with the help of the state out of which the salary of the ministers might be paid.

Hunzinger's book clearly appealed to several leading Mennonite preachers in the Palatinate. Writing in June 1830, Johannes Risser excitedly reported that Hunzinger had personally given him a copy of the book in addition to seven other copies to pass along to local subscribers. "As is well known," commented Risser, the book "is useful to all of us, especially for preachers and elders [who are] implementing the rebuilding of our congregations, whose decay [...] appears to be imminent."[44]

---

[43] The full details of the Union can be followed in Johannes Müller, *Die Vorgeschichte der pfälzischen Union* (Witten: Luther Verlag, 1967). Lutheran and Reformed congregations in Mainz (1802), Koblenz (1803), and Lambrecht (1805) had joined together in local unions already during the period of the French occupation.

[44] Johannes Risser to Johan Jakob Krehbiel, 22 October 1830, 1-536, AMC. Interestingly enough, Hunzinger's book eventually found its way to America and, in 1862, was reprinted by the American Mennonite reformer John Oberholtzer. "Hunzinger, Abraham," *Mennonite Encyclopedia*, ed. Harold S. Bender, 4 vols. (Harrisonburg VA: Herold Press, 1955–1959; supp.

In a similar spirit, progressive Palatine Mennonites in the early 1830s joined forces to publish a new hymnbook. For generations, Mennonites in the region sang from the *Ausbund,* a collection of sixteenth-century hymns whose lyrics, sung slowly and in unison, reminded congregants that following Christ would entail persecution. But now that Mennonites were no longer living under the shadow of persecution, progressives increasingly regarded the songs of the *Ausbund* as anachronistic and tedious. In February 1827, Johannes Risser noted in a letter that Leonhard Weydmann, pastor at the Monsheim congregation, had offered to take on the task of compiling a new hymnal. "We and our churches," concluded Risser, "have an obligation to extend him a helping hand in bringing this pleasant prospect to fruition."[45] Three years later in 1830, Weydmann presented a draft of the book—which integrated the best "old core-songs" *(Kernlieder)* with a host of popular new songs borrowed from Reformed and Lutheran hymnals—to a meeting of local ministers who agreed that it should be further circulated among the preachers and elders.[46]

When the *Christliches Gesangbuch* was published in 1832, it appeared in versions—alike in all respects except for the title page and foreword. The standard version lacked a foreword and included the subtitle, "Primarily for Use among the Baptism-Minded" (*Zunächst für den Gebrauch der Taufgesinnten*). Progressive Mennonites in Friedelsheim and Sembach, however, had protested against the use of the term *Taufgesinnten* in the title, fearing that the name still carried connotations in the popular mind of the discredited Täuferreich (Anabaptist kingdom) at Münster. Indeed, the Sembach congregation had been so adamant about the concern that they refused to accept them until a "correction" had been made on the books destined for use in their setting.[47] Thus a variant print run of some 200 copies of the new hymnal was arranged in which the word *Taufgesinnten* in the title page was replaced with the phrase *evangelischen Mennoniten-Gemeinen.* To their ears, "evangelical Mennonites" sounded more modern, more in line with their *evangelischen*—or Protestant—neighbors.[48]

---

vol. 5 1990) 2:845.

[45] Johannes Risser to Cousin, 14 February 1827, 1-536, 5/4, AMC.

[46] Johannes Galle and other conservatives opposed the new songbook from the outset, claiming that it had "eliminated all the good core-songs on the themes of suffering and the cross." Indeed, in Galle's judgment, the book was so bad that "if someone would hack off the arms and legs or cut away the nose and ears of a person, his body would not be so mutilated as the songbook has been mutilated" (quoted in Neff, "Männer der alten Richtung," 96).

[47] Johannes Weber to [?], 28 October 1832, 1-536, 4/5, AMC.

[48] A 1839 republication of the hymnal simplified *Evangelischen Mennoniten-Gemeinen* to *Mennoniten.* The 1832 hymnal found ready acceptance in the leading Mennonite congregations in South Germany. Katharina Krehbiel, writing from the Weierhof early in 1833 to her brother Daniel, a recent emigrant to New York, said that the congregation there had started singing through the book, beginning with the "new" songs in the middle, learning all the new

Around the same time, several congregations began to express frustration with the traditional model of uneducated, unsalaried ministers, selected randomly by lot. In 1835, following a pattern established at Monsheim, Sembach, and Ibersheim, the Weierhof congregation hired its first paid minister. Hermann Reeder was educated at a Baptist seminary in London and had heard about Mennonites from William Heinrich Angas. Shortly after his ordination as a Mennonite minister in Neuwied, he moved to Kirchheimbolanden with the expressed intention of deepening the spiritual life of the Mennonites there and of cultivating their newly awakened interest in missions. Almost immediately after arriving in the Palatinate, Reeder determined that his first project would be the construction of a new churchhouse. To that end, he embarked on a fundraising tour among North German Mennonite churches and the Baptists in England. By 1837 he had collected enough money to finance the construction of a new Mennonite church at the Weierhof. In contrast to the plain meetinghouses Mennonites had traditionally constructed, the new structure was modeled directly on a Baptist church Reeder had seen in Tottenham, England, and was built on an elevation that featured an imposing stairway. In 1837, Joseph Galle described the new construction at the Weierhof in sharply critical tones to his brother Johannes. "It seems that just because they installed a new, educated missionary preacher (Pfarrer)," he wrote, "they must also have a new elegant church." Galle went on to quote a passage from the prophet Hosea where Israel "forgot their creator and built a temple."

The architectural novelties did not end there. The new building at Ibersheim included a belltower—a feature consciously borrowed from the state churches. Many of the new churches introduced organs for the first time, which called for the specialized skills of a trained musician and introduced a significant shift in congregational singing. And even though Reeder insisted that the introduction of a raised pulpit (*Kanzel*) was for acoustical reasons, the innovation inevitably helped to underscore the new authority of the professional preacher as well as the centrality of the sermon in the worship service.

3. New Theological Emphases. Not surprisingly, these changes in Mennonite practice in the Palatinate in the years following Angas' visit found theological expression as well. The most visible measure of that shift can be seen in a controversial initiative to revise the church's catechism.

For at least fifty years, Mennonites in the region had been using the thirty-five questions and answers of the *Christliches Gemüthsgespräch* as their basic text for catechal instruction. Written in 1702 by the highly respected North German

---

melodies as they went. "Every evening people sing. Whole families gather to practice singing new melodies in four parts and some of them have even been sung in church" (addendum by Katharina Krehbiel to a letter from Johannes Krehbiel to Daniel Krehbiel, 6 January 1833, 1-536, 7/6, AMC).

Mennonite preacher and elder Gerrit Roosen, the catechism had found favor among Mennonites in the Palatinate who frequently reprinted it, along with the *Anleitung zum christliches Glauben*, a similar catechism written by the Dutch Mennonite Johannes Deknatel.[49]

Progressive ministers, however, chafed at several specific questions in the Roosen catechism—particularly article 26, which restricted marriage to other Mennonites, article 27 against divorce, and articles 31–33 on church discipline. So Leonhard Weydmann set about to write his own new and improved catechism, openly enlisting the help of local Protestant (*evangelisch*) clergy in the process. Even before the new catechism appeared in 1836, conservative ministers raised their voices in protest. Their concerns are illuminating. In a letter to Christian Krehbiel at the Weierhof, a proponent of the new catechism, Johannes Galle contrasted the manner of its presentation with an earlier era:

> Fifty or one hundred years ago when our congregations were scattered from 30–60 hours apart, everyone was informed and worked together with the Holy Spirit's leading whenever anything important was decided. But this new catechism was prepared in such secrecy and released like a whirlwind on innocent and unsuspecting congregations. Now disunity has arisen because many ministers and deacons—indeed most Mennonite congregations—find it impossible to agree with you in calling light darkness and darkness light, or sweet sour and sour sweet.[50]

On 25 February 1835, ministers from six congregations of the conservative union met to consider an invitation to meet with Weydmann and others for an extended discussion of the new catechism. Rejecting the offer, they dismissed the new book as an effort to reduce salvation to the Ten Commandments and the Lord's Prayer, something that the Catholics, Reformed and Lutheran, could all accept as well. "Christ called us to the narrow way. [...] Therefore we will stay by those old catechisms that we value most."[51] The statement was signed by eighteen ministers.

In April 1835 Kägy organized another gathering of conservative ministers at Sinsheim, where he was more specific in his critique. The new catechism was clearly "not for Mennonites," he argued, since it left out any mention of church discipline, the selection of leaders, marriage, and nonresistance.[52] In a letter the

---

[49] The most recent publication of the book at the time had been orchestrated (and likely paid for) by David Kägy, a wealthy conservative farmer from Offstein who, in fall 1828, ordered 400 copies of the book from Kranzbuhler printers in Worms (David Kägy to Herrn Kranzbuhler, 26 November 1828, 1-536, AMC). The edition appeared in 1829.

[50] Johannes Galle to Christian Krehbiel, 19 December 1835, 1-536, AMC.

[51] Quoted in Neff, "Die Männer der alte Richtung," 98.

[52] David Kägy to friend (in Bruchhausen), 18 April 1835, 1-536, AMC.

following month, he wrote that "all of our doctrines and church discipline (*Ordnungen*) are contained within the 35 Questions and Answers and every member and leader can understand them." Weydmann, he claimed to yet another correspondent, "has thrown out the doctrinal basis that separates us from the Protestant denominations (*Evangelischen Glaubensgenossen*)." In the same letter, he cast the new catechism in the broadest perspective: "[B]ecause we Mennonites have sat for such a long time in proud peace and have had the gospel without the Passion of Christ, we know nothing of the persecution and suffering of our forefathers. Thus many despise the old teaching books which they are now trying to destroy [...]." Our basis, Kägy continued, "is none other and none newer than the Apostle Paul who says in Hebrews 13:5— be happy with what you have."[53] "The Mennonites and the Protestants," lamented Johannes Galle, "continue to melt together."[54]

The protests of the conservatives met with little success. By 1836 the large congregations of Monsheim, Ibersheim, Friedelsheim, Sembach, and the Weierhof all had adopted the new catechism, titled *Christliche Lehre, zunächst zum Gebrauch der Taufgesinnten in Deutschland.*[55] In subsequent years, Mennonites in the Sembach and Friedelsheim congregations began celebrating Reformation Sunday; and in 1850, Weydmann published a glowing biography of Martin Luther titled *Luther: Ein Charakter- Und Spiegelbild Für Unsere Zeit.*

Conclusion

The opening decades of the nineteenth century were a tumultuous time for all inhabitants of the Palatinate, but especially for the small community of Mennonites in the region. Thanks to the legal reforms introduced by the French, Mennonites were no longer merely "tolerated" subjects of a feudal prince, subject to burdensome legal restrictions and fears of renewed persecution or expulsion. The reforms invited—indeed compelled—Mennonites to join with their Catholic and Protestant neighbors in a modern secular society made up of citizens equal under the law. Yet at the same time, Mennonites were ill-prepared to understand, critique, or creatively engage these new realities. Conservatives saw no reason why the convictions, practices, and postures inherited from the past should suddenly change to reflect the new context. On the other hand, progressives like Johannes Risser and Leonhard Weydmann were convinced that the cognitive dissonance between the inherited language of suffering and the reality of religious freedom simply could not be sustained.

---

[53] David Kägy to "Brother Galle," 16 May 1835, 1-536, AMC.

[54] Johannes Galle to John Lapp, 20 March 1838, 1-536, AMC.

[55] The title clearly mirrored that of the recently published songbook. Weydmann apparently was not among those who resisted the use of the term *Taufgesinnten.*

When William Henry Angas arrived in summer 1824 preaching a gospel of personal spiritual renewal and active engagement in overseas missions, his message immediately appealed to progressives. In the free marketplace of religion, it made sense to develop budgets, organizations, and long-term strategies to win the souls of the lost. In an increasingly bureaucratized culture—organized around principles of efficiency, professional training, and competence—trained and salaried ministers offered clear competitive advantages over the barely literate farmer-preachers chosen by lot. In a context where religion had increasingly become a private matter of individual conscience, the Protestant language of forensic salvation and a personal relationship with God seemed more compelling than the communitarian themes of Mennonite ecclesiology. In short, engagement in world missions, ecumenical contacts, a professional pastorate, new hymnbooks, and revised catechisms all offered a better "fit" with the emerging public culture. Mennonites were no longer sectarians; they could now rightly claim their new status as Protestants.

From a longer theological and historical perspective, the consequences of this new posture remain rather ambiguous. Weydmann's reworked catechism, for example, retained passing references to the traditional Mennonite themes of nonresistance and adult baptism; but by consciously dropping the principle of church discipline, these distinctive themes became options for individual discernment, no longer a test of church membership. The fundamental organizing principle of Weydmann's new catechism was now the doctrine of personal salvation. Teachings on moral regeneration had virtually disappeared and instruction regarding the nature of the church had become generically Protestant.

Not surprisingly, within a generation or so, the principle of nonresistance had virtually disappeared from the German Mennonite vocabulary. Today, the cemeteries of many German Mennonite congregations are filled with the graves of those who "died for the Fatherland" in deadly combat with fellow Christians from France or England or North America.

Clearly, William Henry Angas was not personally responsible for the concerted efforts by many nineteenth-century Mennonites in the Palatinate to assimilate into the mainstream Protestant churches of their day. Nor should the sobering consequences of that assimilation undermine the importance of ongoing ecumenical conversations between Mennonites, Baptists, and other Protestant denominations. But Angas' visit to the Palatinate in summer 1824 was a catalytic moment in the history of Mennonites in southwest Germany. The larger questions it raised about Mennonite identity—and the relationship between the Anabaptist-Mennonite tradition and the broader currents of Reformation Protestantism—are still relevant today.[56]

[56] This essay is dedicated to William Brackney, whose scholarship, ecumenical commitments, and enduring friendships have immeasurably strengthened ecclesial relations between the Baptists and the Mennonites.

FIGHTING, FAITH, AND FREEDOM: 1914 AND TODAY

Keith Clements

1914: WAR AND THE CHURCHES

It is no exaggeration to say that in August 1914 the British churches went to war, along with the nation as a whole, and the Free Churches overall were as committed as any others. It has to be said also, however, that the outbreak of war came as a great shock, and at first within the church constituency there were doubts about whether Britain should get involved. Indeed, on 1 August there was convening at Constance on the German-Swiss border a long-awaited conference of peace-minded church figures from many countries in Europe and North America. A fruit of the North American peace movement and of the exchange visits of the British and German churches dating from 1908–1909, it barely had time to resolve on the setting up of the World Alliance for Promoting International Friendship through the Churches before dismissing the delegates who had to hurry home across a Europe now mobilising for war.

Among the British participants was the Baptist John Clifford, the "uncrowned of militant nonconformity," veteran peace campaigner who had dared publicly to oppose the Boer War of 1899–1901. He journeyed home having prepared a draft opposing British involvement, but on arrival in London and hearing the government's case, changed his mind. The government must have been relieved that such a conspicuous figure on the public stage was not going to head an opposition movement. The vital factor in swinging opinion was Germany's violation of Belgian neutrality. A typical reaction was that of the Congregationalist A.E. Garvie, principal of the Hackney Theological College: "On August 2, I believed that Great Britain could and should keep out of the European conflict, but the violation of Belgian neutrality made me waver, and the speeches in the House of Commons of Mr. Asquith and Sir Edward Grey convinced me that duty and honour called to participation."

"Duty and honour" were watchwords of the hour. This was not just flag-waving patriotism. There was a deeper sense of morality at issue. Clifford declared that Germany had "deliberately and of express purpose [...] broken into Belgium, flung to the winds as veriest chaff her solemn treaty obligations, flouted public law, and trampled underfoot with ineffable scorn the rights of small nationalities as not even the small dust of the balance."

This high moral tone cannot simply be dismissed as a fig-leaf covering the chauvinist excitement of the hour. It was consistent with the responses of liberal

Christianity, among the Free Churches especially, to a whole series of international episodes during the 1900s where human dignity and basic freedoms were held to be under attack: for example, forced Chinese labour in the Transvaal; Turkish atrocities in Armenia and Macedonia; and from 1903, Belgian brutal treatment of forced African labourers in the Congo. Clifford declared of the Congolese and the Congo itself: "Their rights have been most cruelly trampled underfoot, Leopold and his satellites have never seen it, but they have violently annexed it, and barbarously sacked it." This was exactly the same language Clifford was to use in 1914! Only, it was now Belgium itself that was being cruelly treated. Albeit that many (though not all) atrocity stories were greatly exaggerated and multiplied beyond measure, it would have been extraordinary if there had been no moral anger.

The German "Appeal to Evangelical Christians Abroad"

At first there was an inclination by British church leaders to distinguish between their German counterparts and the "Prussian militarism" that had taken over the country. This stance became harder to maintain once it emerged that German church opinion was solidly behind the Kaiser and the whole German war effort. In September 1914 there arrived at Lambeth Palace an open "Appeal to Evangelical [i.e., Protestant] Christians Abroad" signed by leading Protestant leaders and academics, including many—such as Julius Richter, Adolf Deissmann, and Adolf von Harnack—who had been involved either in the 1910 Edinburgh World Missionary Conference or the Anglo-German churches' peace organisation. It protested strongly against the "network of lies" being spread abroad through the international telegraph system about German responsibility for the war. It asserted the absolute right, allegedly denied to her by her enemies, to call on the assistance of God as Germany struggled to defend her lands against "Asiatic barbarism." It deplored the sundering of relationships between British and German missions in Africa and Asia. No mention was made of Belgium.

Archbishop Randall Davidson's reply, endorsed by a wide spectrum of Anglican and Free Church signatories, was restrained and measured but, no less than was the German appeal, supportive of the respective government's policy. It expressed amazement that there could be such a different view of the matter and to what appeared in British eyes to be the plain facts of the case. It shared the Germans' distress at the rupturing of relationships and expressed the hope that, in due course, this might be healed. The thirteen Free Church signatories were R.J. Campbell, John Clifford, P.T. Forsyth, T.R. Glover, R.F. Horton, F. Scott Lidgett, T.M. Lindsay, F.B. Meyer, G. Campbell Morgan, W. Robertson Nichol, W.B. Selbie, Alexander Whyte, and F. Luke Wiseman.

Much more virulent than the "appeal" was the "Manifesto of the 93," a declaration by 93 German intellectuals, artists, and writers—including leading theologians—violently denouncing all who had criticised Germany's actions, and passionately defending the country's cause. This was the manifesto that so alarmed the young Swiss pastor Karl Barth, who saw nearly all his esteemed German theological teachers among the signatories. This was, he said, almost as bad as the violation of Belgian neutrality and opened his eyes to how Protestant theology, in Germany at any rate, had been totally subsumed into Western so-called Christian culture and values, and thereby lost its distinct calling and prophetic voice.

For their part, as has been shown, British Free Church leaders largely supported the British entry into the war, on moral grounds. There was a paradox here. They were being true to the nonconformist line of moral protest against injustice—but also conforming to the prevailing national mood. They were being both nonconformist and conformist.

Alan Wilkinson, in his *Dissent or Conform?*,[1] suggests that the Free Churches' response to the First World War resulted in their greater acceptance into the mainstream of British public life, but at the cost of their having little distinctive to say thereafter or any alternative vision of society to offer. At the end of the war the Free Churches held a thanksgiving service attended by King George V and Queen Mary. Some felt that their day had arrived at last. Others may have felt that it signalled the end of the truly nonconformist era.

What cannot be denied in 1914 was the *voluntary* rush to the colours from within the churches. The strength of this commitment may be judged by the fact that even 30 percent of Quakers of military age volunteered, or accepted conscription when it came in from early 1916. How far was recruitment aided from the pulpit? That is not clear. Many Baptist churches, for example, certainly expressed pride and gratitude at the numbers of their young men enlisting, but that does not mean they were specifically exhorted to do so by the sermons they heard, which for the most part probably declaimed in general terms on the righteousness of the cause. The most explicit recruiting address I have come across was that of a certain judge who, as reported in the *Baptist Times* in 1915, urged theological students in Manchester to leave their studies and go to the colours, since after the war a VC would matter much more than a BD in gaining a large and prestigious congregation, and if they did not return alive, then it wouldn't matter anyway.

A Fight for Freedom? A Further Fateful Paradox

John Clifford, in his *Our Fight for Freedom and What It Means*, sought to unite the nonconformist principle so dear to his heart with the national cause. The fact of so much *voluntary* enlistment taking place in the first year of the war,

[1] Alan Wilkinson, *Dissent or Conform?* (London: SCM Press, 1986).

the sight of so many young men freely offering themselves soul and body—knowing that this could mean the ultimate sacrifice—was, indeed, deeply moving. To many, it carried a religious aura and confirmed the moral case for the war. By late 1915, however, the casualty rate had risen to such an extent as to outrun the numbers enlisting, and the War Office felt impelled to bring in conscription from the start of 1916. Clifford was appalled. A fight for freedom was now turning into a war requiring a coercion of wills and possibly even the disregard of that most hallowed freedom of all, the freedom of conscience. The issue of conscientious objection divided Free Church opinion. A.E. Garvie reports how in the Free Church Council executive there were fierce debates between those arguing that "absolutists"—those refusing any form of war service at all—deserved no sympathy, and those pleading that even those had rights to be respected. Clifford was among those church leaders who protested strongly when a group of conscientious objectors was transported to France under martial law and would have been summarily executed for "refusing to obey orders" had not the War Office, under pressure from church leaders and others, intervened. But there was now a genuine dilemma for the nonconformist conscience. The fight for "freedom" had now to be fought by illiberal means. War was losing any lofty romance it might have had. There is a strong case for saying this was the point at which the old nonconformist conscience really died, with the realisation that going in with the national cause meant going all the way. It was no longer enough to state "ideals," when one ideal might clash with another, or be thrown back on the rocks of political necessity. In relation to another context of the war, the historian A.J.P. Taylor refers to "the enthusiasts for a better world: men convinced that the war was being fought for great ideals, and almost convinced that these ideals would win the war of themselves" (*English History*, 107).

WHAT WAS THE WAR ACTUALLY FOR?

"Freedom," "honour," and "duty" are big words, like "democracy" is today. If the violation of Belgium was the prime factor bringing Britain into the war, how would this actually help Belgium once Belgium was overrun? What is remarkable, looking at the records of the time, is that there seems to have been hardly any public discussion of the actual war aims other than simply "defeat" of Germany. It presently became clear that this would have to be by a war of attrition. Then, after the armistice, by a blockade, which in the hunger, malnutrition, and disease it inflicted on Germany and other continental countries, violated all sense of decency, all in the interests of forcing Germany to accept the unacceptable and humiliating terms of the Versailles Treaty. Thankfully, the blockade was opposed by the "Fight the Famine" council and the campaign led by those remarkable Quaker sisters Dorothy Buxton and Eglantyne Jebb—"Fight the Famine." This was the situation brought about by the absence of any real attempt, from August 1914 onwards, to set out precisely what the war was being fought for apart from the grandiosities of "freedom," "honour," "king and country," and so forth. This was where real prophecy from the churches should have been heard. Prophecy was not entirely absent. There was the "Papers in Wartime Group" led by William Temple, which called for a much more self-critical attitude to the war and its implications for British society. In 1915, one member of the group, the Scottish lay theologian and ecumenical missionary statesman J.H. Oldham, stated in a letter sent to one of his German missionary colleagues that, in the event of an allied victory, any attempt to humiliate Germany or to impose conditions denying her legitimate aspirations would be "to sow the seeds of another war." That was indeed prophetic in every sense. It was not heeded at Versailles in 1919.

In fact, it is extraordinary that no actual official statement of war aims by any of the allied belligerent powers appeared until January 1918, when United States President Woodrow Wilson issued his famous "Fourteen Points," declaring that the World War was being fought for a moral cause and calling for post-war peace in Europe. He laid out in some detail a policy of free trade and open agreements, democracy and self-determination for all countries in Europe and at least parts of the Ottoman Empire. European governments generally welcomed Wilson's intervention, but British Prime Minister David Lloyd George, like his French and Italian counterparts, was sceptical about its idealistic vision. In fact, a few days before Wilson's speech, Lloyd George, evidently having gotten wind of it, addressed a conference of Trades Union leaders in Westminster Central Hall. He sounded all the right notes that resonated with his left-wing audience: an emphasis on reconciliation with Germany, self-government for all countries, the rights of minorities, etc. But the first thing to be said about this speech was that it was not made to Parliament! Second, it was laden with ambiguity, and was not as idealistic as appeared on the surface. The German colonies, for example, were to be afforded "self-determination," but that appeared to mean being handed to Britain for safe-keeping. Moreover, "Arabia, Armenia, Syria, and Palestine are in our judgment entitled to a recognition of their separate national identities," which, being translated, meant little more than being portioned between Britain and France.

As an aside, I may mention that that foremost Freechurchman, Baptist leader, and ecumenical statesman, Dr. Ernest Payne, once mentioned to me that he was slightly disappointed that the armistice came when it did in 1918. As an 18-year-old, he was due for military call-up, and was all ready to go to a tribunal as an objector: not on pacifist grounds, but declaring that if the allied war aims were as stated thus far, he was not prepared to fight for them. A dissenter indeed!

A "JUST WAR"?

One of the striking differences between today and a century ago is that, today, the "Just War" doctrine is endlessly and in great detail debated whenever a conflict situation arises. In 1914–1918 we seem to find it scarcely mentioned at all, despite its venerability and its origins as far back as Augustine of Hippo in the fifth century. Perhaps, for those who supported the war, the fact that Germany had grossly and with evil intent violated Belgian neutrality both provided and ended any argument about the justice of Britain's cause. Would a strict application of the doctrine of Just War have made any difference? It is worth recalling just how the doctrine—developed over many centuries from Augustine, St. Thomas Aquinas, Francisco de Vitoria, and Hugo Grotius—has attempted greater precision as well as scope in the criteria that must be satisfied. Thus, the intervention must:

- Be good in intent—to make peace (St. Augustine of Hippo).
- Be for good and just purpose, not exercise for self-gain or power or revenge.
- Be waged by properly instituted authority, such as the prince or state. Hold to peace as the central motive even in the midst of violence.
- Seek the redressing of a wrong, not conquest.
- Achieve a good outweighing any evil unleashed.
- Restrain violence and destruction within the limits of proportionality.

The Just War doctrine is certainly an attempt to give a moral framework to behaviour in a violent world. Against this, critics argue that while the criteria seem noble and quite clear, each and every one of them is open to quite different interpretations as to their meaning in general, and even more so in particular cases. *Of course* a ruler or government will *always* say its intentions are honourable. *Of course* they will say that its means are just—collateral damage is just a regrettable necessity. *Of course* they will claim that going to war is the lesser of evils, and "think of what it would have been like if we did *not* go to war." So, is the Just War doctrine a real restraint on war, or does it simply provide a sweetener for going to war?

Therefore, does it have any more meaning today? One argument sometimes voiced is that modern weaponry makes the Just War doctrine meaningless, because it obliterates any notion of proportionality, any distinction between combatants and civilian populations. But not all modern weapons are of mass destruction. There are, for example, missiles that can target with extraordinary precision. But more to the point, the most horrific and indiscriminate slaughters of recent times have actually been carried out by small arms—even machetes, as in the Rwanda genocide of 1994, where up to 1 million died.

The biggest question mark against the Just War doctrine concerns its underlying presupposition. In favour of the doctrine it is often said that its presumption is against war. This is scarcely credible. In fact, its presumption is that war is basically "okay" and that here is a checklist, a series of boxes to be ticked, just to be sure. It is rather like putting out to sea in a boat. The conditions have got to be right, the craft must be seaworthy, its equipment in good order and its crew competent. But, basically, ocean sailing is a good thing to be doing. So, too, on the Just War doctrine that war is all right—or at least there is no objection to it. War is an okay thing to do providing that these conditions are met. Left to itself, the Just War doctrine is defenceless against the presumption that war in principle is acceptable—a view that is incompatible with the biblical injunction against the taking of life. This also must be applied to the term that has been at the centre of much debate in the last twenty years, ever since the first "Gulf War," namely "humanitarian intervention." When is military intervention for humanitarian causes justified? In fact, all the strictures against the Just War doctrine can be applied to the theory of humanitarian intervention. The main criticism is that *even* if the intent is said to be for "humanitarian" motives (to which, of course, other ambitions can easily be attached), it is still basically dealing with the rights of the would-be intervener rather than the needs of the population in whose interest it is claimed the intervention is being made. As an alternative, a great deal of exploration is taking place, not only in U.N.-related circles but in ecumenical discussion, on the *responsibility to protect* rather than the right to intervene. This places the needs of the threatened population as first consideration, with the onus elsewhere than on those wishing to intervene, and encourages a look at a variety of alternatives if action from the start.[2]

The question needs to be reframed. Not, "Is this war just?" but "What is the best way to maintain and strengthen a moral international order?" This means a search for alternatives to war from the beginning, not leaving that search till we are on the brink of war when often it is too late. We need to talk much more about a Just *Peace*, and the things that make for peace. Is there not, in fact, in our whole modern way of life—economically, culturally, politically, and even religiously—a presumption towards war, seen for example in the power of the military-industrial complex, the privilege given by governments (including our own) to arms manufacture and arms exports? According to the World Bank, the world spends fifteen times as much on weapons as on development. It is hard to avoid concluding that we are basically presumed towards war. This points us to the uncomfortable fact that Just War doctrine does not do much to expose not just the "aim" but the deeper motivation of going to war. We need a study of national corporate psychology. What script are we acting out? In a *Guardian* newspaper

[2] For material on this, see *Just Peace Companion* (Geneva: WCC, 2012).

article in April 2012, Simon Jenkins (son of a notable Congregational theologian) stated apropos of the Afghanistan debacle:

Unlike most European countries, sucked into the Afghan vortex by NATO blackmail, the U.S. and Britain were willing warriors, with belligerence in their cultural genes. Discussing "what must be done" to order the rest of the world is second nature to their political class. The Afghan war has not made the West one jot safer, almost certainly the reverse. Islamist terrorism and its obverse, panicky security, is polluting this year's Olympic Games in London. Yet the war clearly responded to a yearning in many Britons to see the world as still their ancestral responsibility. To them a war that turns out right, such as Libya, "proves" Britain's manifest destiny.

There is surely an agenda for the churches here, especially for the Free Churches who should be the most alert to the way the national narrative, in the service of the state, co-opts the big, grandiose words like "freedom" and "democracy" for its own purposes, even glad when a religious aura attaches to them. In 1914–1918 the national patriotic narrative took over and exploited the peaceable nurse Edith Cavell, just as in 2009 it attempted (with perhaps less success) to do the same with the anti-war Harry Patch, last survivor of the Western Front, in according him what amounted to a state funeral. Herein lies a mission and a prophetic task for us. We might then be true dissenters again.

POSTLUDIUM

WADE IN THE WATER: A BAPTISMAL SERMON

Horace O. Russell

Jesus left Galilee for the Jordan to be baptized by John, but John would not do it and instead asked Jesus to baptize him. Jesus then reminded John that together they had to "fulfill all righteousness."

Matthew 3:13–16

WHAT DOES YOUR BAPTISM MEAN AND WHAT DOES IT DEMAND?

Today we will celebrate the ordinance of Holy Baptism, and as it happens this year, we celebrate on the Sunday marked for the remembrance of the Baptism of Jesus. This is a happy day for our family as two of our grandchildren, Lisa and Julian, are among those to be baptized. I am sure if you ask them or any Christian, "Why baptism?", the response would be, "To follow the example of Jesus." If that be so, then it is important that we try to understand what the baptism of Jesus entails so that we may model our baptism on his. When we speak like this, however, we are confronted with an immediate challenge. The baptism which John was administering was a baptism of repentance for the forgiveness of sin, and we know from the Holy Scriptures that Jesus was without Sin. Why, then, did Jesus come for baptism? This is a puzzle. The only reasonable explanation appears to be that Jesus accepted John's baptism because he had decided to begin his ministry in solidarity with the human predicament, which is the separation of humankind from a Holy God. So, Jesus who was the forgiver of Sin identified himself with us, lost sinners who stand in need of forgiveness.

Still, we must not diminish the importance of John's baptism because it was a rite which promised the forgiveness of sin and mercy from a God who is Holy and Just. While Jesus did not need the assurance that the baptism of John gave, John's hearers did. The Scriptures tell us that crowds went to the Jordan to be baptized by John. John's baptism gave to his hearers a promise which still echoes from pulpits and lecterns in today's world and is still sought by the followers of many faith communities. Men and women still need to know that God is merciful. Still, although we seek the assurance of a merciful God deep down, we know that we need more assurance than that to live by. We need more because we also know that God is just and this gives us pain. In our quiet moments we tremble inwardly and at times outwardly when we remember that God is just. The Holy Bible tells us that in speaking with Moses on Mt. Sinai, God said, "I am Jehovah, the Lord, a compassionate and gracious God," and continues, "I am the One who punishes the children and grandchildren to the third and fourth generation for the sins of their ancestors" (Ex. 34:5–7). Yes, God is merciful, and God is also just, so we need more to live by if we are not to live in daily fear. Thank God for, Jesus, in and through him we got more.

It is because of this, that on this Sunday the Church celebrates for He "who had no sin" so identified himself with humankind that Jesus became Sin for all of us in a personal, particular yet universal way and so became and assumed in every sense, Sin for all Creation. So not only in the manger, but also here at his baptism Jesus makes manifest to all creation that He is indeed, Immanuel, God with us.

Now, water is not always as calm as it appears in this pool this Sunday morning. Water is often the symbol of the chaotic. Just ask those who have lived through a Caribbean hurricane or a Jersey nor'easter. The Bible in the book of Genesis begins with the waters of Chaos and the taming of those waters by the Spirit of God moving over them to bring order out of chaos. This idea is also present in the drama of Job and repeated in several Psalms. The miracles of Jesus also demonstrate the same reordering of the created order as well as human behavior itself in the Stilling of the Storm, for instance. The Apocalypse is full of references to the taming of chaos and disorder to usher in the divine order and peace. In his baptism, Jesus, it seems to me, in a dramatic way in his immersion into the dark brown waters of the river Jordan, divided with his body the waters of the Jordan, in the same way as God divided the Red Sea to let his people free. And as his ancestors came through unscathed and alive, so did Jesus emerge—wet, yes, but unscathed and alive—that in and through him we, too, will live. The Bible tells us that as he emerged from the water a voice from heaven declared, "Son, you have done well," and the Holy Spirit, like a dove, rested upon him.

Today I am telling you that just as it was with Jesus at his baptism, so it is with every believer who passes through the waters of baptism. You, too, challenge the chaos of life, the life of Sin which manifests itself in separation from God and in the daily dysfunction of all relationships. Today, in your baptism it is an open declaration that by God's grace all your relationships are being reordered and the Holy Dove hovers and rests, confirms and secures. Today is one of those significant days for you; life is not going to be the same. Today in your baptism, today in these waters, today in this rite is authenticated for you the renewal of the image of God in your very person, and you are incorporated into the new humanity.

Our baptism, yours and mine, should therefore give us the divine assurance of God's presence in every situation, whether they be times of trouble, temptation, or distress. It is reported that Martin Luther, the reformer, used to counsel his hearers that when they experienced times of temptation and alienation from God, they should remind themselves that they had been baptized, and because they were baptized, the stamp of God was upon them. Since they belonged to God, there was then no need to fear. The victory, whatever that victory needs to be, is already ours in Christ, by faith. So we live our lives with the assurance and confidence of knowing that the Creator of the universe has a special and unique relationship with us. Still, it is not a relationship in which we "Sit at ease in Zion." We are, as a consequence, stewards or caretakers of each other and, indeed, of all creation by virtue of our baptism in order to bring order to the chaos of life engendered by the Evil One.

Look, the symbols of chaos and death and dying seem to bombard us these days from every quarter. Still we need not be afraid. I believe it was the theologian Karl Barth who is reported to have called baptism "a threat to death." We know that if any candidate for baptism is held long enough under the water, he or she will drown. Indeed, in some sections of the church the candidate is held long enough under the water that they struggle to come up for air. Always remember that the baptism of Jesus was his identification with the human struggle to come up for air in the face of the threats of the drowning of daily living. Your baptism and mine is an affirmation that the meaning of Life is living life in all its fullness in this neverending confrontation with chaos and death. Chaos and death manifest themselves in the seven deadly sins—murder, greed, lust, pride, envy, jealousy, and laziness—which by God's mercy and grace will give way to the virtues of love, joy, peace, patience, kindness, gentleness, and self-control.

I have a colleague and friend whose wife died four years ago now. We were in conversation at the beginning of this year and in the conversation he confessed how much he missed his wife at Christmas. I understood full well what he meant since our families had spent many Christmases together. His wife was an excellent homemaker and the life of the party. In response I lamely replied, "Such is Life." To which he replied, "Not only Life, my friend, but Death and Resurrection." My friend got it right because the baptized believer confesses in baptism the resurrection life which Jesus demonstrated in his baptism. The baptism of Jesus in the Jordan pointed to his death and resurrection on the Easter weekend. His death on Calvary was his baptism in blood for the sake of all humanity. It was the entrance of God into far more murky waters than the river Jordan and was also the facing down of the ultimate threat which chaos poses to all creation, disintegration, and non-existence. "Death was swallowed up in victory."

In baptism we also receive the freedom of becoming or being sanctified. This gift of grace rests upon the divine promise of a new life in which the chaotic and disordered have no place. That is why as Christians we have an optimistic view of the world, because we know that good has already had the last word. This does not mean that as believers we live perfect lives each day, although we strive to do. What it means is that, in a universal way, all humankind and all creation are moving toward a common goal of goodness. Sometimes it is almost impossible to recognize this movement, but occasionally it is made clear in the life of Christian leaders like a St. Theresa of Avila, a Desmond Tutu of South Africa, or a Pope John Paul on the world stage; and by persons like my Sunday-school teacher Mother Briscoe, a humble seamstress who also ran the school canteen at the high school I attended. I am sure you know someone in your own life who represents this trend to goodness.

It is important to bear this in mind because to be baptized is not an individual and personal act only. Your baptism in church today is an initiation into a fellowship of believers which transcends both space and time. The confessions of all Christian believers affirm in some form a belief in what the Nicene Creed calls "the One, Holy, Catholic and Apostolic Church." Your baptism and mine is our entrance into the universal Church, the Body of Christ, and not into any particular expression of the Church. In baptism, we are incorporated into the body of Christ, and we become in a sense little "Christs." This is both exhilarating and frightening. It is exhilarating because we now share in the divine nature, not by nature but by grace, and that is out of this world, but it is precisely this sharing that is frightening. It is almost as if we are being "set up" for failure by our baptism. Still we can take heart, for in baptism we were also given the gift of the Holy Spirit, and the Spirit stays with and in us.

This communal aspect of the Christian faith places upon us as baptized believers certain obligations. It requires that our daily lifestyle reflect "kingdom values" or the Christian virtues. This ethical dimension of Christian baptism is clearly articulated in the New Testament scriptures. Some aspects are not unique and bear some resemblance to the demands of the baptism of John, although the motivation is not the same. The unique ethical motivation of Christian baptism is the love of God manifested in the ultimate baptism of Jesus on Calvary and its vindication on the Easter weekend. Christian baptism is not a personal or communal response motivated by the fear of retribution by a just, angry, and somewhat reluctantly merciful God. Rather, the Christian ethic is rooted in a love which responds in amazement to the divine act of self-giving. "Love so amazing, so divine, demands my life, my soul, my all." This in turn obliges the believer to respond in the same way to other believers within their contexts as God acted in theirs.

There is one more word I wish to leave with you today. Christian Baptism, by whatever name we call it, whether sacrament or ordinance, cannot be treated in isolation from our other theological understandings of the Faith. Baptism is an empty act when it is detached from the need for the reordering and redemption of a sinful and chaotic world (Rom. 8:18–23). Your baptism and mine are also eschatological activities in which, as Christian believers, we are engaged in, acts which are the last and the first. Our baptism in a sense is our imitation of the

Alpha and Omega of Jesus and an identifying with his final promise to his disciples in the Upper Room as he dined with them: "Take this and divide it among you. For I tell you I will not drink again of the fruit of the vine until the Kingdom of God comes" (Luke 22:19). Today you will have your first communion, and this is fitting since your baptism links you directly to the events in Upper Room. For every time we participate in the Breaking of Bread, it is our last time and our first. It is the last act in time and space and the first act of eternity.

My brothers and sisters, I also leave you with words from the Book of Revelation:

> Behold I am coming soon and my reward is with me, and I will give to everyone according what he (or she) has done. I am Alpha and Omega, the first and the last, the beginning and the end. Blessed are those who wash their robes that they may have the right to the tree of life and may go through the gates into the city [...] the Spirit and the Bride say, "Come" and let him who hears say, "Come." Whoever is thirsty let him come and let him take of the water of life freely. (Rev. 22:12 and17)[1]

[1] Sermon, preached on the occasion of the baptism of our grandchildren, Lisa and Julian, and others at the Saints Memorial Baptist Church in Bryn Mawr, Pennsylvania, on the celebration of the Baptism of Our Lord, edited for this *Festschrift* in honor of a scholar and friend.

INDEX